Master C++ for Windows

Let the PC Teach You Object-Oriented Programming

REX WOOLLARD Training Innovations

WAITE GROUP PRESS™
Corte Madera, CA

PUBLISHER   Mitchell Waite
EDITOR-IN-CHIEF   Charles Drucker
ACQUISITIONS EDITOR   Jill Pisoni
EDITORIAL DIRECTOR   John Crudo
MANAGING EDITOR   Dan Scherf
CONTENT EDITOR   Carol Henry
COPY EDITOR   Cathy Carlyle
TECHNICAL REVIEWER   David Calhoun
PRODUCTION DIRECTOR   Julianne Ososke
PRODUCTION MANAGER   Cecile Kaufman
PRODUCTION   Jude Levinson
COVER PHOTOGRAPH   © J. Share

© 1995 by The Waite Group, Inc.® Published by Waite Group Press™, 200 Tamal Plaza, Corte Madera, CA 94925

Waite Group Press™ is distributed to bookstores and book wholesalers by Publishers Group West, Box 8843, Emeryville, CA 94662, 1-800-788-3123 (in California 1-510-658-3453).

All rights reserved. No part of this manual shall be reproduced, stored in a retrieval system, or transmitted by any means, electronic, mechanical, photocopying, desktop publishing, recording, or otherwise, without permission from the publisher. No patent liability is assumed with respect to the use of the information contained herein. While every precaution has been taken in the preparation of this book, the publisher and author assume no responsibility for errors or omissions. Neither is any liability assumed for damages resulting from the use of the information contained herein.

All terms mentioned in this book that are known to be registered trademarks, trademarks, or service marks are listed below. In addition, terms suspected of being trademarks, registered trademarks, or service marks have been appropriately capitalized. Waite Group Press cannot attest to the accuracy of this information. Use of a term in this book should not be regarded as affecting the validity of any registered trademark, trademark, or service mark.

The Waite Group is a registered trademark of The Waite Group, Inc.

Printed in the United States of America

95 96 97 98 • 10 9 8 7 6 5 4 3 2 1

Library of Congress Cataloging-in-Publication Data

Woollard, Rex.
    Master C++ for Windows / Rex Woollard, Robert Lafore, Harry Henderson.
              p.   cm.
    Includes index.
    ISBN 1-57169-000-X
    1. Object-oriented programming (Computer science) 2. C++ (Computer program language) 3. Master C++.   I. Lafore, Robert (Robert W.) II. Henderson, Harry, 1951-   .   III. Title.
QA76.64.W668   1995
005.13'3--dc20   95-38015
                                                                                           CIP

DEDICATION

To Laurie, Robyn and Jay
— *Rex Woollard*

Message from the Publisher

WELCOME TO OUR NERVOUS SYSTEM

Some people say that the World Wide Web is a graphical extension of the information superhighway, just a network of humans and machines sending each other long lists of the equivalent of digital junk mail.

I think it is much more than that. To me the Web is nothing less than the nervous system of the entire planet—not just a collection of computer brains connected together, but more like a billion silicon neurons entangled and recirculating electro-chemical signals of information and data, each contributing to the birth of another CPU and another Web site.

Think of each person's hard disk connected at once to every other hard disk on earth, driven by human navigators searching like Columbus for the New World. Seen this way the Web is more of a super entity, a growing, living thing, controlled by the universal human will to expand, to be more. Yet unlike a purposeful business plan with rigid rules, the Web expands in a nonlinear, unpredictable, creative way that echoes natural evolution.

We created our Web site not just to extend the reach of our computer book products but to be part of this synaptic neural network, to experience, like a nerve in the body, the flow of ideas and then to pass those ideas up the food chain of the mind. Your mind. Even more, we wanted to pump some of our own creative juices into this rich wine of technology.

TASTE OUR DIGITAL WINE

And so we ask you to taste our wine by visiting the body of our business. Begin by understanding the metaphor we have created for our Web site—a universal learning center, situated in outer space in the form of a space station. A place where you can journey to study any topic from the convenience of your own screen. Right now we are focusing on computer topics, but the stars are the limit on the Web.

If you are interested in discussing this Web site, or finding out more about the Waite Group, please send me email with your comments and I will be happy to respond. Being a programmer myself, I love to talk about technology and find out what our readers are looking for.

Sincerely,

Mitchell Waite

Mitchell Waite, C.E.O. and Publisher

200 Tamal Plaza
Corte Madera CA 94925
415 924 2575
415 924 2576 fax

Internet E-mail:
mwaite@waite.com

CompuServe E-mail:
75146,3515

Website:
http://www.waite.com/waite

CREATING THE HIGHEST QUALITY COMPUTER BOOKS IN THE INDUSTRY

Waite Group Press
Waite Group New Media

Come Visit
WAITE.COM
Waite Group Press
World Wide Web Site

Now, find all the latest information on Waite Group books at our new Web site, **http://www.waite.com/waite**. You'll find an online catalog where you can examine and order any title, review upcoming books, and send E-mail to our authors and editors. Our ftp site has all you need to update your book: the latest program listings, errata sheets, most recent versions of Fractint, POV Ray, Polyray, DMorph, and all the programs featured in our books. So download, talk to us, ask questions, on **http://www.waite.com/waite**.

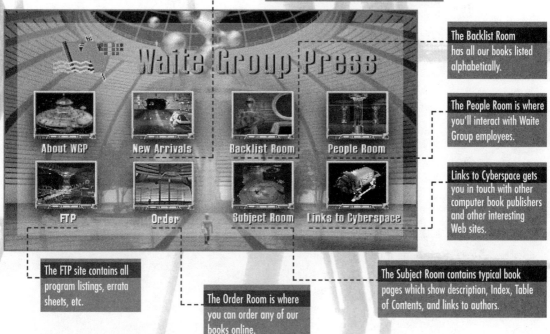

The New Arrivals Room has all our new books listed by month. Just click for a description, Index, Table of Contents, and links to authors.

The Backlist Room has all our books listed alphabetically.

The People Room is where you'll interact with Waite Group employees.

Links to Cyberspace gets you in touch with other computer book publishers and other interesting Web sites.

The FTP site contains all program listings, errata sheets, etc.

The Order Room is where you can order any of our books online.

The Subject Room contains typical book pages which show description, Index, Table of Contents, and links to authors.

World Wide Web:

COME SURF OUR TURF—THE WAITE GROUP WEB

http://www.waite.com/waite
Gopher: gopher.waite.com
FTP: ftp.waite.com

ABOUT THE AUTHOR

Rex Woollard is a co-author of The Waite Group's *Master C* and *Master C++*, the Waite Group Press' first computer-based tutorials. He has taught for many years as a professor of Information Systems at a Canadian college and is currently President of Training Innovations Inc., a multimedia, software development firm specializing in computer-based training (CBT) solutions. When not working with students and computers, you can often find him in a canoe, plying the white waters of the Canadian wilderness with his wife and children.

TABLE OF CONTENTS

1 WHAT IS *MASTER C++ FOR WINDOWS* 1

2 INSTALLATION 11

3 EXPLORING *MASTER C++ FOR WINDOWS* 17

4 USING *MASTER C++ FOR WINDOWS* TO LEARN C++ 29

5 COURSE MAP 39

6 IN CASE OF TROUBLE 59

7 DEVELOPING C++ PROGRAMS 65

8 REVIEW EXERCISES 87

9 REFERENCE OVERVIEW 163

10 ALPHABETICAL REFERENCE 189

APPENDIX A *MASTER C++ FOR WINDOWS* COMMAND REFERENCE .. 393

APPENDIX B FURTHER READING 397

INDEX 399

CONTENTS

1 WHAT IS *MASTER C++ FOR WINDOWS* 1

Master C++ for Windows Book & Software 3
Features of *Master C++ for Windows* Software 5
Strategies for Using *Master C++ for Windows* 5
How *Master C++* Encourages Learning 7
Let's Get Started 9

2 INSTALLATION 11

Preliminaries 13
    Using the README.TXT File 13
    System Requirements 14
Installation Overview 14
Installing 15
    Steps for the First Installation 15
    Steps for a Subsequent Installation 16

3 EXPLORING *MASTER C++ FOR WINDOWS* 17

Getting Started 19
The Main Table of Contents Screen 20
Lesson Screens 21
    The Main Instructional Area 21
    The Button Bar 21
    The Status Bar 22
The Button Bar and Its Functions 22
    Forward and Back 23
    Help 23
    Refresh 23
    Progress 23
    Options 24
    Glossary 24
    Note and Example 25
    Edit 26

CONTENTS

    Memo... 26
    Exit... 26
    How *Master C++ for Windows* Numbers Screens.............. 27
  What Is Mastery?.. 27

4 USING *MASTER C++ FOR WINDOWS* TO LEARN C++ 29

  How *Master C++ for Windows* Asks Questions 31
    Questions in Different Formats............................. 32
    Acceptance of Abbreviated and Shortened Answers 32
    Questions That Get Progressively Easier 33
    Recognizing Incomplete Answers 35
    Guided Practice in Building Programs....................... 36
  Recording Your Achievement 36
    Approaching Mastery..................................... 36
    Understanding the Progress Information..................... 36
    Resetting Achievement Info 37
  Other Ways to Learn with *Master C++ for Windows* 37
    Using the Glossary....................................... 37
    Using the Review Lessons 38
    Making a Hard Copy of *Master C++ for Windows* Screens 38
    Setting Out on Your Own 38

5 COURSE MAP 39

  How *Master C++ for Windows* Is Organized 41
  1: The Big Picture 42
    Overview of Contents 42
    Objectives... 43
    Topics... 43
  2: Compiling and Linking 43
    Overview of Contents 43
    Objectives... 43
    Topics... 43
  3: C++ Basics.. 44
    Overview of Contents 44
    Objectives... 44
    Topics... 44
  4: Loops and Decisions 45
    Overview of Contents 45
    Objectives... 45
    Topics... 45
  5: Structures 46
    Overview of Contents 46

    Objectives. 46
    Topics. 46
6: Functions 47
    Overview of Contents 47
    Objectives. 47
    Topics. 48
7: Objects and Classes 48
    Overview of Contents 48
    Objectives. 48
    Topics. 49
8: Arrays 49
    Overview of Contents 49
    Objectives. 49
    Topics. 50
9: Operator Overloading 50
    Overview of Contents 50
    Objectives. 51
    Topics. 51
10: Inheritance. 51
    Overview of Contents 51
    Objectives. 52
    Topics. 52
11: Pointers. 52
    Overview of Contents 52
    Objectives. 53
    Topics. 53
12: Virtual Functions 54
    Overview of Contents 54
    Objectives. 54
    Topics. 55
13: Streams and Files 55
    Overview of Contents 55
    Objectives. 55
    Topics. 56
14: Larger Programs. 56
    Overview of Contents 56
    Objectives. 56
    Topics. 56
15: Templates and Exceptions. 57
    Overview of Contents 57
    Objectives. 57
    Topics. 57

CONTENTS

6 IN CASE OF TROUBLE 59
Installation Problems 61
Problems While Running the Software 62

7 DEVELOPING C++ PROGRAMS 65
The Borland Compilers 67
    EasyWin 68
    Installing the Compilers 68
    The Installation Dialog 69
Turbo C++ for Windows 70
    Visual Tools 71
    Libraries 72
    Examples 73
    Help 73
Borland C++ 74
    Debuggers 76
    Visual Tools 76
    Libraries 76
    Examples 78
    Help 78
Finishing the Installation 79
Your First Program 79
    Creating a Project 80
    Using the Editor 82
    Saving Your Program 83
    Compiling and Linking 83
    Running the Program 84
    Exiting the IDE 84
    Opening an Existing Project 84
    Errors 84
    Link Errors 84
    Conceptual Errors 85
Summary 85

8 REVIEW EXERCISES 87
CHAPTER 3 89
    Exercise 1 89
    Exercise 2 90
    Exercise 3 90
    Exercise 4 90
    Exercise 5 91

xi

CHAPTER 4	91
Exercise 1	91
Exercise 2	92
Exercise 3	93
Exercise 4	94
Exercise 5	95
CHAPTER 5	95
Exercise 1	95
Exercise 2	96
Exercise 3	97
Exercise 4	98
Exercise 5	99
CHAPTER 6	100
Exercise 1	100
Exercise 2	101
Exercise 3	101
Exercise 4	102
Exercise 5	104
Exercise 6	105
Exercise 7	107
CHAPTER 7	108
Exercise 1	108
Exercise 2	109
Exercise 3	110
Exercise 4	111
Exercise 5	112
Exercise 6	113
Exercise 7	114
CHAPTER 8	116
Exercise 1	116
Exercise 2	117
Exercise 3	118
Exercise 4	119
Exercise 5	121
CHAPTER 9	122
Exercise 1	122
Exercise 2	123
Exercise 3	124
Exercise 4	126
Exercise 5	127
Exercise 6	128
CHAPTER 10	130
Exercise 1	130
Exercise 2	131

Exercise 3	134
Exercise 4	135
Exercise 5	137
CHAPTER 12	140
Exercise 1	140
Exercise 2	141
Exercise 3	142
Exercise 4	142
Exercise 5	144
Exercise 6	145
CHAPTER 13	146
Exercise 1	146
Exercise 2	148
Exercise 3	151
Exercise 4	153
Exercise 5	155
CHAPTER 14	156
Exercise 1	156
Exercise 2	157
Exercise 3	158
Exercise 4	159
Exercise 5	161

9 REFERENCE OVERVIEW 163

C++, an Emerging Standard	166
C++ and ANSI C	166
Overview of Language Elements	166
Language Keywords	166
Operators and Precedence	167
Preprocessor Directives and Macros	170
Other Predefined Values and Data Types	172
Escape Sequences	172
Library Classes and Functions	173
C++ Streams and Files	174
Process Control and Locale Routines	179
Variable Argument List Routines	181
Memory Allocation Routines	181
Data Conversion Routines	182
Math Routines	183
Character Classification and Conversion Routines	184
String and Buffer Manipulation Routines	185
Searching and Sorting Routines	187
Date and Time Routines	187

10 ALPHABETICAL REFERENCE 189
Alphabetization 191
Format of Entries. 192
Master C++ for Windows Alphabetical Reference 193

APPENDIX A   *MASTER C++ FOR WINDOWS* COMMAND REFERENCE . . 393
Toolbar Commands 393

APPENDIX B   FURTHER READING. 397
C++ in General 397
C++ Compilers and Development Environments 398
Resources from C 398

INDEX. 399

ACKNOWLEDGMENTS

Rex Woollard would, first and foremost, like to thank his wife Laurie for her support throughout the months of development effort, and his young daughter Robyn, whose innocent delight lifted his spirits when he was particularly overwhelmed. His thanks also go to his parents, who were always there to help when pressures began to mount.

In addition, he would like to thank many colleagues at Training Innovations whose work and ideas have contributed to a polished final product—Susan Morrison for her creativity and unending energy, John Kerr and Chris Clark for their incredible programming skills. Special thanks go to Richard Wright, Jr. for updating Part II to the latest C++ standard. Finally, Rex would like to thank Dan Scherf and Jill Pisoni of Waite Group Press for getting this product to press.

PREFACE

The Waite Group is well-known for bringing tutorial and reference materials to C and C++ programmers—helping make these languages accessible to everyone. The success of books such as Stephen Prata's *C Primer Plus* and Robert Lafore's *Object-Oriented Programming in C++* was very gratifying to us and to our authors, but we knew that we could not rest on our laurels.

A printed book, no matter how well organized and lucidly written, cannot provide the kind of interactive learning that a student experiences with a real teacher. So back in 1987 The Waite Group began thinking about what a "computer book of the future" would be like. We decided that it would be as much as possible "a teacher on a disk." The software would be smart enough to teach you and test you, to probe for your weaknesses and offer remedial work when necessary. With questions that have a range of possible correct answers, the software would accept a wide variety of responses, so you wouldn't have to guess the exact wording. With questions requiring precise answers, the software would use an "expert system" to identify problems and guide you to the correct answer. To help provide variety and reinforcement in learning, questions would be presented in a variety of forms. Perhaps most importantly, you would write real program code, solving problems step by step.

Our teaching software would also take advantage of the organizational flexibility of the computer medium. Students would choose chapters from a menu. Within a chapter, sub-menus would offer major topics. But we would also provide a way to "jump" to any topic of interest so that advanced students could skip material they already knew, and students who had already completed the course could review material selectively.

The first two computer-based training (CBT) products were *Master C* and *Master C++*. Even though both products were DOS-based and text-oriented, they met with widespread and enthusiastic acceptance. But the nature of computing hardware and software is rapidly changing, and our approach to (CBT) has evolved to embrace the multimedia capabilities of the Windows environment. Thus, it was a natural next step to build on the success of *Master C* and *Master C++* by creating *Master C++ for Windows*.

This new software package is much more than a simple revision of our earlier work. The software has been completely redesigned, bringing the best of desktop publishing, graphics, and animation to the world of C++ programming. We sincerely believe that *Master C++ for Windows* provides one of the most effective ways to master the object-oriented technology of C++. As always, we welcome your feedback and suggestions about *Master C++ for Windows* and all other Waite Group Press products.

INTRODUCTION

This book is designed to get you up and running with *Master C++ for Windows*, a computer-based training (CBT) product that turns a PC into a friendly and intelligent C++ instructor.

The book is divided into two parts. The first part, consisting of Chapters 1-6, is the user's manual for the software. Chapter 1 explains what *Master C++ for Windows* is and outlines the minimum hardware configuration. Chapter 2 covers the simple process of installing the software on your PC. Chapter 3 surveys the main features of the software and explains its menus and screen layout. Chapter 4 suggests how you can use the features of *Master C++ for Windows* to help you learn C++ in a systematic and enjoyable way. Chapter 5 provides an overview and outline of each lesson set in the software. An estimated completion time is given for each lesson as an aid in scheduling and curriculum planning. Finally, Chapter 6—organized in a question-and-answer format—is designed to help you identify and solve any problem you may encounter in installing or using *Master C++ for Windows*.

The second part of this book provides supplemental and reference materials that you can use as you develop your own C++ programs. Chapter 7 gives an overview of the process of developing C++ programs and introduces and illustrates some of the important programming tools provided with many C++ compilers. Chapter 8 provides extensive supplemental exercises to test and reinforce the concepts studied in the software.

Chapter 9 provides an overview of the many standard ANSI C library functions and C++ stream input/output classes that are provided with most C++ compilers. The overview includes alphabetical lists of keywords, operators, and functions organized according to topic, as well as lists that can help you identify which functions your program needs in a given situation.

Chapter 10 is a detailed reference for C++ and ANSI C keywords, operators, preprocessor directives, standard values, functions, and streams classes. Each reference entry gives a definition, syntax description, example call, and other details of using the language element or library function. You can use the alphabetical reference when you need to quickly look up a C++ function you can't remember, or when you are away from the computer and wish to study or review C++ "vocabulary."

Two appendices are also provided: Appendix A is a summary of the *Master C++ for Windows* option bar commands. Appendix B is a brief guide to further reading about the C++ language and Borland/Turbo C++.

MASTER C++ FOR WINDOWS

We recommend that you read Chapter 2 completely before installing the software so you will understand the entire process. Then install *Master C++ for Windows* on your PC, and look at Chapters 3 and 4 to familiarize yourself with the program's features and various strategies for using them. You then will be ready to begin learning C++.

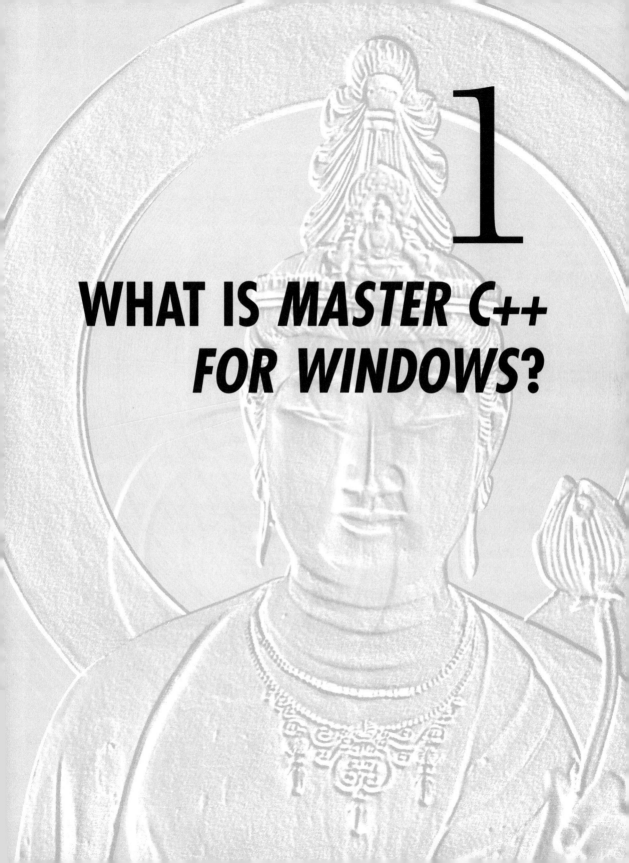

1

WHAT IS *MASTER C++* FOR WINDOWS?

1
WHAT IS *MASTER C++* FOR WINDOWS?

The C programming language has proven to be powerful, versatile, and popular, and it will no doubt be with us for many years to come. However, recent years have seen the coming of age of its likely successor, C++. C++ provides the conceptual and organizational benefits of object-oriented programming while preserving the skills and talents of large numbers of trained C programmers and building on huge libraries of working C code. C++ is, therefore, a natural migration for many thousands of C programmers. And with the help of *Master C++ for Windows*, this exciting new language also becomes an easily accessible first language for students and beginners.

MASTER C++ FOR WINDOWS BOOK AND SOFTWARE

Master C++ for Windows is a package consisting of a book and software on disk. This Windows-based software takes you through a systematic course on the C++ language—a course that uses computer-based training (CBT) to present C++ topics *interactively*. When you work with *Master C++ for Windows*, you don't just *read* about programming in C++—you interact with a comprehensive expert system that guides your learning experience. The *Master C++ for Windows* system includes many elements:

◆ You learn important concepts as you watch animated diagrams of computer memory maps.

MASTER C++ FOR WINDOWS

- You write real C++ code.

- Your understanding is checked with each topic.

- Your progress is evaluated with a variety of testing techniques that reinforce key concepts while avoiding a boring sameness and repetition.

- *Master C++ for Windows* ensures that you truly understand each lesson by evaluating your progress and offering reviews when necessary.

Contents of the Book

The book you are now reading serves as both a guide to using *Master C++ for Windows* and as a detailed reference to the C++ language. The first four chapters help you get started with *Master C++ for Windows* by taking you through the installation and use of all the features of the software. Chapter 5, *Course Map* presents an outline and overview of the topics covered in each lesson set. An estimated completion time is given for each lesson-set, so students and teachers can use the course map as an aid in devising a study plan. Chapter 6, *In Case of Trouble*, is designed to get you back on track in the rare cases that something goes wrong when you install or try to use *Master C++ for Windows*.

The remainder of the book is designed to aid your transition from student to working C++ programmer. Chapter 7, *Working with C++*, gives an overview of the process of developing a C++ program, and guides you in the use of the compiler, linker, libraries, and tools found in a modern C++ program development environment. Chapter 8, *Review Exercises*, provides an extensive set of supplemental exercises to help you practice your coding skills. Chapter 9, *Reference Overview*, gives an overview of the keywords and operators of C++. There is also a summary (by name and task category) of the libraries of ANSI C functions commonly available to the C++ programmer, as well as the C++ streams class library used for console and disk I/O. Finally, Chapter 10, *Alphabetical Reference*, includes every C++ keyword and operator as well as the ANSI C library and a selection of C++ streams functions. The book concludes with two appendices covering further reading on C++ and a summary of *Master C++ for Windows* features.

Taken as a whole, *Master C++ for Windows* explains everything from the broad concepts of object-oriented programming to the actual steps and techniques used in the design and development of C++ programs. When you complete the lessons in this package, you will have covered all the fundamentals of proficient C++ programming.

A Note About Implementation Specifics

Nearly all the examples in *Master C++ for Windows*, with the exception of some graphics and file operations, are "generic" C++; that is, they're meant to run on any standard C++ implementation, including all those that compile for the IBM PC, Apple Macintosh, minicomputers, and mainframe computers. Occasionally, *Master*

CHAPTER 1 WHAT IS *MASTER C++ FOR WINDOWS*?

C++ for Windows discusses implementation-dependent matters, such as differences in the ways files are stored.

FEATURES OF *MASTER C++ FOR WINDOWS* SOFTWARE

Master C++ for Windows has evolved over a period of several years. Our first edition, *Master C++*, was designed for a text-based MS-DOS environment. Using this earlier version, tens of thousands of programmers have learned the essentials of C++. This Windows-based rewrite embraces the best of desktop publishing, graphics animation, and expert system design to bring programming concepts to life.

The underlying software engine for *Master C++ for Windows* was developed after years of research at three educational institutions. The content is based on the best-selling book, *Object-Oriented Programming in Turbo C++, 2nd Edition,* by Robert Lafore (Waite Group Press, 1995). The learning software was further enhanced with the aid of feedback from earlier users and by noting important trends in C++ programming. By blending this powerful software engine with the excellent writing of a proven book, Waite Group Press has created an effective learning tool.

Interactive Lesson Sets

Master C++ for Windows is organized into 15 lesson sets, each covering a broad topic such as "loops and decisions" or "objects and classes." Each lesson set is presented as a sequence of text, graphics, and animated screens. After you have worked through each screen or series of screens, *Master C++ for Windows* asks questions and finds out if you understand the topic. The questions may be true/false, multiple choice, or fill-in-the-blank. Often the questions are repeated in different formats. One time a question might require a complete word to be typed in, another time it might be presented in true/false format. Varying the type of question helps keep your learning experience from falling into a rut, and ensures that you are really thinking.

Master C++ for Windows presents concepts in a sequence found to be easiest for most students. If you have trouble answering particular questions, *Master C++ for Windows* will detect that and go into the *Recall* mode, sending you to the point in the tutorial where your knowledge is weak. After you successfully complete the recalled lesson, you return to where you stumbled and then proceed with additional material. *Master C++ for Windows* won't let you become "stuck" or confused. It is a dynamically adaptive learning environment that tailors the path of instruction to your particular strengths and weaknesses—something no book can do.

STRATEGIES FOR USING *MASTER C++ FOR WINDOWS*

Following are several strategies for using *Master C++ for Windows* that accommodate students with varying backgrounds and interests. It is likely you will want to experiment with more than one of them.

Using *Master C++ for Windows* Like a Book

You can use the *Master C++ for Windows* software much as you would a regular book, starting at the beginning and moving linearly through its material, from Lesson-set 1 to Lesson-set 15. The lesson sets in the software parallel the chapters in the related book, *Object-Oriented Programming in Turbo C++, 2nd Edition.* You can buy that book and read the corresponding chapters when you are away from the computer, to reinforce your learning.

Jumping Directly to Tutorials

An ideal learning environment balances the need to give you a guided learning experience while also leaving you in control. *Master C++ for Windows* strikes this balance. It lays out a path of learning that is well suited to most people, but you are still in control. You can jump directly to those C++ topics that are of interest to you. You can skip the preliminary sections of instruction if you want, and move right into the areas you want to understand. This can be particularly helpful if you are an experienced C programmer and don't need to learn about loops and decisions, for instance. (Note, however, that C++ adds features to many areas of C programming. Experienced C programmers may want to examine Chapter 5 of this book, *Course Map*, and check for concepts that are new to them.)

Master C++ for Windows will analyze your work in the review lessons, and if your answers to recent questions indicate that you may be confused, it will send you to the proper lesson, so you can't leave the course confused. Once inside a *Master C++ for Windows* lesson, you have control over moving forward and backward through the screens of material. At any time, you can branch off to use related *Master C++ for Windows* features—and you will always be returned to your original position when done.

Studying a Single Concept via the *Master C++ for Windows* Glossary

Master C++ for Windows' built-in Glossary provides a third way to use this powerful learning tool. After looking up a related C++ keyword in the Glossary, you can request a lesson on the defined word. This can provide a special training path that is finely tuned to what you want to learn, on an as-needed, "just-in-time" basis.

Using *Master C++ for Windows* Review Sections

If you already have some familiarity with C++ and just want to check for weaknesses in your knowledge, you can use the review sections of each lesson set. These reviews present a condensed summary of the content of the lesson set, along with quizzes to test your understanding. Taking the entire course can consume several days of work, so the reviews provide a way to quickly digest certain lesson sets.

CHAPTER 1   WHAT IS *MASTER C++ FOR WINDOWS?*

HOW *MASTER C++ FOR WINDOWS* ENCOURAGES LEARNING

Master C++ for Windows has several features that customize your course in the same way a good personal teacher would. You will come to appreciate these features as you work with the learning package. Here is an overview of them.

Sophisticated Answer Judging

Master C++ for Windows' skills are most apparent in the way it assesses your responses. It contains an integrated expert system that is designed to accept a wide range of possible user responses. You can misspell the answer, abbreviate it, and even give it in a poorly structured sentence, and the software will still recognize a correct answer. Some questions are open-ended and there may be many ways to phrase a correct response. *Master C++ for Windows* is able to figure out what you mean if you are close. This is unlike most CBT systems, which require that you type the exact answer before moving forward.

Retention of Student Progress Information

As you complete various lessons, *Master C++ for Windows* retains information about your progress—information that is summarized on each menu screen. *Master C++ for Windows* tells you which lessons have been completed and what your "score" is. The score is the percentage of correct answers, with 80% being considered "mastery." The course will also identify the lessons you have finished, and ones on which you still need to work.

Master C++ for Windows also retains much additional detailed information about your progress. When you access this information, you get a graphical window showing your scores and the time taken for every attempt.

Digital Bookmarks

You can quit *Master C++ for Windows* at almost any point in its tutorials. When you return later, it will take you back to the exact point you were working on in the last lesson.

Meaningful Feedback on Wrong Answers

Master C++ for Windows' feedback to answers varies depending on the nature of the questions. With particularly easy questions, a wrong answer causes the system to respond immediately—telling you the correct answer and providing some additional feedback.

With more demanding questions, *Master C++ for Windows* brings more of its expertise to bear. For example, if you answer a question incorrectly, the answer is analyzed and checked against anticipated problem areas. The system then responds with relevant hints designed to help you clarify your understanding. You are then given an opportunity to try the question again.

In some cases, if you are still having difficulty with a particular question, *Master C++ for Windows* presents the same question again, but in a simpler, multiple choice format. If you still have trouble with the question, the system switches into the Recall mode.

Recall Mode

Master C++ for Windows' Recall mode is one of its most powerful learning elements. Following presentation of a question and subsequent answer analysis and helpful hints, you might still be having difficulty with a particular topic. Here, the course automatically jumps to a mini-tutorial covering that topic. You then have a chance to review this related material before trying to answer the question again.

Online Glossary

Because you may encounter unfamiliar terms or keywords, *Master C++ for Windows* includes an online Glossary. At any point in the course, you can look up related C++ terms for additional information. For many of the terms, you can link to related instructional material. If you choose to work with the related material, afterward you will be able to return to your jumping-off point—the place where you first invoked the Glossary.

This feature provides an alternate and powerful learning path. Ordinarily, you are likely to access learning material by choosing lesson items from a menu. Using the Glossary, you can jump directly to instructional material by selecting the desired term or keyword. There is no need to walk back and forth through menus. This feature is useful in a variety of circumstances. You may, for instance, already be familiar with the C++ language, but need to reference the learning material on some specific topic.

Even if you are using the menus as your primary path to learning material, you can make good use of the Glossary path. Imagine that you are working through a lesson on control loops, and you encounter references to the ++ operator. Without leaving the lesson, you can use the Glossary to explore others covering the ++ operator. When finished with the ++ operator, you will automatically be brought back to your jumping-off point—the lesson on loops.

The "Personality" of the Course

When *Master C++ for Windows* responds to your answers, its feedback will have a particular tone or "personality." Feedback may have a "friendly" quality, or something that is more concise and businesslike. Or, if you prefer, you can hear something that is a bit more "off-the-wall." The choice is always yours. The friendly personality may be helpful for students who may be anxious about their performance. The more terse businesslike personality saves a little time for experienced students who are reviewing previously mastered material. And the off-the-wall style is for those who like to be different.

CHAPTER 1   WHAT IS *MASTER C++ FOR WINDOWS*?

Calculator

An online scientific calculator is also included. It supports standard trigonometric functions and constants such as *pi*. It will also work with hexadecimal, octal, and binary number systems, though it does not allow you to do segment math for the Intel family of microprocessors. Nevertheless, it can be a useful tool for your programming work.

LET'S GET STARTED

Now that you've been introduced to the features of *Master C++ for Windows* it's time to get started. Please turn to Chapter 2, *Installation*, to learn how to install the software on your PC.

2
INSTALLATION

2

INSTALLATION

The installation steps for *Master C++ for Windows* have been tested with common PC configurations, and the installation software is designed to work automatically with a minimum of work on your part.

PRELIMINARIES

Before you begin installing *Master C++ for Windows*, you should review the system requirements and note any special circumstances that may apply to you. The README.TXT file on your *Master C++ for Windows* disk and the following discussion provide the necessary information.

Using the README.TXT File

Take a few minutes to read the README.TXT file on the diskette from your *Master C++ for Windows* package. This file may contain information that was obtained after this book was printed, as well as notes on the use of *Master C++ for Windows* with particular hardware or software environments. After inserting the floppy into your floppy drive, you can display the contents of the README.TXT file in one of several ways.

- From the DOS prompt, you can enter the MORE command with the following syntax:

    C:\>MORE < A:\README.TXT [ENTER] or C:\>MORE < B:\README.TXT

This will let you read the file a screen at a time. (Note that DOS commands are shown in all capital letters for clarity, but you can type any command in lowercase if you want. The [ENTER] symbol means to press the [ENTER] key to send the command to DOS.)

* Alternatively, you can turn on your printer and use the PRINT command to get hard copy.

C:\>PRINT A:\README.TXT [ENTER]

* If you are already inside of Windows, you can view the README.TXT file through Windows' Notepad application. In Windows 95, you can click the Start button at the bottom left of the screen and select Run. In Windows 3.x, you can open the File Menu and select Run from the Program Manager. You should see a dialog box something like Figure 2-1.

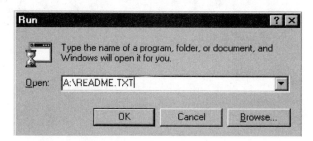

Figure 2-1 Running the README.TXT File

As shown here, you must enter the drive letter, a colon, and the backslash followed by the file name README.TXT. This will automatically open the Notepad application and load the README.TXT file.

Alternatively, you can double-click on the Notepad icon (normally found in the Accessories group) to open an empty notepad. Select File, Open. Using the mouse, you can then select your floppy drive and the README.TXT file.

Note: You can also consult the README.TXT file for help with installation problems or if *Master C++ for Windows* does not run properly after installation. (Also see Chapter 6, *In Case of Trouble*, for answers to common questions and problems.)

System Requirements

Master C++ for Windows can be installed on virtually any PC running Windows 3.1 or higher. A minimum of 4 MB of RAM, a floppy drive, a hard drive, and a color monitor are recommended. Although a monochrome monitor can be used, *Master C++ for Windows* makes extensive use of color in text and graphics to highlight key elements. *Master C++ for Windows* requires approximately 4 MB of storage space when installed on your hard disk.

CHAPTER 2   INSTALLATION

INSTALLATION OVERVIEW

The programs for *Master C++ for Windows* and their associated data files are supplied on one 1.44 MB IBM-PC floppy disk in a compressed format. This means you must use the SETUP program on the *Master C++ for Windows* disk to get the software up and running; simply copying the files will not work. You can, however, make a backup copy of the disk using the DOS DISKCOPY command, using the Windows 3.1 (or higher) File Manager, or using the Copy Disk feature in Windows 95. (Refer to your DOS or Windows manual if you aren't sure how to do this.) You can then install *Master C++ for Windows* from this backup disk.

The first time you install *Master C++ for Windows*, you will be asked to enter your name. Your copy of the software will then be updated to include this registration information. Later, if you choose to install the course on another computer system, the registration information will already be recorded; you will not be asked to enter your name again. *Master C++ for Windows* can legally be used only on one computer system at a time. Be sure to fill out and mail the enclosed registration card, so you will be informed about possible updates and related products that might be of interest.

INSTALLING *MASTER C++ FOR WINDOWS*

Before starting this installation, make sure you have at least 4 MB of free space on your hard disk to hold the *Master C++ for Windows* files.

Steps for the First Installation

Follow these steps to install *Master C++ for Windows* for the first time:

1. Start your computer and get into Windows.

2. Place the disk in drive A or B.

3. In Windows 95, click the Start button at the bottom left of the screen and select Run. In Windows 3.x, from the Program Manager, select the File Menu, then choose Run. You should see a dialog box something like Figure 2-2. In the text box, type A:\setup or B:\setup, then click OK.

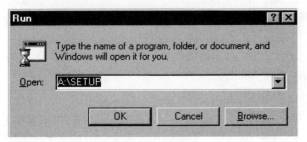

Figure 2-2 Starting the Installation

15

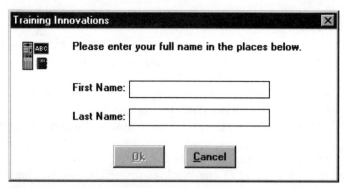

Figure 2-3 Registering Your Product

4. Once the installation program is running, it will ask you a number of questions, beginning with your name (See Figure 2-3). After entering your name, click OK.

5. The next dialog (see Figure 2-4) will ask you to identify where you want to install *Master C++ for Windows*. The dialog will already have the disk and directory reference, C:\MCPPW, because this is an appropriate location. If you prefer, you can change the destination drive or directory.

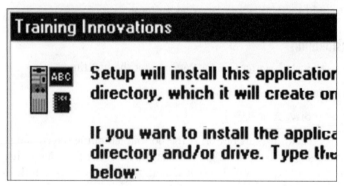

Figure 2-4 Defining the Destination Directory

6. As the installation program proceeds, progress information will appear. When the installation is done, a Program Menu is added to Windows 95; if you're running Windows 3.x, a Program group is created.

Steps for a Subsequent Installation

If you need to reinstall *Master C++ for Windows*, you will follow the same steps outlined above, except for step 4. You will have already registered your copy of the program, so you will not be asked to enter your name a second time.

3

EXPLORING MASTER C++ FOR WINDOWS

3
EXPLORING *MASTER C++ FOR WINDOWS*

Before you continue, make sure you have followed the installation steps given in Chapter 2, *Installation*.

GETTING STARTED

Naturally, to start *Master C++ for Windows* you need to be running Windows. The setup routine will have already created a new group window in Program Manager, and placed the *Master C++ for Windows* icon in that group window. Of course, you can resize that group window or drag it to some other location on the screen, just as you can with any other Program Manager group window. You can also move the *Master C++ for Windows* icon to a different group window using the standard drag-and-drop technique.

To start *Master C++ for Windows*, find the icon and double-click on it. The splash screen (shown in Figure 3-1) appears briefly while several additional program and data files are loaded into your computer. (The version number shown on your computer screen may be higher than the number shown here, indicating that you have a more recent version of the software.)

After the splash screen is displayed, you'll see the main table of contents screen.

Figure 3-1 Splash Screen

THE MAIN TABLE OF CONTENTS SCREEN

This table of contents screen or "main menu" (see Figure 3-2) is used for accessing the 15 lesson sets of *Master C++ for Windows*.

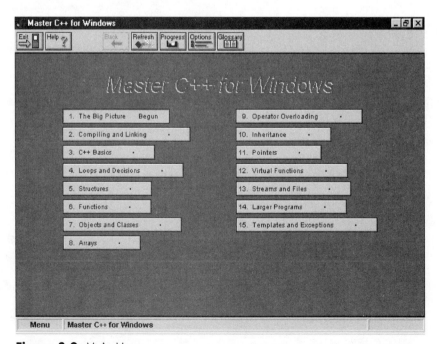

Figure 3-2 Main Menu

From the main menu, you can go to a given lesson set in any one of several ways: by typing the lesson number; by clicking on the appropriate button with the mouse; or by using the cursor keys and then pressing [ENTER]. Each lesson set offers a series of topics in a submenu that is similar to the table of contents menu. Again, you can press the number of the topics you want to explore, or click on the appropriate button with the mouse, or use the cursor keys and press [ENTER].

You'll probably want to tackle the topics in the order presented, because some topics may require knowledge of preceding ones, but the choice is always yours. If you already have some experience with C or C++, you may want to jump directly to topics of particular interest. Chapter 5, *Course Map,* outlines and summarizes the main points covered in each lesson. You can use the Course Map to help you find particular topics without having to examine all the menus.

Each numbered item on the main menu represents a corresponding chapter in the book *Object-Oriented Programming in Turbo C++.* Likewise, the topics offered in the submenu for each lesson set correspond to the main headings in that book. (Note that a few of the final chapters in the book are not included in *Master C++ for Windows,* due to their specialized nature.)

In case you're unsure about where you are when viewing a menu in the software, you can always identify the *main menu* by the flying *Master C++ for Windows* logos. Individual lesson-set submenus have a stationary C++ logo.

LESSON SCREENS

Master C++ for Windows presents a consistent screen layout (see Figure 3-3) to simplify "navigation" of the learning system. Every screen has these three general areas:

◆ Main instructional area

◆ Button bar

◆ Status bar

Each of these areas serves several different functions.

The Main Instructional Area

The large center part of the screen is used to present all learning material. This material includes text explanations, graphics, notes, and examples, as well as questions and feedback.

The Button Bar

The button bar consists of a number of symbols and keywords that identify specific functions. These give you control over your learning environment as you use *Master C++ for Windows.* You can move forward and backward through the lesson screens,

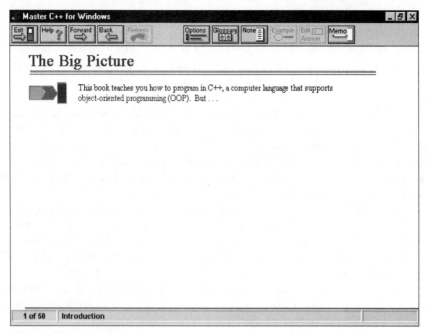

Figure 3-3 Sample Screen

explore the Glossary, review your progress (scores), create personal memos, and use other features of *Master C++ for Windows*.

The Status Bar

You can see the status bar at the bottom of the screen in Figure 3-2 (Main Menu) and Figure 3-3 (Sample Screen). The status bar always displays location information. When you're viewing a menu (Figure 3-2), the left corner shows the label "Menu," and the center section displays the title of the menu. When you're working through a thread of instructional material (see Figure 3-3), the left corner indicates the current screen number and total number of screens. The center section displays the title of the lesson.

THE BUTTON BAR AND ITS FUNCTIONS

In this section, we will explain the purpose of all the available buttons, though not all of them are always visible. As you can see in Figure 3-2, the Back button is grayed and several other buttons are not even visible, leaving obvious gaps in the line of buttons. If a button is visible and in full color, it is active and available. If a button is grayed or absent, then no meaningful action is available at that point in the course. In our first sample screen, the Back button is grayed because this particular screen is the main menu, and you can go back no further. Let's consider each button in more detail.

Forward and Back

The Forward and Back buttons are the two most common ways of moving through lessons. Use the Forward button to move to the next element in the lesson. Sometimes more information is added to the material already shown in the main instructional area. In other cases, a completely new screen is generated. Naturally, you can use the mouse to click on the Forward button, but you can also move forward by pressing [ENTER].

The Back button takes you back one step at a time to each preceding screen, allowing you to review material as desired. If you move back while at the first screen, you will be taken back to the point where you entered the lesson. Usually, this is a menu, because menu access is the most common path into lessons. If you entered Recall lesson material after answering a question incorrectly, or entered through the Glossary, then you would be taken back to that starting point. You can also invoke the Back button by pressing [ESC], instead of using the mouse.

Help

The Help button provides general help about the learning environment, not about C++ terms or concepts.

Refresh

The Refresh button replays a sound, video, or animation sequence when one is available at the current course location.

Progress

The Progress button displays a graph of detailed achievement information about the currently displayed menu. The upper bargraph contains pairs of bars: the green bar (on the left) shows your percentage achievement; the red bar (on the right) shows the time taken. Each pair corresponds to one item on the currently displayed menu. This upper bargraph summarizes the information generated by all your attempts. The lower graph displays a detailed view of achievement and time for the currently selected menu item. Each dot on a line graph marks one attempt. (If the currently selected item points to a submenu instead of instructional material, you will see small bargraphs in the lower graph area.)

When the progress window is open, the menu buttons behave differently. Ordinarily, when you select a menu item, you jump into that selected section of material (either a submenu or instructional material). When you select menu items while the progress window is open, the progress window changes to show you detailed information about the newly selected menu item. You must close the progress window to use the menu buttons in the normal way. To close the window, press the Progress button again, or press the small button in the top-left corner of the progress window.

Options

 The Options button opens a drop-down button bar that contains the following additional features.

Calc

The Calc button launches a calculator, which implements standard scientific functions. It can perform its work in decimal, hexadecimal, octal, or binary number systems.

Goal

 By pressing the Goal button, you can see a statement of objectives associated with the current learning material. In addition, this window displays an estimate of the time required to complete the material, and the percentage you must achieve to be credited with mastery. As you move from lesson to lesson, you can invoke this Objective window to list the essential elements of the each active lesson.

Settings

The Settings button opens a dialog box where you can change some of the course characteristics.

- For Course Personality, you can choose a "friendly" tone of feedback, one which is more businesslike or one that is a bit more "off-the-wall."

- Progress Detail controls the visibility of progress information. Initially, the software displays progress information directly on each menu item button. When you have mastered a particular section, you will see the percentage achieved at the end of the button. When you have started, but not yet finished a section, you will see Begun. A dot implies that you have not yet worked in that section. Figure 3-2 shows an example of this.

You can hide your progress information with the Partial setting if you prefer to keep your progress confidential. Of course, you can always access detailed progress information with the Progress button.

Glossary

The *Master C++ for Windows* Glossary (see Figure 3-4) provides online access to a collection of C++ terms and concepts. You can select the desired term using the list box. This presents a single screen of instructional material. With most of these terms, you can then launch to more detailed, related information before returning to your original course material. In this way, you can use the Glossary as a cross-referenced index to access related information, without having to walk through the standard menu structure.

CHAPTER 3   EXPLORING *MASTER C++ FOR WINDOWS*

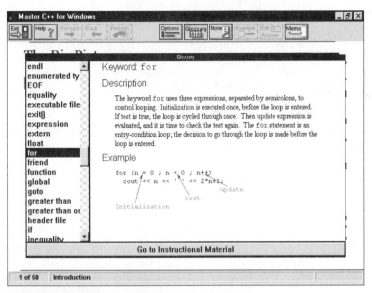

Figure 3-4 Glossary Window

Note and Example

When the animated Note or Example button appears, you can open an additional window that contains related information about the current concept. Once you have left a screen that contains a note or example, the animated button will become grayed.

You should read all available notes and examples the first time you go through a lesson. (You may want to skip them when reviewing the highlights of a lesson.) Notes and examples that are considered essential will pop open automatically. Those that are less critical will remain closed unless you explicitly open them.

A Note window (See Figure 3-5) might contain additional information that further clarifies a point, or presents a different approach to coding some operation. A Note window might also address the issue of machine dependency (for example, the differences between UNIX and MS-DOS implementations); it might amplify the details of some underlying organization and structure; or it might be an interesting aside.

An Example window usually contains a specific C++ example that extends the idea displayed in the main instructional area. It might also contain the output of a program.

With both Note and Example windows, only a portion of the original main screen information will remain visible behind the windows. To view all of the original main screen information again, you can use one of several techniques. To move a Note or Example window, click and hold the mouse button while pointing to the window's title bar, drag the window to the new location, and then release the mouse

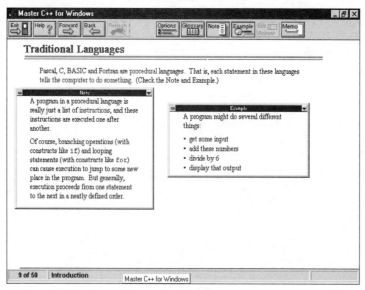

Figure 3-5 Note and Example Windows

button. To close the window, click on the Note or Example button again, or click on the system menu button in the top-left corner of the Note or Example window.

Edit

The Edit button comes in two forms: one with a blue arrow and one without. When the blue arrow is visible, you can press it to jump back to the most recently answered question, so you can edit the answer. When the blue arrow is not visible, you are sitting at a spot that has a question (probably one that you've just finished answering). By pressing the Edit button here, you can reedit the answer at the current location.

Memo

The Memo button invokes a simple notepad facility where you can make notes about the learning material. These notes accumulate from session to session and are accessible from any instructional screen.

Exit

The Exit button allows you to leave the course entirely, or to exit only from the current lesson. When you use this button, you will see the dialog box in Figure 3-6.

If you choose the first exit option, your progress information is saved and you exit the tutorial, returning to your standard Windows environment. Later, when you

Figure 3-6 Exit Dialog

restart *Master C++ for Windows*, you return to the point where you were last working. By exiting in this manner, you will be using the Bookmark feature of *Master C++ for Windows*.

The second option, Return to Menu, will return you to the section of *Master C++ for Windows* where you entered the current lesson or menu. This option will *not* save any progress information about your work in the active instructional material. You may want to use this option in the middle of instructional material when you are merely reviewing and don't need to complete all the screens. This may be during Recall mode or when using the Glossary.

HOW *MASTER C++ FOR WINDOWS* NUMBERS SCREENS

Obviously, the total number of screens per lesson varies. That's pretty well expected. But because of the way *Master C++ for Windows* is designed, the total number of screens may vary even for a given lesson, depending on when and how that lesson is entered. Therefore, a complete lesson as entered from the main menu may have 26 screens, so the first screen you see will be numbered *1 of 26*. If in the course of the lesson you answer a question incorrectly and seem to be confused, *Master C++ for Windows* will guide you through a review of the relevant material. This review "minilesson" might have only 4 screens, the first of which will be numbered *1 of 4*.

WHAT IS MASTERY?

You are credited with achieving mastery in a lesson when you answer 80% of the questions correctly. This 80% standard was chosen because it seemed to be the best compromise between passing knowledge of C++ (70% mastery) and a rigorous understanding of the language (90% to 100% mastery).

A few lessons contain no questions because the lessons are introductory in nature. When a lesson has questions, the mastery level will be displayed in the Objective window; when there are no questions in a lesson, no mastery level is set or displayed.

Now that you understand how to navigate in *Master C++ for Windows*, turn to the next chapter to find out how the program works, and how to best use it.

4

USING *MASTER C++* FOR WINDOWS TO LEARN C++

4

USING *MASTER C++* *FOR WINDOWS* TO LEARN C++

You have seen that the *Master C++ for Windows* menu screens are easy to understand and that navigation is simple using the commands on the button bar. In this chapter, you will look at what is going on "behind the scenes" when you interact with *Master C++ for Windows*. By understanding how the course asks questions and responds to your answers, you will be better able to use it as an effective learning tool. The way the system keeps track of your progress will also be explained to you. Finally, some alternative approaches to studying and reviewing material with *Master C++ for Windows* will be suggested.

HOW *MASTER C++ FOR WINDOWS* ASKS QUESTIONS

Master C++ for Windows uses an age-old method of teaching: it presents facts, and then it presents questions to see if you really understand the facts. Questions may be fill-in-the-blank, where you must complete a sentence or type in a specific word or phrase; multiple choice, where there are three or four buttons labelled with possible answers; or true/false. Most other teaching software stops here, but *Master C++ for*

Windows is unique. This expert system anticipates possible wrong answers and gives detailed feedback finely tuned to your current understanding. With some incorrect answers, *Master C++ for Windows* will intelligently alter the question and ask it again in another form.

Questions in Different Formats

Suppose the first time you take a lesson you get the question, *What is the name of the computer part that can store large amounts of information even when the computer is turned off?* Because this is a fill-in-the-blank style, you would also see a dialog box with a spot for you to enter your answer. One correct answer could be "disk," but *Master C++ for Windows* would also accept "floppy" and several other related responses.

If you encountered this question again, it might be rephrased as, *In a computer, RAM can store large amounts of your information, even when the computer is turned off.* This time the text would be accompanied with two buttons labelled True and False. Even though this question requires a true or false response, it essentially deals with the same material as the original question. This technique of question alteration does two things. It makes the test less repetitive, and it aids understanding by presenting the same material in different ways.

Acceptance of Abbreviated and Shortened Answers

Master C++ for Windows asks many open-ended questions. For these, there may be many ways to phrase the correct response. This is particularly true with fill-in-the-blank questions. *Master C++ for Windows* allows you to approximate the complete answer much as a human teacher would; if your response consists of shortened words or partial phrases that still contain the basic meaning of the answer, it will be judged correct. This allows the course to consider the widest possible range of correct answers and not penalize you for not typing the answer exactly as the computer expected it.

In the question about computer storage, the complete answer is considered to be "floppy or hard disk," but you could answer "disk," "hard drive," "floppy," and dozens of other variations of these terms. So when questions deal with definitions and concepts, feel free to use shortened answers. When you respond with a correct but partial answer, *Master C++ for Windows* will also give you the complete answer for reference.

As you can see from the preceding discussion, in answers to questions about programming concepts, *Master C++ for Windows* is very forgiving about your spelling and grammar. But sometimes spelling really does matter. As you probably know, computer languages are less forgiving than English when it comes to specifying something. When questions deal with the details of C++ programming code, be sure to include all the required elements: all punctuation and complete words—paying particular attention to uppercase and lowercase. Remember, C++ *is* a case-sensitive language.

CHAPTER 4 USING *MASTER C++ FOR WINDOWS* TO LEARN C++

Questions That Get Progressively Easier

In some cases, a question may be structured so that it becomes progressively easier if you enter an incorrect answer. As a first step, *Master C++ for Windows* will usually offer some helpful hint that relates to your particular incorrect answer. Consider the example in Figure 4-1. Suppose you are working in Lesson 3.2, *Preprocessor Directives and Comments*. The system asks you:

What is the purpose of the #include directive?

and you type the answer:

to let you edit the program

Master C++ for Windows responds:

The name of the directive implies its purpose.

Please try again.

Therefore, *Master C++ for Windows* gives you a hint. (Look at the name *#include* itself for a clue to the directive's purpose.)

Another way *Master C++ for Windows* simplifies a question is to accompany it with a series of possible answers (essentially a multiple choice question). For example, consider Figure 4-2 which shows the question:

Imagine that you are writing some source code for a program. What line would you use to include the contents of the header file named FSTREAM.H in your code?

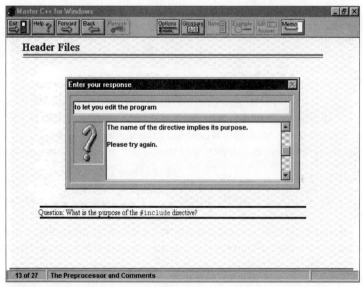

Figure 4-1 *Master C++ for Windows:* The Intelligent Tutor

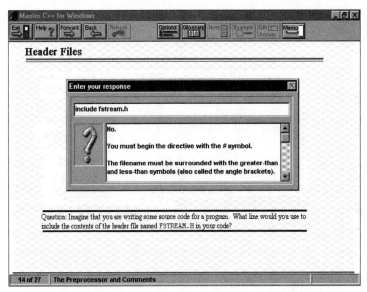

Figure 4-2 *Master C++ for Windows:* The Expert System

Suppose that you answer this question by typing:

include fstream.h

Because this is incorrect, the system will analyze the answer, identify the two problems, present a "hint," and then give you another chance:

You must begin the directive with the # symbol.

The filename must be surrounded with the greater-than and less-than symbols (also called the angle brackets).

Please try again

Notice that *Master C++ for Windows* has identified two different problems with your response, and gives specific feedback for both problems. Because your original answer is still accessible for editing, you can make the minor changes without having to reenter your complete answer. Suppose you tried again and typed this answer:

#include [fstream.h]

This is still wrong. (Angle brackets instead of square brackets must surround the file name *fstream.h*.) *Master C++ for Windows* recognizes that you are having problems, and like a wise teacher it simplifies the matter for you by presenting a multiple-choice question with a series of buttons that include the actual answer (as shown in Figure 4-3).

Multiple-choice questions are easier than equivalent fill-in-the-blank questions. With a fill-in-the-blank question, you must recall the answer without any cueing. For

CHAPTER 4 USING *MASTER C++ FOR WINDOWS* TO LEARN C++

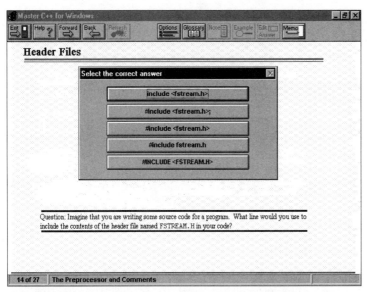

Figure 4-3 *Master C++ for Windows:* Simplifying Questions

a similar multiple-choice question, you can survey the five choices and select the best answer (the final answer is correct here). When the original question was first presented, skills of recall were required; with the multiple-choice form, skills of recognition are needed.

Finally, if you still haven't answered correctly after several tries, *Master C++ for Windows* takes you back to some earlier learning material so that you can review the lesson on the *#include* directive.

Recognizing Incomplete Answers

Master C++ for Windows employs an interesting technique to accept incomplete answers and prompt you for the remaining parts. For example, in answer to:

All C++ programs begin execution with a function that is always called _____.
suppose you type

main

Master C++ for Windows will present this text in its *Feedback* window:

You are correct so far. Continue.

The course is telling you that you have typed an almost complete answer, but something more is still needed. If you follow this by typing the ( ) needed to complete the header of the *main* function, *Master C++ for Windows* will say you are correct and move to the next question. Otherwise, the answer is judged incorrect.

Guided Practice in Building Programs

One of the strengths of *Master C++ for Windows* is the technique used to lead you through the process of building complete working programs, and smaller sections of program code. The course begins by explaining the nature of the programming problem to be solved. It then asks you to enter the lines of code required to solve that problem—prompting you for each line. In the early stages of your learning process, *Master C++ for Windows* gives very clear explicit explanations and expects you to enter each line. Later, as you gain more proficiency, sections of code that are clearly easier material will be filled in automatically. You will only be asked to enter new material that you are currently learning. This "fast-track" approach to learning ensures that you know all the required material, without forcing you to answer endless questions about material that you already know.

RECORDING YOUR ACHIEVEMENT

Master C++ for Windows provides you with a record of your achievement—a "grade" that measures your mastery of the material presented. Because everyone has trouble at one time or another, the system also makes it easy to review material and take tests again.

Approaching Mastery

Each time a question is presented, your attempt at an answer is recorded by the software. If you get it right you are given credit for that question. However, if you get it wrong or use the Review option to repeat it, you don't get credit. You must go completely through a lesson and answer at least 80% of the questions correctly. If at the end of a *Master C++ for Windows* lesson more than 20% of the questions were answered incorrectly or have been reviewed, you will need to repeat those questions to "pass."

Understanding the Progress Information

A record of your progress is saved in two files in a subdirectory called REGISTER. A summary of this information is displayed on the menu buttons for each lesson set. As you work through the learning material, *Master C++ for Windows* updates your progress continually. In cases where you prefer that this progress information remain private, you can specify this using the Options button bar Settings option (see Chapter 3, *Exploring Master C++ for Windows*).

Here's a list of progress information that can be displayed:

    80%-100%   A number between 80% and 100% indicates that you have successfully completed the lesson. Any score of less than 80% displays the word Repeat in front of the section title.

Begun	Indicates that you used the Exit or Back buttons to leave a lesson before reaching its end.
Done	Displayed in front of sections that were completed but did not have any questions, and hence had no scores.
Repeat	Displayed in front of sections that were completed with a score of less than 80%.
• (Dot)	Displayed in front of sections that have not been started.

Resetting Achievement Info

If you want to remove all your achievement information (scores) so that you can start *Master C++ for Windows* over, you must delete the two files in the C:\MCPPW\MCPPW\REGISTER directory. Both these files will be named whatever you typed into the First Name field of the dialog box at installation. One will have the .MKS extension; the other .VAR. You can delete these two files through File Manager or from the DOS prompt with this DOS command:

C:\>DEL C:\MCPPW\MCPPW\REGISTER*.* [Enter]

(Note that you do not remove the directory itself, only its contents.) You can then start *Master C++ for Windows* and work "from scratch." All records of previous achievement will be lost.

OTHER WAYS TO LEARN WITH *MASTER C++ FOR WINDOWS*

Computer-based training systems are often criticized for being too linear. With some programs, you have only one prescribed path of learning even though you may already know some of the material. But *Master C++ for Windows* is different. Although its menu system provides fixed sequences of topics, there are several alternative ways to approach material. You can use *Master C++ for Windows* in a more direct manner than studying its contents lesson by lesson.

Using the Glossary

You can look up a specific concept or keyword in the Glossary, and jump to the location in *Master C++ for Windows* where that concept or keyword is covered. The system doesn't just jump from the keyword to a specific concept. Rather, it locates only those screens that are relevant to the keyword or concept and presents them so you can choose where to go next. When finished, you will be returned to the point where you first launched into the Glossary.

Using the Glossary can be helpful when you want to study or review a particular concept in depth.

Using the Review Lessons

The final item in most lesson-set menus is called Review. If you are somewhat familiar with C++ programming or you want to test your knowledge before embarking on detailed study in all the lessons, you can use this Review item.

As you work through the material, you are presented with information and given a chance to answer questions. Whenever you answer a question incorrectly, after prompting by *Master C++ for Windows* you will be taken to the parts of earlier lessons where you are weak. This is a quick way to let the course diagnose your problems and structure an individualized review.

Making a Hard Copy of *Master C++ for Windows* Screens

If you have a printer, you can study a *Master C++ for Windows* screen away from the computer by using the Windows capability of capturing screen images. While viewing the *Master C++ for Windows* window (that is, the title bar of the window is highlighted), you can press [ALT]-[PRINT SCREEN]. This captures an image of the active window to the Windows Clipboard. You can then move over to Paintbrush (or some other suitable graphics program) and paste in the captured image. From there, you can use the normal printing facilities of the graphics package.

Setting Out on Your Own

A number of features of *Master C++ for Windows* have been outlined, and a number of strategies for accessing information have been suggested. Not everyone learns in the same way, so experiment to find the learning approach that best suits your needs. The best technique for many users is to use a combination of reading sections in a sequence; alternating with reading the book; jumping into specific lessons via the Glossary; and studying just the Review sections.

The next chapter of this manual presents the course map—an overview of the material covered in the course.

5 COURSE MAP

5
COURSE MAP

This chapter provides a "map" of the material covered by *Master C++ for Windows*. You can use the accompanying lesson overviews to get a broad sense of the topics involved in mastery of the C++ language. The topic list for each chapter lets you zero in on specific interests. You might also want to read more about a topic by checking the corresponding chapter in the Waite Group Press book *Object-Oriented Programming in Turbo C++*.

HOW *MASTER C++ FOR WINDOWS* IS ORGANIZED

The *Master C++ for Windows* CBT consists of 15 lesson sets, which are presented on the main table of contents menu screen. Table 5-1 shows all 15 lesson sets and the estimated time for the average student to cover each lesson. Remember that the numbers generally correspond to the chapter numbers in *Object-Oriented Programming in Turbo C++* (though the section on graphics is not included here).

Table 5-1 *Master C++ for Windows* lessons and course time requirements

CHAPTER	LESSON TITLE	HOURS
1	The Big Picture	1.0
2	Compiling and Linking	0.5
3	C++ Basics	3.5
4	Loops and Decisions	3.5
5	Structures	2.0

continued on next page

continued from previous page

CHAPTER	LESSON TITLE	HOURS
6	Functions	3.0
7	Objects and Classes	2.5
8	Arrays	2.0
9	Operator Overloading	2.0
10	Inheritance	2.5
11	Pointers	3.5
12	Virtual Functions	2.0
13	Streams and Files	1.5
14	Larger Programs	1.5
15	Templates and Exceptions	2.0
	Total:	33.0

1: THE BIG PICTURE

Overview of Contents

C++ is a superset of the C language—that is, it includes all of C's features and syntax and adds many features of its own. But C++ is not merely an improved C with added features. Rather, C++ is designed to be a vehicle for *object-oriented programming (OOP)*—a new way to think about data and the things you need to do with data. OOP came as a response to the problems increasingly encountered in trying to manage large programs written in traditional *procedural* languages such as BASIC, Pascal, and C. Although these languages provide features for breaking down large programs into smaller pieces, they do not provide an effective mechanism for controlling access to data and hiding irrelevant details.

In C, the building block for program development was the function—a set of instructions for manipulating certain data in a specified way. In C++, programs are organized as a set of *classes*. Each class is a blueprint for the *objects* that a program needs to work with—for example, a geometric figure, a bank account, or a screen window.

Each class *encapsulates* the necessary data items and functions. A class also provides controlled access to the data from other parts of the program, making the overall program easier to understand (and as a result, easier to maintain).

In addition, the mechanism of *inheritance* allows specialized classes to be *derived* from more general ones. Through inheritance and derivation, the C++ language provides easy *reusability* of well-tested code.

C++ is *extensible* because the new data types and operators you define become integral parts of the language. Finally, the *polymorphism* of C++ allows operators and functions to work appropriately under different circumstances.

CHAPTER 5   COURSE MAP

Objectives

- Identify the conceptual differences between the C++ language and more traditional procedural languages.
- Identify the advantages of object-oriented programming.
- Understand the essential characteristics of object-oriented languages.

Topics

1.1	Introduction	
1.2	The Object-Oriented Approach	
1.3	The Major Elements	
1.4	Review	

Time Requirements: 1.0 hours

2: COMPILING AND LINKING

Overview of Contents

The *segmented* architecture used by the Intel family of 8086-based processors on the IBM PC complicates programming. As a programmer, you must decide how memory will be divided among program code, the stack (used to pass data to and from functions), and *near* and *far* data areas. Standard configurations called *memory models* are provided to meet most needs. The *small* memory model should be quite adequate for learning C++, though you'll likely outgrow it as you generate larger applications.

    Creating an executable program involves many steps, though modern *integrated development environments (IDE)* automate many of the detailed tasks. C++ compiler products from companies such as Borland, Microsoft, and Symantec have made great strides in simplifying what was once a fairly complex process. Nevertheless, you should have a conceptual understanding of the steps involved in compiling, linking, and running C++ code.

Objectives

- Understand how Intel-based C++ compilers organize memory.
- Understand the steps involved in building an executable program.

Topics

2.1	Memory Models	
2.2	Compiling, Linking, and Running	
2.3	Review	

Time Requirements: 0.5 hour

3: C++ BASICS

Overview of Contents

In this chapter you will learn how to put together simple but complete C++ programs. Each C++ program must have a function called *main()*, where execution begins. By following simple rules, you construct a series of program *statements* that define the tasks to be performed. Each statement must end with a semicolon. Statements often contain *expressions*, which use variables, constants, and operators to express values.

You use *preprocessor directives* to give the compiler special instructions. The *#include* directive gives your program access to the rich library of ANSI C functions and C++ classes that come with modern compilers. You will begin to use the simple output facilities C++ provides through the IOSTREAM.H header file.

You will also learn how to create and name variables, based on the basic data types. These variables can represent numbers and characters, and can be used to perform calculations with arithmetic operators. You will learn the rules C++ uses for converting one type of variable to another, and how to use *type casts* to convert a value to a specific type.

Objectives

- Understand the basic organization of a C++ program.
- Use the preprocessor to control compilation and processing of your program.
- Understand the structure and use of the fundamental numeric and character data types.
- Use the standard arithmetic operators to compute values.
- Use header files and library files to bring needed functionality into your program.

Topics

3.1	Program Construction Basics
3.2	The Preprocessor and Comments
3.3	Integer Variables
3.4	Character Variables
3.5	Floating-Point Variables
3.6	Manipulators
3.7	Variable Type Summary
3.8	Arithmetic Operators
3.9	Header Files and Library Files
3.10	Review

Time Requirements: 3.5 hours

4: LOOPS AND DECISIONS

Overview of Contents

In most real-world processes, decisions are made on the basis of changing conditions. In this lesson set, you will learn how to have your program test for one or more specified conditions. Based on the result of the test, the program can perform some other specified action (via a *decision statement*). A *loop* allows for the conditional or unconditional repetition of an operation.

C++ provides three loop statements: *for, while,* and *do while*. You generally use the *for* loop when you know how many times a particular operation should be performed. The *while* and *do while* loops are "open ended," running until some specified condition is met or not met. With the *while* loop, the loop body might never be executed (if the test condition at the top of the loop is false). The *do while* loop, on the other hand, is always executed at least once, because the test occurs at the bottom of the loop. The *break* and *continue* statements can be used to interrupt a loop if a specified situation arises during execution.

The *if* and *if else* statements test one or more conditions and perform the specified actions if the conditions are met. The *if else* construct allows several alternatives to be considered in the same statement, but the *switch* statement is easier to use and clearer to read when there are many conditions being tested.

You can use *logical operators* to express complex conditions that have two or more parts. The *AND* and *OR* operators test two conditions and are true if both (*AND*) or at least one (*OR*) of them is true. The *NOT* operator can be used to negate (reverse) the truth of a condition.

Objectives

- Use relational operators to compare data values.
- Control repeated program actions with the *for, while,* and *do while* loops.
- Decide how the program will test and respond to data.
- Make simple and complex branching decisions with the *if* and *if else* statements.
- Use the *switch* statement for multibranching.
- Employ logical operators to express complex conditions.

Topics

4.1 Relational Operators
4.2 Loops
    4.2.1 The *for* Loop
    4.2.2 *for* Loop Variations
    4.2.3 The *while* Loop

           4.2.4   Precedence
           4.2.5   The *do while* Loop
   4.3   Decisions
           4.3.1   The *if* Statement
           4.3.2   The *if else* Statement
           4.3.3   The *switch case* Statement
   4.4   Logical Operators
   4.5   Other Control Structures
   4.6   Review
Time Requirements: 3.5 hours

5: STRUCTURES

Overview of Contents

This lesson set begins the exploration of structures and classes in C++. Structures provide a powerful technique of program organization by allowing you to group data items together in a single unit (sometimes called a "record" in other languages). As examples, applications might deal with data that is organized as "records" of customer information, as bank account information, or as the location and size of a graphics figure.

You will learn to define simple data *structures* and access individual "fields" or *members* of those structures. A simple card game will illustrate the manipulation of structures. You will also learn how to use *enumerated variables* to manipulate items that have a small number of possible values, such as the suits in a card deck.

Objectives

- Use structures to group related items of data together.
- Access and change data in a structure.
- Use enumerated variables to specify items that have one of a specified list of values.

Topics

   5.1   An Introduction
   5.2   Other Structure Features
   5.3   Structures Inside Structures
   5.4   A Card Game Example
   5.5   Enumerated Data Types
   5.6   Review
Time Requirements: 2.0 hours

6: FUNCTIONS

Overview of Contents

Now that you've learned how to represent and organize data into simple variables and structures, it's time to define functions to manipulate the data. You will learn how to define a function and how to specify its *arguments* (data in the form of variables or constants being passed to the function for processing). You specify the name and arguments of the function in a *prototype*. You write the executable statements that perform the function's work in the function *definition*.

A function can return only a single data value, but that value can be a more complex entity such as a structure. A function can also work with *references* to actual variables, rather than just using a copy of the data. Passing a reference allows the function to change the value of the original variable. The use of references in C++ provides a more convenient syntax for accessing data than is possible through the use of pointers. (In contrast, the C language does not support references.)

You will also learn about other powerful function features that C++ adds to C. By declaring a function to be *inline*, you can have its code repeatedly inserted wherever the function is named, avoiding the processing delay caused by a function call. Because an inline function is a true function with a prototype, C++ can still check the types of values being passed to it. This gives the inline function a significant advantage over preprocessor macros that are commonly used in C. You will also learn how to define functions that set default values for certain variables. This can make function calls easier to write.

Finally, you will survey the *storage classes*, which determine the parts of a program that can use a variable and how long values stored in the variable are kept. By default, variables defined in a function are *automatic* and exist only while the function is executing. Variables can be made *static* instead, so that they will retain their value between function calls. *External* variables defined outside functions exist as long as the program is running.

Objectives

- Define simple functions.
- Pass values to functions for processing.
- Get results back from a function.
- Use references to pass actual variables to a function for modification.
- Define inline functions for faster processing.
- Establish default values for data being passed to a function.
- Understand storage classes and visibility of variables.

Topics

	6.1	Simple Functions
	6.2	Passing Arguments to Functions
	6.3	Returning Values from Functions
	6.4	Reference Arguments
	6.5	Overloaded Functions
	6.6	Inline Functions
	6.7	Default Arguments
	6.8	Variables and Storage Classes
	6.9	Returning Reference Arguments
	6.10	Review

Time Requirements: 3.0 hours

7: OBJECTS AND CLASSES

Overview of Contents

Now that you've mastered data and functions, you can put them together into classes and objects—the heart of object-oriented programming. A *class* specifies a blueprint for creating actual *objects*. A class normally includes both data items and the functions that manipulate the data. You can restrict access to the data members and member functions of a class, making selected data and functions invisible to other parts of a program. *Private* members can be accessed only by an object of the class. *Public* members can be accessed by other functions in the program. Just like simple variables, objects can be sent to a function or used as a return value.

Each class has two special member functions—a *constructor* that creates new objects of the class, and a *destructor* that cleans up after an object is no longer needed. C++ provides default, built-in constructors and destructors, but you will commonly provide your own explicit constructor. Explicit destructors are required less often, except when using extensive pointers and memory allocation.

Classes provide a powerful tool for representing the data with which your program works and the operations that must be performed on the data. There are few hard-and-fast rules for defining appropriate classes, so object-oriented programming is more of an art than a science.

Objectives

✦ Understand the parts of a class and how a class defines objects.

✦ Use constructors and destructors to create and manage objects.

✦ Give class objects to a function and return an object from a function.

✦ Understand how a C++ program manages the use of memory by objects.

CHAPTER 5 COURSE MAP

Topics

7.1	A Simple Class	
7.2	C++ Objects	
7.3	Constructors and Destructors	
7.4	Objects As Function Arguments	
7.5	Returning Objects from Functions	
7.6	Classes, Objects, and Memory	
7.7	Static Class Data	
7.8	What Does It All Mean?	
7.9	Review	

Time Requirements: 2.5 hours

8: ARRAYS

Overview of Contents

A structure or class is the best way to group together related data items that are of different data types. For example, you might create a structure or class to hold a person's name, address, phone number, and age. On the other hand, when you have many instances of the same kind of data item (for example, test scores for a group of students), an *array* is the appropriate organizational tool. With an array, individual items can be searched, sorted, or copied easily by manipulating a value called the *index*, which is a number identifying a particular location or *element* in the array. An array can have more than one *dimension*; therefore, you can have an array of arrays. For example, a calendar can be represented as an array of 12 months, with each month being an array of days.

Arrays can be used in the same ways as simple data types. The array name stands for the starting address of the array. You can therefore, pass an array to a function for modification. You can have an array of any sort of data object—simple numeric variables, characters, strings, or class objects.

A *character string* is just an array of characters. An array of strings is particularly useful for storing and manipulating text. As you work through the more complex and interesting examples in this lesson set, you will learn more about the string formatting capabilities of the C++ *streams library* and the useful string manipulation functions inherited from the C library. Finally, you will begin to develop a string object that improves on the traditional way of working with strings.

Objectives

- Use arrays to hold collections of similar data items.

- Create arrays of arrays (multidimensional arrays).

- Use structures and objects in arrays.
- Define a string array.
- Use the string manipulation functions in the standard library.
- Include strings as members of a class.

Topics

8.1	Array Fundamentals	
8.2	Multidimensional Arrays	
8.3	Passing Arrays As Arguments	
8.4	Arrays of Structures	
8.5	Arrays of Objects	
8.6	Strings	
	8.6.1	String Variables and Constants
	8.6.2	Reading Multiple Lines
	8.6.3	Copying Strings
	8.6.4	Arrays of Strings
	8.6.5	Strings As Class Members
8.7	Review	

Time Requirements: 2.0 hours

9: OPERATOR OVERLOADING

Overview of Contents

The ability to redefine or *overload* operators is a key feature of C++. You can take many of the standard operators (such as +) and make them work with objects. Therefore, you can extend the C++ language to include syntax such as *string1* + *string2* to combine two strings, or *C1* + *C2* to add two complex numbers. You can use *Obj1* > *Obj2* to check whether one graphic object is farther from the center of the screen than the other.

You redefine operators by providing an appropriate *operator function* as part of the class with whose objects you want to work. Redefining operators requires understanding the difference between *unary* operators (that take only one operand) and *binary* operators (that use two operands). When creating overloaded operators, you should define them with actions that are analogous to the ordinary use of the operator. In this way, the expressions you write will make more sense to the reader of your program.

You will often need to convert between your defined objects and real-world data expressed in different units. (For example, you may need to convert between metric and English distance units.) You will learn how to use constructors to convert values when initializing objects, and how to write conversion functions that can convert your objects into other specified units.

Objectives

- Understand the difference between unary and binary operators.
- Redefine (overload) operators to work with the new objects you define.
- Define useful operations such as string concatenation and comparison.
- Understand issues involving type conversion.

Topics

9.1 Unary Operators
9.2 Binary Operators
9.3 Concatenating Strings
9.4 Comparison Operators
9.5 Arithmetic Operators
9.6 Data Conversion
9.7 Pitfalls of Operator Overloading
9.8 Review
Time Requirements: 2.0 hours

10: INHERITANCE

Overview of Contents

Most programs require more than one class to represent the real-world objects being manipulated. *Inheritance* provides one way to express the relationship between classes. For example, a graphic circle can be *derived* from the *base class* called Point by adding a radius data member to the x-and y-coordinates it receives from the Point class.

You can control the access that derived classes have to the data in the base class. The keyword *protected* specifies that a derived class can access data or functions from the base class, but they cannot be accessed from the outside. You can also control access by making the class derivation *public* (allowing access to the base class' public members) or *private* (prohibiting such access). Access control makes it possible to safely distribute classes without risking corruption of their internal structure.

When you create a hierarchy of classes, you must understand how constructors and destructors are called for an object of a derived class. When an object is created, the base constructor is called first (or more than one base constructor in the case of multiple inheritance). When the object is destroyed, however, the derived destructor is called first, then the base destructor. When working with a class hierarchy you can use the *scope resolution operator* to explicitly call a member function at a particular point in the hierarchy.

In addition to the inheritance relationship, you can also put one class inside another, expressing *containership*. Derivation says, in effect, "B *is a* kind of A," but containership says "A *has a* B."

Objectives

- Understand the concept of class inheritance and how it can help you represent a hierarchy of concepts.
- Derive a new class from an existing one.
- Control access to inherited class members.
- Use multiple inheritance, where one class can share characteristics from two "parent" classes.
- Contain one class inside another.
- Understand the difference between *Is A* and *Has A* relationships.
- Understand issues in program design with classes.

Topics

10.1   Derived Class and Base Class
10.2   Derived Class Constructors
10.3   Inheritance with the Distance Class
10.4   Class Hierarchies
10.5   Public and Private Inheritance
10.6   Multiple Inheritance
10.7   Containership: Classes Within Classes
10.8   Inheritance and Program Development
10.9   Review

Time Requirements: 2.5 hours

11: POINTERS

Overview of Contents

Pointers hold the addresses where values are stored. By adding to or subtracting from a pointer you can quickly retrieve a series of values stored in adjacent locations in memory (for example, array elements or characters in a string). The * (asterisk)

CHAPTER 5   COURSE MAP

operator is used to *dereference* a pointer and return the value stored in the location pointed to by the address in the pointer.

When a pointer is used as an argument to a function, the function has direct access to the original variable (rather than only a copy of the variable's value). In this respect, pointers are an alternative to the C++ reference operator. Strings and arrays can be accessed either using *array notation* (with an index value) or through dereferencing a pointer (with the * asterisk). Class objects can also be referenced with pointers. Giving a class a pointer to itself makes it possible to have linked data structures such as stacks and lists. You can even have pointers to other pointers.

Although pointers offer great flexibility, it is easy to make mistakes in working with them. Also, complex expressions involving pointers may be hard to read.

Objectives

- Understand pointers and how to access addresses and the value stored at an address.
- Use pointers as an alternate way to access arrays.
- Use pointers to pass variables to a function.
- Manipulate values with pointers inside a function.
- Use pointers to access strings.
- Use pointers with class objects.
- Understand issues involved with debugging common problems involving pointers.

Topics

- 11.1 Addresses and Pointers
    - 11.1.1 Introduction
    - 11.1.2 Finding the Address
    - 11.1.3 Pointer Variables
    - 11.1.4 Accessing the Variable Pointed To
    - 11.1.5 Pointer to void
- 11.2 Pointers and Arrays
- 11.3 Pointers and Functions
    - 11.3.1 Passing Simple Variables
    - 11.3.2 Passing Arrays
    - 11.3.3 Sorting Array Elements
- 11.4 Pointers and Strings
- 11.5 The *new* Operator
- 11.6 Pointers to Objects

11.7   An Array of Pointers to Objects
11.8   Pointers to Pointers
11.9   Debugging Pointers
11.10 Review
Time Requirements: 3.5 hours

12: VIRTUAL FUNCTIONS

Overview of Contents

Imagine that you have a hierarchy of derived classes, but no virtual functions, and you are accessing those member functions using pointers. C++ uses the declared type of the pointer to determine which class member function to call. This can cause problems when a program is using a reference or pointer of the *base class* type that refers to an object of a *derived class* type. By default, the member function from the *base* type will be called, losing the added functionality in the derived type. A solution to this problem is the use of a *virtual* base class function. With a virtual function the correct call to the correct derived class function will be made at runtime.

Sometimes you will create a class that needs to access members of two classes that aren't otherwise related. In this situation you can make your new function or class a *friend* to the existing one, allowing access to private members. Friends are typically defined to allow the streams to work with overloaded functions from user-defined classes.

If a class has data values shared by all of its objects (for example, a "flag" used to indicate a mode of processing), you can define and access such common data through *static* functions.

Assignment operators and copy constructors can be overloaded in order to manage the creation of a new copy of an object during assignment. This is often necessary when memory must be allocated for a complex object.

You can use the predefined *this* pointer to refer to "the object itself" within a member function. This allows you to return the object itself from a function.

Objectives

- Use virtual functions for runtime flexibility.
- Define friend functions to allow controlled access to unrelated classes.
- Use static functions to manage data values common to all objects of a class.
- Understand problems involved with creation of copies of objects during assignment.
- Have an object refer to itself with the *this* pointer.

Topics

12.1	Virtual Functions
12.2	Pure Virtual Functions
12.3	Friend Functions
12.4	Static Functions
12.5	Assignment and Copy
12.6	The Copy Constructor
12.7	The *this* Pointer
12.8	Review

Time Requirements: 2.0 hours

13: STREAMS AND FILES

Overview of Contents

As you have seen previously, C++ provides a *streams library* of Input/Output (I/O) functions that can replace the traditional C I/O facilities. C++ streams are often more efficient because you can put together the components you need rather than relying on a few large "all-purpose" I/O and formatting functions. You will first review I/O with the keyboard and screen (*cin* and *cout*) and then look at I/O with disk files.

Stream I/O can also be combined with operating system facilities such as the command-line processing and I/O redirection available with MS-DOS and UNIX. This can enable you to write programs that can be used flexibly at the command line.

By overloading the << and >> operators you can tailor I/O operations to work with the class objects you design.

Objectives

- Understand how the C++ streams library provides facilities for input and output (including access to files).

- Use streams for input and output of single characters and strings.

- Read and write data from files.

- Handle file processing errors.

- Redirect file input and output and send output to a printer.

- Use command-line arguments.

- Overload the << and >> operators to work with new classes.

Topics

    13.1   Streams
    13.2   String, Character, Binary I/O
    13.3   Object I/O
    13.4   File Pointers
    13.5   Error Handling
    13.6   Overloading the << and >> Operators
    13.7   Redirection
    13.8   Command-Line Arguments
    13.9   Printer Output
    13.10   Review
Time Requirements: 1.5 hours

14: LARGER PROGRAMS

Overview of Contents

In all earlier examples, program code was placed in a single source file. This approach is fine for small sample programs, but it is unsuitable for real application development. Larger programs must be broken into a series of smaller, source code modules, each of which sits in its own file.

With larger programs, development can proceed much faster. For example, a small code change in a .CPP source code file will only necessitate recompilation of that single file, even though there may be dozens of other related source code files.

This lesson set explains the techniques of organization when building larger programs.

Objectives

- Understand the role of header files.

- Understand the uses of *public* and *private* declarations when creating class libraries for distribution.

- Build a small multifile application to implement a new numeric data type that can manipulate very large numbers.

Topics

    14.1   Reasons for Multiple File Programs
    14.2   Creating a Multiple File Program
    14.3   A Very Long Number Class
    14.4   Review
Time Requirements: 1.5 hours

CHAPTER 5   COURSE MAP

15: TEMPLATES AND EXCEPTIONS

Overview of Contents

Templates allow you to generate a family of functions or a family of classes to handle different data types. Whenever you find yourself writing several identical functions that perform the same operation on different data types, you should consider using a *function template* instead. Similarly, whenever you find yourself writing several different class specifications that differ only in the type of data acted on, you should consider using a *class template*. You'll save yourself time, and the result will be a more robust and more easily maintained program that is also (once you understand templates) easier to understand.

Exceptions are a mechanism for handling C++ errors in a systematic OOP-oriented way. An exception is typically caused by a faulty statement in a try block that operates on objects of a class. The class member function discovers the error and throws an exception, which is caught by exception-handler code following the try block.

Objectives

- Implement templates to create a common body of code for different data types.
- Use templates with multiple arguments.
- Implement templates as part of a class design.
- Understand the advantages of formal exception handling.
- Implement a simple exception handler.
- Implement multiple exception handlers in a class.

Topics

15.1	Templates: An Introduction	
15.2	A Simple Template	
15.3	Templates with Multiple Arguments	
15.4	Class Templates	
15.5	Exceptions: An Introduction	
15.6	Exceptions: A Simple Example	
15.7	Exceptions: Distance Class	
15.8	Exception Notes	
15.9	Review	

Time Requirements: 2.0 hours

6
IN CASE OF TROUBLE

6

IN CASE OF TROUBLE

Master C++ for Windows has been thoroughly tested with a number of different PC configurations. In 99% of the cases, it should install and run without problems. But just in case something is wrong, this chapter presents answers to possible questions about installing and running *Master C++ for Windows*.

This discussion is divided into two categories. First, the problems that might prevent proper installation of the software are covered, and then problems that might occur while you are using *Master C++ for Windows* are discussed.

INSTALLATION PROBLEMS

The first step in dealing with installation problems is to review Chapter 2, *Installation*, which discusses the steps involved in installing the *Master C++ for Windows* software. You may find that you accidentally skipped a step, and you can start over and complete the installation successfully. If that is not the case, look among the following questions for possible answers to your problem.

If none of these issues is what you are facing, you can call Waite Group Press for technical support.

I've copied *Master C++ for Windows* to my hard disk but it won't run.

You cannot run *Master C++ for Windows* directly from the distribution disk. Nor can you run it by copying the files to your hard disk. The program files are compressed and have to be processed by the Install program. Follow the directions in Chapter 2.

Why won't the Install program work? Insufficient disk space?

Check to make sure you have at least 4 MB of space available on your hard disk. If you use a disk compression utility on your hard drive, then the reported free space may not accurately reflect the amount of available space. In addition, Windows often creates temporary files while it works, and these temporary files may consume additional free space during the installation process.

Why won't the Install program work? Using copied disks?

The installation disks are organized with a complete directory structure. If you are using backup disks, your backups must have the identical directory structure. This will always be the case if you use the Windows File Manager and its Disk Copy menu item.

PROBLEMS WHILE RUNNING THE SOFTWARE

Suppose you've installed *Master C++ for Windows* but it doesn't run as described in Chapter 3, *Exploring Master C++ for Windows*, and Chapter 4, *Using Master C++ for Windows to Learn C++*.

I don't have Windows 3.1 and *Master C++ for Windows* won't run.

Master C++ for Windows uses TrueType fonts and requires Windows version 3.1 or later. If you are running with an earlier version of Windows, you will have to upgrade to at least version 3.1.

I've installed *Master C++ for Windows* but it won't run.

Check the hardware requirements for *Master C++ for Windows* listed at the beginning of Chapter 2, *Installation*. In general, if you can run other Windows applications, you should be able to run *Master C++ for Windows*. This application uses standard Windows API function calls.

If you have a large number of device drivers or TSR programs loaded, Windows may not have sufficient base memory to run all its applications. Eliminate any unnecessary device drivers and TSR programs from your CONFIG.SYS and AUTOEXEC.BAT files. You can also increase base memory by using a high memory manager such as EMM386.EXE. Check your DOS manual for details about its installation.

Master C++ for Windows starts up but the dialog boxes are white instead of gray.

Master C++ for Windows uses a DLL file called CTL3DV2.DLL to enhance dialog boxes. This file is installed in your \WINDOWS\SYSTEM directory during the installation process. If this file has been deleted, you can reinstall it by reinstalling *Master C++ for Windows*.

CHAPTER 6 IN CASE OF TROUBLE

I can't read the characters on the screen very well.

Master C++ for Windows was designed to work with all standard display drivers. In a few rare cases, proprietary display drivers may not always show all text correctly. First, try changing your Windows display driver to standard VGA. Restart Windows and try *Master C++ for Windows* again. With the standard VGA driver, your display should now appear normal. You should also be able to use the Super VGA (800 X 600, 16-color) driver that comes with Windows.

I can't tell which text is highlighted.

As you learned in Chapter 3, *Exploring Master C++ for Windows*, *Master C++ for Windows* uses highlighting to call your attention to certain parts of a lesson or to parts of the program code that are under discussion. If you cannot see a difference between regular and highlighted text, you may have to work with your computer's brightness and contrast controls—adjusting one a little, then the other—until a suitable balance is obtained.

7

DEVELOPING C++ PROGRAMS

7

DEVELOPING C++ PROGRAMS

Once you've completed the Master C++ for Windows lessons, you'll have a good grasp of the elements of the C++ language and the mechanics of writing a C++ program. But learning a programming language is like learning a foreign language in this respect: There's no substitute for experience. When you work through the questions and exercises in Chapter 8, *Review Exercises*, you'll have a chance to sharpen your new programming skills. After that, the next step in learning C++ is to try out the language on a variety of small to medium-sized projects of your own choosing. Only by writing lots of code will you figure out what works and what doesn't.

Of course, you'll need a C++ compiler to develop C++ programs. Which one should you buy? You may also have some questions about developing C++ programs. What are the steps involved in using a C++ compiler? What features and tools are provided to help you?

THE BORLAND COMPILERS

There is probably no better platform for learning C++ than Borland's C++ compilers. Borland C++ version 4.51 is a complete professional development environment. With it you can develop programs for DOS, Windows 3.1, Windows NT, and Windows 95. It includes many tools and options for heavy-duty development. The more economical Turbo C++ for Windows, version 4.5, is a stripped-down version of its bigger sibling. With Turbo C++ for Windows you can build programs that will run under

Windows 3.1 only (you cannot target DOS, Windows NT, or Windows 95). Turbo C++ for Windows looks and works virtually identically to the Borland C++ environment. Their Windows-hosted Integrated Development Environment (IDE) puts all the tools you need for C++ program development into a single, convenient screen.

This chapter describes how to install both of these compilers, how to use them to write your own programs, and how to run the programs you'll develop in the exercises in Chapter 8.

EasyWin

The purpose of this book and accompanying software lessons is to teach you to write programs in C++, but not necessarily programs specifically for Windows. Windows programming is a very large and complex topic that is well beyond the scope of this book. Just creating your first window and displaying some text can take two pages of code!

For the purposes of teaching the C++ language, it would be far easier to build DOS-based programs that require no special "windowing" code than it would be to write full-fledged Windows-based applications. A short program that demonstrates some feature or concept and prints its output on the screen is all that is needed to demonstrate the various language elements. Under the new Windows operating systems (Windows NT and Windows 95) these are called *console mode* applications. Under Windows 3.1, these were called DOS *text mode* applications (although Windows NT and Windows 95 are perfectly able to run the older DOS applications, as well).

As mentioned previously, Borland C++ is capable of building DOS and Windows programs (3.1, NT, and 95), and the newer console mode applications. Turbo C++ for Windows, however, can only be used to write Windows 3.1 based programs. Fortunately, both Borland C++ and Turbo C++ for Windows support a special kind of windows program called an *EasyWin* program.

An EasyWin program opens a normal-looking window, but the contents behave just as if the program were written for DOS or console mode. This means you can write your program as if it were DOS based, and the compiler will take care of the details of formatting your output for a window. In addition to showing you how to install your compiler, this chapter will show you how to select the options required to build an EasyWin application.

Installing the Compilers

This section describes how to install Borland C++ or Turbo C++ for Windows on your computer's hard drive. These programming environments have many options, tools, additional libraries, and capabilities that could be installed, but only a minimal installation capable of building EasyWin programs will be discussed here.

First, you must start Windows. If you are installing from floppies, insert Disk 1 into your disk drive. If you are installing from CD-ROM, insert the CD into the CD-ROM

CHAPTER 7 DEVELOPING C++ PROGRAMS

drive. Using File Manager (or the Windows Explorer if you're running Windows 95), select the drive with the disk.

If you are doing a floppy install, you will see an installation program INSTALL.EXE in the root directory of the floppy. If you are doing a CD install, you will find the INSTALL.EXE program in the \INSTALL subdirectory. Double-click on INSTALL.EXE to run the program and start the installation process.

The Installation Dialog

The installation program presents the dialog shown in Figure 7-1. This dialog allows you to select one of three installation options: Full, Custom, or CD Only (for CD version of software only). You can also choose the drive on which to install. If you want to install all the tools, help files, and sample programs on your hard disk, choose Full. This will take up a lot of precious hard disk space, however—over 100 MB for Borland C++, and 65 MB for Turbo C++. You won't need portions of the development environment for a long while, so a good alternative is the "CD Only" option. This allows full access to all the tools and options that come with the environment, but requires only a minimum of your hard drive space (25 MB for Borland C++, 7 MB for Turbo C++).

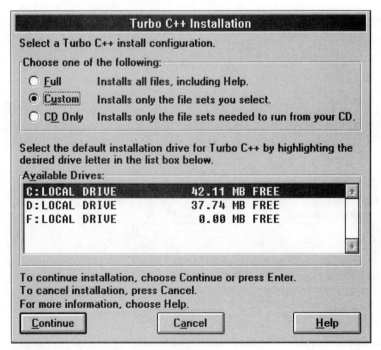

Figure 7-1 The Borland installation dialog

MASTER C++ FOR WINDOWS

If you choose the Custom installation, you will have to manually weed out any unneeded components and tools. This is also where the Turbo C++ and Borland C++ installations differ. Remember, all we really want is enough to build an EasyWin program.

The next two sections describe the Custom installation process for both compilers, installing only what is needed for EasyWin programs. If you are installing from floppies, you may be required to supply additional disks during this process.

TURBO C++ FOR WINDOWS

Figure 7-2 shows the next dialog displayed for a Turbo C++ for Windows installation from CD-ROM. Note that Turbo C++ for Windows uses the Adobe Acrobat reader for some of its help files, so you will also need to install this product (included with Turbo C++).

The next dialog you will see, Figure 7-3, allows you to choose the general categories of the components you want to install. The Quick Tour check box installs an automated demonstration of the IDE. The four buttons are for the Visual Tools,

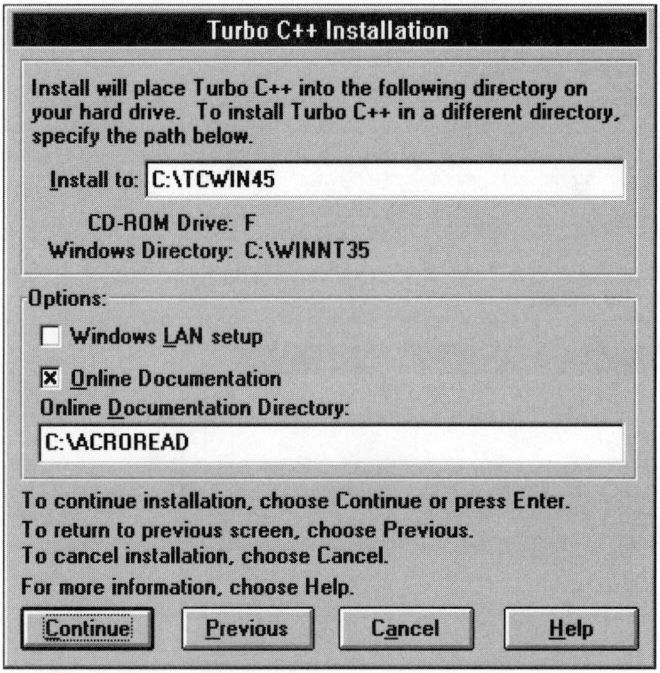

Figure 7-2 Turbo C++ for Windows destination dialog

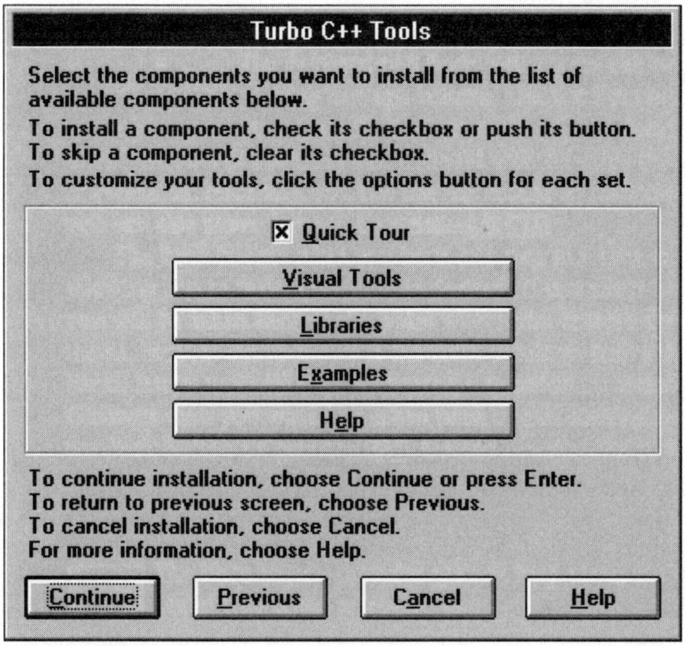

CHAPTER 7 DEVELOPING C++ PROGRAMS

Figure 7-3 Turbo C++ Tools

Libraries, Examples, and Help categories. Let's take a look at each of the dialogs for an EasyWin installation.

Visual Tools

The Visual Tools dialog contains the following six check boxes.

- Integrated Development Environment (IDE)
- Resource Workshop
- Winsight
- Control 3D Look
- Winspector
- Miscellaneous Tools

You only need to select the first check box, for the IDE. This automatically selects the Resource Workshop check box, although you don't need it for EasyWin programs.

Libraries

The Libraries dialog contains the following five check boxes.

- Run-Time Libraries
- ObjectWindows Libraries
- ObjectComponents Libraries
- Class Libraries
- OLE 2

Only the first two items need to be checked. The second two will be checked and disabled by default, and the last item (OLE 2) will be unchecked and disabled by default.

When you click on Continue in the Libraries dialog, the Run-Time Libraries dialog appears. This has two sets of check boxes. The first contains these check boxes:

- Header Files
- Static Libraries
- Dynamic Libraries

You will only need to check the Header Files and the Static Libraries.

The second set of check boxes contains the Memory Model choices for the libraries you selected.

- Small
- Compact
- Medium
- Large

The memory model influences how the compiled code is organized and how memory is accessed. Memory models are explained further in the software course; however, this concept is becoming less important with the new, 32-bit operating systems (Windows NT and Windows 95), and you can safely ignore them for the purposes of this course. You should check the Large memory model because it is the most similar to the flat memory model of the 32-bit operating environments, and has no special implications for your programs.

This dialog also contains two text boxes to allow you to change the locations of the libraries and header files. You should accept the default locations.

The next library dialog, library source, allows you to install the class library source code. You don't need this for EasyWin or any other type of programs you may develop. You may at some future time want to examine them, but you can always install them later.

CHAPTER 7 DEVELOPING C++ PROGRAMS

Finally, you are presented with the Object Windows options dialog. This dialog contains five check boxes:

- Static ObjectWindows Libraries
- Dynamic ObjectWindows Libraries
- ObjectWindows 1.0 Conversion Tool
- ObjectComponents Source
- ObjectWindows Source

Again, to build EasyWin programs you only need to check the first box.

Examples

The examples dialog contains five check boxes to help you install various types of example programs that come with Turbo C++ for Windows.

- ObjectWindows
- ObjectComponents
- Class Libraries
- Windows
- IDE

You don't need any of these examples for EasyWin programs. You may at some future time want to examine them, but you can always install them later.

Help

Finally, the Help Options dialog lets you select which help files you want to be accessible from within the Turbo C++ for Windows environment. Eleven options are available:

- TCW and Library Reference
- ObjectWindows
- ObjectComponents
- Windows 3.1 Reference
- Resource Workshop
- Visual Utilities
- Class Library Reference
- Creating Windows Help
- OpenHelp

- Documentation
- Programming Tips

For building EasyWin programs, you only need the first option, TCW and Library Reference. This provides help on using the IDE and the C++ library functions.

BORLAND C++

Figure 7-4 shows the dialog displayed for a Borland C++ installation from CD-ROM. Unless you want to change the drive and directory in which Borland C++ is installed, you should accept the default selections.

Figure 7-5 shows the Target Platforms dialog for Borland C++. Here you select the targets for which you want to write programs. EasyWin is a 16-bit Windows target application, so make sure the first check box is selected.

The next dialog you will see, Figure 7-6, allows you to choose the general categories of the components you want to install. You can deselect the Command Line Tools, because you won't need them for this book. The five buttons are for the Debuggers, Visual Tools, Libraries, Examples, and Help categories. Let's take a look at each of the dialogs for an EasyWin installation.

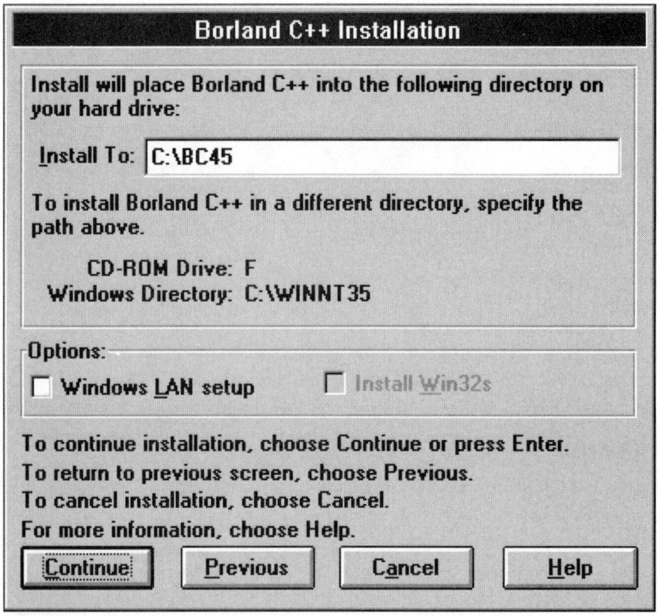

Figure 7-4 Borland C++ destination dialog

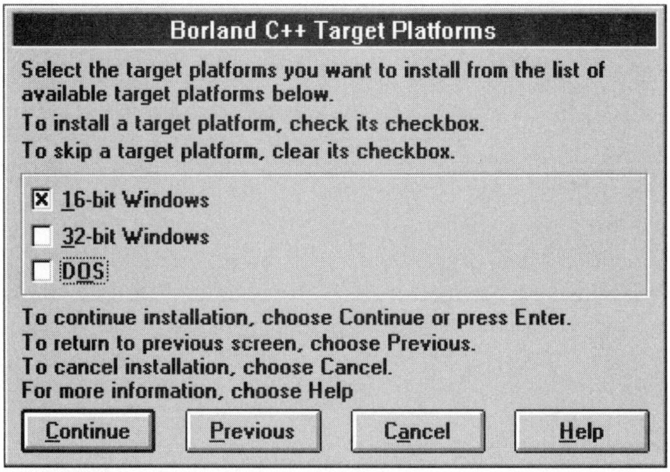

CHAPTER 7 DEVELOPING C++ PROGRAMS

Figure 7-5 Target Platforms dialog

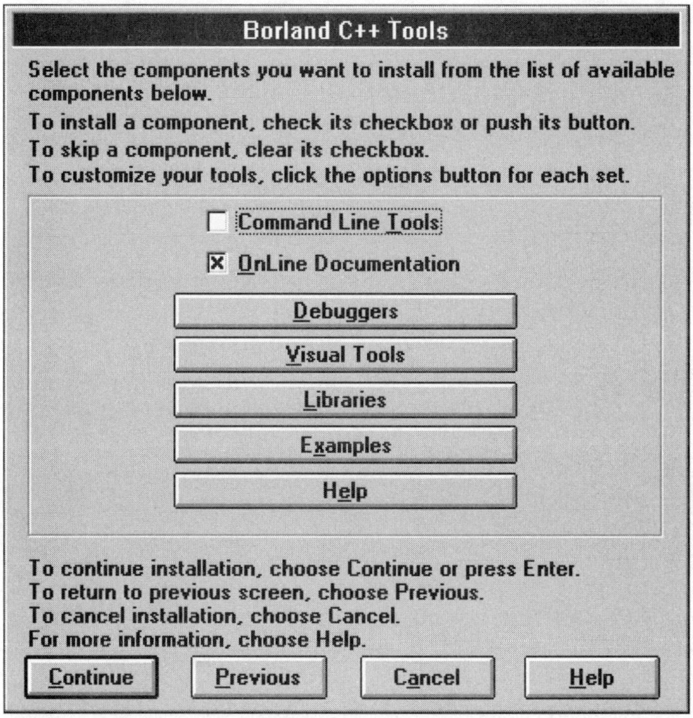

Figure 7-6 Borland C++ Tools section dialog

Debuggers

The Borland C++ Debuggers dialog has three check boxes:

- Turbo Debugger
- Remote Debugging
- Turbo Profiler

You won't need Remote Debugging or the Profiler, but you may want to use the Turbo Debugger to trace through and debug your EasyWin programs. The use of the debuggers is beyond the scope of this book, and you can safely choose not to install it.

Visual Tools

The Visual Tools dialog presents the following six check boxes.

- Integrated Development Environment (IDE)
- Resource Workshop
- Winsight
- Control 3D Look
- Winspector
- Miscellaneous Tools

You only need to select the first check box, for the IDE. This automatically selects the Resource Workshop check box too, although you don't need it for EasyWin programs.

Libraries

The Libraries dialog contains the following five check boxes.

- Run-Time Libraries
- ObjectWindows Libraries
- ObjectComponents Libraries
- Class Libraries
- OLE 2

Only the first two items need to be checked. The second two will be checked and disabled by default, and the last item (OLE 2) will be unchecked and disabled by default as well.

When you click on Continue in the Libraries dialog, a second Run-Time Libraries dialog will be displayed. This has two sets of check boxes. The first contains these check boxes:

CHAPTER 7   DEVELOPING C++ PROGRAMS

- Header Files
- Static Libraries
- Dynamic Libraries
- Graphics BGI

You will only need to check the Header Files and the Static Libraries.

The second set of check boxes contains the *Memory Model* choices for these libraries:

- Tiny
- Small
- Compact
- Medium
- Large
- Huge

The memory model influences how the compiled code is organized and how memory is accessed. Memory models are explained further in the software course. However, this concept is becoming less important with the new, 32-bit operating systems (Windows NT and Windows 95), and you can safely ignore them for the purposes of this course. You should check the Large memory model because it is the most similar to the flat memory model of the 32-bit operating environments, and has no special implications for your programs.

This dialog also contains two text boxes to allow you to change the locations of the libraries and header files. You should accept the default locations.

In the next dialog, Borland C++ Class Libraries, you'll see these choices:

- Static Class Libraries
- Dynamic Class Libraries
- Class Library Source
- Obsolete Class Libraries

You'll only need to check the first option: Static Class Libraries.

Finally, you are presented with the Object Windows options dialog. This dialog contains five check boxes:

- Static ObjectWindows Libraries
- Dynamic ObjectWindows Libraries
- ObjectWindows 1.0 Conversion Tool

- ObjectComponents Source
- ObjectWindows Source

Again, to build EasyWin programs you only need to check the first box.

Examples

The examples dialog contains seven check boxes to help you install various types of example programs that come with Borland C++.

- ObjectWindows
- ObjectComponents
- Class Libraries
- Turbo Profiler
- Windows
- DOS
- IDE

You don't need any of these examples for EasyWin programs. You may at some future time want to examine these, but you can always install them later.

Help

Finally, the Help Options dialog lets you select which help files you want to be accessible from within the Borland C++ environment. Eleven options are available:

- BCW and Library Reference
- BC DOS and Library Reference
- ObjectWindows
- ObjectComponents
- Win32 and Windows 3.1 Reference
- Resource Workshop
- Visual Utilities
- Class Library Reference
- Creating Windows Help
- OpenHelp
- Documentation

For building EasyWin programs, you only need the first option, BCW and Library Reference. This provides help on using the IDE and the C++ library functions.

CHAPTER 7   DEVELOPING C++ PROGRAMS

FINISHING THE INSTALLATION

When you have finished selecting your custom installation options, the installation program will start copying the needed files to your computer's hard drive. If you are installing from floppy disks, you will have to swap disks whenever the installation program instructs you to do so. If you are installing from a CD-ROM, you are in luck: time for a break! The installation program may have additional instructions after all the files are copied; it may want to allow you to electronically register your product, or display some final installation notes. After this you are done and ready to begin writing programs.

YOUR FIRST PROGRAM

As far as building EasyWin programs is concerned, the IDE for both Borland C++ and Turbo C++ for Windows look and work virtually the same. Before you can begin doing any programming, you must start the IDE. Do this simply by double-clicking on the Borland C++ or Turbo C++ for Windows icon created by the installation program in the Program Manager. The IDE window will appear as shown in Figure 7-7.

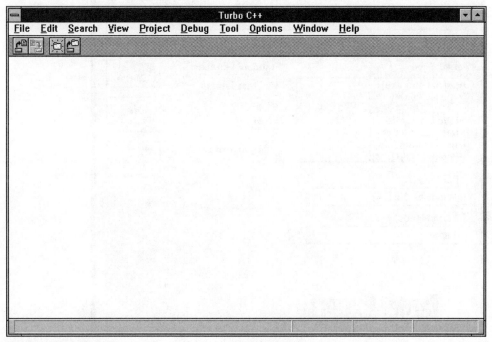

Figure 7-7 The Turbo C++ for Windows or Borland C++ IDE

Creating a Project

All program development is based on *projects*. A project contains a list of source files for a program, with compile and link instructions for them. For most of the programs in Chapter 8, *Review Exercises*, you will have only a single source file, so your project will contain one source file (with the extension .cpp), and the compiler settings to tell the IDE that you are building an EasyWin program (the IDE automatically saves these settings for you).

To create a new project (let's use the first example in Chapter 8), select New Project from the Project drop-down menu (the fifth menu item from the left at the top of the IDE). The dialog shown in Figure 7-8 is displayed.

Type the path and file name of your project file into the Project Path and Name text box. When creating the project file, the IDE will automatically put a .ide extension on the file name if you do not specify it yourself. The Target Name field changes automatically to show the name of the program you are creating. You may override this with another entry if you want.

Figure 7-8 New project dialog

CHAPTER 7   DEVELOPING C++ PROGRAMS

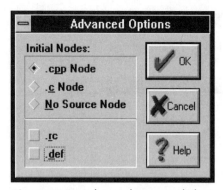

Figure 7-9 Advanced Options dialog

Before you create the project, bring up the Advanced Options dialog (see Figure 7-9) by clicking on the Advanced button. Deselect the .rc and .def check boxes. This tells the IDE that you will not be using any special Windows Resource Files for your project. This also eliminates the need for a .def file which contains special commands to the linker. When you build the project, you will receive a warning that there was no .def file and that the IDE is going to assume default values; this is fine.

Click OK to create the project. Your IDE should look something like the one shown in Figure 7-10.

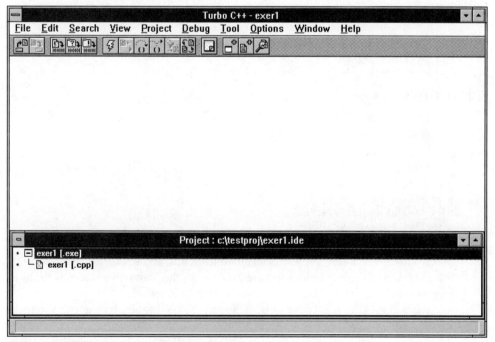

Figure 7-10 IDE after newly created project

81

MASTER C++ FOR WINDOWS

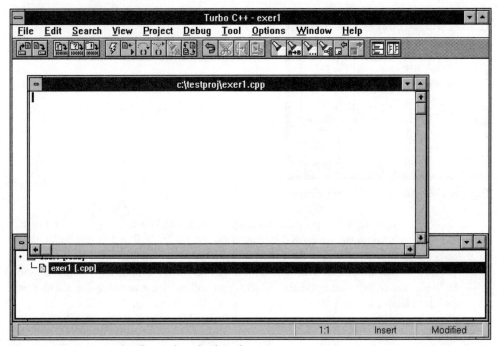

Figure 7-11 IDE with Edit window displayed

Double-click on the exer1.cpp line in the project window. The IDE displays the edit window as shown in Figure 7-11.

Using the Editor

The cursor should be in the upper-left corner of the edit window. Type the following program from Chapter 8, *Review Exercises*, exactly as shown here:

```
#include <iostream.h>

void main()
  {
  cout << "\nIma Coder";
  cout << "\n2123 Object Ave.";
  cout << "\nClasstown, OP 10101";
  }
```

Be sure to use lowercase letters for **main** and **cout**, and to enter the paired braces ({ }) and the semicolons. Figure 7-12 shows the Turbo C++ screen with the program entered; the Borland C++ screen is virtually identical.

You will find the IDE editor to be quite intuitive. What you type appears in the window, and you can use the arrow keys or mouse to move the cursor anywhere in the window. If you have used a word processor or text editor, you will find that the

CHAPTER 7   DEVELOPING C++ PROGRAMS

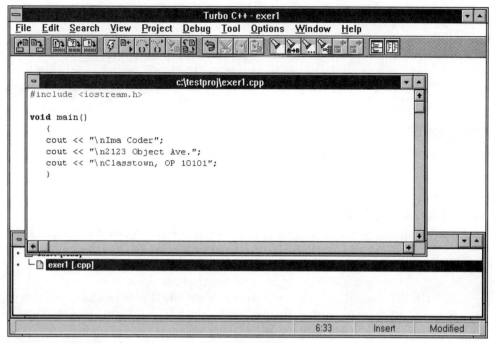

Figure 7-12 IDE with program typed into edit window

keyboard behaves much as you would expect. You can get a complete list of keyboard commands by selecting Keyboard from the Help menu, then click on the links Default, then Editor.

Saving Your Program

When you've entered your program, save it to disk by selecting Save from the File menu. It is usually a good idea to save your work before you attempt to compile or run your program. That way, if a bug crashes the IDE, you will not lose your source file. Whenever you save a new version of a program file, a backup with the .BAK extension is created automatically.

Compiling and Linking

Now that you have a working source file, you must *compile* and *link* it before you have a working program. From the Project drop-down menu, select Make All to compile and link your program. The term Make refers to compiling any files that you have changed. If you have a multifile project, Make recompiles only the source files you have changed. The Build All menu option tells the IDE to unconditionally recompile all files in the project, whether they have been changed or not.

83

Running the Program

After you successfully build your program, you will want to run it and see its output. Within the IDE, you can do this in one of two ways: by pressing [Ctrl]-[F9], or by selecting Run from the Debug drop-down menu. Of course, you now have a real .EXE program file that you can run from the Program Manager as well.

Exiting the IDE

To exit the IDE, select Exit from the File menu. If you haven't saved your latest changes, the IDE will prompt you to do so before closing.

Opening an Existing Project

Rarely will you ever sit down at your computer, type in a program, build it, and be done with it. You may work on large projects for days, weeks, or even months. Perhaps you will think of some great modifications to make to your program in the middle of the night and the next day want to implement them.

The IDE would be of little use if you could not reload your project to work on it at some later time. To open an existing project, choose Open Project from the Project drop-down menu. A File dialog will display the project files saved on the hard disk. Double-click the desired project to load it.

Errors

No one writes error-free code all the time (or even most of the time). You are sure to make an occasional typing mistake or leave out some important character in a function call. Most of these *syntax errors* can be caught by the compiler or linker.

For instance, suppose you omitted a semicolon from the end of one of the statements in the sample program discussed earlier. After trying to compile your program, the IDE would look something like the one shown in Figure 7-13.

Notice the error message displayed in the message window at the bottom, telling you where the error occurred (line 7) and what kind of error it was. You can double-click on the error message, and the IDE will automatically switch to the edit window and place the cursor on the line with the error. This is very useful when you have a large source file with several errors.

Link Errors

Even if your program compiles OK, you can still get an error during the link process. Link errors are often more difficult to track down. They usually occur because you used a function that is declared in your program (or in a header file), but not included in any library or source modules.

CHAPTER 7   DEVELOPING C++ PROGRAMS

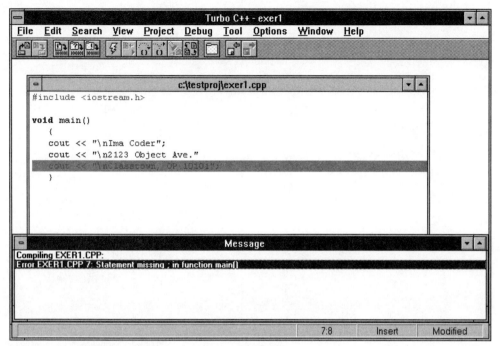

Figure 7-13 Message window showing a syntax error

Conceptual Errors

Conceptual errors are logic errors in your program code. Even when a program compiles and links successfully, it may still behave in ways you did not expect. For instance, a loop from one to ten may only count off nine times (old-timers know this as the famous fencepost error). No matter how many years you spend programming, you will rarely be able to avoid this type of error.

SUMMARY

In this chapter, you learned how to install Borland C++ and Turbo C++ for Windows. You were shown how to create projects and program source files using the IDE, and how to compile, link, and execute your programs. Now the rest is up to you. Work through the examples in this book, but don't be afraid to dream up your own examples as well. You may start timidly, by expanding one of our samples into a working and useful program, and then later start something from scratch. Many programmers have begun by writing small programs and utilities for their work, friends, and family. Good luck and enjoy!

8

REVIEW EXERCISES

8
REVIEW EXERCISES

This chapter of exercises provides a valuable way to consolidate your understanding of C++. Each exercise corresponds to a lesson on the *Master C++ for Windows* disks. For most of the chapters on the disk, there are a few simple exercises to test your fundamental knowledge of the material, and several more challenging ones to give you practice in applying the principles to more-or-less practical problems.

Use these exercises after you complete a *Master C++ for Windows* chapter to reinforce what you've learned. Try not to look at the solutions before you've tried the exercise yourself. Each exercise provides only one possible solution. Of course, there are many ways to implement each solution.

Note that when example programs are referred to as "Example X in Chapter N on the disk" the examples referred to are from the *Master C++ for Windows* disk tutorial. "Exercise X in Chapter N" means an exercise in the chapter you're reading right now.

Disk chapters 1, 2, 11, and 15 did not require additional exercises.

CHAPTER 3
Exercise 1

Write a program that displays your name and address on the screen. Use a separate program statement to generate each line of the address.

```
// address1.cpp
// outputs name and address using three statements
#include <iostream.h>

void main()
```

continued on next page

continued from previous page
```
   {
   cout << "\nIma Coder";
   cout << "\n2123 Object Ave.";
   cout << "\nClasstown, OP  10101";
   }
```

Exercise 2

Modify the ADDRESS1 exercise so that it uses only one program statement to display the entire address. Use a separate << operator for each line of the address.

```
// address2.cpp
// outputs name and address using one statement
#include <iostream.h>

void main()
   {
   cout << "\nIma Coder"
           << "\n2123 Object Ave."
           << "\nClasstown, OP  10101";
   }
```

Exercise 3

Write a program that asks the user to input exactly three characters. The program should then print the three characters in reverse order: last one first.

```
// revlets.cpp
// reverses three characters
#include <iostream.h>

void main()
   {
   char first, second, third;

   cout << "\nInput first character: ";
   cin >> first;
   cout << "Input second character: ";
   cin >> second;
   cout << "Input third character: ";
   cin >> third;
   cout << "Reversed word is " << third << second << first;
   }
```

Exercise 4

Here's a handy program for astronomers. Write a program that converts light-years to inches. There are 5.878e12 (that is, 5,878,000,000,000) miles in a light-year, 5,280 feet in a mile, and 12 inches in a foot. The program should take a value in light-years input by the user, and generate the corresponding value in inches.

```
// lightyrs.cpp
// converts light-years to inches
```

```
#include <iostream.h>

void main()
    {
    const float MPLY = 5.878e12;
    const float FPM = 5280;
    const float IPF = 12;
    float ltyears;

    cout << "Enter distance in light-years: ";
    cin >> ltyears;
    cout << "Distance in inches is ";
    cout << ltyears * MPLY * FPM * IPF;
    }
```

Exercise 5

Sometimes the increment operator (++) can produce surprising results. To test this, write a program that, in a single statement, prints the same variable three times. Each appearance of the variable should include a postfix increment operator (as in *joe*++).

```
// incagain.cpp
// demonstrates increment operator
#include <iostream.h>

void main()
    {
    int joe=10;
    cout << endl << joe++ << " " << joe++ << " " << joe++;
    }
```

Examine the output. Note that although the variables are printed from left to right, the increment operators are applied from right to left. The moral: Operations are not always performed in the order you think they may be. In this case, be careful when using the increment (or decrement) operator more than once on the same variable in a given statement.

CHAPTER 4

Exercise 1

Write a program to see how fast your computer performs integer addition. Use two *for* loops, one nested inside the other. The inner loop should always cycle 32,767 times (the maximum for integers). The outer loop should cycle a number of times selected by the user, so it can be adjusted for different speed ranges.

In the inner loop, add the two loop variables together and assign them to a dummy variable:

dummy = k + j;

This should be the only statement in the nested loops.

Have the program wait for a keystroke before starting the test, and display "Done" when the test is over.

The variable that holds the sum is called a dummy variable because you don't really care about its value. However, you'll need to do something with this value following the loops, or the compiler will complain that "dummy is assigned a value that is never used." For instance, you can display its value when the test is over.

For comparison, a Compaq DeskPro 386/20e takes 20 seconds to run this test when the outer loop limit is 500.

```
// speedtst.cpp
// tests computer speed
#include <iostream.h>
#include <conio.h>              // for getch()
void main()
    {
    int cycles;                 // number of times through outer loop
    int dummy;                  // dummy variable for dummy arithmetic
    int j, k;                   // loop variables
    const int MAX = 32767;      // maximum value of type int

    cout << "\nEnter the number of times to cycle: ";
    cin >> cycles;
    cout << "Press any key to begin: ";
    getch();
    cout << "\nRunning test...";
    for(j=0; j<cycles; j++)         // outer loop counts to cycles
        for(k=0; k<MAX; k++)        // inner loop counts to MAX
            dummy = k + j;                      // dummy statement
    cout << "\nDone (dummy=" << dummy << ")";
    }
```

Exercise 2

Write a program that enables the computer to play the old game of NIM against a human opponent. In this game you start with a certain number of sticks, say 25. Two players alternate turns. Each can select either one, two, or three sticks from the pile. Whoever is forced to take the last stick is the loser. The program should make the human play first.

Assume that the original number of sticks is a special kind of number: 1 added to a multiple of 4, such as 25=1+(6∗4). Then the winning strategy for the program is to subtract from 4 however many sticks the human chose, and take that many sticks. For example, if the human takes 3, the program should take 1; if the human takes 2, the program should take 2. This guarantees there will be one stick left on the human's last turn.

Try the game on your friends as an example of the computer's infallibility. Use a *do* loop, which exits and prints the *You lose* message when the number of sticks equals 1.

CHAPTER 8 REVIEW EXERCISES

```
// nim.cpp
// plays the game of nim against a human player
#include <iostream.h>

void main()
   {
   int sticks=25;                             // multiple of 4, plus 1
   int human, machine;                        // sticks to remove

   do
      {
                              cout << "\nThere are " << sticks << " sticks.";
                              cout << "\nYou can take 1, 2 or 3. Enter choice: ";
      cin >> human;                           // get human move
      sticks -= human;                        // subtract it from total
      machine = 4 - human;                    // calculate machine move
                              cout << "There are " << sticks << " sticks.";
                              cout << "\nI'll take " << machine << " stick(s).";
      sticks -= machine;                      // subtract it from total
      }
   while( sticks != 1 );                      // quit if 1 stick left
   cout                       << "\nThere is 1 stick left, and you must take it."
                              << " You lose.";
   }
```

Exercise 3

Write a program that calculates the greatest common divisor (GCD) of two numbers. This number has many uses. A common one is reducing a fraction to lowest terms by dividing the numerator and denominator by their GCD. For example, to express 12/21 in lowest terms, find the GCD of 12 and 21. This turns out to be 3, because there is no larger number that divides into both 12 and 21 with no remainder. Dividing both numbers by 3 gives you 4/7, which is 12/21 reduced to lowest terms. Other examples: the GCD of 8 and 6 is 2, the GCD of 42 and 66 is 6, and the GCD of 387 and 153 is 9.

You can find the GCD using Euclid's Algorithm. Here's how it works. Get the two numbers from the user. If necessary, switch them so the first is larger. Subtract the second from the first, and assign the result to the first number. Again, switch if necessary, and subtract the second from the first. Repeat this process until the first and second numbers are equal. Both numbers now equal the GCD.

Use a *while* loop that terminates when the first and second numbers are equal. Use an assignment operator to perform the subtraction of the second number from the first, assigning the result to the first. You'll need a temporary variable to help with swapping.

```
// gcd.cpp
// computes the greatest common divisor of two numbers

#include <iostream.h>
```

continued on next page

continued from previous page

```
void main()
    {
    long int first, second, temp;
    cout << "\nEnter two numbers: ";
    cin >> first >> second;
    while( first != second )         // done when they're equal
        {
        if( first < second )         // if first isn't bigger,
            {
            temp=first;              // swap them
            first=second;
            second=temp;
            }
        first -= second;             // first = first - second
        }
    cout << "Greatest Common Divisor is ";
    cout << first;
    }
```

Exercise 4

Write a program that simulates a TV remote-control channel-selector. The user should be able to enter a digit from 2 to 9 (don't worry about multidigit channel numbers), or press the U key to increment the channel number or the D key to decrement it. After each keypress the program should display the new channel number. You might use a *while* loop that encloses both an *if* statement to check for digits and a *switch* statement to check for 'u' and 'd.' Use the *getche()* function to read the digits.

```
// remote.cpp
// simulates TV remote-control channel-switcher
#include <iostream.h>
#include <conio.h>         // for getche()

void main()
    {
    const int ESC = 27;                    // ascii code for escape key
    int channel=2;                         // channel number
    char ch;                               // character typed by user

    while( (ch=getche()) != ESC )          // get the character
        {                                  // exit on escape key
        if( ch<58 && ch>47 )               // if it's a digit
            channel = ch - 48;             // set channel to it
        else                               // otherwise
            switch(ch)                     // go up or down
                {
                case 'u': channel++; break;    // 'u' key
                case 'd': channel-; break;     // 'd' key
                default:  cout << "\nError";   // anything else
                }                              // display channel
```

```
      cout << "\nchannel=" << channel << endl;
      }
   }
```

Exercise 5

Write a program that accepts individual digits in the form of characters (from 0 to 9). These digits should be read in with *getche()* in a loop, and assembled into a number of type *int*. The program should accept digits that form any positive number up to 32,767, the maximum size for this type. The input part of the program should terminate on any nondigit character. The program should then print the entire number using *cout* in the usual way.

You can create the number from individual digits by starting with zero, multiplying by 10 whenever a new digit is typed (to shift the number one place to the left), and adding the new digit (therefore, inserting it in the one's column). The ASCII codes for the digits from 0 to 9 run from 48 to 57 (decimal).

```
// makenumb.cpp
// makes a number out of digits
#include <iostream.h>
#include <conio.h>                 // for getche()

enum boolean { false, true };      // make a "true" value for loop

void main()
   {
   int numb = 0;                       // final number
   char ch;                            // character typed by user

   cout << "\nEnter a number: ";
   while( true )                       // loop ends with break
      {
      ch=getche();                     // get character from user
      if( ch<48 || ch>57 )             // if it's not a digit
         break;                        // exit loop
      int digit = ch - 48;             // convert ASCII to digit
      numb *= 10;                      // shift number one place left
      numb += digit;                   // put digit in one's column
      }
   cout << "\nNumber is " << numb;
   }
```

The foregoing routine emulates, in part, such input routines as the one built into *cin* that accepts digits from the user and creates a multidigit number.

CHAPTER 5

Exercise 1

Create a structure to store time values. It should have three members of type *int*; one each for hours, minutes, and seconds. Also write a *main()* program that allows the user to input values for these three members, and then displays the result in the 12:59:59 format.

Don't worry about leading zeros in single-digit numbers; that is, 12:5:5 is all right.

```
// timestrc.cpp
// models time data type using structure
#include <iostream.h>

struct time                          // specify a structure template
    {
    int hrs;
    int mins;
    int secs;
    };

void main()
    {
    time t1;                         // declare structure of type time

    cout << "Enter hours: ";         // get values from user
    cin >> t1.hrs;
    cout << "Enter minutes: ";
    cin >> t1.mins;
    cout << "Enter seconds: ";
    cin >> t1.secs;
    cout << "Time entered is ";
                                     // display time (format 12:59:59)
    cout << t1.hrs << ":" << t1.mins << ":" << t1.secs << endl;
    }
```

Exercise 2

Create an enumerated data type called *change* that contains United States coins and their values. For instance, *nickel*=5. Use this in a program that makes change; that is, the user types an amount in cents, like 295, and the program tells how many pennies, nickels, dimes, quarters, half-dollars, and dollars are equal to this amount.

```
// changer.cpp
// makes change; uses enumerated type for coin values
#include <iostream.h>

enum change { penny=1, nickel=5, dime=10,
                             quarter=25, half=50, dollar=100 };

void main()
    {
    int cents, whole, remain;

    cout << "\n\nEnter an amount in cents: ";
    cin >> cents;

    whole = cents / dollar;          // find how many dollars
    cout << "\nThat's " << whole << " dollars, ";
```

```
        remain = cents % dollar;        // find how much left over

        whole = remain / half;          // find how many half-dollars
        cout << whole << " half-dollars, ";
        remain %= half;                 // find how much left over

        whole = remain / quarter;       // find how many quarters
        cout << whole << " quarters, ";
        remain %= quarter;              // find how much left over

        whole = remain / dime;          // find how many dimes
        cout << whole << " dimes, ";
        remain %= dime;                 // find how much left over

        whole = remain / nickel;        // find how many nickels
        cout << whole << " nickels, ";
        remain %= nickel;               // find how much left over

        cout << remain << " pennies.";  // pennies is what's left
        }
```

Exercise 3

A compass rose is the rotating circular card in a compass that has the directions (N, NE, E, and so on) printed on it. Create an enumerated data type called *rose* that holds eight such directions. Within the definition of the enumerated type, set each symbol equal to the number of degrees it represents. Degrees are measured clockwise from 0 around to 360, so N (north) is 0, NE (northeast) is 45, E (east) is 90, and so on through SE, S, SW, W, and NW, which is 315.

Write a program that allows the user to input a course in degrees, and then display the course, using "N," "NE," and so on if the course is exactly equal to one of these directions, but simply displays the number of degrees if the course is some other direction, such as 10 degrees.

```
// rose.cpp
// enumerated data type holds compass directions
#include <iostream.h>

enum rose { N=0, NE=45, E=90, SE=135,
            S=180, SW=225, W=270, NW=315 };

void main()
    {
    int degrees;

    while( degrees >= 0 )
        {
        cout << "\n\nEnter a course in degrees: ";
        cin >> degrees;
        cout << "Course is ";
        switch(degrees)
            {
            case N:  cout << "N";  break;
```

continued on next page

continued from previous page
```
            case NE: cout << "NE"; break;
            case E:  cout << "E";  break;
            case SE: cout << "SE"; break;
            case S:  cout << "S";  break;
            case SW: cout << "SW"; break;
            case W:  cout << "W";  break;
            case NW: cout << "NW"; break;
            default: cout << degrees << " degrees";
            }
        }
    }
```

Exercise 4

Stock prices are usually presented in terms of a whole number and a fraction. For example, the closing price of General Motors stock on a certain day was thirty-six and five-eighths, written 36-5/8.

Create a structure called *fracpri* that holds the three parts of this price: the whole number (36 in the example shown), the numerator of the fraction (5), and the denominator of the fraction (8).

Write a *main()* program that creates at least two *fracpri* structures, prompts the user to place values in them (three numbers for each structure), and then displays the contents of each structure in the form "36-5/8."

```
// fracstr.cpp
// structure used to hold stock prices
#include <iostream.h>

struct fracpri                          // structure holds fractional prices
    {
    int whole;                          // whole number part of price
    int numer;                          // numerator (top) of fraction
    int denom;                          // denominator (bottom) of fraction
    };

void main()
    {
    fracpri fp1, fp2;                   // make two structures
    char dummy;                         // for hyphen and slash

    cout << "\nEnter first price: ";    // get first
    cin >> fp1.whole;                   // get whole number
    cin >> dummy;                       // get hyphen
    cin >> fp1.numer;                   // get numerator
    cin >> dummy;                       // get slash
    cin >> fp1.denom;                   // get denominator

    cout << "\nEnter second price: ";   // get second
    cin >> fp2.whole;                   // get whole number
    cin >> dummy;                       // get hyphen
    cin >> fp2.numer;                   // get numerator
```

```
        cin >> dummy;                        // get slash
        cin >> fp2.denom;                    // get denominator

        cout << "\nFirst price is ";         // display first
        cout << fp1.whole << "-"
             << fp1.numer << "/"
             << fp1.denom;

        cout << "\nSecond price is ";        // display second
        cout << fp2.whole << "-"
             << fp2.numer << "/"
             << fp2.denom;
        }
```

Exercise 5

Suppose you're on a fishing boat, motoring through the fog, looking at the radar screen. The display shows other ships as spots of light, called blips. Each ship is a certain distance—called its range—away from your boat, and at a certain angle—called the bearing—to you. The bearing is measured in degrees, starting at 0 for a ship straight ahead of you, 90 for a ship to the right, 180 for a ship behind you, and 270 for a ship to the left. Bearings are never negative, and never exceed 360 degrees.

The range and bearing of a ship can be inferred by the position of its blip on the radar screen. Your boat is in the center of the screen, and the up direction on the screen represents the forward direction for your boat. The range of a ship is shown by the distance of the blip from the center of the radar screen, and its bearing is shown by the direction of the blip. If the blip is above the center, the ship is in front of you, at 0 degrees. If the blip is to the right, the ship is to your right at 90 degrees, and so on.

Create a structure called *target* that contains members that represent the range and bearing of a blip. Use type *float* for the range (because a ship could be 2.4 miles away), and type *int* for the bearing (fractions of a degree are not necessary). Write a *main()* program that creates a target 10 miles away directly on our right. Now assume your boat can turn. Ask the user to enter the number of degrees to turn. Positive numbers represent a right turn, and negative numbers represent a left turn. When you turn, the bearing of the target will change. Alter the target's bearing, and print the range and the new bearing.

```
// radar.cpp
// structure models ship as seen on a radar set
#include <iostream.h>

struct target
    {
    float range;                // miles from our location
    int bearing;                // relative to our heading, from 0 to 360
    };

void main()
```

continued on next page

continued from previous page

```
   {
   target t1 = { 10.0, 90 };   // 10 miles away, on our right
   int turn = 10;              // can't start at 0

   cout << endl << endl;
   while( turn != 0 )          // exit if no turn
      {
      cout << "Range and bearing of target 1 is "
           << t1.range << " miles, "
           << t1.bearing << " degrees.";

      cout << "\nEnter number of degrees to turn "
           << "(negative numbers indicate left turn): ";
      cin >> turn;             // get degrees to turn

      t1.bearing -= turn;      // subtract turn from bearing
      if(t1.bearing < 0)       // if result is negative,
         t1.bearing += 360;    // add 360 for positive bearing
      if(t1.bearing >= 360)    // if result 360 or more,
         t1.bearing -= 360;    // subtract 360
      }
   }
```

CHAPTER 6

Exercise 1

An easy (but slow) way to clear the screen is to write 2,000 spaces to it (for an 80x25 screen). Create a function called *clear()* that does this, and a *main()* program to test the function.

```
// clear.cpp
// clears screen by writing blank lines to it
#include <iostream.h>

void clear();                  // prototype

void main()
   {
   clear();                    // clear the screen
   cout << "This message appears on an otherwise blank screen.";
   }

// clear()
// clears screen by writing 2000 spaces to it
void clear()
   {
   for(int j=0; j<2000; j++)   // print a blank 2000 times
      cout << ' ';
   cout << endl;               // put cursor at beginning of line
   }
```

CHAPTER 8 REVIEW EXERCISES

Exercise 2

Write a function that acts like the *getch()* library function, except that it returns 0 if the user presses the ENTER key. (Your function can call *getch()* to get the character.) Like *getch()*, your function should return any other character unchanged. Write a *main()* program that tests your function by using it in a loop. Note that it's easier to write the test condition for the loop with this function than it is *getch()*, because you don't need to test for equality with '\r', but only for truth (not zero).

```
// getachar.cpp
// places getch() in user-written function
#include <iostream.h>
#include <conio.h>                         // for getch()

char getachar();                           // prototype

void main()
   {
   char ch;

   while( ch=getachar() )                  // get a character
      cout << ch;                          // display it
   }

// getachar()
// return character typed by user
char getachar()
   {
   char ch = getch();                      // get a character
   if( ch == '\r' )                        // if it's Enter,
      return 0;                            // return 0
   else                                    // otherwise,
      return ch;                           // return the character
   }
```

Exercise 3

The FRACSTR exercise from Chapter 5 on the disk modelled stock prices, using a structure called *fracpri* to represent the three parts of the price: the whole number, the numerator of the fractional part, and the denominator of the fractional part.

Modify this program so that functions get data from the user to put into the structure, and then display the data from the structure. You'll need to pass a structure variable to the function that displays the data, and return a structure from the function that gets the data from the user.

```
// fraction.cpp
// structure used to hold stock prices
#include <iostream.h>

struct fracpri                   // structure holds fractional prices
   {
```

continued on next page

continued from previous page
```
    int whole;                  // whole number part of price
    int numer;                  // numerator (top) of fraction
    int denom;                  // denominator (bottom) of fraction
    };

void dispfrac(fracpri);         // prototypes
fracpri getfrac();

void main()
    {
    fracpri fp1, fp2;                       // make two structures

    cout << "\nEnter first price: ";    // prices in fp1 and fp2
    fp1 = getfrac();
    cout << "\nEnter second price: ";
    fp2 = getfrac();
    cout << "\nFirst price is ";        // display fp1 and fp2
    dispfrac(fp1);
    cout << "\nSecond price is ";
    dispfrac(fp2);
    }

// dispfrac()
// displays fractional price, in form 37-1/8
void dispfrac(fracpri fp)
    {
    cout << fp.whole << "-"
         << fp.numer << "/"
         << fp.denom;
    }

// getfrac()
// function gets fractional price from user
// returns fracpri structure
fracpri getfrac()
    {
    fracpri temp;               // make a temporary structure
    char dummy;                 // for hyphen and slash

    cin >> temp.whole;          // get whole number
    cin >> dummy;               // get hyphen
    cin >> temp.numer;          // get numerator
    cin >> dummy;               // get slash
    cin >> temp.denom;          // get denominator
    return temp;                // return temp structure
    }
```

Exercise 4

The data for a company's stock, shown in the newspaper each day, includes the number of shares traded, the closing or last price of the day, and the change in price from the day before. Create a structure that holds these three values. Use the *fracpri* structure from the FRACTION exercise in this chapter to hold the *last* and *change*

CHAPTER 8   REVIEW EXERCISES

prices. Use type *long int* to hold *sales*, the number of shares traded (which is the actual number divided by 100).

Write a *main()* program that creates at least two structures to hold stock data, asks the user for the data for the stocks, fills it in, and displays it. You'll need the functions used with the *fracpri* structure in the FRACTION exercise as well as the structure itself.

```
// stocks.cpp
// uses structure to hold stock data
#include <iostream.h>

struct fracpri              // structure holds fractional prices
   {
   int whole;               // whole number part of price
   int numer;               // numerator (top) of fraction
   int denom;               // denominator (bottom) of fraction
   };

struct stock                // structure holds stock data
   {
   long sales;              // number of shares sold (div by 100)
   fracpri last;            // closing price
   fracpri chng;            // change from previous day
   };

void dispfrac(fracpri);     // prototypes
fracpri getfrac();
void dspstock(stock);
stock getstock();

void main()
   {
   stock stk1, stk2;                        // create two stocks

   cout << "\nEnter data for first stock";  // get data
   stk1 = getstock();
   cout << "\nEnter data for second stock";
   stk2 = getstock();
   cout << "\nFirst stock: ";               // display data
   dspstock(stk1);
   cout << "\nSecond stock: ";
   dspstock(stk2);
   }

// dspstock()
// displays data for one stock
void dspstock(stock s)
   {
   cout << "sales=" << s.sales;             // display sales
   cout << ", last=";                       // display closing price
   dispfrac(s.last);
   cout << ", change=";                     // display change
   dispfrac(s.chng);
   }
```

continued on next page

103

continued from previous page
```cpp
// getstock()
// get stock data from user,
// return data in stock structure
stock getstock()
    {
    stock temp;

    cout << "\n   Enter sales: ";           // get sales
    cin >> temp.sales;
    cout << "   Enter closing price";       // get closing price
    temp.last = getfrac();
    cout << "   Enter change";              // get change
    temp.chng = getfrac();
    return temp;                            // return stock struct
    }

// dispfrac()
// displays fractional price, in form 37-1/8
void dispfrac(fracpri fp)
    {
    cout << fp.whole << "-"                 // display whole number
         << fp.numer << "/"                 // display top of fract
         << fp.denom;                       // display bottom
    }

// getfrac()
// function gets fractional price from user
// returns price in fracpri structure
fracpri getfrac()
    {
    fracpri temp;   // make a temporary structure

    cout << "\n   Enter whole number part of price: ";
    cin >> temp.whole;
    cout << "   Enter top of fraction: ";
    cin >> temp.numer;
    cout << "   Enter bottom of fraction: ";
    cin >> temp.denom;
    return temp;
    }
```

Exercise 5

Combine the MAKENUMB and REMOTE exercises from Chapter 4 so the user can enter multidigit channel numbers. The MAKENUMB program should be made into a subroutine that is called from the modified REMOTE program at the appropriate point.

```cpp
// remote2.cpp
// simulates TV remote-control channel-switcher
// accepts multidigit channel numbers
#include <iostream.h>
#include <conio.h>              // for getche()
```

```cpp
enum boolean { false, true };
int makenumb(char);                       // prototype

void main()
   {
   const int ESC = 27;                    // ascii code for escape key
   int channel=2;                         // channel number
   char ch;                               // character typed by user

   cout << "\nchannel=" << channel << endl;
   while( (ch=getche()) != ESC )          // get the character
      {                                   // exit on escape key
      switch(ch)
         {
         case 'u': channel++; break;      // 'u' key; go up
         case 'd': channel-; break;       // 'd' key; go down
         default:                         // might be number
            if( ch>47 && ch<58 )          // if digit,
               channel = makenumb(ch);    // get complete number
            else                          // otherwise,
               cout << "\nError";         // error
         }                                // display channel
      cout << "\nchannel=" << channel << endl;
      }
   }

// makenumb()
// makes a number out of digits
int makenumb(char c)                      // enter with first digit
   {
   int numb = c-48;                       // put first digit in number

   while( true )                          // loop ends with break
      {
      c=getche();                         // get next char from user
      if( c<48 || c>57 )                  // if it's not a digit
         break;                           // exit loop
      numb *= 10;                         // shift number one place left
      numb += c-48;                       // put digit in one's column
      }
   return(numb);                          // return final number
   }
```

Exercise 6

To the FRACTION exercise in this chapter, add a function that adds two fractions of type *fracpri*. Adding two fractions involves first representing both fractions with a common denominator, and then adding the numerators, as you learned in grade school.

```cpp
//addfracs.cpp
// adds two fraction structures
#include <iostream.h>
```

continued on next page

```
continued from previous page
struct fracpri                      // structure holds fractional prices
   {
   int whole;                       // whole number part of price
   int numer;                       // numerator (top) of fraction
   int denom;                       // denominator (bottom) of fraction
   };

void dispfrac(fracpri);             // prototypes
fracpri getfrac();
fracpri addfracs(fracpri, fracpri);

void main()
   {
   fracpri fp1, fp2, fp3;           // make three structures

   cout << "\n\nEnter first price: ";   // prices in fp1 and fp2
   fp1 = getfrac();
   cout << "Enter second price: ";
   fp2 = getfrac();

   fp3 = addfracs(fp1, fp2);        // fp3 = fp1 and fp2

   cout << "\nSum of fp1 and fp2 is ";
   dispfrac(fp3);
   }

// dispfrac()
// displays fractional price, in form 37-1/8
void dispfrac(fracpri fp)
   {
   cout << fp.whole;                // print whole number
   if( fp.numer )                   // if not 0, print fraction
      cout << "-" << fp.numer << "/" << fp.denom;
   }

// getfrac()
// function gets fractional price from user
// returns fracpri structure
fracpri getfrac()
   {
   fracpri temp;       // make a temporary structure
   char dummy;         // for hyphen and slash

   cin >> temp.whole;            // get whole number
   cin >> dummy;                 // get hyphen
   cin >> temp.numer;            // get numerator
   cin >> dummy;                 // get slash
   cin >> temp.denom;            // get denominator
   return temp;                  // return temp structure
   }

// addfracs()
// adds two fractions sent as arguments, returns sum
// (for comments, assume f1 = 7-2/3, f2 = 11-3/4)
```

```
fracpri addfracs(fracpri f1, fracpri f2)
   {
   fracpri temp;
   int newnum1, newnum2, newnumer, carry;

   temp.whole = f1.whole + f2.whole;      // 18 = 7 + 11
   temp.denom = f1.denom * f2.denom;      // 12 = 3 * 4
   newnum1 = f1.numer * f2.denom;                         // 8 = 2 * 4
   newnum2 = f2.numer * f1.denom;                         // 9 = 3 * 3
   newnumer = newnum1 + newnum2;                          // 17 = 8 + 9
   carry = newnumer / temp.denom;                         // 1 = 17 / 12
   temp.whole += carry;                                   // 19 = 18 + 1
   temp.numer = newnumer % temp.denom;    // 5 = 17 % 12
   return temp;                                           // return 19-5/12
   }
```

Exercise 7

Write a function called *fraclow()* that reduces a fraction to lowest terms (that is, it changes 20/32 to 5/8). You can do this by dividing both the numerator and the denominator by their greatest common divisor, which can be calculated using the algorithm of the GCD exercise from Chapter 4.

Use reference arguments, so that the original fraction in the calling program is reduced to lowest terms. Write a *main()* program that allows the user to input values for a fraction, which is then stored, reduced to lowest terms by calling *fraclow()*, and displayed.

Before beginning Euclid's algorithm, you might want to check to make sure the user didn't enter a 0 for the numerator, because the algorithm would cycle endlessly in this case. If the numerator is 0, set the fraction to 0/1.

```
// fraclow.cpp
// reduces fraction to lowest terms
#include <iostream.h>

void fraclow(long& numerator, long& denominator);      // prototype

void main()
   {
   long numerator, denominator;
   char dummy;                                         // for slash

   cout << "\nEnter fraction: (format 20/32): ";
   cin >> numerator >> dummy >> denominator;           // get fraction
   fraclow(numerator, denominator);                    // to lowest terms
   cout << "In lowest terms that's "                   // display
        << numerator << '/' << denominator;
   }

// fraclow()
// reduces fraction to lowest terms, uses reference arguments
void fraclow(long& numer, long& denom)
```

continued on next page

```
continued from previous page
     {
     if( numer == 0 )                      // check for special case of
         { denom=1; return; }              // zero numerator

     long first=numer;                     // find greatest common divisor
     long second=denom;                    // of numerator and denominator
     long temp;                            // (compute with local vars)

     while( first != second )              // done when they're equal
         {
         if( first < second )              // if first isn't bigger,
             {
             temp=first;                   // swap them
             first=second;
             second=temp;
             }
         first -= second;                  // first=first-second
         }
                                           // first is now gcd
     numer /= first;                       // divide both numer and denom
     denom /= first;                       // by gcd to get lowest terms
     }
```

CHAPTER 7
Exercise 1

Convert the structure from the TIMESTRC example for Chapter 5 to an object. Member functions should get and display the time entered from the user.

```
// timclass.cpp
// models time data type using class
#include <iostream.h>

class time
    {
    private:
        int hrs;
        int mins;
        int secs;
    public:
        void gettime()                   // get time from user
            {
            char dummy;
            cout << "\nEnter time (format 12:12:59): ";
            cin >> hrs >> dummy >> mins >> dummy >> secs;
            }
        void disptime()                  // display time (format 12:59:59)
            {
            cout << hrs << ":" << mins << ":" << secs;
            }
    };
```

CHAPTER 8 REVIEW EXERCISES

```
void main()
   {
   time t1, t2;                            // create two objects of class time

   cout << "\nTime number 1: ";            // get two times from user
   t1.gettime();
   cout << "\nTime number 2: ";
   t2.gettime();

   cout << "\nTime number 1 is ";          // display two times
   t1.disptime();
   cout << "\nTime number 2 is ";
   t2.disptime();
   }
```

Exercise 2

Add a constructor to the *time* class in the foregoing exercise TIMCLASS so that objects of this class can be initialized when they are created, using statements of the form

> time t1(10,59,59);

```
// timconst.cpp
// adds constructor to time class
#include <iostream.h>

class time
   {
   private:
      int hrs;
      int mins;
      int secs;
   public:
      time()                                             // constructor
         { }
      time(int h, int m, int s)      // constructor initializes time
            { hrs=h; mins=m; secs=s; }
      void gettime()                                     // get time from user
                           {
                           char dummy;
                           cout << "\nEnter time (format 12:12:59): ";
                           cin >> hrs >> dummy >> mins >> dummy >> secs;
                           }
      void disptime()            // display time (format 12:59:59)
                           {
                           cout << hrs << ":" << mins << ":" << secs;
                           }
   };

void main()
   {
   time t1;                     // create a time but don't initialize it
   time t2(10,33,45);           // create another time and initialize it
```

continued on next page

continued from previous page

```
    cout << "\nTime number 1: ";      // get time 1 from user
    t1.gettime();

    cout << "\nTime number 1 is ";    // display both times
    t1.disptime();
    cout << "\nTime number 2 is ";
    t2.disptime();
    }
```

Exercise 3

Use a class to represent the TV remote-control unit from the REMOTE2 exercise in Chapter 6. It should have the same capabilities, but encapsulate the channel number as data, and the input and display routines as member functions. It should also have a constructor that initializes each channel object to channel 2. (Note: The member function that gets input cannot be inline if it incorporates a *switch* statement.)

```
// remclass.cpp
// uses class to simulate TV remote-control channel-switcher
#include <iostream.h>
#include <conio.h>              // for getche()

enum boolean { false, true };
int makenumb(char);             // prototype

class remote
    {
    private:
        int channel;            // channel number
    public:
        remote()                // initialize channel to 2
            { channel = 2; }
        void displaychan()      // display current channel
            { cout << "\nchannel=" << channel << endl; }
        int getchan();          // get user input
    };

int remote::getchan()
    {
    const int ESC = 27;         // ascii code for escape key
    char ch;                    // character typed by user

    ch=getche();                // get the character
    if( ch == ESC)              // return 0 if it's ESC key
        return 0;
    switch(ch)
        {
        case 'u': channel++; break;   // 'u' key; go up
        case 'd': channel-; break;    // 'd' key; go down
        default:                              // might be number
            if( ch>47 && ch<58 )              // if digit,
                channel = makenumb(ch);       // get complete number
            else                                      // otherwise,
```

```cpp
            cout << "\nError";           // error
        }
    return 1;                            // return non-zero
    }

void main()
    {
    remote rem;                  // create a remote object

    cout << endl << endl;        // skip two lines
                                 // get channel from user
    while( rem.getchan() )       // cycle until zero
        rem.displaychan();       // display channel
    }

// makenumb()
// makes a number out of digits
int makenumb(char c)             // enter with first digit
    {
    int numb = c-48;             // put first digit in number

    while( true )                // loop ends with break
        {
        c=getche();              // get next char from user
        if( c<48 || c>57 )       // if it's not a digit
            break;               // exit loop
        numb *= 10;              // shift number one place left
        numb += c-48;            // put digit in one's column
        }
    return(numb);                // return final number
    }
```

Exercise 4

Create a *fracpri* class based on the *fracpri* structure from the FRACTION example in Chapter 6. Give it the same capabilities called for in that program. A fraction should be able to display itself, and get a value for itself from the user.

```cpp
// fraclass.cpp
// class used to hold stock prices
#include <iostream.h>

class fracpri                    // class for fractional prices
    {
    private:
        int whole;               // whole number part of price
        int numer;               // numerator (top) of fraction
        int denom;               // denominator (bottom) of fraction
    public:
        void dispfrac()          // display fraction (format 31-3/8)
            {
            cout << whole << "-"
                 << numer << "/"
                 << denom;
```

continued on next page

111

continued from previous page

```
        }
    void getfrac()            // get fraction from user
        {
        char dummy;           // for hyphen and slash

        cin >> whole;         // whole number
        cin >> dummy;         // hyphen
        cin >> numer;         // top part of fraction
        cin >> dummy;         // slash
        cin >> denom;         // bottom part of fraction
        }
    };
void main()
    {
    fracpri fp1, fp2;                    // make two objects

    cout << "\nEnter first price: ";     // prices in fp1 and fp2
    fp1.getfrac();
    cout << "\nEnter second price: ";
    fp2.getfrac();
    cout << "\nFirst price is ";         // display fp1 and fp2
    fp1.dispfrac();
    cout << "\nSecond price is ";
    fp2.dispfrac();
    }
```

Exercise 5

Use a class to represent the NIM game in the NIM example for Chapter 4. It should hold the number of counters remaining as private data, and have member functions to get the human's move and display the machine move. The machine-move routine can return the number of sticks remaining so the *main()* program can issue appropriate messages, such as "you lose" if there is only one stick remaining.

```
// nimclass.cpp
// plays the game of nim against a human player
#include <iostream.h>

class nim                         // class holds state of nim
    {
    private:
        int sticks;               // number of sticks left
    public:
        nim()                     // constructor
            {
            sticks = 25;          // initialize to 25 sticks
            }
        void humanmove()          // get human move
            {
            int human;
            cout << "\nThere are " << sticks << " sticks.";
            cout << "\nYou can take 1, 2 or 3. Enter choice: ";
```

```
                cin >> human;           // get human move
                sticks -= human;        // subtract it from total
                }
            int machinemove()           // calculuate machine move
                {
                int machine;
                machine = (sticks+3) % 4;   // calculate machine move
                cout << "There are " << sticks << " sticks.";
                cout << "\nI'll take " << machine << " stick(s).";
                sticks -= machine;      // subtract it from total
                return sticks;          // return remaining sticks
                }
    };
void main()
    {
    nim n;                              // make object n of class nim

    do
        {
        n.humanmove();                  // get human move
        } while( n.machinemove() != 1 );    // quit if 1 stick left
    cout << "\nThere is 1 stick left, and you must take it."
         << " You lose.";
    }
```

Exercise 6

Use a class to represent an object of type *target* that represents a radar target's position in terms of range and bearing, as seen in the RADAR example for Chapter 5. Member functions should display the current target and alter its bearing if the ship turns.

```
// rbclass.cpp
// class models range and bearing of radar targets
#include <iostream.h>

class target
    {
    private:
        float range;    // miles from our location
        int bearing;    // relative to our heading, from 0 to 360
    public:
        target(float ra, int be)        // initialize target info
            { range=ra; bearing=be; }
        void display()                  // display target info
            {
            cout << range << " miles, "
                 << bearing << " degrees.";
            }
        void rotate(int turn)           // rotate target
            {
            bearing -= turn;            // subtract turn from bearing
            if(bearing < 0)             // if result is negative,
```

continued on next page

continued from previous page

```
                bearing += 360;        // add 360 for positive bearing
            if(bearing >=360)          // if result is 360 or more,
                bearing -= 360;        // subtract 360
        }
    };

void main()
    {                                  // initialize targets
    target t1(10.0, 90);               // 10 miles away, on our right
    target t2(4.5, 0);                 // 4.5 miles away, straight ahead
    int turn = 10;                     // (can't start at 0 degrees)

    cout << endl << endl;
    while( turn != 0 )                 // exit if no turn
        {
        cout << "\nTarget t1: ";       // display targets'
        t1.display();                  // range and bearing
        cout << "\nTarget t2: ";
        t2.display();

        cout << "\nEnter number of degrees to turn "
             << "(negative numbers indicate left turn): ";
        cin >> turn;                   // get degrees to turn
        t1.rotate(turn);               // tell the targets to rotate
        t2.rotate(turn);
        }
    }
```

Exercise 7

Extend the *fracint* class in the FRACLASS example in this chapter so that two fractions can be added together. That is, a member function will add two fractions given to it as arguments, and will set itself to the sum. The addition routine from the ADDFRACS example in Chapter 6 can be used.

Another member function should reduce the resulting fraction to lowest terms. You can use the *fraclow()* function from the FRACLOW exercise of Chapter 6 to do this. Note, however, that as a member function, the new *fraclow()* need not take any arguments, reference or otherwise.

```
// fracladd.cpp
// add two fractions, reduce result to lowest terms
#include <iostream.h>

class fracpri                          // class for fractional prices
    {
    private:
        int whole;                     // whole number part of price
        int numer;                     // numerator (top) of fraction
        int denom;                     // denominator (bottom) of fraction
    public:
        void dispfrac()                // display fraction (format 31-3/8)
            {
```

```
            cout << whole << "-"
                 << numer << "/"
                 << denom;
            }
        void getfrac()                      // get fraction from user
            {
            char dummy;                     // for hyphen and slash
            cin >> whole >> dummy >> numer >> dummy >> denom;
            }
        void addfracs(fracpri, fracpri);    // add two fractions
        void fraclow();                     // reduce ourself to lowest terms
    };

// addfracs()
// member function adds two fractional prices
void fracpri::addfracs(fracpri f1, fracpri f2)   // this=f1+f2
    {
    int newnum1, newnum2, newnumer, carry;

    whole = f1.whole + f2.whole;         // find new whole number
    denom = f1.denom * f2.denom;         // find new denominator
    newnum1 = f1.numer * f2.denom;       // cross multiply
    newnum2 = f2.numer * f1.denom;
    newnumer = newnum1 + newnum2;        // add the new numerators
    carry = newnumer / denom;            // find how much to carry
    whole += carry;                      // add to whole number part
    numer = newnumer % denom;            // find new numerator
    }

// fraclow()
// member function reduces fraction to lowest terms
void fracpri::fraclow()
    {
    if( numer == 0 )                     // check for special case of
        { denom=1; return; }             // zero numerator

    long first=numer;                    // find greatest common divisor
    long second=denom;                   // of numerator and denominator
    long temp;                           // (compute with local vars)

    while( first != second )             // done when they're equal
        {
        if( first < second )             // if first isn't bigger,
            {
            temp=first;                  // swap them
            first=second;
            second=temp;
            }
        first -= second;                 // first=first-second
        }                                // first is now gcd
    numer /= first;                      // divide both numer and denom
    denom /= first;                      // by gcd to get lowest terms
    }

void main()
```

continued on next page

continued from previous page
```
   {
   fracpri fp1, fp2, fp3;              // make three objects

   cout << "\n\nEnter first price: ";  // get prices for fp1, fp2
   fp1.getfrac();
   cout << "Enter second price: ";
   fp2.getfrac();

   fp3.addfracs(fp1, fp2);             // fp3 = fp1 + fp2;

   fp3.fraclow();                      // fp3 to lowest terms
   cout << "Sum is ";                  // display fp3
   fp3.dispfrac();
   }
```

CHAPTER 8
Exercise 1

Write a function *getmax()* that finds the maximum value in an array of integers passed to it as an argument. (The number of valid elements in the array may be passed as the second argument.)

A *main()* program should first fill an array with test scores entered by the user, then call *getmax()* to find the highest score, and finally display this score.

```
// scores.cpp
// find highest score from array of scores
#include <iostream.h>
int getmax(int[], int);
const int SIZE = 100;                 // size of array

void main()
   {
   int scores[SIZE];                  // array of scores
   int sc;                            // score entered by user
   int j=0;                           // array index

   cout << endl;
   while(1)
      {
      cout << "Enter score: ";
      cin  >> sc;                     // get a score
      if(( sc < 0 )||(j>(SIZE-1)))    // if negative entry,
         break;                       // no more entries
      scores[j++] = sc;               // put entry in array
      }
   int m = getmax(scores, j);         // return maximum score
   cout << "\nMaximum score is " << m;
   }

// getmax()
```

```
// function to find maximum score
int getmax(int arr[], int n)
    {
    int max=0;                      // holds maximum value
    int k;                          // array index

    for(k=0; k<n; k++)              // if any array element
        if( arr[k] > max )          // is greater than max,
            max = arr[k];           // max becomes that element
    return max;
    }
```

Exercise 2

Write a function called *compstr()* that compares two strings sent to it as arguments. Use a character-by-character comparison to determine if the strings match. Return a 1 if the strings are the same, and a 0 if they are different.

Write a *main()* program that tests this function by inviting the user to compare two strings. You can use the *cin.gets(str, MAX)* function to get the string; this enables you to read strings with embedded blanks. Unfortunately, this function leaves a delimiter in the *istream* after use, so insert *cin.ignore()* between calls to *cin.gets()* to get rid of the delimiter.

```
// compstr.cpp
// function compares two strings passed as arrays
#include <iostream.h>
#include <string.h>                             // for strlen(), etc.

const int MAX = 80;                             // maximum length of words
int compstr(char string1[], char string2[]);   // prototype
void main()
    {
    char s1[MAX], s2[MAX];

    cout << "\nEnter first string: ";
    cin.get(s1, MAX);
    cin.ignore();                               // clear istream

    cout << "Enter second string: ";
    cin.get(s2, MAX);
    if( compstr(s1, s2) )
        cout << "These strings are the same.";
    else
        cout << "These strings are different.";
    }

// compstr()
// compares two strings passed as arguments
// returns 0 if different, 1 if the same
int compstr(char s1[], char s2[])
    {
    int j;                                      // loop variable
    int len1 = strlen(s1);                      // get string lengths
```

continued on next page

continued from previous page
```
    int len2 = strlen(s2);

    if( len1 != len2 )                  // if different lengths,
        return 0;                       // strings not the same
    for(j=0; j<len1; j++)               // step through characters
        if( s1[j] != s2[j] )            // if any mismatch,
            return 0;                   // strings not the same
    return 1;                           // otherwise they are the same
    }
```

Exercise 3

Create a class of addresses called *address*. There should be three items of data in this class: a string holding the street number and name, a string holding the city and state, and a long integer holding the zip code. A member function *putaddr()* should display the address, and a member function *getaddr()* should prompt the user to type in a new address.

Write a *main()* program that creates an array of *address* objects, prompts the user to enter as many addresses as desired, and then displays all the addresses.

```
// addrarr.cpp
// create an array of address objects
#include <iostream.h>
#include <conio.h>                      // for getche()

const int MAX = 80;                     // length of input buffer

class address
    {
    private:
        char street[MAX];               // street number and name
        char city[MAX];                 // city and state
        long zip;                       // zip code
    public:
        void putaddr()                  // display address
            {
            cout << "\n     " << street
                 << "\n     " << city
                 << "  "  << zip;
            }
        void getaddr()                  // get address from user
            {
            cout << "\n   Enter street name and number: ";
            cin.get(street, MAX);
            cin.ignore();               // clear istream
            cout << "   Enter city and state: ";
            cin.get(city, MAX);
            cout << "   Enter zip code: ";
            cin >> zip;
            }
    };

void main()
```

CHAPTER 8   REVIEW EXERCISES

```
   {
   address adlist[10];          // array of 10 address objects
   int j=0;                     // set to start of array
   char ch;                     // for user choice

   do
      {
      cout << "\nEnter address number " << j+1;
      adlist[j++].getaddr();    // get address, put it in array
      cout << "Input another (y/n)? ";
      ch = getche();
      cin.ignore();             // clear istream
      }
   while((ch == 'y' )++(j<10));  // cycle until user types 'n'

   cout << "\n\nAddress list:";
   for(int k=0; k<j; k++)       // display array of addresses
      {
      cout << "\n\nAdress number " << k+1;
      adlist[k].putaddr();
      }
   }
```

Exercise 4

Modify the FRACLADD exercise from Chapter 7 so that you can store objects of type *fracpri* in an array. Get a series of fractions from the user, and store them in the array. Then total the contents of the array, using the *addfracs()* member function and keeping a running total. Finally, display the result.

```
// fracarr.cpp
// adds elements in array of fraction objects
#include <iostream.h>
#include <conio.h>                 // for getche()

class fracpri                      // class for fractional prices
   {
   private:
      int whole;                   // whole number part of price
      int numer;                   // numerator (top) of fraction
      int denom;                   // denominator (bottom) of fraction
   public:
      fracpri()                    // initialize to 0 (except denom!)
         { whole=numer=0; denom=1; }
      void dispfrac()              // display fraction (format 31-3/8)
         {
         cout << whole << "-" << numer << "/" << denom;
         }
      void getfrac()               // get fraction from user
         {
         char dummy;               // for hyphen and slash
         cin >> whole >> dummy >> numer >> dummy >> denom;
         }
      void addfracs(fracpri, fracpri);  // add two fractions
      void fraclow();              // reduce ourself to lowest terms
```

continued on next page

continued from previous page
```
   };

void fracpri::addfracs(fracpri f1, fracpri f2)    // add fracs
   {
   int newnum1, newnum2, newnumer, carry;

   whole = f1.whole + f2.whole;             // find new whole number
   denom = f1.denom * f2.denom;             // find new denominator
   newnum1 = f1.numer * f2.denom;           // cross multiply
   newnum2 = f2.numer * f1.denom;
   newnumer = newnum1 + newnum2;            // add the new numerators
   carry = newnumer / denom;                // find how much to carry
   whole += carry;                          // add to whole number part
   numer = newnumer % denom;                // find new numerator
   }

void fracpri::fraclow()                     // reduce to lowest terms
   {
   if( numer == 0 )                         // check for special case of
      { denom=1; return; }                  // zero numerator

   long first=numer;                        // find greatest common divisor
   long second=denom;                       // of numerator and denominator
   long temp;                               // (compute with local vars)

   while( first != second )                 // done when they're equal
      {
      if( first < second )                  // if first isn't bigger,
         { temp=first; first=second; second=temp; }      // swap
      first -= second;                      // first=first-second
      }                                     // first is now gcd
   numer /= first;                          // divide both numer and denom
   denom /= first;                          // by gcd to get lowest terms
   }

void main()
   {
   fracpri fracarr[100];                    // make array of fractions
   fracpri total;                           // total amount (set to 0)
   int j = 0;                               // array index

   do
      {
      cout << "\nEnter price (format 31-3/8): ";
      fracarr[j++].getfrac();               // get price, put in array
      cout << "   Do another (y/n)? ";
      } while( j<100++getche() == 'y' );    // repeat until 'n'

   for(int k=0; k<j; k++)                   // total=total+fracarr[k];
      total.addfracs(total, fracarr[k]);
   total.fraclow();                         // total to lowest terms
   cout << "\nTotal is ";                   // display total
   total.dispfrac();
   }
```

CHAPTER 8   REVIEW EXERCISES

Exercise 5

A queue is like a stack except that when you take an item out of a queue, it is the first item that was placed in the queue, rather than the last. The queue is like the line at the checkout counter in the supermarket: it operates on a first in, first out (FIFO) basis, as opposed to a stack, which operates on a last in, first out (LIFO) basis.

Create a class called *Queue* that models a queue, using an array to hold the data, which can consist of integers (assumed to be positive). This is slightly more complicated than a stack, because you need two indexes into the array: *head* points to the place where the next input will be placed, and *tail* points to the place from which the next output will be taken. Both these indexes move forward through the array. When either one reaches the end of the array, it must be reset to the beginning. This gives the effect of a circular buffer. If the tail catches the head it should return an error code (such as a negative number) to indicate there is no more data to read.

Write a *main()* program to test this class by letting the user choose whether to put an item in the queue, or take it out. This way the user can experiment with the queue, seeing how it works under different circumstances. Try putting in a few items, then taking them out. When you have put in MAX items (even if some have been taken out), you've reached the end of the buffer and the head pointer goes back to the beginning.

Don't worry about such unusual cases as when the head catches up with itself and writes over data that has not yet been read by the tail.

```
// queue.cpp
// models a queue, using an array
#include <iostream.h>
#include <process.h>           // for exit()
#include <conio.h>             // for getche()

const int MAX = 10;            // size of array for queue
const int ESC = 27;            // ascii code for 'Esc' key

class Queue                    // class models FIFO queue
    {
    private:
        int queue[MAX];        // array holds queue
        int head;              // array index for input
        int tail;              // array index for output
    public:
        Queue()                // constructor
            {
            head=tail=0;       // initialize head and tail
            }
        void put(int var)      // put item in queue
            {
            queue[head++] = var;   // put item in array
            if( head >= MAX )      // if head past end of array,
                head = 0;          // reset it to beginning
            }
        int get()              // take item from queue
```

continued on next page

continued from previous page

```
         {
         if( tail >= MAX )         // if tail past end of array,
             tail = 0;             // reset it to beginning
         if( tail == head )        // if tail catches head,
             return(-1);           // return "error code"
         return queue[tail++];     // normally, return item at tail
         }
   };

void main()
   {
   Queue Q;                           // make a queue
   int item;                          // item to put in queue
   char choice;                       // user's choice: get or put

   while(1)
      {
      cout << "\nEnter p to put item in queue, g to get an item: ";
      choice = getche();
      switch(choice)
         {
         case 'p':
            cout << "\nEnter item to put in queue: ";
            cin >> item;
            Q.put(item);
            break;
         case 'g':
            cout << "\nItem is " << Q.get();
            break;
         case ESC:
            exit(1);
         default:
            cout << "\nType 'p' or 'g'";
         }
      }
   }
```

CHAPTER 9
Exercise 1

Sometimes it's necessary to bump a counter; that is, increase it by a number larger than 1. This might represent a tour group arriving all at once in a bank teller's line, rather than individual people arriving.

Modify the COUNTPP3 example from Chapter 9 on the disk so that it adds an integer value to a *Counter* object. Overload the '+' operator so you can do this with an expression like

c2 = c1 + 9;

where *c1* and *c2* are *Counter* objects. The *Counter* object should not modify its own value, but rather that of the unnamed temporary object that it returns.

CHAPTER 8 REVIEW EXERCISES

```cpp
// countadd.cpp
// add integer to count variable with '+' operator
#include <iostream.h>

class Counter
   {
   private:
      unsigned int count;                      // count
   public:
      Counter()          { count = 0; }        // constructor  no args
      Counter(int c)     { count = c; }        // constructor, one arg
      int get_count()    { return count; }     // return count

      Counter operator + (int i)               // add integer to Count
         {
         return Counter(count+i);              // return temp Count
         }                                     // initialized to sum
   };

void main()
   {
   Counter c1(2), c2;                          // c1=2, c2=0

   cout << "\nc1=" << c1.get_count();          // display
   cout << "\nc2=" << c2.get_count();

   c2 = c1 + 17;                               // add 17 to c1,
                                               // put result in c2
   cout << "\nc1=" << c1.get_count();          // display: c1=2
   cout << "\nc2=" << c2.get_count();          // c2=19
   }
```

Exercise 2

Suppose you want to know whether two *Counter* objects are equal. Overload the '==' operator so you can compare two *Counters* with an expression like

   if(c1 == c2)

Write a *main()* program to test this operator by creating several *Counter* objects with the same and different values, and comparing them in an *if* expression.

```cpp
// countcmp.cpp
// overload '==' operator to compare two counters
#include <iostream.h>

enum boolean { false, true };

class Counter
   {
   private:
      unsigned int count;              // count
   public:
      Counter()          { count = 0; }        // constructor  no args
```

continued on next page

```
continued from previous page
        Counter(int c)    { count = c; }         // constructor, one arg
        int get_count()   { return count; }      // return count

        boolean operator == (Counter c)          // compare two Counters
            {
            if( count == c.count )               // if count data is
                return true;                     // equal, then the
            else                                 // Counters are equal
                return false;
            }
    };
void main()
    {
    Counter c1(27), c2(27), c3(33);              // initialize
    cout << "\nc1=" << c1.get_count();
    cout << "\nc2=" << c2.get_count();
    cout << "\nc3=" << c3.get_count();

    if( c1 == c2 )
        cout << "\nc1 equals c2";
    else
        cout << "\nc1 not equal to c2";

    if( c2 == c3 )
        cout << "\nc2 equals c3";
    else
        cout << "\nc2 not equal to c3";
    }
```

Exercise 3

Modify the FRACLADD exercise for Chapter 7 so that the overloaded '+' operator is used in the *main()* part of the program to add two fractions (*fracpri* objects). That is, the statement

fp3 = fp1 + fp2;

should add the fractions *fp1* and *fp2* and assign the result to *fp3*. You may need to add a three-argument constructor to the *fracpri* class so that the '+' operator can create a temporary *fracpri* object whose value it can return.

```
// fracplus.cpp
// overloads '+' operator to add two fractions
#include <iostream.h>

class fracpri                           // class for fractional prices
    {
    private:
        int whole;                      // whole number part of price
        int numer;                      // numerator (top) of fraction
        int denom;                      // denominator (bottom) of fraction
    public:
        fracpri()                       // constructor, no args
```

```cpp
        { whole=numer=0; denom=1; }
      fracpri(int w, int n, int d)    // constructor, 3 args
        { whole=w, numer=n, denom=d; }
      void dispfrac()                 // display fraction (format 31-3/8)
         {
         cout << whole << "-"
              << numer << "/"
              << denom;
         }
      void getfrac()                  // get fraction from user
         {
         char dummy;                  // for hyphen and slash
         cin >> whole >> dummy >> numer >> dummy >> denom;
         }
      fracpri operator + (fracpri);   // add two fractions
      void fraclow();                 // reduce ourself to lowest terms
   };

// overloaded '+' operator adds this fraction to argument,
// returns the sum as a fraction
fracpri fracpri::operator + (fracpri farg)// ans=this+farg
   {
   int w, d, n;                       // three parts of temp frac
   int newnum1, newnum2, newnumer, carry;

   w = whole + farg.whole;            // find new whole number
   d = denom * farg.denom;            // find new denominator
   newnum1 = numer * farg.denom;      // cross multiply
   newnum2 = farg.numer * denom;
   newnumer = newnum1 + newnum2;      // add the new numerators
   carry = newnumer / d;              // find how much to carry
   w += carry;                        // add to whole number part
   n = newnumer % d;                  // find new numerator
   return fracpri(w, n, d);           // return temporary fraction
   }

// fraclow()
// member function reduces this fraction to lowest terms
void fracpri::fraclow()
   {
   if( numer == 0 )                   // check for special case of
      { denom=1; return; }            // zero numerator

   long first=numer;                  // find greatest common divisor
   long second=denom;                 // of numerator and denominator
   long temp;                         // (compute with local vars)

   while( first != second )           // done when they're equal
      {
      if( first < second )            // if first isn't bigger,
        { temp=first; first=second; second=temp; } // swap'em
      first -= second;                // first=first-second
      }                               // first is now gcd
   numer /= first;                    // divide both numer and denom
   denom /= first;                    // by gcd to get lowest terms
   }
```

continued on next page

continued from previous page
```
void main()
    {
    fracpri fp1, fp2, fp3;                  // make three objects

    cout << "\nEnter first price: ";        // get prices for fp1, fp2
    fp1.getfrac();
    cout << "Enter second price: ";
    fp2.getfrac();

    fp3 = fp1 + fp2;                        // add fp1 and fp2
                                            // put result in fp3
    fp3.fraclow();                          // set fp3 to lowest terms
    cout << "Sum is ";                      // display fp3
    fp3.dispfrac();
    }
```

Exercise 4

Modify the RBCLASS exercise for Chapter 7 so that the overloaded '*' operator is used in the *main()* part of the program to rotate a target. That is, the statement

*t1 * turn;*

should rotate the target *t1* by *turn* degrees (remember that a right turn causes the target to rotate left).

```
// rbtimes.cpp
// overloads '*' operator to rotate target
#include <iostream.h>

class target
    {
    private:
        float range;                // miles from our location
        int bearing;                // relative to our heading, from 0 to 360
    public:
        target(float ra, int be)    // initialize target info
            { range=ra; bearing=be; }
        void display()                          // display target info
            {
            cout<< range << " miles, "
                << bearing << " degrees.";
            }
        void operator * (int turn)          // rotate target
            {
            bearing -= turn;                    // subtract turn from bearing
            if(bearing < 0)                     // if result is negative,
                bearing += 360;                 // add 360 for positive bearing
            if(bearing >=360)                   // if result is 360 or more,
                bearing -= 360;                 // subtract 360
            }
    };

void main()
```

```
   {                              // initialize targets
   target t1(10.0, 90);           // 10 miles away, on our right
   target t2(4.5, 0);             // 4.5 miles away, straight ahead
   int turn = 10;                 // (can't start at 0 degrees)

   cout << endl << endl;
   while( turn != 0 )             // exit if no turn
      {
      cout << "\nTarget t1: ";    // display targets'
      t1.display();               //      range and bearing
      cout << "\nTarget t2: ";
      t2.display();

      cout << "\nEnter number of degrees to turn "
           << "(negative numbers indicate left turn): ";
      cin >> turn;                // get degrees to turn
      t1 * turn;                  // tell the targets to rotate
      t2 * turn;
      }
   }
```

Exercise 5

Modify the FRACPLUS exercise from this chapter so that it compares two fractions using the overloaded '<' operator. That is, the expression

fp1 < fp2

should evaluate to 1 (true) if *fp1* is numerically less than *fp2*, and to 0 otherwise. Test this operator with a *main()* program that lets the user enter two fractions, and then reports whether the first is smaller than the second.

```
// fracomp.cpp
// overloads '<' operator to compare two fractions
#include <iostream.h>

enum boolean { false, true };

class fracpri                      // class for fractional prices
   {
   private:
      int whole;                   // whole number part of price
      int numer;                   // numerator (top) of fraction
      int denom;                   // denominator (bottom) of fraction
   public:
      void dispfrac()              // display fraction (format 31-3/8)
         {
         cout    << whole << "-"
                 << numer << "/"
                 << denom;
         }
      void getfrac()               // get fraction from user
         {
         char dummy;               // for hyphen and slash
         cin >> whole >> dummy >> numer >> dummy >> denom;
```

continued on next page

continued from previous page
```
        }
        boolean operator < (fracpri);   // compare two fractions
    };

// overloaded '<' operator compares this fraction with argument
// returns true if this is less than arg, false if not less than
// (assumes fractions are in lowest terms)
boolean fracpri::operator < (fracpri farg)
    {
    if( whole < farg.whole )            // if whole number less,
            return true;                // then fraction irrelevent
    if( whole > farg.whole )            // if whole number greater,
            return false;               // then fraction irrelevent
                                        // whole numbers are equal
    int newnum1 = numer * farg.denom;   // cross multiply
    int newnum2 = farg.numer * denom;
    if( newnum1 < newnum2 )             // compare new numerators
            return 1;                   // first is less
    else
            return 0;                   // second is less or equal
    }
void main()
    {
    fracpri fp1, fp2;                   // make two fractions

    cout << "\nEnter first price: ";    // get prices for fp1, fp2
    fp1.getfrac();
    cout << "Enter second price: ";
    fp2.getfrac();

    if( fp1 < fp2 )                     // compare the fractions
            cout << "First price is less than second.";
    else
            cout << "First price not less than second.";
    }
```

Exercise 6

Modify the *fracpri* class so it can convert floating-point (decimal) numbers into fractions, and fractions into floating-point numbers. That is, it should figure out that 7.3 is 7-19/64, and that 2-7/8 is 2.875.

You can assume that the denominator of a fraction never needs to be smaller than 64. Therefore, any decimal number evaluates to some number of sixty-fourths, reduced to lowest terms if necessary.

```
// fraconv.cpp
// converts fractions to real numbers and back again
#include <iostream.h>

void fraclow(int&, int&);       // prototype (not a member func)

class fracpri                   // class for fractional prices
```

CHAPTER 8   REVIEW EXERCISES

```cpp
    {
    private:
        int whole;              // whole number part of price
        int numer;              // numerator (top) of fraction
        int denom;              // denominator (bottom) of fraction
    public:
        fracpri()                              // constructor, no args
            { whole=numer=0; denom=1; }
        fracpri(float flo)                     // constructor, 1 arg
            {                                  // (float to fraction)
            flo += 0.0078125;                  // adjust: add 1/128
            whole = int(flo);                  // whole is integer part
            float flofrac = flo - whole;  // frac is what's left
            numer = flofrac * 64;              // how many 64ths?
            denom = 64;                        // denominator always 64
            fraclow(numer, denom);        // to lowest terms
            }
        void dispfrac()         // display fraction (format 31-3/8)
            {
            cout << whole << "-" << numer << "/" << denom;
            }
        void getfrac()          // get fraction from user
            {
            char dummy;         // for hyphen and slash
            cin >> whole >> dummy >> numer >> dummy >> denom;
            }
        operator float()        // conversion function
            {                   //    (fraction to float)
            return whole + float(numer)/denom;
            }
    };

// fraclow()
// function reduces fraction to lowest terms (not a member func)
void fraclow(int& numer, int& denom)
    {
    if( numer == 0 )            // check for special case of
        { denom=1; return; }    // zero numerator

    long first=numer;           // find greatest common divisor
    long second=denom;          // of numerator and denominator
    long temp;                  // (compute with local vars)

    while( first != second )    // done when they're equal
        {
        if( first < second )    // if first isn't bigger,
            {
            temp=first;         // swap them
            first=second;
            second=temp;
            }
        first -= second;        // first=first-second
        }                       // first is now gcd
    numer /= first;             // divide both numer and denom
    denom /= first;             // by gcd to get lowest terms
    }
```

continued on next page

continued from previous page
```
void main()
    {
    fracpri fp1;                    // create fraction
    float decimal;                  // create decimal number

    cout << "\nEnter decimal number (format 7.75): ";
    cin >> decimal;

    fp1 = decimal;                  // convert decimal to fraction

    cout << decimal << " = ";       // display fraction
    fp1.dispfrac();

    decimal = fp1;                  // convert back to decimal

    cout << " = " << decimal;       // display decimal
    }
```

CHAPTER 10
Exercise 1

Instead of adding the overloaded '+' operator to the *Counter* class as a member function, as was done in the COUNTADD exercise in Chapter 9, add this operator to the *Counter* class using inheritance, by creating a derived class called *Countadd* that contains this operator. In *main()* add an integer to an object of type *Countadd* instead of type *Counter*.

```
// counplus.cpp
// add integer to count variable using inheritance
#include <iostream.h>

class Counter
    {
    protected:                                          // note: not private
        unsigned int count;                             // count
    public:
        Counter()           { count = 0; }              // constructor  no args
        Counter(int c)      { count = c; }              // constructor, one arg
        int get_count()     { return count; }           // return count
    };
class Countadd : public Counter
    {
    public:
        Countadd() : Counter()
            { }                                         // constructor, no args

        Countadd(int c) : Counter(c)
            { }                                         // constructor, 1 arg
        Countadd operator + (int i)                     // add integer to Count
```

```
            {
            return Countadd(count+i);          // return temp Count
            }                                  //   initialized to sum
   };
void main()
   {
   Countadd c1(2), c2;                         // c1=2, c2=0

   cout << "\nc1=" << c1.get_count();          // display
   cout << "\nc2=" << c2.get_count();

   c2 = c1 + 17;                               // add 17 to c1,
                                               //    put result in c2
   cout << "\nc1=" << c1.get_count();          // display: c1=2
   cout << "\nc2=" << c2.get_count();          // c2=19
   }
```

Exercise 2

Imagine that you're running a hardware store in Hayfork, Idaho. You need a database program to keep track of your inventory. Start with a base class called *item* that includes data for the name of the item (a string); the price (type *float*); and the quantity in stock (type *int*). From this derive four other classes, called *pipe, lightbulbs, tools,* and *paint.* The *pipe* class should add data for the length (expressed in feet, type *float*); the size (the diameter in inches, type *float*); and the type (galvanized, ABS, and so on, a string). The *lightbulbs* class should add data for the wattage of the bulb (type *int*). The *tools* class doesn't need any additional data. The *paint* class should add data for the size in pints (type *int*) and the color (a string).

Write a *main()* program to get data from the user for several items of different types, and then display these items. (See the EMPLOY program in Chapter 10 on the disk for an approach to this situation.)

```
// hardware.cpp
// models hardware store inventory using inheritance
#include <iostream.h>

const int LEN = 80;              // maximum length of names

class item                       // base class for all items
   {
   private:
      char name[LEN];            // item name
      float price;               // item price
      int quantity;              // number in stock
   public:
      void getdata()             // get data from user
         {
         cout << "\n   Enter item name: ";
         cin >> name;
```

continued on next page

continued from previous page

```
            cout << "   Enter price (format 12.95): ";
            cin >> price;
            cout << "   Enter quantity in stock: ";
            cin >> quantity;
            }
        void putdata()             // display data
            {
            cout << "\n   Name: " << name;
            cout << "\n   Price: " << price;
            cout << "\n   Quantity: " << quantity;
            }
    };

class pipe : public item          // pipe class
    {
    private:
        float length;              // length of pipe
        float size;                // size of pipe
        char type[LEN];            // type of pipe
    public:
        void getdata()             // get data from user
            {
            item::getdata();
            cout << "   Enter length: "; cin >> length;
            cout << "   Enter size: ";   cin >> size;
            cout << "   Enter type: ";   cin >> type;
            }
        void putdata()                 // display data
            {
            item::putdata();
            cout << "\n   Length: " << length;
            cout << "\n   Size: " << size;
            cout << "\n   Type: " << type;
            }
    };
class lightbulbs : public item    // lightbulbs class
    {
    private:
        int watts;                     // wattage of light bulbs
    public:
        void getdata()                 // get data from user
            {
            item::getdata();
            cout << "   Enter wattage: "; cin >> watts;
            }
        void putdata()                 // display data
            {
            item::putdata();
            cout << "\n   Wattage: " << watts;
            }
    };

class tools : public item             // tools class
    {                                 // (no additional data)
```

```cpp
    };
class paint : public item            // paint class
    {
    private:
        int size;                    // size in pints
        char color[LEN];             // color of paint
    public:
        void getdata()               // get data from user
            {
            item::getdata();
            cout << "   Enter size (pints): "; cin >> size;
            cout << "   Enter color: "; cin >> color;
            }
        void putdata()               // display data
            {
            item::putdata();
            cout << "\n   Size: " << size;
            cout << "\n   Color: " << color;
            }
    };

void main()
    {
    pipe p1;                                    // make one item
    lightbulbs b1;                              // of each class
    tools t1;
    paint pnt1;

    cout << endl;
    cout << "\nEnter data for pipe item ";     // get data for
    p1.getdata();                               // items

    cout << "\nEnter data for light bulb item";
    b1.getdata();

    cout << "\nEnter data for tool item";
    t1.getdata();

    cout << "\nEnter data for paint item";
    pnt1.getdata();

    cout << "\nItem 1";                         // display data for
    p1.putdata();                               // items

    cout << "\nItem 2";
    b1.putdata();

    cout << "\nItem 3";
    t1.putdata();

    cout << "\nItem 4";
    pnt1.putdata();
    }
```

MASTER C++ FOR WINDOWS

Exercise 3

Use inheritance to add the capability to handle negative fractions to the *fracpri* class from the FRACLASS.CPP exercise for Chapter 7. The derived class can be called *signfrac*. In this class a no-argument constructor should set the sign to positive and call the no-argument constructor in *fracpri*. A four-argument constructor should set the sign to '+' or '-' and call the three-argument constructor in *fracpri*. A *dispfrac()* function should display the sign "(+)" or "(-)" and call *dispfrac()* in *fracpri*. A *getfrac()* function should get the sign ('+' or '-') from the user and call the *getfrac()* function in *fracpri*. Don't worry about how to add signed fractions.

```
// negfrac.cpp
// uses inheritance to add sign ('+' or '-') to fractions
#include <iostream.h>

class fracpri                       // class for fractional prices
   {
   private:
      int whole;                    // whole number part of price
      int numer;                    // numerator (top) of fraction
      int denom;                    // denominator (bottom) of fraction
   public:
      fracpri()                                       // constructor, no args
         { whole=numer=0; denom=1; }
      fracpri(int w, int n, int d)                    // constructor, 3 args
         { whole=w, numer=n, denom=d; }
      void dispfrac()               // display fraction (format 31-3/8)
         {
         cout << whole << "-"
              << numer << "/"
              << denom;
         }
      void getfrac()                // get fraction from user
         {
         char dummy;     // for hyphen and slash
         cin >> whole >> dummy >> numer >> dummy >> denom;
         }
   };

enum posneg { pos, neg };      // values for sign

// new class derived from fracpri
class signfrac : public fracpri                  // adds sign to fracpri
   {
   private:
      posneg sign;
   public:
      signfrac() : fracpri()                        // constructor, no args
         { sign = pos; }
                                                    // constructor, 4 args
      signfrac(posneg s, int w, int n, int d) : fracpri(w, n, d)
         { sign = s; }
      void dispfrac()                               // display sign and fraction
         {
```

```
                cout << ((sign==pos) ? "(+)" : "(-)");   // display sign
                fracpri::dispfrac();                     // rest of frac
                }
        void getfrac()                                   // get sign and fraction
                {
                char ch;                                 // get sign
                cout << "(format +31-3/8 or -31-3/8): ";
                cin >> ch;
                sign = (ch=='-') ? neg : pos;            // set sign
                fracpri::getfrac();                      // rest of frac
                }
    };

void main()
    {
    signfrac fp1;                              // make signed fraction
    signfrac fp2( neg, 1, 7, 8 );              // initialize signed frac

    cout << "\nEnter price ";                  // get price for fp1
    fp1.getfrac();

    cout << "\nfp1 = "; fp1.dispfrac();        // display signed
    cout << "\nfp2 = "; fp2.dispfrac();        // fractions
    }
```

Exercise 4

Start with the ENGLEN example in Chapter 10 on the disk, which adds a sign ('+' or '-') to the *Distance* class using inheritance. Assume that you don't like the input and output routines. You would prefer distances to be entered by the user using the format +3´4˝ or –3´4˝, rather than answering individual questions for feet, inches, and the sign. You also would like distances output in the same format, rather than with a hyphen between the feet and inches and parentheses around the sign.

Create a third-generation class, derived from the *DistSign* class (which is derived from the *Distance* class) that incorporates new versions of the *getdist()* and *showdist()* member functions to allow for input and output in this new format. Don't modify *Distance* and *DistSign* (except for one small item). Assume the user will always type a sign before the feet and inches, whether '+' or '-.' Don't forget that when you use the single quote (') or double quote (") in string or character constants, they must be preceded by a backslash (e.g., \' and \").

```
// engliop.cpp
// modify I/O routines by deriving new class
#include <iostream.h>

class Distance                                 // English Distance class
    {
    protected:                                 // note: can't be private
        int feet;
        float inches;
    public:
```

continued on next page

continued from previous page
```
        Distance()                      // constructor (no args)
            { feet = 0; inches = 0.0; }
        Distance(int ft, float in)      // constructor (two args)
            { feet = ft; inches = in; }
        void getdist()                  // get length from user
            {
            cout << "\nEnter feet: ";  cin >> feet;
            cout << "Enter inches: ";  cin >> inches;
            }
        void showdist()                 // display distance
            { cout << feet << "\'-" << inches << '\"'; }
    };

enum posneg { pos, neg };               // for sign in DistSign

class DistSign : public Distance        // adds sign to Distance
    {
    protected:                          // note: can't be private
        posneg sign;                    // sign is pos or neg
    public:
                                        // constructor (no args)
        DistSign() : Distance()         // call base constructor
            { sign = pos; }             // set the sign to +

                                        // constructor (2 or 3 args)
        DistSign(int ft, float in, posneg sg=pos) :
                Distance(ft, in)        // call base constructor
            { sign = sg; }              // set the sign

        void getdist()                  // get length from user
            {
            Distance::getdist();        // call base getdist()
            char ch;                    // get sign from user
            cout << "Enter sign (+ or -): ";  cin >> ch;
            sign = (ch=='+') ? pos : neg;
            }

        void showdist()                 // display distance
            {
            cout << ( (sign==pos) ? "(+)" : "(-)" );    // show sign
            Distance::showdist();                       // ft and in
            }
    };

class DistIO : public DistSign
    {
    public:
        DistIO()                        // one-arg constructor
            { }                         // 2- or 3-arg constructor
        DistIO(int f, float i, posneg s=pos) : DistSign(f, i, s)
            { }
        void getdist()                  // get distance from user
            {                           // format +7'4" or -7'4"
            char ch, dummy;
```

CHAPTER 8 REVIEW EXERCISES

```
                    cin >> ch              // get sign    (in DistSign)
                        >> feet            // get feet    (in Distance)
                        >> dummy           // get feet mark (')
                        >> inches          // get inches (in Distance)
                        >> dummy;          // get inches mark (")
                    sign = (ch=='-') ? neg : pos;
                    }
         void showdist()                   // display distance
                    {                      // format -7'4" or +7'4"
                    cout << ( (sign==pos) ? '+' : '-' )
                         << feet << '\''
                         << inches << '\"';
                    }
         };

void main()
    {
    DistIO alpha;                          // no-arg constructor
    cout << "\n\nEnter distance (format +7\'4\"): ";
    alpha.getdist();                       // get alpha from user

    DistIO beta(11, 6.25);                 // 2-arg constructor

    DistIO gamma(100, 5.5, neg);           // 3-arg constructor

                                           // display all distances
    cout << "\nalpha = ";   alpha.showdist();
    cout << "\nbeta = ";    beta.showdist();
    cout << "\ngamma = ";   gamma.showdist();
    }
```

Exercise 5

Start with the ENGLEN example in Chapter 10 on the disk, which adds a sign ('+' or '-') to the *Distance* class. Then add a new overloaded '+' routine to the *DistSign* class so that two signed distances can be added together.

To do this you may want to add to the *Distance* class the routine for the overloaded '+' operator from the ENGLPLUS example and the routine for the overloaded '<' operator from the ENGLESS example, both in Chapter 9 on the disk. Also, you will want to write a member function that overloads the '-' operator so you can subtract two *Distance* objects. Finally, you may find that you need a constructor for the *DistSign* class that takes two arguments: a *Distance* and a sign.

When signed quantities (call them *a* and *b*) are added, there are several possible results, depending on the signs of *a* and *b*. If they are both positive, they are added and given a positive sign. If both are negative, they are added and given a negative sign. If the signs are different and *a* is less than *b*, then *a* is subtracted from *b* and the result is given the sign of the larger quantity. If *a* is greater than *b*, then *b* is subtracted from *a* and the result is given the sign of the larger quantity. The new addition routine in *DistSign* will need to consider these possibilities by examining the signs of the

DistSign objects and by using the overloaded '<' operator in *Distance*. It can then call the overloaded '+' and '-' routines in *Distance* to carry out the arithmetic.

```cpp
// negengl.cpp
// use inheritance to add sign ('+' or '-') to Distance class,
// modify overloaded '+' operator to work with signed Distances
#include <iostream.h>

enum boolean { false, true };

class Distance                      // English Distance class
    {
    protected:                      // NOTE: can't be private
        int feet;
        float inches;
    public:
        Distance()                  // constructor (no args)
            { feet = 0; inches = 0.0; }
        Distance(int ft, float in)           // constructor (two args)
            { feet = ft; inches = in; }
        void getdist()                       // get length from user
            {
            cout << "\n   Enter feet: ";  cin >> feet;
            cout << "   Enter inches: ";  cin >> inches;
            }
        void showdist()                      // display distance
            { cout << feet << "\'-" << inches << '\"'; }
        Distance operator + (Distance);      // add Distances
        Distance operator - (Distance);      // subtract Distances
        boolean operator < (Distance);       // compare Distances
    };
                                             // add this Distance to d2
Distance Distance::operator + (Distance d2)  // return the sum
    {
    int f = feet + d2.feet;        // add the feet
    float i = inches + d2.inches;            // add the inches
    if(i >= 12.0)                            // if total exceeds 12.0,
        {                                    // then decrease inches
        i -= 12.0;                           // by 12.0 and
        f++;                                 // increase feet by 1
        }                                    // return a temporary Distance
    return Distance(f,i);                    // initialized to sum
    }
                                             // subtract d2 from this Dist
Distance Distance::operator - (Distance d2)  // return difference
    {                                        // (assume this > d2)
    int f = feet - d2.feet;                  // subtract feet
    float i = inches - d2.inches;            // subtract inches
    if( i < 0 )                              // if carry needed,
        {                                    // increase inches by 12.0
        i +=12.0;                            // and
        f-;                                  // decrease feet by 1
        }
    return Distance(f,i);                    // return difference
    }
                                             // compare this with d2
```

```cpp
boolean Distance::operator < (Distance d2)         // true or false
   {
   float bf1 = feet + inches/12;
   float bf2 = d2.feet + d2.inches/12;
   return (bf1 < bf2) ? true : false;
   }

enum posneg { pos, neg };         // for sign in DistSign

// class inherited from Distance
class DistSign : public Distance                   // adds sign to Distance
   {
   private:
      posneg sign;                // sign is pos or neg
   public:
                                  // constructor (no args)
      DistSign() : Distance()     // call base constructor
         { sign = pos; }          // set the sign to +
                                  // constructor (Distance+sign)
      DistSign(Distance d, posneg sg) : Distance(d)
         { sign = sg; }
                                  // constructor (2 or 3 args)
      DistSign(int ft, float in, posneg sg=pos) :
             Distance(ft, in)     // call base constructor
         { sign = sg; }           // set the sign

      void getdist()              // get length from user
         {
         Distance::getdist();     // call base getdist()
         char ch;                 // get sign from user
         cout << "   Enter sign (+ or -): ";  cin >> ch;
         sign = (ch=='+') ? pos : neg;
         }

      void showdist()             // display distance
         {
         cout << ( (sign==pos) ? "(+)" : "(-)" );   // show sign
         Distance::showdist();                      // ft and in
         }
      DistSign operator + (DistSign);   // add signed Distances
   };

DistSign DistSign::operator + (DistSign d2)        // add signed dists
   {
   posneg tsign;
   Distance t1(feet, inches);       // Distance version of this
   Distance t2(d2);                 // Distance version of d2
   Distance sum;                    // Distance to hold sum
   // (need these so we can use Distance arithmetic functions)

   if( sign==pos && d2.sign==pos )  // if both signs positive
      {                             // add Distances
      sum = t1 + t2;                // sign is positive

      tsign = pos;
      }
```

continued on next page

continued from previous page

```
    else if( sign==neg && d2.sign==neg )  // if both signs neg
        {                                 // add Distances
        sum = t1 + t2;
        tsign = neg;
        }
    else if( t1 < t2 )                    // signs are different
        {                                 // if this < d2
        sum = t2 - t1;                    // subtract this from d2
        tsign = (d2.sign==pos) ? pos : neg;   // use sign of larger
        }
    else                                  // if d2 < this
        {
        sum = t1 - t2;                    // subtract d2 from this
        tsign = (sign==pos) ? pos : neg;  // use sign of larger
        }                                 // return sum
    return DistSign(sum, tsign);          //    in DistSign form
    }

void main()
    {
    DistSign a, b, c;         // make 3 signed distances

    cout << "\n\nEnter Distance a: ";     // get values for two
    a.getdist();
    cout << "Enter Distance b: ";
    b.getdist();
    c = a + b;                // add two signed distances
    cout << "Sum is ";
    c.showdist();             // display the sum
    }
```

CHAPTER 12
Exercise 1

Here's a program that lets you see another way in which pointers work.
    Start by creating five integer variables, and initialize them to constants like 1, 2, 3, 4, and 5. Create a pointer to *int*. Set the pointer to point to the middle variable. Now, in a loop, allow the user to enter either 'i' or 'd,' to increment or decrement the pointer (as in *ptr++* and *ptr–*). Quit the loop by pressing the ESC key.
    Also in the loop, print out the address pointed to, and the contents of that address. Now the user can roam back and forth in the program's data, examining the data items and their corresponding addresses. Notice that you can easily go beyond the program's data. Such out-of-bounds data won't mean much, because it is program code or garbage left over from other programs. Remember that local data is stored in descending order in memory, with the highest address getting the first data item; global data is stored in ascending order.

```
// ptrtest.cpp
// allows user to increment and decrement address pointer
```

CHAPTER 8 REVIEW EXERCISES

```cpp
#include <iostream.h>
#include <conio.h>

const char ESC = 27;

void main()
    {
    int avar = 111;                             // five integer
    int bvar = 222;                             // variables,
    int cvar = 333;                             // initialized
    int dvar = 444;
    int evar = 555;

    char ch = 'a';
    int* ptr = &cvar;                           // set ptr to cvar

    while( ch != ESC )                          // quit on Esc key
        {
        cout << "\n\nContents of " << ptr << " = " << *ptr;
        cout << "\nType i to increment address, "
             << "or d to decrement address: ";
        ch = getche();                          // get character
        if( ch == 'i' )
            ptr++;             // increment ptr
        if( ch == 'd' )
            ptr-;              // decrement ptr
        }
    }
```

Exercise 2

It is said that a woman's ideal weight can be found by multiplying her height in inches by 3.5 and subtracting 110 from the result. (This and all such formulas should be taken with a grain of salt.) Write a function that takes two arguments: a height in inches, and a pointer to a weight. The function should calculate the ideal weight based on this formula, and insert it into the appropriate variable in the calling program, using the pointer. You can use type *int* throughout. See the PASSPTR example from Chapter 12 on the disk for the general idea.

```cpp
// weight.cpp
// passing one argument by pointer
#include <iostream.h>

void main()
    {
    void ideal(int, int*);        // prototype

    int height;
    int weight;

    cout << "\nEnter height in inches: ";
    cin >> height;
```

continued on next page

```
continued from previous page
    ideal(height, &weight);         // send address of weight
    cout << "Ideal weight is " << weight;
    }

void ideal(int h, int* ptrw)
    {
    *ptrw = (3.5 * h) - 110;        // *ptrw is the same as weight
    }
```

Exercise 3

Using the COPYSTR example in Chapter 12 on the disk as a starting point, create a function that concatenates two strings to form a third. That is, if the first string is "cats" and the second is " and dogs," the resulting string should be "cats and dogs." The prototype for the function should be of the form

void concastr(char* dest, char* src1, char* src2);

Within this function, move the source strings to the destination string on a character-by-character basis, using pointers. The destination string should already exist as an empty array, sized large enough to hold the concatenated strings.

```
// concat.cpp
// concatenates two strings to form a third; uses pointers
#include <iostream.h>

void main()
    {
    void concastr(char*, char*, char*);       // prototype

    char* str1 = "\nThe quality of mercy ";   // Shakespeare
    char* str2 = "is not strained;";
    char str3[80];                            // empty string

    concastr(str3, str1, str2);               // concatenate str1 and str2
    cout << endl << str3;                     // display str3
    }

void concastr(char* dest, char* src1, char* src2)
    {
    while( *src1 )                            // until null character,
        *dest++ = *src1++;                    // copy chars from src1 to dest
    while( *src2 )                            // until null character,
        *dest++ = *src2++;                    // copy chars from src2 to dest
    *dest = '\0';                             // terminate dest
    }
```

Exercise 4

Write a member function for the *String* class from the NEWSTR example in Chapter 12 on the disk. This function should take two *String* objects as

CHAPTER 8 REVIEW EXERCISES

arguments, and concatenate them to make a new string in the *String* object of which it is a member. The function will need to erase whatever string its object currently holds, copy the first *String* object into its object, and concatenate the second *String* object.

```
// stringca.cpp
// concatenates two String objects
#include <iostream.h>
#include <string.h>                // for strlen(), strcpy(), strcat()

class String                       // user-defined string class
   {
   private:
      char* str;                   // pointer to string
   public:
      String(char* s)              // constructor, one arg
         {
         int length = strlen(s);   // length of string argument
         str = new char[length+1]; // get memory
         strcpy(str, s);           // copy argument to it
         }
      ~String()                    // destructor
         {
         delete str;               // release memory
         }
      void display()               // display the String
         {
         cout << str;
         }
      void concat(String, String); // concatenate strings
   };
void String::concat(String s1, String s2)  // concatenate strings
   {
   delete str;                     // forget current string
   int len = strlen(s1.str) + strlen(s2.str);
   str = new char[len];            // get space for both
   strcpy(str, s1.str);            // copy first into space
   strcat(str, s2.str);            // add the second
   }

void main()
   {
   String str1 = "Now is the time ";   // initialize Strings
   String str2 = "for all good men.";
   String str3 = "";                   // empty String

   str3.concat(str1, str2);            // concatenate old Strings
   cout << endl << "str3 = ";
   str3.display();                     // display new String
   }
```

MASTER C++ FOR WINDOWS

Exercise 5

Make an array of pointers to fractional price objects. Start with the *fracpri* class from the FRACLASS exercise from Chapter 7, and use the array of pointers to objects as seen in the PTROBJS example from Chapter 12 on the disk.

```
// ptrfracs.cpp
// array of pointers to fracpri (fraction) objects
#include <iostream.h>
#include <conio.h>              // for getche()

class fracpri                   // class for fractional prices
   {
   private:
      int whole;                // whole number part of price
      int numer;                // numerator (top) of fraction
      int denom;                // denominator (bottom) of fraction
   public:
      void dispfrac()           // display fraction (format 31-3/8)
         {
         cout << whole << "-" << numer << "/" << denom;
         }
      void getfrac()            // get fraction from user
         {
         char dummy;            // for hyphen and slash
         cin >> whole >> dummy >> numer >> dummy >> denom;
         }
   };

void main(void)
   {
   fracpri* fracPtr[100];       // array of pointers to fractions
   int n = 0;                   // number of fractions in array
   char choice;                 // user's choice

   do                                                   // put fractions in array
      {
      cout << "\nEnter fractional price: ";
      fracPtr[n] = new fracpri;                 // make new object
      fracPtr[n]->getfrac();                    // get fraction from user
      n++;                                      // count new fraction
      cout << "Enter another (y/n)? ";  // enter another
      choice = getche();                        // fraction?
      }
   while(( choice=='y' )++(n<100));             // quit on 'n'

   for(int j=0; j<n; j++)                       // display all fractions
      {
      cout << "\nFractional price number " << j+1 << " is ";
      fracPtr[j]->dispfrac();
      }
   }  // end main()
```

144

CHAPTER 8 REVIEW EXERCISES

Exercise 6

Make a linked list of *person* objects. Start with the linked list structure from the LINKLIST example and the *person* class from the PERSORT example, both in Chapter 12 on the disk. You won't need to modify the *person* object, but you'll need to change the *additem()* and *display()* member functions in *linklist* so they call the appropriate routines in *person*, rather than getting data from an argument and displaying it directly. For example, the appropriate statement in *additem()* is

  newlink->data.setName();

and in *display()* it's

  current->data.printName();

Write a *main()* program that, in a loop, asks the user for a name, using the *setName()* member function from *person* (which is embedded in the *additem()* member function from *linklist*). The new *person* object should then be added to the linked list. When the user has added as many names as desired to the list, display all the names using the *printName()* member function in *person* (which is embedded in the *display()* member function from *linklist*).

Notice that the same linked list class can be used to hold data from different classes, with few modifications to the linked list class itself. Container class libraries are based on this principle.

```
// linkpers.cpp
// linked list with person objects
#include <iostream.h>
#include <conio.h>                              // for getche()

class person                                    // class of persons
    {
    private:
        char name[40];                          // person's name
    public:
        void setName(void)                      // set the name
            { cout << "\n   Enter name: "; cin >> name; }
        void printName(void)                    // display the name
            { cout << endl << name; }
        char* getName()                         // return the name
            { return name; }
    };

struct link                                     // one element of list
    {
    person data;                                // data item is a person
    link* next;                                 // pointer to next link
    };
```

continued on next page

```cpp
continued from previous page
class linklist                                   // a list of links
    {
    private:
       link* first;                              // pointer to first link
    public:
       linklist()                                // no-argument constructor
           { first = NULL; }                     // no first link
       void additem();                           // add data item (one link)
       void display();                           // display all links
    };
void linklist::additem()                         // add data item
    {
    link* newlink = new link;                    // make a new link
    newlink->data.setName();                     // person gets own data
    newlink->next = first;                       // it points to next link
    first = newlink;                             // now first points to this
    }

void linklist::display()                         // display all links
    {
    link* current = first;                       // set ptr to first link
    while( current != NULL )                     // quit on last link
       {
       current->data.printName();     // person shows own data
       current = current->next;       // move to next link
       }
    }

void main()
    {
    linklist li;                                 // make linked list
    char ch;                                     // for user choice
    do
       {
       cout << "\nEnter data for person";
       li.additem();                             // add person to list
       cout << "\nAdd another person (y/n)? ";
       ch = getche();
       }
    while(ch != 'n');                            // quit loop on 'n'

    li.display();                                // display persons on list
    }
```

CHAPTER 13
Exercise 1

Start with the VIRTPERS example from Chapter 13 on the disk. Remove the *isOutstanding()* member function from both the *student* and *professor* classes, and substitute a *printData()* function that displays a student's GPA or a professor's number of publications. Make whatever other changes are necessary so that the *main()* program, using the same basic loop approach as in VIRTPERS, will display a list of students and professors, showing the name (using the *printName()* function) followed by either the GPA or the number of publications, as appropriate (using the *printData()* function).

```
// virtpez.cpp
// virtual functions with person class
#include <iostream.h>
enum boolean { false, true };

class person                                          // person class
    {
    protected:
        char name[40];                                // person's name
    public:
        void setName()                                // get name from user
            { cout << "   Enter name: "; cin >> name; }
        void printName()                              // display name
            { cout << "Name is: " << name << endl; }
        virtual void printData() = 0;    // pure virtual function
    };

class student : public person               // student class
    {
    private:
        float gpa;                                    // grade point average
    public:
        void setData()                                // get GPA from user
            { cout << "   Enter student's GPA: "; cin >> gpa; }
        void printData()                              // display GPA
            { cout << "   GPA is: " << gpa << endl; }
    };

class professor : public person             // professor class
    {
    private:
        int numPubs;                // number of papers published
    public:
        void setData()              // get number of papers from user
            {
            cout << "   Enter number of professor's publications: ";
            cin >> numPubs;
            }
        void printData()            // display number of papers
            { cout << "   Number of pubs is: " << numPubs << endl; }
    };

void main(void)
    {
    person* persPtr[100];       // list of pointers to persons
    student* stuPtr;            // pointer to student
    professor* proPtr;          // pointer to professor
    int n = 0;                  // number of persons on list
    char choice;                // user's choice

    do
```

continued on next page

continued from previous page

```cpp
    {
    cout << "Enter student or professor (s/p): ";
    cin >> choice;
    if(choice=='s')                          // it's a student
       {
       stuPtr = new student;                 // make new student
       stuPtr->setName();                    // set student name
       stuPtr->setData();                    // set GPA
       persPtr[n++] = stuPtr;     // put pointer in list
       }
    else                                     // it's a professor
       {
       proPtr = new professor;   // make new professor
       proPtr->setName();                    // set professor name
       proPtr->setData();                    // set number of pubs
       persPtr[n++] = proPtr;     // put pointer in list
       }
    cout << "   Enter another (y/n)? ";      // do another person?
    cin >> choice;
    } while((n<100)++( choice=='y' ));       // cycle until not 'y'
 for(int j=0; j<n; j++)                      // for each person,
    {
    persPtr[j]->printName();        // display name
    persPtr[j]->printData();        // display GPA or pubs
    }
 } // end main()
```

Exercise 2

Start with the HARDWARE exercise from Chapter 10. Your goal is to create a list in which you can store items from these four hardware categories: pipe, lightbulbs, tools, and paint. Each of these categories corresponds to a class derived from the *item* class. The program should repeatedly ask the user to select one of these four categories, and then prompt the user to fill in the specifics of the item, which depend on the category. For example, you ask for the length and size of pipe, but the color of paint.

The *main()* part of the program should create an array of type *pointer-to-item*, as in the VIRTPERS example from Chapter 13 on the disk. This array will hold pointers to items from the derived classes. In a loop the program should ask the user what category a new item should be, and then create the item using *new*. The pointer to the item should be placed on the list, where it can be used to ask the user for the details of the item. When the user has finished entering items, the program, in a *for* loop, should display all the items, using the pointers stored in the array.

Only two lines need to be changed in the *item* class, and no changes are necessary in the derived classes *pipe, lightbulbs, tools,* and *paint*.

```cpp
// virthard.cpp
// virtual functions in hardware store inventory
#include <iostream.h>
#include <conio.h>                  // for getche()
```

CHAPTER 8   REVIEW EXERCISES

```cpp
const int LEN = 80;                    // maximum length of names

class item                             // base class for all items
   {
   private:
      char name[LEN];                  // item name
      float price;                     // item price
      int quantity;                    // number in stock
   public:
      virtual void getdata()           // get data from user (virtual)
         {
         cout << "\n   Enter item name: ";
         cin >> name;
         cout << "   Enter price (format 12.95): ";
         cin >> price;
         cout << "   Enter quantity in stock: ";
         cin >> quantity;
         }
      virtual void putdata()           // display data (virtual)
         {
         cout << "\n   Name: " << name;
         cout << "\n   Price: " << price;
         cout << "\n   Quantity: " << quantity;
         }
   };

class pipe : public item               // pipe class
   {
   private:
      float length;                    // length of pipe
      float size;                      // size of pipe
      char type[LEN];                  // type of pipe
   public:
      void getdata()                   // get data from user
         {
         item::getdata();
         cout << "   Enter length: "; cin >> length;
         cout << "   Enter size: ";   cin >> size;
         cout << "   Enter type: ";   cin >> type;
         }
      void putdata()                   // display data
         {
         item::putdata();
         cout << "\n   Length: " << length;
         cout << "\n   Size: " << size;
         cout << "\n   Type: " << type;
         }
   };

class lightbulbs : public item   // lightbulbs class
   {
   private:
      int watts;                       // wattage of light bulbs
   public:
      void getdata()                   // get data from user
         {
```

continued on next page

continued from previous page
```
            item::getdata();
            cout << "   Enter wattage: "; cin >> watts;
            }
        void putdata()                 // display data
            {
            item::putdata();
            cout << "\n   Wattage: " << watts;
            }
    };

class tools : public item              // tool class
    {                                  // (no additional data)
    };

class paint : public item              // paint class
    {
    private:
        int size;                      // size in pints
        char color[LEN];               // color of paint
    public:
        void getdata()                 // get data from user
            {
            item::getdata();
            cout << "   Enter size (pints): "; cin >> size;
            cout << "   Enter color: "; cin >> color;
            }
        void putdata()                 // display data
            {
            item::putdata();
            cout << "\n   Size: " << size;
            cout << "\n   Color: " << color;
            }
    };

void main()
    {
    item* itemPtr[100];         // array of pointers to items
    pipe* pipePtr;              // pointer to pipe
    lightbulbs* bulbPtr;        // pointer to lightbulbs
    tools* toolPtr;             // pointer to tools
    paint* paintPtr;            // pointer to paint
    int n=0;                    // number of items on list
    int nchoice;                // user's choice (1, 2, 3, or 4)
    char cchoice;               // user's choice (y or n)

    do
        {
        cout << "\n1-Pipe\n2-Lightbulbs\n3-Tools\n4-Paint";
        cout << "\nEnter number for category: ";
        cin >> nchoice;
        switch(nchoice)
            {
            case 1:
                pipePtr = new pipe;     // make ptr to new pipe
                itemPtr[n] = pipePtr;   // put ptr in array
```

```
            itemPtr[n++]->getdata();    // use it to get data
            break;
        case 2:
            bulbPtr = new lightbulbs; // make ptr to new bulb
            itemPtr[n] = bulbPtr;        // put ptr in array
            itemPtr[n++]->getdata();    // use it to get data
            break;
        case 3:
            toolPtr = new tools;         // make ptr to new tool
            itemPtr[n] = toolPtr;        // put ptr in array
            itemPtr[n++]->getdata();    // use it to get data
            break;
        case 4:
            paintPtr = new paint;        // make ptr to new paint
            itemPtr[n] = paintPtr;       // put ptr in array
            itemPtr[n++]->getdata();    // use it to get data
            break;
        }
    cout << "\nEnter another (y/n)? ";
    cchoice = getche();
    cin.ignore();
    } while((n<100)++(choice != 'n' ));

   for(int j=0; j<n; j++)
      {
      cout << "\nItem number " << j+1; // use ptrs from array
      itemPtr[j]->putdata();                         // to display data
      }                                              // for all items
   }
```

Exercise 3

Modify the FRACPLUS exercise from Chapter 9 on the disk so that you can execute statements of the form

   fp2 = floatvar + fp1;

where *floatvar* is a variable of type *float*. You'll need to add the one-argument constructor from the FRACONV exercise of Chapter 9, so you can convert from type *float* to type *fracpri*. You'll also need to change the form of the overloaded '+' operator; otherwise, you'll get the discouraging *Operator cannot be applied to these operand types* error message.

```
// fracfren.cpp
// uses friend function to add two fractions
#include <iostream.h>

class fracpri                          // class for fractional prices
   {
   private:
      int whole;                       // whole number part of price
      int numer;                       // numerator (top) of fraction
      int denom;                       // denominator (bottom) of fraction
   public:
```

continued on next page

continued from previous page
```
        fracpri()                               // constructor, no args
                           { whole=numer=0; denom=1; }
        fracpri(float flo)                      // constructor, 1 arg
            {                                   //   (float to fraction)
            flo += 0.0078125;                   // adjust: add 1/128
            whole = int(flo);                   // whole is integer part
            float flofrac = flo - whole;        // frac is what's left
            numer = flofrac * 64;               // how many 64ths?
            denom = 64;                         // denominator always 64
            fraclow();                          // to lowest terms
            }
        fracpri(int w, int n, int d)    // constructor, 3 args
            { whole=w, numer=n, denom=d; }
        void dispfrac()                 // display fraction (format 31-3/8)
            {
            cout << whole << "
                 << numer << "/"
                 << denom;
            }
        void getfrac()          // get fraction from user
            {
            char dummy;         // for hyphen and slash
            cin >> whole >> dummy >> numer >> dummy >> denom;
            }
                                // add two fractions
        friend fracpri operator + (fracpri, fracpri);
        void fraclow();         // reduce ourself to lowest terms
    };

// friend function
// overloaded '+' operator adds two arguments, returns sum
fracpri operator + (fracpri farg1, fracpri farg2)
    {                                           // ans=farg1+farg2
    int w, d, n;                                // three parts of temp frac
    int newnum1, newnum2, newnumer, carry;

    w = farg1.whole + farg2.whole;              // find new whole number
    d = farg1.denom * farg2.denom;              // find new denominator
    newnum1 = farg1.numer * farg2.denom;        // cross multiply
    newnum2 = farg2.numer * farg1.denom;
    newnumer = newnum1 + newnum2;               // add the new numerators
    carry = newnumer / d;                       // find how much to carry
    w += carry;                                 // add to whole number part
    n = newnumer % d;                           // find new numerator
    return fracpri(w, n, d);                    // return temporary fraction
    }

// fraclow()
// member function reduces this fraction to lowest terms
void fracpri::fraclow()
    {
    if( numer == 0 )                    // check for special case of
        { denom=1; return; }            // zero numerator
    long first=numer;                   // find greatest common divisor
```

```
        long second=denom;                  // of numerator and denominator
        long temp;                           // (compute with local vars)

        while( first != second )             // done when they're equal
            {
            if( first < second )             // if first isn't bigger,
                { temp=first; first=second; second=temp; }        // swap'em
            first -= second;                 // first=first-second
            }                                // first is now gcd
        numer /= first;                      // divide both numer and denom
        denom /= first;                      // by gcd to get lowest terms
        }

void main()
    {
    fracpri fp1, fp2, fp3;                   // make three objects
    float decipri;                           // decimal price

    cout << "\nEnter fractional price: ";    // get price for fp1
    fp1.getfrac();
    cout << "Enter decimal price: ";         // get decimal price
    cin >> decipri;

    fp2 = fp1 + decipri;                     // add fp1 and float
    fp3 = decipri + fp1;                     // add float and fp1

    fp2.fraclow();                           // set fp2 to lowest terms
    fp3.fraclow();                           // set fp3 to lowest terms
    cout << "Adding decimal to fraction gives ";
    fp2.dispfrac();                          // display fp2
    cout << "\nAdding fraction to decimal gives ";
    fp3.dispfrac();                          // display fp3
    }
```

Exercise 4

One reason to write your own function for an overloaded '=' operator is to monitor the amount of memory used by objects in your program. For example, suppose that you need to create a class of objects that hold a great deal of data. Let's call this the *bigdata* class. For simplicity, assume that the amount of data is the same for all *bigdata* objects, say 5,000 integers.

Let's further suppose that it's sometimes desirable to create an object without actually allocating memory space for its data. For instance, if you use a no-argument constructor, you might want to bring an object into existence, so you can refer to it by name in the program, but not actually allocate memory at that time. We can call an object with no data an empty object. You would allocate memory for data when, for instance, the object was set equal to another object that did contain data (a full object).

This exercise models such a *bigdata* class. Its private data should consist only of a pointer that can point to a block of memory 5,000 *ints* long. The class should have a no-argument constructor that creates an object but does not allocate memory for any data. Also, it should have a *putdata()* member function that creates memory space using *new* and fills it with data, therefore, changing the object from empty to full. (This can be arbitrary data, such as the integers from 0 to 4,999. In a real application the data would come from an external source, such as a disk file.)

Finally, there should be an overloaded '=' operator to set the data in an empty object equal to the data in a full object. The empty object goes on the left of the equal sign and the full object on the right. The '=' operator should allocate memory and copy the data into this space from the full object.

In the *main()* program, create an object of type *bigdata* (call it *abig*) and initialize its data with *putdata()*. Then create an array of pointers to *bigdata* objects. For each one, create a *bigdata* object with *new*, and (using its pointer) set the object equal to *abig*, with a statement like this:

*bigPtr[j] = abig;

Let the user decide whether to create each new object.

```
// bigequal.cpp
// overloads assignment operator to allocate memory after construction
#include <iostream.h>
#include <conio.h>              // for getche()

const unsigned int SIZE = 32000;        // data size in bigdata object

class bigdata
    {
    private:
            int* ptr;                   // pointer to memory for data
    public:
            bigdata()                   // no-arg constructor
                { }
            bigdata(int* p)             // one-arg constructor
                { ptr = p; }
            void putdata();             // fill memory with data
            void operator = (bigdata&); // overloaded = operator
    };

void bigdata::putdata()                 // put data in memory
    {
    ptr = new int[SIZE];                // Get big chunk of memory

    for(unsigned k=0; k<SIZE; k++)      // fill it with dummy data
         *(ptr+k) = k;                  // (0, 1, 2, 3...)
    }
void bigdata::operator = (bigdata& bg)  // overloaded =
    {
    ptr = new int[SIZE];                // get big chunk of memory

    for(unsigned k=0; k<SIZE; k++)      // copy data from bg
         *(ptr+k) = *(bg.ptr+k);
    }
```

CHAPTER 8 REVIEW EXERCISES

```
void main()
    {
    bigdata* bigPtr[10];            // array of ptrs to bigdata objects
    int j = 0;                      // count the objects created so far
    cout << "\nSize of data = " << sizeof(int[SIZE]);
    bigdata abig;                   // create a bigdata object
    abig.putdata();                 // fill it with data

    while(1)
        {
        cout << "\nj=" << j;
        cout << "\nCreate another object(y/n)? ";
        char choice;                // get permission from
        choice = getche();          // user to create
        if( choice == 'n' || j > 9 )    // another object
            break;
        bigPtr[j] = new bigdata;    // make a new bigdata object
        *(bigPtr[j++]) = abig;      // set it equal to abig
        }
    }
```

Exercise 5

Modify the foregoing BIGEQUAL exercise to include an overloaded copy constructor for the *bigdata* class. You can use this new constructor to create new *bigdata* objects with the statement

    bigPtr[j] = new bigdata(abig);

which uses the copy constructor to initialize the new object pointed to by *bigPtr[j]*.

```
// bigcopy.cpp
// overloads copy contructor to allocate memory on copy
#include <iostream.h>
#include <conio.h>      // for getche()

const unsigned int SIZE = 5000;    // data size in bigdata object

class bigdata
    {
    private:
        int* ptr;                  // pointer to data
    public:
        bigdata()                  // no-arg constructor
            { }
        bigdata(int* p)            // one-arg constructor
            { ptr = p; }
        bigdata(bigdata&);   // copy constructor
        void putdata();            // fill memory with data
    };

void bigdata::putdata()            // put data in memory
    {
```

continued on next page

continued from previous page
```
            ptr = new int[SIZE];                   // get big chunk of memory
            for(unsigned k=0; k<SIZE; k++)  // fill it with dummy data
                *(ptr+k) = k;                      // (0, 1, 2, ...)
            }

bigdata::bigdata(bigdata& bg)            // overloaded copy constructor
            {
            ptr = new int[SIZE];                   // get big chunk of memory
            for(unsigned k=0; k<SIZE; k++)  // copy data from bg
                *(ptr+k) = *(bg.ptr+k);
            }

void main()
            {
            bigdata* bigPtr[10];    // array of ptrs to bigdata objects
            int j = 0;              // count the objects created so far
            cout << "\nSize of data = " << sizeof(int[SIZE]);

            bigdata abig;                    // create a bigdata object
            abig.putdata();                  // fill it with data

            while(1)
                    {
                    cout << "\nj=" << j;
                    cout << "\nCreate another object(y/n)? ";
                    char choice;                    // get permission from
                    choice = getche();              // user to create
                    if( choice == 'n' || j > 9 )    // another object
                        break;

                    // make new bigdata object
                    bigPtr[j++] = new bigdata(abig);    // initialize it with
                    }                                    // copy constructor
            }
```

CHAPTER 14
Exercise 1

In this exercise, you'll write an array of *fracpri* objects to the disk. Use the *fracpri* class from the FRACLASS exercise in Chapter 7 on the disk. In the *main()* function, have the user enter an arbitrary number of *fracpri* objects. Then store them in an array, and write them to the disk with a single statement. Write only as many objects as there are in the array; don't write any empty array spaces. You may want to precede this data with the number (an integer) of fractions that will be written. Having this number in the disk file will simplify things for a program that must read this file.

```
// fracout.cpp
// writes array of fractions to a disk file
#include <fstream.h>            // for file streams
#include <conio.h>              // for getche()
```

CHAPTER 8   REVIEW EXERCISES

```
class fracpri                    // class for fractional prices
   {
   private:
      int whole;                  // whole number part of price
      int numer;                  // numerator (top) of fraction
      int denom;                  // denominator (bottom) of fraction
   public:
      void dispfrac()             // display fraction (format 31-3/8)
         {
         cout << whole << "-" << numer << "/" << denom;
         }
      void getfrac()              // get fraction from user
         {
         char dummy;
         cin >> whole >> dummy >> numer >> dummy >> denom;
         }
   };

void main(void)
   {
   fracpri farray[100];                  // array of fractions
   int n = 0;                            // number of fracs in array
   char ch;                              // user's response
   do
      {
      cout << "\nEnter fraction: ";
      farray[n++].getfrac();             // get frac, put in array
      cout << "Enter another (y/n)? ";
      ch=getche();
      }
   while(ch != 'n'++ n<100);             // loop until user types 'n'

   ofstream outfile("FRACA.DAT");        // create file for output
                                         // write number of fracs
   outfile.write( (char*)&n, sizeof(int) );
                                         // write array from 0 to n
   outfile.write( (char*)&farray, n * sizeof(fracpri) );
   }
```

Exercise 2

Write a program that reads the file generated by the foregoing FRACOUT exercise. Your new program should first read the integer that tells how many fractions there are in the file. Then, in a single statement, it should read all the fractions into an array. It can then use a *for* loop to display all the fractions from the array.

```
// fracin.cpp
// reads fractions from a disk file into an array
#include <fstream.h>              // for file streams

class fracpri                      // class for fractional prices
   {
```

continued on next page

```
continued from previous page
   private:
      int whole;                      // whole number part of price
      int numer;                      // numerator (top) of fraction
      int denom;                      // denominator (bottom) of fraction
   public:
      void dispfrac()                 // display fraction (format 31-3/8)
         {
         cout << whole << "-" << numer << "/" << denom;
         }
      void getfrac()                  // get fraction from user
         {
         char dummy;
         cin >> whole >> dummy >> numer >> dummy >> denom;
         }
   };

void main(void)
   {
   fracpri farray[100];                // array of fractions
   int n;                              // number of fracs in array

   ifstream infile("FRACA.DAT");       // open file for input
   infile.read( (char*)&n, sizeof(int) );   // read number into n
                                       // read file into array
   infile.read( (char*)&farray, n * sizeof(fracpri) );

   for(int j=0; j<n; j++)              // for each of n fractions
      {
      cout << "\nFraction " << j << " is ";
      farray[j].dispfrac();            // display it
      }
   }
```

Exercise 3

Write a program that compares two text files (such as .CPP files) that are entered as command-line arguments. If there is a mismatch in the files, the program should display some characters following the mismatch so the user can figure out where the error is in the file. If the files match, the program should say so.

```
// ocomp.cpp
// compares two text files, displays difference
#include <fstream.h>            // for file functions
#include <process.h>            // for exit()

void main(int argc, char* argv[] )
   {
   char ch1, ch2;                // characters to read
   ifstream file1, file2;        // files for input
   char buffer[100];             // buffer for input

   if( argc != 3 )
      {
      cerr << "\nFormat: ocomp file1 file2";
```

```
        exit(-1);
        }

    file1.open( argv[1] );        // open file 1
    if( !file1 )                           // check for errors
       { cerr << "\nCan't open " << argv[1]; exit(-1); }

    file2.open( argv[2] );        // open file 2
    if( !file2 )                           // check for errors
       { cerr << "\nCan't open " << argv[2]; exit(-1); }

                                         // read a character
    while( (file1.get(ch1) != 0) && (file2.get(ch2) != 0)  )
       if( ch1 != ch2 )                  // if mismatch
          {                              // display file 1
          cout << "\n\nFile 1:\n--------\n";
          file1.read( (char*)&buffer, 70);
          buffer[70] = '\0';
          cout << ch1 << buffer;
          cout << "\n\nFile 2:\n--------\n";         // display file 2
          file2.read( (char*)&buffer, 70);
          buffer[70] = '\0';
          cout << ch2 << buffer;
          exit(0);                                      // exit program
          }
    cout << "\nFiles match.";
    }
```

Exercise 4

The idea in this exercise is to modify the *linklist* class from the LINKLIST example in Chapter 12 on the disk so a *linklist* object can write itself to a disk file, or add objects to itself by reading them from a disk file. Add *read()* and *write()* member functions to the *linklist* class that will carry out these activities. Write a *main()* program that creates a linked list, adds some data items to it, and writes the resulting list to a disk file. It should then create a second linked list, read the disk file back in, and display the list.

Hint: The *read()* and *write()* functions are somewhat similar to the *display()* and *additem()* functions, at least as far as the interaction with the list itself is concerned.

```
// linkdisk.cpp
// reads and writes linked list to disk
#include <fstream.h>                          // for file streams

struct link                                   // one element of list
    {
    int data;                                 // data item
    link* next;                               // pointer to next link
    };

class linklist                                // a list of links
    {
```

continued on next page

continued from previous page
```cpp
    private:
        link* first;                        // pointer to first link
    public:
        linklist()                          // no-argument constructor
            { first = NULL; }               // no first link
        void additem(int d);                // add data item (one link)
        void display();                     // display all links
        void write(char*);                  // write this list to file
        void read(char*);                   // add file to this list
    };

void linklist::additem(int d)               // add data item
    {
    link* newlink = new link;               // make a new link
    newlink->data = d;                      // give it data
    newlink->next = first;                  // it points to next link
    first = newlink;                        // now first points to new
    }

void linklist::display()                    // display all links
    {
    link* current = first;                  // set ptr to first link
    while( current != NULL )                // quit on last link
        {
        cout << endl << current->data;      // print data
        current = current->next;            // move to next link
        }
    }
void linklist::write(char* fname)           // write this list to file
    {
    ofstream outfile;                       // make file
    outfile.open(fname);                    // open file
    link* current = first;                  // set ptr to first link
    while( current != NULL )                // quit on last link
        {                                   // write link to file
        outfile.write( (char*)&current->data, sizeof(int) );
        current = current->next;            // move to next link
        }
    outfile.close();
    }

void linklist::read(char* fname)            // add file to this list
    {
    int tempint;
    ifstream infile;                        // make file
    infile.open(fname, ios::nocreate);      // open it
    while( 1 )
        {                                   // read data
        infile.read( (char*)&tempint, sizeof(int) );
        if( infile.eof() )                  // break on eof
            break;
        additem(tempint);                   // insert data in list
        }
    }
void main()
```

```
    {
    linklist list1;                  // make linked list

    list1.additem(25);               // add items to list
    list1.additem(36);
    list1.additem(49);
    list1.additem(64);
    list1.write("LIST.DAT");         // write items from list to disk

    linklist list2;                  // make another linked list
    list2.read("LIST.DAT");          // read items from disk into list
    list2.display();                 // display list
    }
```

Exercise 5

Here's a generalization of the foregoing LINKLIST exercise. Create a class called *objfile* that models a disk file which can hold objects of any class. For each *objfile*, all the objects are from the same class, and are, therefore, of the same size. The *objfile* class should have a member function that adds an object to the file, and another member function that reads back an object at an arbitrary record number in the file. For example, if you write five objects to the file, you should be able to read back the third one without reading the first or second.

You'll need to give each of your *objfile* objects a file name, and you may want to tell it the size of the objects that will be read from it or written to it. A statement to create or "open" an object of class *objfile* might be

objfile ob1.("NAME.EXT", sizeof(testclass));

When you add or "write" an object to an *objfile* object, you'll need to indicate to the routine the address of the object to be added, as in

ob1.add(&testobj);

When you read an object from an *objfile* object, you'll need to tell it not only the address where you want the object placed (the address of an empty object), you'll need to specify which object in the file you want to read: 1 for the first, 2 for the second, and so on. A statement to read the third object might be

ob1.get(&emptytestobj, 3);

In the *main()* program, create a class that can be used to test the *objfile* class. As a minimum this test class should be able to create objects with initialized data, and should have a member function to display that data. (Alternatively, you could use an object from a class in this section, such as the *person* or *fracpri* class.) Create an object of class *objfile* and store several test objects in it. Then read them back from the disk and display them in an arbitrary order.

```
// bigequal.cpp
// overloads assignment operator to allocate memory after construction
```

continued on next page

continued from previous page

```cpp
#include <iostream.h>
#include <conio.h>                      // for getche()


const unsigned int SIZE = 32000;        // data size in bigdata object

class bigdata
        {
        private:
                int* ptr;               // pointer to memory for data
        public:
                bigdata()               // no-arg constructor
                        { }
                bigdata(int* p)         // one-arg constructor
                        { ptr = p; }
                void putdata();                 // fill memory with data
                void operator = (bigdata&);     // overloaded = operator
        };

void bigdata::putdata()                         // put data in memory
        {
        ptr = new int[SIZE];            // Get big chunk of memory

        for(unsigned k=0; k<SIZE; k++)  // fill it with dummy data
                *(ptr+k) = k;                   // (0, 1, 2, 3...)
        }

void bigdata::operator = (bigdata& bg)          // overloaded =
        {
        ptr = new int[SIZE];            // get big chunk of memory

        for(unsigned k=0; k<SIZE; k++)  // copy data from bg
                *(ptr+k) = *(bg.ptr+k);
        }

void main()
        {
        bigdata* bigPtr[10];            // array of ptrs to bigdata objects
        int j = 0;                      // count the objects created so far
        cout << "\nSize of data = " << sizeof(int[SIZE]);
        bigdata abig;                           // create a bigdata object
        abig.putdata();                         // fill it with data

        while(1)
                {
                cout << "\nj=" << j;
                cout << "\nCreate another object(y/n)? ";
                char choice;                    // get permission from
                choice = getche();              // user to create
                if( choice == 'n' || j > 9 )    // another object
                        break;
                bigPtr[j] = new bigdata;        // make a new bigdata object
                *(bigPtr[j++]) = abig;          // set it equal to abig
                }
        }
```

9 REFERENCE OVERVIEW

9

REFERENCE OVERVIEW

The printed reference materials for *Master C++ for Windows* are divided into two major parts. This chapter is a reference overview, and Chapter 10, *Alphabetical Reference*, is a detailed alphabetical listing of the elements of the C++ and ANSI C languages.

This chapter briefly introduces each of the following elements of C++, which are covered more thoroughly in the detailed reference.

- Language keywords, such as *char*, *while*, and *class*
- Operators, such as +, ::, and size of
- Preprocessor directives, such as *#include* and *#define*
- Predefined values, such as _ _DATE_ _ and BUFSIZ
- Predefined data types, such as *time_t* and *va_list*
- Predefined standard classes such as *istream* and *ostream*, and their most commonly used member functions
- Character escape sequences, such as \n and \t
- Functions from the ANSI C library, such as *fopen()* and *printf()*

This overview presents groups of related items and a summary of their use. Mastering the use of the predefined streams classes and ANSI library functions is particularly important, so the overview divides them into functionally related groups (such as C++ Streams, ANSI C Streams and Files, Process Control, and Data Conversion). Most function groups are presented with two tables: one that lists the functions in the group alphabetically, and one that organizes them according to the task performed, such as opening a file, reading data from a file, and writing data to a file.

The bulk of the reference is the alphabetical list in Chapter 10. If you are interested in a particular keyword, function, macro, class, data structure, or other item, you can go directly to its entry. Each entry includes a description of the item's purpose, a summary of its use, and often an illustrative example. Before using the alphabetical list for the first time, please read the notes at the beginning of Chapter 10 about using the reference.

C++, AN EMERGING STANDARD

Unlike the older C language, C++ does not yet have an ANSI standard. *Master C++ for Windows* is, therefore, based on the C++ language as embodied in AT&T C++ Release 2.1 (the de facto standard) and reflects the common features found in such C++ implementations as Borland C++, Turbo C++ (also by Borland), and available C++ compilers for UNIX.

C++ and ANSI C

C++ is largely a superset of ANSI C. That is, the language keywords and syntax of ANSI C are included in that of C++. Put another way, a legal ANSI C program should also be a legal C++ program. Because *Master C++ for Windows* is specifically about C++, no attempt is made to distinguish the elements of ANSI C from the important new features added in C++.

As with C, much of the power of C++ comes from the addition of predefined libraries that include the functionality needed to handle real-world hardware in areas such as file I/O, arithmetic, and graphics. Although ANSI C offers a generous library of such predefined functions, C++ doesn't really have such a standard library, except in the important area of stream I/O. Most C++ implementations, therefore, include the ANSI C function library, the streams class library, and often additional proprietary class libraries. The *Master C++ for Windows* reference (Chapter 10) includes the ANSI C and streams libraries. You will need to consult your compiler documentation for information about other included class libraries, as well as any additions to the ANSI C library. (Borland C++, for example, includes both the extensive Borland C library (a superset of ANSI C) and a set of useful class libraries. See Appendix B, *Further Reading*, for recommended books on Borland C++ and the ANSI C library.)

OVERVIEW OF LANGUAGE ELEMENTS

Each of the kinds of items that make up the C++ language and environment, are discussed here, and are covered in the alphabetical reference.

Language Keywords

C++ language keywords are used to provide control structures (such as *if* and *while*), data types (such as *char* and *float*), structure types (such as *struct*, *class*, and terms used to specify class access and relationships), and qualifying terms that specify how

CHAPTER 9 REFERENCE OVERVIEW

data types or variables will be handled (such as *unsigned* and *volatile*). Keywords are also sometimes called *reserved words* because they are reserved for the use of the compiler—you can't use them as variable names. It is, however, all right to embed a keyword in a variable name—for example, *chart*. Here is a list of the C++ keywords, each of which has its own entry in the alphabetic reference.

asm	double	new	switch
auto	else	operator	template
break	enum	private	this
case	extern	protected	throw
catch	float	public	try
char	for	register	typedef
class	friend	return	union
const	goto	short	unsigned
continue	if	signed	virtual
default	inline	sizeof	void
delete	int	static	volatile
do	long	struct	while

Note that while all of the listed C++ keywords have entries in the alphabetical reference, some of them are not covered in *Master C++ for Windows* because they are esoteric or not yet implemented in most C++ compilers.

Operators and Precedence

Operators are language elements that manipulate variables or data in some way, such as by adding data items together, getting the address of a variable, comparing the size of two numbers, and so on. Each operator has an entry in the alphabetical reference. Because all of the operators except *sizeof*, *new*, and the type cast (*<type>*) consist of nonalphabet characters, all the nonalphabetic operators in Chapter 10 precede the letter A. Remember that in C++ you can also use the mechanism of *overloading* to extend the meaning of operators so that they handle objects of classes that you define. Table 9-1 lists all of the predefined C++ operators, grouped by category.

Table 9-1. Operators in C++

OPERATOR	NAME	EXAMPLE	EXPLANATION
Arithmetic Operators			
*	Multiplication	x*y	Multiply x and y
/	Division	x/y	Divide x by y

continued on next page

continued from previous page

OPERATOR	NAME	EXAMPLE	EXPLANATION
%	Modulo	x%y	Remainder of x divided by y
+	Addition	x+y	Add x and y
–	Subtraction	x–y	Subtract y from x
++	Increment	x++	Increment x after use
– –	Decrement	– –x	Decrement x before use
–	Negation	–x	Negate the value of x
+	Unary plus	+x	Positive value of x

Relational and Logical Operators

>	Greater than	x>y	1 if x exceeds y, else 0
>=	Greater than or equal to	x>=y	1 if x is greater than or equal to y, else 0
<	Less than	x<y	1 if x is less than y, else 0
<=	Less than or equal to	x<=y	1 if x is less than or equal to y, else 0
==	Equal to	x==y	1 if x equals y, else 0
!=	Not equal to	x!=y	1 if x and y are unequal, else 0
!	Logical NOT	!x	1 if x is 0, else 0
||	Logical OR	x||y	0 if both x and y are 0, else 1

Assignment Operators

=	Assignment	x=y;	Put value of y into x
o=	Compound	x+=y;	Equivalent to x = assignment x oy; assignment where o is one of the operators: + – * / · % << >> & ^ |

Data Access and Size Operators

[ ]	Array element x	[0]	First element of array x
.	Member selection	s.x	Member x in class or struct s
–>	Member selection	p–>x	Member named x in a class or struct to which p points
–>*	Class member selection	p–>*x	Member x of class pointed to p>
.*	Class member selection	(c.*f)	Pointer to member function f in class c
*	Indirection	*p	Contents of location whose address is in p
&x	Address of	&x	Address of variable x
<type>& x=y	Reference to x	int & x=y	x refers to same location as y
sizeof	Size in bytes	sizeof(x)	Size of x in bytes

CHAPTER 9   REFERENCE OVERVIEW

OPERATOR	NAME	EXAMPLE	EXPLANATION
Bitwise Operators			
~	Bitwise complement	~x	Flip 1 bits to 0 and complement 0 bits to 1
&	Bitwise AND	x&y	Bitwise AND of x and y
|	Bitwise OR	x|y	Bitwise OR of x and y
^	Bitwise XOR	x^y	Value with 1's at exclusive OR bits. Where corresponding bits of x and y differ
<<	Left shift	x<<y	x shifted to the left (by y bit positions)
>>	Right shift	x>>y	x shifted to the right (by y bit positions)
Miscellaneous Operators			
()	Function call	sqr(10)	Call sqr with argument 10
type()	Type cast	double(i)	Convert i to double
(type)	Type cast	(double) i	Converted to a double (older syntax)
? :	Conditional	x1 ? x2 : x3	If x1 is not 0, x2 is evaluated, else x3 is evaluated
,	Sequential evaluation	i++, m++	First increment i, then increment m
::	Scope resolution	a::b()	Call member function b of class a
new	Memory allocation	p=new x	Allocate new object of type x, return pointer
delete	Delete object	delete(x)	Destroy (deallocate) object x
<<	Insert to stream	cout << x	Put value of x to cout
>>	Extract from stream	cin >> x	Put value of input stream in x

An important consideration in using operators is the precedence, or order in which operators take effect. Within a given level of precedence the order in which operators take effect is called *associativity*. Table 9-2 gives both the precedence and associativity of all of the C++ operators.

Table 9-2. Operator precedence and associativity in C++

OPERATOR TYPE	OPERATORS	ASSOCIATIVITY
Expression	() [] . ->	Left to right
Unary	− + ~ ! * & ++ --	Right to left
	sizeof (type)	
	* (dereference),	
	typecast	
	new, delete	
Member selection	., ->	Right to left
Pointer to member	.*, ->*	Right to left
Multiplicative	* / %	Left to right

continued on next page

continued from previous page

OPERATOR TYPE	OPERATORS	ASSOCIATIVITY
Additive	+ −	Left to right
Shift	<< >>	Left to right
Relational (inequality)	< <= > >=	Left to right
Relational (equality)	== !=	Left to right
Bitwise AND	&	Left to right
Bitwise XOR	^	Left to right
Bitwise OR	|	Left to right
Logical AND	&&	Left to right
Logical OR	||	Left to right
Conditional	? :	Right to left
Assignment	= *= /= %=	Right to left
	+= −= <<= >>= &= |= ^=	
Sequential evaluation	,	Left to right

Therefore, the expression $a * b / c + d$ is evaluated by doing multiplication and division first, because they have a higher precedence than addition. Because the associativity for the multiplicative operators is from left to right, $a * b$ is performed first, then the result is divided by c. Finally d is added to the result. Of course you can use parentheses to override precedence: In the expression $(a * b) / (c + d)$ the multiplication and addition in parentheses are performed first, and then the division.

As mentioned earlier, most C++ operators can be overloaded or redefined to work with new data types. Here is a list of operators that can be overloaded. Remember that overloading cannot change the nature (unary or binary), precedence, or associativity of the operator.

+	−	*	/	%	^	&	|
~	!	=	<	>	+=	−=	*=
/=	%=	^=	&=	|=	<<	>>	>>=
<<=	==	!=	<=	>=	&&	||	++
--	,	->*	->()	[]			

Preprocessor Directives and Macros

The preprocessor processes the source text of a program file and acts on commands, called *preprocessor directives*, embedded in the text. These directives begin with the character #. Usually the compiler automatically invokes the preprocessor before beginning compilation, but most compilers will allow you to invoke the preprocessor alone by using compiler options.

CHAPTER 9   REFERENCE OVERVIEW

The preprocessor provides three important services that enable users to make their programs modular, more easily readable, and easier to customize for different computer systems. The services are full inclusion (including the contents of a file into a C++ program), token replacement and macro processing (replacing one string with another), and conditional compilation (compiling selected portions of a program). Table 9-3 summarizes the preprocessor directives. Each preprocessor directive also has an entry in the alphabetical reference.

Table 9-3. C++ Preprocessor directives

DIRECTIVE	MEANING
# operator	String forming operator
	Example: #define show(x) printf(#x)
	show(me); expands to printf("me");
## operator	Token-pasting operator
	Example: #define version(x) BC##x
	version(5) results in the token BC5
#define	Define a symbol or a macro (you can redefine a macro with the same expression as often as you want)
	Example: #define double(x) ((x)+(x))
	r=double(2.0); sets r to 4.0
#elif	Else if operator (see example for #if)
#else	Else operator (see example for #if)
#endif	Mark the end of an #if directive
#error	Produce diagnostic message
	Example: #if defined(WRONG_OPTION)
	#error Recompile with correct option
	#endif
#if	Conditional directive
	Example: #if !defined(FILE_1_INCLUDED)
	#include <file1.h>
	#elif defined(INCLUDE_FILE_2)
	#include <file2.h>
	#else
	#include <file3.h>
	#endif
#ifdef	Equivalent to #if defined
#ifndef	Equivalent to #if !defined
#include	File inclusion

continued on next page

continued from previous page

DIRECTIVE	MEANING
	Example: #include <stdio.h>
#line	Set the current line number
#pragma	Instruct the compiler
#undef	Remove the definition of a symbol

C++ essentially inherits the preprocessor directives from ANSI C. Note, however, that use of the CONST keyword is preferable to *#define* for creating constants, because constants created with CONST can be type-checked and the compiler will guard against the value of such a constant being changed. Similarly, the use of inline functions is preferred in C++ over traditional macros when it is desirable to avoid the overhead of function calls. Most C++ implementations include a number of standard predefined preprocessor symbols, as listed in Table 9-4. Note that the predefined macros begin with an underscore character (_). You cannot use *#undef* to remove the definitions of these macros. Each of these macros also has an entry in the alphabetical reference.

Table 9-4. Common predefined macros

MACRO NAME	DEFINED TO BE
__cplusplus	Tells combined C and C++ compilers that the source file is for C++
__DATE__	The date of translation of the source file in the form of a string of the form "MMM DD YYYY" (such as "Jul 12 1992")
__FILE__	A string containing the name of the source file
__LINE__	The line number of the current source file, as a decimal constant
__STDC__	The decimal constant 1 to indicate that the compiler conforms to some specified standard
__TIME__	The time of translation of the source file as a string of the form "HH:MM:SS"

Other Predefined Values and Data Types

C++ implementations also provide predefined values that allow the programmer to access implementation-dependent values, such as the minimum and maximum sizes for various character and numeric data types, the locale (national format) in use, and so on. There are also many data types defined in the header files for use by various library functions, such as file information, time, and date formats. Many of these values, both those inherited from ANSI C and those added by C++, have individual entries in the alphabetical reference.

Escape Sequences

Escape sequences allow you to include special characters (such as a newline or tab) in strings. A backslash (\) introduces each escape sequence. Table 9-5 lists the escape

CHAPTER 9   REFERENCE OVERVIEW

sequences supported by C++. Note that you can specify any character in your machine's character set by following the backslash with the octal (base 8) character code, or with an *x* followed by the hexadecimal character code.

Table 9-5. Standard character escape sequences

SEQUENCE	NAME	MEANING WHEN PRINTED
\a	alert	Produce an audible alert
\b	backspace	Move character position backward
\f	form feed	Move to the beginning of a new page
\n	newline	Move to beginning of next line
\r	carriage return	Move to beginning of current line
\t	horizontal tab	Move to next tabulation position on this line
\v	vertical tab	Move to next vertical tabulation point
\\		Interpret as a single backslash
\'		Interpret as '
\"		Interpret as "
\?		Interpret as ?
\<octal digits>		Specified octal ASCII character
\x<hexadecimal digits>		Specified hexadecimal ASCII character

Library Classes and Functions

As noted earlier, C++ compilers inherit a standard function library from ANSI C, often with proprietary enhancements. In traditional C, functions are the building blocks of C programs. They are independent collections of declarations and statements you mix and match to create stand-alone applications. Each C or C++ program has at least one function: the *main()* function. The library specified in ANSI C consists mostly of functions (in addition to quite a few macros). For the most part, developing software in C involves writing functions.

In C++, however, the basic building block is not the function but the class: a structure bundling together a set of data and functions that manipulate the data. While a C library consists of functions (and accompanying constants, predefined macros, and so on), a true C++ library consists of one or more classes that are designed to solve particular problems. Most C++ implementations include both an older C library and one or more C++ libraries. Predefined functions and classes are accessed through include files.

Table 9-6 lists the header files that are required by the ANSI standard and the most basic ones added by C++ implementations. Many compilers provide additional header files for graphics, calls to operating system functions, and other hardware-dependent matters.

Table 9-6. Standard header files

HEADER FILE NAME	DESCRIPTION
assert.h	Defines the assert macro and NDEBUG symbol. Used for program diagnostics.
complex.h	Defines complex number operations (in most C++ compilers).
ctype.h	Declares character classification and conversion routines.
errno.h	Defines macros for error conditions, EDOM and ERANGE, and the integer variable *errno*.
float.h	Defines symbols for the maximum and minimum values of floating-point numbers.
fstream.h	Defines file-oriented stream classes.
iomanip.h	Defines manipulator functions for C++ streams classes (used for data formatting).
iostream.h	Defines C++ I/O streams classes (pre C++ 2.0 implementations use *stream.h* instead).
limits.h	Defines symbols for the limiting values of all integer data types.
locale.h	Declares functions necessary for customizing a C program to a particular locale. Defines the *lconv* structure.
math.h	Declares the math functions and the HUGE_VAL constant.
setjmp.h	Defines the *jmp_buf* data type used by the routines *setjmp* and *longjmp*.
signal.h	Defines symbols and routines necessary for handling exceptional conditions.
stdarg.h	Defines the macros that facilitate handling variable-length argument lists.
stddef.h	Defines the standard data types *ptrdiff_t*, *size_t*, *wchar_t*, the symbol NULL, and the macro offsetof.
stdlib.h	Declares the utility functions such as the string conversion routines, random number generator, memory allocation routines, and process control routines.
string.h	Declares the string manipulation routines.
time.h	Defines data type *time_t*, the *tm* data structure, and declares the *time* functions.

Note: Some C++ implementations use the extension .hpp rather than .h for C++ header files.

The following sections present the library functions in ten categories. For each category two tables—one alphabetical and one organized by task—give you an overview of each set of related functions.

C++ Streams and Files

The C++ and C programming languages have no built-in capability to perform any input and output (I/O). This task is the responsibility of the library accompanying your C++ compiler. Fortunately, all C++ implementations include a set of classes designed to perform a variety of I/O operations. The ANSI standard for C also specifies a set of I/O functions that must be present in a standard-conforming compiler. Table 9-7 lists all the C++ streams I/O routines alphabetically, and Table 9-8 groups them by task. Similarly, Table 9-9 lists the traditional C stream I/O functions alphabetically, and Table 9-10 groups them by task.

CHAPTER 9 REFERENCE OVERVIEW

Notes: The following table does not include functions that are primarily for internal use, or that are involved in low-level programming of streambufs. Many manipulators have alternative member functions. To use general stream functions, include iostream.h or stream.h; to use specialized file functions, include fstream.h.

Table 9-7. Alphabetical list of C++ stream I/O classes and routines

NAME	CLASS	DESCRIPTION
!	ios	Returns "true" if there has been a stream error; else returns "false."
*	ios	Returns null pointer if error in stream processing, else returns "true" pointer.
>>	istream	Extracts value from input stream into an object.
<<	ostream	Inserts value of object into output stream.
bad	ios	Returns "true" if badbit or hardfail flag is on.
cerr	ostream_withassign	Provides standard error stream.
cin	istream_withassign	Provides standard input stream.
clear	ios	Sets all ios status bits to specified value (clears them by default).
clog	ostream_withassign	Provides buffered error stream (useful for retrieving error messages).
close	fstream	Closes a file stream.
cout	ostream_withassign	Provides standard output stream.
dec	<manip.>	Sets conversion base to decimal.
endl	<manip.>	Inserts newline and flushes stream.
ends	<manip.>	Inserts terminal null character in string.
eof	ios	Returns "true" if at end of file.
fail	ios	Returns "true" if an operation has set failbit, badbit, or hardfail flag.
filebuf	streambuf	Class that does I/O with file descriptors.
fill	ios	Reports and/or sets fill character.
flags	ios	Reports or sets ios formatting flags.
flush	<manip.>	Flushes an ostream.
fstream	streambuf	Class used for file I/O.
fstreambase	ios	Base class for fstream.
get	istream	Reads single character or specified character from input.

continued on next page

continued from previous page

NAME	CLASS	DESCRIPTION
getline	istream	Gets line (including last character) from input.
good	ios	Returns "true" if no ios error flags are on.
hex	<manip.>	Sets conversion base to hexadecimal.
ifstream	fstreamsbase, istream	File stream for input.
ignore	istream	Skips specified number of chars. in input.
ios		Class that contains variables for tracking stream state and for error handling.
iostream	istream, ostream	Class that provides biodirectional I/O using same stream.
istream	ios	Class that manages input from streambufs.
istream	istream_withassign	Provides standard input streams and assignment ops.
oct	<manip.>	Sets conversion base to octal (base 8).
ofstream	fstreambase, ostream	Class that provides file stream for output.
open	fstream	Opens a file stream.
ostream	ios	Class that manages output stream going to a streambuf.
ostream_	ostream_withassign	Provides standard streams and assignment ops.
peek	istream	Reads next character in input without removing it.
precision	ios	Reports and/or sets floating point precision.
put	ostream	Puts character in output stream.
putback	istream	Puts last character read back into input stream.
rdstate	ios	Returns values of stream state flags.
read	istream	Reads binary data from input stream.
resetiosflags	<manip.>	Clears specified bits in ios format flags.
seekg	istream	Sets read position for file.
seekp	ostream	Sets write position for file.
setbase	<manip.>	Sets conversion base to specified number (0,8,10, or 16).
setf	ios	Reports or sets formatting flags.
setfill	<manip.>	Sets fill character.
setiosflags	<manip.>	Sets specified bits in stream status flags.
setprecision	<manip.>	Sets floating-point precision.
setw	<manip.>	Sets character field width.
streambuf		Base class for unformatted streams.
tellg	istream	Gives current read location in file.
tellp	ostream	Gives current write location in file.
unsetf	ios	Reports and sets specified formatting flags.
width	ios	Sets width in characters.

CHAPTER 9 REFERENCE OVERVIEW

NAME	CLASS	DESCRIPTION
write	ostream	Puts multiple characters or bytes in output stream.
ws	<manip.>	Removes whitespace (blanks, tabs, etc.) from stream.

Notes: <manip.> means function is a manipulator.

Table 9-8. C++ stream I/O routines classified by task

I/O TASK	ROUTINE NAMES
Create or open a file	open
Close a file	flush, close
Put value from objects into input	<<
Get value from input to object	>>
Formatted read	Set format with manipulators or ios member functions, then pass stream to read routine
Formatted write	Set format with manipulators, then write
Set conversion base	dec, oct, hex, setbase
Set or change floating-point precision	precision, setprecision
Specify fill character	fill, setfill
Set field width	setw, width
Set or get formatting flags	setf, flags
Read a character	get
Read character without removing from input	peek
Skip input characters	ignore
Remove whitespace from input	ws
Write a character	put
Write last character back to input	putback
Read a line	getline
Write a line	write, then use endl
Binary read	read
Add end character to string	ends
Set or get read position	setg, tellg
Set or get write position	setp, tellp
Check EOF condition	eof
Check error conditions	*, !, bad, fail, good, rdstate
Set error flags	setiosflags, resetiosflags

Table 9-9. Alphabetical list of ANSI C file I/O

NAME OF ROUTINE	DESCRIPTION
clearerr	Clears the error indicator of a stream.
fclose	Closes a stream.
feof	A macro that returns a nonzero value if current position in a stream is at the end of file.
ferror	A macro that returns a nonzero value if an error had occurred during read/write operations on a stream.
fflush	Writes to the file the contents of the buffer associated with a stream.
fgetc	Reads a character from a stream.
fgetpos	Returns current position of a stream in an internal format suitable for use by fsetpos.
fgets	Reads a line (up to and including the first newline character) from a stream.
fopen	Opens a named file as a buffered stream (includes options for selecting translation modes and access types).
fprintf	Performs formatted output to a stream.
fputc	Writes a character to a stream.
fputs	Writes a string of characters to a stream.
fread	Reads a specified amount of binary data from a stream.
freopen	Closes a stream and reassigns it to a new file.
fscanf	Performs formatted input from a stream.
fseek	Sets current position to a specific location in the file.
fsetpos	Sets current position of a stream using value returned by an earlier call to fgetpos.
ftell	Returns the current position in the file associated with a stream.
fwrite	Writes a specified number of bytes of binary data to a stream.
getc	Reads a character from a stream.
getchar	Reads a character from the stream stdin.
gets	Reads a string up to a newline character from the stream stdin.
printf	Performs formatted output to the stream stdout.
putc	Writes a character to a stream.
putchar	Writes a character to the stream stdout.
puts	Writes a C string to the stream stdout.
remove	Deletes a file specifed by its name.
rename	Changes the name of a file to a new one.
rewind	Sets the current position to the beginning of the file associated with a stream.
scanf	Performs formatted input from the stream stdin.
setbuf	Assigns a fixed-length user-defined buffer to an open stream.
setvbuf	Assigns a variable-length user-defined buffer to an open stream.
sprintf	Performs formatted output to a buffer.

NAME OF ROUTINE	DESCRIPTION
sscanf	Performs formatted input from a buffer.
tmpfile	Creates a temporary file open for buffered stream I/O.
tmpnam	Generates a temporary file name.
ungetc	Pushes a character back into the buffer associated with a stream.
vfprintf	Version of fprintf that accepts a pointer to a list of arguments and performs formatted output to a stream.
vprintf	Version of printf that accepts a pointer to a list of arguments and performs formatted output to the stream stdout.
vsprintf	Version of sprintf that accepts a pointer to a list of arguments and performs formatted output to a buffer.

Table 9-10. File I/O routines in ANSI C classified by task

I/O TASK	ROUTINE NAMES
Create or open a file	fopen, freopen
Close a file	fclose
Delete or rename a file	remove, rename
Formatted read	fscanf, scanf
Formatted write	fprintf, printf, vfprintf, vprintf, vsprintf
Read a character	fgetc, fgetchar, getc, getchar
Write a character	fputc, fputchar, putc, putchar
Read a line	fgets, gets
Write a line	fputs, puts
Set read/write position	fseek, fsetpos, rewind
Get read/write position	fgetpos, ftell
Binary read	fread
Binary write	fwrite
Flush buffer	fflush
Check error/eof	clearerr, feof, ferror
Manage temporary files	tmpfile, tmpnam
Control buffering	setbuf, setvbuf
Push character to buffer	ungetc

Process Control and Locale Routines

The process control routines include the signal-handling functions that take care of error conditions, and utility functions to terminate a process, communicate with the operating system, and set up numeric and currency formats depending on the locale for which your program is customized. These routines are defined in locale.h, signal.h, setjmp.h, and stdlib.h. Table 9-11 lists these routines alphabetically, and Table 9-12 groups them by task.

Table 9-11. Alphabetical list of process control and locale routines

NAME OF ROUTINE	DESCRIPTION
abort	Raises the SIGABRT signal after printing a message to *stderr*. The normal handler for SIGABRT terminates the process without flushing file buffers.
assert	Prints a diagnostic message and aborts program, if a given logical expression is false.
atexit	Installs a routine to a stack of up to 32 routines that will be called in "last in, first out" order when the process terminates.
exit	Calls the functions installed by *atexit*, flushes all buffers associated with streams that are open for I/O, and finally terminates the process and returns to the operating system.
getenv	Returns the definition of an environment variable from the environment of the process.
localeconv	Sets the components of a *lconv* structure with information about numeric and monetary formatting appropriate for the current locale.
longjmp	Restores the context of a process, thus effecting an unconditional jump to the place where *setjmp* was called to save that particular context.
perror	Prints an error message using your message and the system message corresponding to the value in the global variable *errno*.
raise	Generates a signal (an exception).
setjmp	Saves the context of a process in a buffer that can be used by *longjmp* to jump back.
signal	Installs a function to handle a specific exception or signal.
setlocale	Selects a locale for a specified portion of the program's locale-dependent aspects.
system	Executes an operating system command.

Table 9-12. Process control and locale routines by task

TASK	ROUTINE NAMES
Execute an operating system command	system
Terminate a process	abort, exit
Handle errors	assert, perror
Get environment	getenv
Install exception handler and generate an exception	raise, signal
Nonlocal jump from one function to another	longjmp, setjmp
Install routines to be called when the process terminates	atexit
Control locale-specific numeric and currency formatting	localeconv, setlocale

Variable Argument List Routines

In writing C++ programs, you encounter built-in functions such as *printf()* that can take a variable number of arguments. Sometimes it is convenient to write your own custom routines that can process a variable number of arguments. Take, for instance, a routine (*findmax()*) that picks the largest element from an array of integers. If the routine can accept a variable number of arguments, you can use such calls as *findmax(1,2,3)* and *findmax(a,b,c,d)* to find the maximum of any number of arguments. A set of macros in ANSI C makes a straightforward task of handling a variable number of arguments. Table 9-13 lists the variable argument-handling routines alphabetically—because there are only three of them, no task-oriented table is given.

Table 9-13. Alphabetical list of variable argument macros

NAME OF MACRO	DESCRIPTION
va_arg	Gets the next argument from the stack.
va_end	Resets everything so that the function can return normally.
va_start	Initializes the argument pointer to the address of the first argument to the function.

Memory Allocation Routines

Most computer systems store instructions and data in memory and use a central processing unit (CPU) to repeatedly retrieve instructions from memory and execute them. The operating system, itself a program residing in memory, takes care of loading other programs and executing them. The operating system has its own scheme of managing the available memory for its data and that for other programs as well.

In older programming languages, such as FORTRAN, there is no provision for requesting memory at runtime. All data items and arrays have to be declared before compiling the program. You have to guess beforehand the maximum size of an array and there is no way to exceed the maximum other than recompiling the program. This is inefficient because you are locking in the maximum amount of memory your program will ever need.

In most modern languages, including C++, you can request blocks of memory at runtime and release the blocks when your program no longer needs them. A major advantage of this capability is that you can design your application to exploit all available memory in the system. Like most other capabilities in C, this comes in the form of a set of library routines, known as the memory allocation routines. The specific set that comes with ANSI C has four basic memory-allocation routines, cataloged in Table 9-14. (Again, due to the limited number of routines in this category, there is no task-oriented table.)

C++ programmers, however, are encouraged to build memory allocation and disposal into class objects via constructors and destructors. This provides a safer and more orderly way to handle memory within the context of a C++ program.

Table 9-14. Alphabetical list of ANSI C memory allocation routines

NAME OF ROUTINE	DESCRIPTION
calloc	Allocates memory for an array of data elements and initializes them to zero.
free	Frees previously allocated memory.
malloc	Allocates a number of bytes and returns a pointer to the first byte of the allocated memory.
realloc	Enlarges or shrinks a previously allocated block of memory. If necessary, this function will move the block in the physical memory of the system.

Data Conversion Routines

Information management with computers frequently requires crunching numbers. These numbers are represented internally in several forms depending on the type of C++ variable that holds the value. It is more convenient to have users enter numbers as strings, however, because strings can be scanned and otherwise checked using a variety of routines. The ANSI C data conversion routines, declared in the header file stdlib.h, allow strings to be converted to the internal forms needed by numeric variables. These routines are listed alphabetically in Table 9-15 and by task in Table 9-16.

Note that there are a few additional routines in the C library which also provide data conversion facilities. The *sprintf()* and the *sscanf()* functions in the I/O category can respectively convert internal values to strings and strings back to internal representations. The *sscanf()* routine, however, lacks the ability to convert a string to an integer using an arbitrary radix—only decimal, octal, and hexadecimal formats are supported.

Finally, note that C++ programmers can handle many data formatting and conversion tasks through the streams classes described earlier in Tables 9-7 and 9-8.

Table 9-15. Alphabetical list of ANSI C data conversion routines

NAME OF ROUTINE	DESCRIPTION
atof	Converts a string to a double-precision floating-point value.
atoi	Converts a string to an integer.
atol	Converts a string to a long integer.
strtod	Converts a string to a double-precision floating-point value.
strtol	Converts a string to a long integer.
strtoul	Converts a string to an unsigned long integer.

Table 9-16. ANSI C data conversion routines by task

TASK	ROUTINE NAMES
Convert character string to floating-point value	atof, strtod
Convert character string to integer	atoi
Convert character string to long integer	atol, strtol
Convert character string to unsigned long integer	strtoul

Math Routines

In addition to the support for basic, floating-point operations in the language, the ANSI C library also includes a set of common math functions (such as sine and cosine). Table 9-17 lists the math routines alphabetically, and Table 9-18 groups them by task.

Table 9-17. Alphabetical list of ANSI C math routines

NAME OF ROUTINE	DESCRIPTION
abs	Returns the absolute value of an integer argument.
acos	Computes the arc cosine of a value between −1 and 1 and returns an angle between 0 and pi radians.
asin	Computes the arc sine of a value between −1 and 1 and returns an angle between −pi/2 and pi/2 radians.
atan	Computes the arc tangent of a value and returns an angle between −pi/2 and pi/2 radians.
atan2	Computes the arc tangent of one argument divided by the other and returns an angle between −pi and pi radians.
ceil	Finds the smallest integer larger than or equal to the function's floating-point argument.
cos	Evaluates the cosine of an angle in radians.
cosh	Evaluates the hyperbolic cosine of its argument.
div	Divides one integer by another and returns an integer quotient and an integer remainder.
exp	Computes the exponential of a floating-point argument.
fabs	Returns the absolute value of a floating-point argument.
floor	Finds the largest integer smaller than or equal to the function's floating-point argument.
fmod	Computes the floating-point remainder after dividing one floating-point value by another so that the quotient is the largest possible integer for that division.
frexp	Breaks down a floating-point value into a mantissa between 0.5 and 1 and an integer exponent so that the value is equal to the mantissa times two raised to the power of the exponent.
labs	Returns the absolute value of a long integer argument.
ldexp	Computes a floating-point value equal to a mantissa times two raised to the power of an integer exponent.
ldiv	Divides one long integer by another and returns a long integer quotient and a long-integer remainder.
log	Evaluates the natural logarithm of its floating-point argument.
log10	Evaluates the logarithm to the base 10 of its floating-point argument.
modf	Breaks down a floating-point value into its integer part and its fractional part.
pow	Computes the value of one argument raised to the power of a second one.
rand	Returns a random integer between 0 and RAND_MAX (defined in stdlib.h).

continued on next page

continued from previous page

NAME OF ROUTINE	DESCRIPTION
sin	Evaluates the sine of an angle in radians.
sinh	Evaluates the hyperbolic sine of its argument.
sqrt	Computes the square root of a positive floating-point number.
srand	Sets the starting point for the sequence of random numbers generated by rand.
tan	Evaluates the tangent of an angle in radians.
tanh	Evaluates the hyperbolic tangent of its argument.

Table 9-18. ANSI C math routines by task

TASK	ROUTINE NAMES
Evaluate trigonometric functions	acos, asin, atan, atan2, cos, sin, tan
Evaluate hyperbolic functions	cosh, sinh, tanh
Evaluate powers and logarithms	exp, frexp, ldexp, log, log10, pow
Compute square root	sqrt
Compute magnitudes and absolute values	abs, fabs
Find integer limits (lower and upper) for floating-point numbers	ceil, floor
Break down floating-point number into integer and fraction	modf
Find floating-point remainder	fmod
Integer arithmetic	abs, div, labs, ldiv
Generate random numbers	rand, srand

Character Classification and Conversion Routines

Character classification routines (actually macros) beginning with *is* classify a character by various criteria such as whether it is part of the alphabet, a number, a punctuation mark, and so on. The routines *tolower* and *toupper* convert characters to lowercase and uppercase, respectively.

Table 9-19 lists the character classification and conversion routines alphabetically, and Table 9-20 groups them by task.

Table 9-19. Alphabetical list of character classification and conversion routines

NAME OF ROUTINE	DESCRIPTION
isalnum	Tests if a character is alphanumeric.
isalpha	Tests if a character is alphabetic.
iscntrl	Tests if a character belongs to the set of control characters.

NAME OF ROUTINE	DESCRIPTION
isdigit	Tests if a character is a numerical digit.
isgraph	Tests if a character is printable (excluding the space character).
islower	Tests if a character is lowercase.
isprint	Tests if a character is printable (includes space).
ispunct	Tests if a character belongs to the set of punctuation characters.
isspace	Tests if a character belongs to the set of "whitespace" characters.
isupper	Tests if a character is uppercase.
isxdigit	Tests if a character is a hexadecimal digit.
tolower	Converts a character to lowercase only if that character is an uppercase letter.
toupper	Converts a character to uppercase only if that character is a lowercase letter.

Table 9-20. Character classification and conversion routines by task

TASK	ROUTINE NAMES
Classify a character	isalnum, isalpha, iscntrl, isdigit, isgraph, islower, isprint, ispunct, isspace, isupper, isxdigit
Convert from uppercase to lowercase	tolower
Convert from lowercase to uppercase	toupper

String and Buffer Manipulation Routines

Manipulating text is a major part of many computer applications. The manipulation might involve text editing, word processing, or that part of your application which reads commands typed by the user and interprets them. Typically, you read a single line of command into a C++ string and interpret it. Depending on the syntax of your application's command set, the interpretation will involve chores such as extracting the commands and parameters from the string, comparing the command against entries in a stored table, or copying the parameters into separate strings for later use.

Although C++ has no built-in operators for handling strings, the ANSI C standard specifies a set of string manipulation routines that provides all the capabilities needed to process strings. Note that "multibyte characters" are new and are not supported by all otherwise ANSI-compliant compilers. They are useful mainly for dealing with special character sets and international alphabets.

As C++ class libraries continue to be developed, more string functions are likely to be "packaged" as operators or other member functions for use with appropriate string classes.

Table 9-21 lists the string and buffer routines alphabetically, and Table 9-22 groups them by task.

Table 9-21. Alphabetical list of string and buffer manipulation routines

NAME OF ROUTINE	DESCRIPTION
mblen	Returns the number of bytes that make up a single multibyte character.
mbtowc	Converts a multibyte character to wchar_t type.
mbtowcs	Converts a sequence of multibyte characters into a sequence of codes of wchar_t type.
memchr	Searches for a specific character in a given number of bytes of the buffer.
memcmp	Compares a specified number of bytes of two buffers.
memcpy	Copies a specified number of bytes from one buffer to another (*not for overlapping source and destination*).
memmove	Copies a specified number of bytes from one buffer to another (*handles overlapping source and destination*).
memset	Sets specified number of bytes of a buffer to a given value.
strcat	Appends one string to another.
strchr	Locates the first occurrence of a character in a string.
strcmp	Compares one string to another and differentiates between lowercase and uppercase letters.
strcoll	Compares two strings using a collating sequence specified by the LC_COLLATE category of current locale.
strcpy	Copies one string to another.
strcspn	Returns the position in the string, of the first character that belongs to a given set of characters.
strerror	Returns a string containing the system error message corresponding to an error number.
strlen	Returns the length of a string as the number of bytes in the string excluding the terminating null ('\0').
strncat	Appends a specified number of characters of one string to another.
strncmp	Compares a specified number of characters of two strings while maintaining the distinction between lowercase and uppercase letters.
strncpy	Copies a specified number of characters from one string to another. (Note: resulting string will not automatically have a null character '\0' appended.)
strpbrk	Locates the first occurrence of any character from one string in another.
strrchr	Locates the last occurrence of a character in a string.
strspn	Returns the position in the string of the first character that does not belong to a given set of characters.
strstr	Locates the first occurrence of one string in another.
strtok	Returns the next token in a string with the token delimiters specified in a string.
strxfrm	Transforms a string to a new form so that if strcmp is applied to two transformed strings the returned result is the same as that returned when strcoll is applied to the original strings.
wctomb	Converts a character of wchar_t type to a multibyte character.
wcstombs	Converts a sequence of codes of wchar_t type sequence of multibyte characters.

CHAPTER 9   REFERENCE OVERVIEW

Table 9-22. String and buffer manipulation routines by task

TASK	ROUTINE NAMES
Find length of a string	mblen, strlen
Compare two strings or buffers	memcmp, strcmp, strncmp, strcoll, strxfrm
Copy and append	memcpy, memmove, strcat, strcpy, strncat, strncpy
Search for a character or a substring	memchr, strchr, strcspn, strpbrk, strrchr, strspn, strstr
Extract tokens from a string	strtok
Load the same character into every position in a buffer	memset
Prepare error message in a string	strerror
Convert between multibyte and wide character types	mbtowc, mbstowcs, wctomb, wcstombs

Searching and Sorting Routines

Searching and sorting are commonplace tasks in many applications. All commercial database programs have these capabilities. If you implement your own database program tailored to your specific requirements, you will invariably need search and sort capabilities. For example, if your database contains the names and addresses of the customers of your company, you will often need to search the list for information about a certain customer. And for mailings, you might want to print labels for all entries in your database, sorted by the zip code.

If you are developing your database in C++, the ANSI C standard makes your job easier by providing two library routines for sorting and searching lists in memory, as described in Table 9-23. (See the main alphabetical reference for more details.) Again, because there are only two functions in this group, no "by task" table is provided.

C++ programmers will increasingly be able to take advantage of data manipulation classes (such as lists and containers) that are being provided with C++ compilers or as third-party class libraries.

Table 9-23. Alphabetical list of searching and sorting routines

NAME OF ROUTINE	DESCRIPTION
bsearch	Search for an element in a sorted array.
qsort	Sort an array of elements.

Date and Time Routines

The ANSI C library includes a set of routines for obtaining and displaying date and time information. These routines are declared in the header file *time.h*. The *time* function is at the heart of these routines. It returns the current date and time in an implementation-defined encoded form.

Library routines are available to convert this time into a printable string and otherwise manipulate it. A list of the time and date functions in alphabetical order appears in Table 9-24; Table 9-25 groups them by task.

Table 9-24. Alphabetical list of time routines

NAME OF ROUTINE	DESCRIPTION
asctime	Converts time from a structure of type *tm* to a string.
clock	Returns the elapsed processor time in number of ticks.
ctime	Converts time from a value of type *time_t* to a string.
difftime	Computes the difference of two values of type *time_t*.
gmtime	Converts time from a value of type *time_t* to a structure of type *tm* which will correspond to the Greenwich Mean Time.
localtime	Converts time from a value of type *time_t* to a structure of type *tm* which will correspond to the local time.
mktime	Converts the local time from a structure of type *tm* into a value of type *time_t*.
strftime	Prepares a string with date and time values from a *tm* structure, formatted according to a specified format.
time	Returns the current date and time encoded as a value of type *time_t*. The encoding is implementation-dependent.

Table 9-25. Time routines by task

TASK	ROUTINE NAMES
Get current date and time	time
Convert time from one form to another	asctime, ctime, gmtime, localtime, mktime
Compute elapsed time	clock, difftime

10
ALPHABETICAL REFERENCE

10
ALPHABETICAL REFERENCE

The reference in this chapter lists every element of the C++ and ANSI C languages—operators, classes, functions, macros, data types, keywords, and so on—in alphabetical sequence. The following guidelines will help you get started with this easy-to-use reference.

ALPHABETIZATION

Reference entries are alphabetized as follows:

- Items that have only nonalphabetic characters, most of the operators for instance, are placed together in one sequence in ASCII character order before the first *a* entry.

- Nonalphabetic characters such as /, #, or _ at the beginning of alphabetic items are disregarded. Therefore, #*define* is treated as though it were *define*.

- Items that contain underscores are treated as though the underscores divided the name into separate words. Therefore, *L_tmpnam* is handled as *L tmpnam* and comes before *LC_ALL*, because *LC* comes after *L*.

- Case is always disregarded.

FORMAT OF ENTRIES

Each reference entry contains at least some of the following elements—not all entries have all of them.

Name

The name of the item. Beside the name is the type of item (function, macro, keyword, operator, and so on). For operators, the descriptive name of the operator is given beside the operator symbol; for example, & (address-of operator) and & (reference operator).

Purpose

A brief description of the purpose for which the item is used and the essential details of its behavior.

Syntax

The format needed to use or invoke the item. A full prototype is given for ANSI C functions. The parameters in parentheses following the function name specify the kind of arguments used in calling the function. For example,

```
double cos(double x);
```

indicates that the *cos()* function is given a *double* value x and returns a *double* value (in this case the cosine of x).

Because C++ stream functions are often overloaded and can have several prototypes, only the general calling format is given for these functions.

The individual elements in syntax statements are described when they are not obvious.

Within general syntax statements for operators, keywords, and stream functions, the descriptive name for a value is enclosed in angle brackets. For example, the syntax

```
<varname> = <int_value>
```

means that you replace <varname> with an actual variable name, and <int_value> with an actual integer value. Therefore, the statement

```
Total = 0;
```

satisfies the previous syntax.

Any header (include) file needed for use of the item is specified in an *#include* statement.

Example Use

An actual statement or expression using the item. An ellipsis (...) indicates that other statements that usually occur in that part of the program have been omitted.

Returns

The value or values that can be returned by the item. Not all functions or other items return values.

See Also

Related items—either other items that do similar things or other items that do different things with the same type of data or variable.

MASTER C++ FOR WINDOWS ALPHABETICAL REFERENCE

! ◆ Logical NOT operator

Purpose

Use the *logical NOT operator* to change a condition to its opposite truth value. *NOT* makes a true condition false and a false condition true.

Syntax
```
!<condition>
```

Example Use
```
!x      /* 1 (true) if x is 0, else 0 (false) */
```

See Also
&&, ||

! ◆ Stream status operator

Purpose

Use the *! operator* to determine whether an error has occurred when accessing a C++ stream. This is an overloaded version of the regular "not" operator and is found in the *ios* class.

Syntax
```
#include <iostream.h>
!<stream_object>   invoke for stream accessed for reading and/or writing
```

Example Use
```
ifstream in_file;           // declare an input stream
...
if (!in_file)               // error in accessing file
    cout << "\nCannot open input file!";
else
                            // do stuff with the file
```

Returns

The *! operator* returns a nonzero integer "true" value if the *failbit*, *badbit*, or *hardfail ios* status flag has been set (indicating an error); otherwise, the operator returns a 0 (false) value. Note: Use the * operator instead of ! if you want the stream status returned as a pointer value.

See Also
istream, ifstream, ios, * (stream status operator), open()

!= ♦ Not equal operator

Purpose
Use the *not equal operator* to test whether two numeric quantities are not equal to each other, or two strings are not the same.

Syntax
```
<expression1> != <expression2>
```

Example Use
```
x!=y /* 1 (true) if x and y are unequal,
            else 0 (false) */
```

See Also
```
==, <, >
```

♦ String-making preprocessor operator

Purpose
Use the *string-making operator* to have the preprocessor make a string out of the item that immediately follows the operator. It does this by putting the value in quotes in the preprocessed source file.

Syntax
```
#<item>
```

Example Use
```
#define value_now(x) printf(#x"=%d\n",x)
value_now(counter);
/* the preprocessor generates this statement:
    printf("counter""= %d\n", counter);
    which is equivalent to:
    printf("counter = %d\n", counter); */
```

See Also
```
## (token-pasting operator), #define
```

♦ Token-pasting preprocessor operator

Purpose
Use the *token-pasting operator* to join one separate item (token) to another one to form a new token.

Syntax
```
<token1>##<token2>
```

CHAPTER 10 ALPHABETICAL REFERENCE

Example Use
```
#define version(x) BCPP##x
/* version(3) results in the token BCPP3 */
```

See Also
(string-making operator), #define

% ♦ Modulus operator

Purpose
Use the *modulus operator* to obtain the remainder after one quantity is divided by another.

Syntax
`<val1> % <val2>`

Example Use
`Remainder = 18 % 7; /* assigns 4 to Remainder */`

See Also
/, div, ldiv, mod, modf

& ♦ Address-of variable operator

Purpose
Use the *address-of operator* to get the address at which the value of a variable is stored.

Syntax
`&<varname>`

Example Use
`Addr = &x; /* assign address of x to Addr */`

See Also
* (pointer dereferencing operator), & (reference operator), sizeof

& ♦ Bitwise AND operator

Purpose
Use the *bitwise AND operator*, &, to compare two quantities bit by bit. Each bit in the resulting value will be set to 1 if and only if the corresponding bits in the values

being compared were both set to 1. Do not confuse & (bitwise AND) with && (logical AND); the latter compares the whole values, not individual bits.

Syntax
```
val1 & val2
```

Example Use
```
Result = 11 & 8; /* 1011 AND 1000 results in 1000 */
```

See Also
|, ~, &&, ||

& ✦ Reference operator

Purpose
Use the *& operator* to create a reference to a variable. When you create a reference, the reference name and the variable name refer to the same location in memory and, therefore, have the same contents.

Syntax
```
#include <iostream.h>
<typename>& <reference_name> = <varname>
typename                      a valid data type
reference_name                name to be used as a reference
varname                       name of the variable to be referred to
```

Example Use
```
int counter = 10;
int& current = counter;       // current now same as counter
cout << counter << current;   // both are 10
```

Do not confuse a reference (*&* after the type name) with the address-of operator (*&* before a variable name). int& r means "a reference called *r*," but &r means "the address of *r*."

See Also
* (pointer), & (address-of operator)

&& ✦ Logical AND operator

Purpose
Use the *logical AND operator* to check whether two conditions are both true. The AND operator returns a value of 1 (true) only if both of the conditions tested are true (1). Do not confuse && (logical AND) with & (bitwise AND); the latter compares individual bits and sets the bits in the result accordingly.

CHAPTER 10 ALPHABETICAL REFERENCE

Syntax
```
val1 && val2
```

Example Use
```
if (Category == CLERICAL && Years_Served >= 10)
/* True only if clerical category and at least 10
   years have been served */
```

See Also
||, !

() ◆ Function argument list operator

Purpose
Use *parentheses* to enclose arguments in function calls and parameter lists in function declarations. An argument is an actual value sent to a function; a parameter is a formal description of the argument in the function declaration.

Syntax
```
<return_type> <func_name>(<type> <parameter_name>, ...)    function declaration
<func_name>(<argument>, ...)                              function call
```

Example Use
```
void *malloc(size_t num_bytes);    /* declaration of malloc() specifies an
                                      argument of */
                                   /* type size_t called num_bytes that
                                      returns a */
                                   /* pointer to void*/
malloc(10)                         /* call malloc with argument 10 */
```

* ◆ Pointer dereferencing operator

Purpose
Use the *pointer dereferencing operator* (*) to get the value stored at the address, represented by a pointer.

Syntax
```
*pointer_name    value pointed to by pointer
```

Example Use
```
Val = *p;    /* assigns contents of location whose address is stored in
                pointer p */
```

See Also
& (address-of operator), & (C++ reference operator), .*, ->, ->*, []

197

* ✦ Multiplication operator

Purpose
Use the *multiplication operator* to multiply two values.

Syntax
```
<val1> * <val2>
```

Example Use
```
Product = x * y;    /* assigns product of x and y to Product */
```

See Also
+, -, /, %

* ✦ Stream status pointer operator

Purpose
Use the * C++ *stream status pointer operator* to return the error status of a stream as a pointer value. The * (pointer) operator has been overloaded by the *ios* class for this purpose.

Syntax
```
#include <iostream.h>
*<stream_object>
stream_object     a stream accessed for reading and/or writing
```

Example Use
```
if (*my_file ==NULL) handle_error();   // handle error if null pointer returned
```

Returns
The * operator returns a pointer value of 0 (false or *NULL*) if the *failbit*, *badbit*, or *hardfail ios* flags have been set (indicating an error in accessing the stream); otherwise, a non-null (true) value is returned. Note that this is the opposite logical sense to the *!* operator, which returns "true" if an error occurred and false otherwise.

See Also
! (stream status operator), ios, open()

+ ✦ Addition operator

Purpose
Use the *addition operator* to add two values together.

Syntax
```
<val1> + <val2>
```

Example Use
```
Total = Price + Tax;        /* Adds Price and Tax and assigns to Total */
```

See Also
-, *, /, %

+ ❖ Unary plus operator

Purpose
Use the *unary plus operator* to make a value positive.

Syntax
```
+<val>
```

Example Use
```
+x     /* Value of x is positive (new in ANSI C) */
```

See Also
-. (negation operator)

++ ❖ Increment operator

Purpose
Use the *increment operator* to add one to the value of a variable. This is often done to increase loop index variables by one each time through the loop. The ultimate effect of i++ is the same as that of *i = i + 1;*.

When the increment operator precedes the variable name (for example, *++i*) the value of *i* is increased by one before any expression containing *i* is evaluated. When the increment operator follows the variable name (for example, *i++*) the value of *i* is increased by one *after* the expression containing *i* is evaluated.

Syntax
```
++val            pre-increment
val++            post-increment
```

Example Use
```
for (i=0, sum=0; i <= limit; sum += i++)
                /* i is incremented only after it is added to the sum */
++counter       /* counter is incremented before it is used for anything*/
```

See Also

`+`, `+=`

, ◆ Sequential evaluation operator

Purpose

Use the *sequential evaluation operator* (a comma) to group together two or more expressions that will be evaluated in succession from left to right. This operator is often used in *for* loops to perform two or more initializations or updates.

Syntax

```
<expression>, <expression> ...
```

Example Use

```
i++, j++;  /* first increment i, then increment j */
```

Note that the order of evaluation within each statement is not affected by the use of the comma to group statements. In particular the rules for pre-increments, post-increments described in the entries for ++ and –– are not affected.

See Also

`for`

– ◆ Negation operator

Purpose

Use the *negation operator* to make a quantity negative. This operator is sometimes called the unary minus operator. Do not confuse this with ~ (the *bitwise negation operator*). The latter negates (reverses) each bit in the specified value, while the – operator simply makes the value a whole negative.

Syntax

```
-val       same magnitude as val but negative
```

Example Use

```
x = 10;
y = -x;    /* y = -10 */
```

See Also

`~` (bitwise negation operator), `+` (unary plus operator), `-` (subtraction operator), `!` (logical NOT operator)

CHAPTER 10   ALPHABETICAL REFERENCE

− ♦ Subtraction operator

Purpose
Use the *subtraction operator* to subtract one value from another.

Syntax
`<val1> - <val2>`

Example Use
`Diff = X1 - X2    /* subtract X2 from X1 and assign to Diff */`

See Also
- (negation operator), ñ (decrement operator)

−− ♦ Decrement operator

Purpose
Use the *decrement operator* to subtract one from the value of a variable. This is often done to decrease loop index variables by one each time through the loop. The ultimate effect of $i--$ is the same as that of $i = i - 1;$.

When the decrement operator precedes the variable name (for example, $--i$), the value of i is decreased by one before any expression containing i is evaluated. When the decrement operator follows the variable name (for example, $i--$), the value of i is decreased by one *after* the expression containing i is evaluated.

Syntax
```
--val      pre-decrement
val--      post-decrement
```

Example Use
```
for (i=MAX_VAL, sum=0; i >= MIN_VAL; sum += i--)
                    /* i is decremented only after it is added to the sum*/
--counter;          /* counter is decremented before it is used for anything */
i--, j--;           /* first decrement i, then decrement j*/
```

See Also
-, -=

-> ♦ Object pointer member selection operator

Purpose
Use the *object pointer member selection operator* to access a particular data member or member function in a class or structure object pointed to by a pointer. The notation

201

class_pointer -> member accesses the *member* field of the class or structure object pointed to by *class_pointer*. If you want to access a member of a class or structure directly (not through a pointer), use the notation *object_name.member_name* where *object_name* is a variable of a class or struct type and *member_name* is the name of the member. Note that to set up a pointer to a member of a class or struct itself rather than to a member of an object, use the class pointer member selection operator described in the next entry.

Syntax

```
class_ptr->member_name
```

Example Use

```
class corp_info
{       /*define a class */
        char * name;
        ...
        char* getname() {return name;}
};
corp_info corp;                         /* define an object of that type */
corp_info* ptr = &corp;                 /* define pointer to the class */
ptr->name = "Turbo C++";                /* assign value to member through pointer */
char* name = ptr->getname();            /* invoke member function through pointer */
```

See Also

.(member selection operator), .* (pointer member selection operator), :: (scope resolution operator), struct, class

->* ♦ Class pointer member selection operator

Purpose

Use the *class pointer member selection operator* (->*) to dereference member offset pointers when the class portion of the expression is also a pointer.

Note that member offset pointers are distinctly different from object pointers. Whereas, an object pointer points directly to an object in memory, a member offset pointer contains an *offset* to a member relative to an object.

Syntax

```
<type> <class>::* <ptr_name>;           to declare a member offset pointer
<ptr_name> = &<class>::<member>;        to assign it to a member
<object-ptr> ->* <ptr_name>;            to access (dereference) the member
```

The <ptr_name> member offset pointer is set to an offset relative to any object of the same *class* that is the same data or function type as <type>. For example, if <ptr_name> is a member offset pointer to a type *double* member of an object class, then it can be assigned and offset to any type *double* members in that class.

The C++ compiler will assign <ptr_name> with the integer offset to <member> relative to the start of the object in memory, i.e., relative to the "this" pointer for an object. Note that <ptr_name> is not assigned a pointer to a specific object in memory, but it is instead assigned an offset relative to a specific class of objects. This offset is then dereferenced using either the .* operator or the ->* operator as shown in the example.

Note that the notation <object_pointer>->* <member_ptr> (where <object_ptr> is a pointer to an "object" and <member_ptr> is a member offset pointer to a data or function "member" in the same class as <object_ptr>) is equivalent to <object.member>. The ->* operator first dereferences <object_ptr> to the left of the operator and then dereferences the member offset pointer by adding the offset to the first dereference to obtain the second, and final, dereference. Function calls via dereferenced function members must use overriding parentheses around the dereferencing portion of the expression.

Example Use

```
#include <iostream.h>

struct EXAMPLE {
     int one;
     int two;
     int Total() { return(one + two); } };

void main(void) {
     EXAMPLE Exp;

     /* ExpPtr is a pointer to the Exp EXAMPLE object */
     EXAMPLE *pExp = &Exp;

     /* pExpMem is a member offset pointer to an integer EXAMPLE member. */
     int EXAMPLE::* pExpMem;

     /* pExpMem equals the offset to an EXAMPLE objects 'one' member */
     pExpMem = &EXAMPLE::one;

     /* Dereference the pExp pointer and the member */
     /* offset pointer using the ->* operator. */
     pExp->*pExpMem = 1;

     /* pExpMem equals the offset to an EXAMPLE objects 'two' member */
     pExpMem = &EXAMPLE::two;

     /* Set the 'two' member equal to 2 using the .* operator */
     Exp.*pExpMem = 2;

     /* Declare a member offset function pointer called 'pMemFnct' */
     int (EXAMPLE::*pMemFnct)();

     /* Set pMemFnct equal to the offset to the EXAMPLE::Total() function. */
     pMemFnct = &EXAMPLE::Total;

     /* Use the .* and ->* operators with the pMemFnct offset pointer */
     cout << "(Exp.*pMemFnct)()    = " << (Exp.*pMemFnct)() << "\n";
     cout << "(pExp->*pMemFnct)() = " << (pExp->*pMemFnct)() << "\n"; }
```

. ♦ Member selection operator

Purpose
Use the *member selection operator* to access a member (field) of a class or struct directly. The notation *object_name.member_name* accesses member *member_name* of struct or class object *object_name*. To access a class or structure through a pointer, use the pointer member selection operator (->) instead.

Syntax
```
object_name.member_name
```

Example Use
```
object address                    /* define a structure*/
{
    char * name
    ...
};
address this_address;             /*declare a variable of that type*/
this_address.name = "John Q. Public";
                                  /* assign value to member of structure */
```

See Also
->, ::, .*, struct, class

.* ♦ Pointer member selection operator

Purpose
Use the *pointer member selection operator* to access a member (field) of a class or struct through a pointer. The notation *pointer_name.*member_name* accesses member *member_name* of struct or class object pointed to by *pointer_name*. Note that the -> and ->* operators provide other ways to access class or structure members through pointers.

Syntax
```
object_name.*member_name
```

Example Use
For examples of the use of the .* operator and a general discussion of the use of member offset pointers, see the entry for the class pointer member selection operator ->*.

See Also
->, ->*, ::, struct, class

/ ♦ Division operator

Purpose
Use the *division operator* to divide one numeric value by another. For integer values, the whole-number quotient is returned; for floating-point type values, the decimal is returned.

Syntax
```
val1 / val2
```

Example Use
```
quotient = dividend / divisor;    /* Divide dividend by divisor */
```

See Also
+, -, *, %

/* */ ♦ C-style comment

Purpose
Use the /* */ symbol pair to enclose a *nonexecutable comment* source code. The comment can be confined to a single line or extend over several lines. Note that although C++ compilers accept the /* */ style of comments, the preferred comment style in C++ introduces comments with the // symbol. Also, some C and C++ compilers allow nested comments, but nesting is not an ANSI requirement and such code may not be portable.

Syntax
```
/* <text of comment> */           Single-line comment
/* <line of comment text
    ...
    ...    */                     Multiple-line comment
```

Example Use
```
for (day=monday; day <= friday; day++);    /* for each weekday */
    PrintSched (day);                      /* print that day's calendar */
```

See Also
// (C++-style comment)

// ♦ C++-style comment

Purpose
Use the // symbol to introduce a *C++-style comment*. All text following // on the line is considered to be a nonexecutable comment. For multiline comments each line must begin with //.

Syntax
```
// <text of comment>
```

Example Use
```
// This program has been tested with Borland C++
// and runs properly in an MS Windows
// DOS session
class Event { // holds system event info.
```

See Also
`/* */` (C-style comment)

:: ◆ Scope resolution operator

Purpose
Use the :: *scope resolution operator* to define a class member function (other than an inline one). You can also use this operator in general to refer to a member function or data member of a structure or class that is outside the current scope, or one that is global. For example, you can use the :: operator within a class object to refer to a global data item or function that has the same name as the class' own member data item or function.

Syntax
```
<class_name>::<member_name> or ::<global_name>
class_name          name of a class or structure
member_name         name of a function or data member
global_name         name of a global function or data item
```

Example Use
```
class box {
      int num;
      char* stuff;
public:
      int checknum()
};
int box::checknum() {
      // member function defined with :: operator return ::num;
      // access global num rather than class
      // member num
}
```

If *box* had a base class called *container* and a member function in box wanted to call the function *open* in the base class, the call would look like this:

```
container::open(mode);
```

See Also
`class, struct, extern`

< ♦ Less-than operator

Purpose
Use the *less-than operator* to determine whether a numeric value is less than another numeric value, or whether a character or string comes before another character or string in the collating sequence.

The less-than operator returns 1 (true) if the first value is less than (or comes before) the second one; otherwise, the operator returns 0 (false).

Syntax
```
val1 < val2
```

Example Use
```
if (score < goal) printf("You lose!\n");
```

See Also
>, =, !=

<< ♦ Insertion stream operator

Purpose
Use the *insertion* or "put-to" *stream operator* to send the value of a constant, literal, or variable to an object of the *ostream* class. Most commonly, the value is put to the standard output stream, *cout*. This operator is commonly overloaded to work with user-defined class objects.

Syntax
```
#include <iostream.h>
<output stream> << <value>
output stream            an ostream object
value                    a basic data type or overloaded for a user-
                         defined class
```

Example Use
```
cout << total;     /* Puts value of variable total to
                      standard output */
cout << endl;      /* send end of line to output
```

Returns
The insertion operator is left-associative and returns a reference to the *ostream* object for which it is invoked. Therefore, multiple uses of the operator can be "cascaded" to output several pieces of data, as in
```
cout << "The value of n is " << n << "\n" ;
```

See Also
>> (extraction operator), ostream, cout, printf()

<< ♦ Left-shift operator

Purpose
Use the *left-shift operator* to shift all of the bits in a value to the left. Each time you shift, the leftmost bit is discarded. A shift of one bit to the left is equivalent to multiplying the value by 2.

Syntax
```
value << <number of times to shift>
```

Example Use
```
x = 2;
x = x << 4;        /* x shifted to the left by 4
                      bit positions and now equals 32 */
```

See Also
`>>, &, |`

<= ♦ Less-than or equal-to operator

Purpose
Use the *less-than or equal-to operator* to determine whether one numeric value is less than or equal to another. If the first value is less than or equal to the second, the operator returns 1 (true). If the second value is less than the first, the operator returns 0 (false).

Syntax
```
<val1> <= <val2>
```

Example Use
```
if (temperature <= critical_point) printf("Everything's fine!\n");
```

See Also
`==, >, >=`

= ♦ Assignment operator

Purpose
Use the *assignment operator* to assign a value to a variable. Do not confuse = with ==; the latter operator does not assign a value but rather tests the value for equality.

Syntax
```
<varname> = <value>;              assign value to variable
<var1> = <var2> = <value>;        assign same value to both variables
```

You can combine an arithmetic operator (+, -, *, or /) with the assignment operator. When you do so, the indicated arithmetic is performed using the variable and the second value, and the result is assigned to the variable. For example:

```
a += b;    /* add b to a and assign result to a */
a *= 2;    /* multiply a times 2 and make that the
              new value of a */
```

Example Use
```
total = 0;              /* assign 0 to total */
line = word = 1;        /* assign 1 to both line and word*/
counter += value;       /* increase counter by value */
```

See Also
=, ++, -

== ♦ Equal-to operator

Purpose

Use the *equal-to operator* to determine whether the first value is equal to the second one. For numbers this means that both have the same value; for characters or strings equality means that both characters or strings are the same. The operator returns 1 (true) if the values are equal; otherwise, it returns false (0).

Do not confuse == with =. The latter does not compare the second value to the first, but rather assigns the second value to the first.

Syntax
```
<val1> == <val2>
```

Example Use
```
if (cust_no == target_no) flag_account(cust_no);
if (choice == 'a') do_choice_a;
```

See Also
<=, >=, !=

> ♦ Greater-than operator

Purpose

Use the *greater-than operator* to determine whether the first value is greater than the second one. For numbers, this means that the first number is larger than the second; for characters or strings, it means that the first character or string comes later than the second one in the collating sequence. The > operator returns the value 1 (true) if the first value is greater than (or comes later than) the second; otherwise, the operator returns 0 (false).

Syntax
```
val1 > val2
```

Example Use
```
if (line > lines_per page) do_header();
if (choice > 'f') menu_error();
```

See Also
```
<, <=, ==, !=
```

>> ♦ Extraction stream operator

Purpose

Use the *extraction* or "get from" *stream operator* to get a value from a stream (an *istream* object) and store it in an object (such as a variable). Typically, this operator is used to get input from *cin*. This operator is often overloaded to provide suitable input for user-defined objects.

The extraction operator does much the same job as *sprintf()* does in C, but the parsing and formatting of the input data is transparent rather than having to be specified. This is because once C++ recognizes the type of input the appropriate overloaded version of >> is called to handle the input. By default, >> skips whitespace (spaces, tabs, etc.) but this feature can be turned off by clearing the *ios::skipws* flag. Also note that the *ws* manipulator can also be used to "eat" and discard whitespace.

Syntax
```
#include <iostream.h>
<istream object> >> <receiving object>
istream object                an input stream such as cin
receiving object              a variable or class object
```

Example Use
```
cout << "Enter your age, please: ";
cin >> age; // store input value in variable age
```

Returns

The >> operator is left associative and returns a reference to the *istream* object for which it is invoked. This allows the "cascading" of input operations as in

```
cin >> start >> pos;
```

where both *start* and *pos* receive the value from *cin*.

See Also
```
<< (insertion operator), istream, cin, ios, ws
```

>> ✦ Right-shift operator

Purpose
Use the *right-shift operator* to shift all of the bits in a value to the right. Each time you shift, the rightmost bit is discarded. A shift of one bit to the right is equivalent to dividing the value by 2.

Syntax
```
<value> >> <times>        Number of times to shift
```

Example Use
```
x = 16;
x = x >> 1;        /* x shifted to the right by 1 bit
                      position and now equals 8 */
```

See Also
<<, &, |

[] ✦ Array element reference operator

Purpose
Use the *array element reference operator* to access the indicated element of an array using a numeric subscript. Note that arrays in C++ begin with element number 0; for an element declared to have n elements, the highest legal subscript is $n - 1$.

Syntax
```
<array_name>[<element_number>]
```

Example Use
```
int total [10];          /* declare array of integer */
total[1] = 25;           /* assign 25 to element 1 of array*/
total[0] = subtotal;     /* assign value of subtotal to first (0) element
                            of the array*/
```

^ ✦ Bitwise exclusive OR operator

Purpose
Use the *bitwise exclusive OR operator* to compare two values bit by bit such that the resulting value has a 1 only in positions where the compared bit values differ. Note that with the bitwise exclusive OR operator the result has a 0 in any position where the compared values are either both 1 or both 0. The bitwise OR operator, on the other hand, has a 1 in the resulting position where at least one of the compared bits is a 1.

Syntax

```
<val1> ^ <val2>
```

Example Use

```
bitvals = 6 ^ 10;   /* 0110 ^ 1010; bitvals has value 1100 */
```

See Also

|, &, ~

| ◆ Bitwise OR operator

Purpose

Use the *bitwise OR operator* to compare two values bit by bit such that the resulting value has a 1 in positions where one or both of the compared values have a 1. This differs from the bitwise exclusive OR operator in that the latter puts a 1 in the resulting position if one and only one of the compared values has a 1 in that position.

Syntax

```
<val1> | <val2>
```

Example Use

```
bitvals = 6 | 10;   /* 0110 | 1010; bitvals has value 1110 */
```

See Also

^, &, ~

|| ◆ Logical OR operator

Purpose

Use the *logical OR operator* to determine whether at least one of two conditions is true. The operator returns 1 (true) if one or both of the conditions is true, but returns 0 (false) if both are false.

Syntax

```
<condition1> || <condition2>
```

Example Use

```
if ((temperature > BOILING_POINT) || (pressure > BURSTING_POINT)) sound_alarm();
```

See Also

&&, !

~ ◆ Bitwise negation operator

Purpose
Use the *bitwise negation operator* to reverse each bit position in a value such that ones become zeros and zeros become ones.

Syntax
```
~<bit_value>              reverse each bit in bit_value
```

Example Use
```
bitvals =  40;            /* 00101000 */
newvals = ~bitvals;       /* 11010111 */
```

See Also
&, !

?: ◆ Conditional operator

Purpose
Use the *conditional operator* to choose one of two expressions based on the truth of a condition.

Syntax
```
<condition> ? <expression1> : <expression2>
```

If the condition is true, then expression1 is evaluated; otherwise, expression2 is evaluated. The expressions are often alternative assignments as shown here. The previous conditional statement is equivalent to:

```
if (condition)
     expression1;
else
     expression2;
```

Example Use
```
a > b ? max = a : max = b;
/* max becomes a if a is greater, otherwise max becomes b */
```

See Also
if

\a ◆ escape sequence for "alert"

Purpose
Use the \a *escape sequence* to have a string sound an alert (usually a beep) on the system's speaker. The position of the cursor or print head is not changed.

Example Use
```
printf("Do you really want to reformat this disk?\a");
```

See Also
```
printf(), cout, << (insertion stream operator)
```

abort() ♦ function

Purpose
Use *abort()* to abnormally exit your program. *abort()* calls *raise(SIGABRT)*. Note that unlike *exit()*, *abort()* will not flush the file buffers or call the routines set up by *atexit()*. However, you can take care of these chores by appropriately setting up the processing for the SIGABRT signal.

Syntax
```
#include <stdlib.h>
void abort(void);
```

Example Use
```
abort();
```

See Also
```
atexit(), exit(), raise(), signal(), SIGABRT
```

abs() ♦ function

Purpose
Use the *abs()* function to get the absolute value of the integer argument *n*.

Syntax
```
#include <stdlib.h>
int abs(int n);
int n;                  Integer whose absolute value is returned
```

Example Use
```
x = abs(-5); /* x will be 5 now */
```

Returns
The integer returned by *abs()* is the absolute value of *n*.

See Also
```
fabs(), labs()
```

acos() ♦ function

Purpose
Use the *acos()* function to compute the arccosine of an argument *x* whose value lies in the range −1 to 1. The result is an angle with a value between 0 and pi radians. You can convert an angle from radians to degrees by multiplying it by 57.29578.

Syntax
```
#include <math.h>
double acos(double x);
double x;            Argument whose arccosine is to be computed
```

Example Use
```
angle = acos(0.5); /* angle is pi/3 */
```

Returns
When the value of the argument *x* is in the valid range of −1 to 1, *acos()* returns the arccosine. Otherwise, a domain error occurs.

See Also
```
cos()
```

argc ♦ predefined value

Purpose
The value *argc*, supported by many operating systems including UNIX and MS-DOS, is used in the call to *main()* that starts the program. The *argc* value is the number of arguments used on the command line, including the name of the program and any command-line switches, file names, etc. that the user supplied.

Syntax
```
void main (int argc, char **argv);  Typical declaration of main()
```

Example Use
```
if (argc < 3)
{
printf("You must supply at least two arguments\n");
exit (EXIT_FAILURE);     /* return to operating system */
};
```

See Also
```
argv, getenv()
```

argv ◆ predefined value

Purpose
The value *argv*, supported by many operating systems including UNIX and MS-DOS, is used in the call to *main()* that starts the program. The *argv value* is a pointer to an array of character strings; each string is one of the arguments that the user typed on the command line. The *argv[0]* value is usually the name of the program itself, and the successive arguments are the option switches, file names, and so on that the user typed.

Syntax
```
void main (int argc, char **argv); typical declaration of main()
```

Example Use
```
/* one way for a program to access its arguments */
for (i = 1; i < argc; i++)
    printf("%s", argv[i]);
```

See Also
argc, getenv()

asctime() ◆ function

Purpose
Use the *asctime()* function to convert to a character string the value of a time stored in the structure of type *tm* at the address *time*. The structure *tm* is defined in *time.h* as follows.

```
struct tm
{
    int tm_sec;         /* seconds after the minute - [0,60]  */
    int tm_min;         /* minutes after the hour - [0,59]    */
    int tm_hour;        /* hours since midnight - [0,23]      */
    int tm_mday;        /* day of the month - [1,31]          */
    int tm_mon;         /* months since January - [0,11]      */
    int tm_year;        /* years since 1900                   */
    int tm_wday;        /* days since Sunday - [0,6]          */
    int tm_yday;        /* days since January 1 - [0,365]     */
    int tm_isdst;       /* daylight savings time flag         */
};
```

The string prepared by *asctime()* will be 26 characters long, counting the null character (\0) at the end, and has the form:

```
Thu Jul 21 19:02:39 1990\n\0
```

As the example shows, a 24-hour clock is used for the time.

Syntax

```
#include <time.h>
char *asctime(tm *time);
tm *time;          Pointer to a structure containing time to be
                   converted to a string
```

Example Use

```
printf("The time is %s\n", asctime(&timedata));
```

Returns

The *asctime()* function returns a pointer to the static data area where the string is stored.

See Also

```
ctime(), gmtime(), localtime(), time(), tm
```

asin() ♦ function

Purpose

Use the *asin()* function to compute the arcsine of the argument *x* provided its value lies in the range –1 to 1. The result is an angle with a value between –pi/2 and pi/2 radians. You can convert an angle from radians to degrees by multiplying it by 57.29578.

Syntax

```
#include <math.h>
double asin(double x);
double x;          Argument whose arcsine is to be computed
```

Example Use

```
angle = asin(0.707)   /* angle is roughly pi/4 */
```

Returns

For a valid argument *x* with values between –1 and 1, *asin()* returns an angle whose sine is equal to *x*. However, if the argument's value lies outside the acceptable range, a domain error occurs.

See Also

```
sin()
```

asm ♦ keyword

Purpose

Use the *asm* keyword to pass instructions from the compiler to an assembler. The implementation of this keyword is compiler-dependent. Typically, *asm* is followed by one or more statements in assembly language. The statements are compiled directly into machine code by the supported assembler.

Syntax
```
asm <assembly statement>;
or
asm <assembly statement>;
asm <assembly statement>...
or
asm     {
        <assembly statement>
        ...
        }
```

You can put *asm* statements one to a line, with asm followed by the actual assembly language statement and ending with a semicolon. You can put more than one *asm* statement on the same line, with each statement beginning with *asm* and ending with a semicolon. You can also precede a set of lines of assembly language statements with the keyword *asm* and enclose the statements with curly braces (like a regular block of C++ statements).

Example Use
```
asm mov ax, [sp + 4];     // Example of single-line use

asm { // Example of multi-line use
    pop ax        // Get stack top into AX
    inc ax        // increment AX
    push ax       // put result back on stack
    }
```

Note that you cannot use assembly language comments introduced by semicolons. Use one of the C++ comment styles instead.

See Also
/* */ (comment), // (comment), inline

assert() ♦ macro

Purpose
Use the *assert()* macro to print an error message and abort the program if the <expression> is false. The *assert()* macro is typically used to identify program errors during the debugging phase. After the program is debugged, you can disable all occurrences of the *assert()* macro by defining the preprocessor macro NDEBUG.

Syntax
```
#include <assert.h>
void assert(<expression>);
<expression>            C++ statements specifying assertion being tested
```

Example Use
```
assert(arg_value >= 0);
```

See Also
abort(), NDEBUG

atan() ◆ function

Purpose
Use the *atan()* function to compute the arctangent of the argument *x*. The result will be an angle with a value between –pi/2 and pi/2 radians. You can convert an angle from radians to degrees by multiplying it by 57.29578.

Syntax
```
#include <math.h>
double atan(double x);
double x;               Argument whose arctangent is to be computed
```

Example Use
```
angle = atan(1.0);   /* angle is pi/4 */
```

Returns
The *atan()* function returns the angle in the range –pi/2 and pi/2 whose tangent is equal to *x*.

See Also
atan2(), tan()

atan2() ◆ function

Purpose
Use the *atan2()* function to compute the arctangent of the ratio of the arguments *y/x*. The result will be an angle with a value between –pi and pi radians. You can convert an angle from radians to degrees by multiplying it by 57.29578. In contrast to *atan()*, which takes a single argument, *atan2()* takes two arguments and uses the sign of the two arguments to determine the quadrant (90 degree sector in Cartesian coordinates) in which the angle should lie.

Syntax
```
#include <math.h>
double atan2(double y, double x);
double x, y;            Arctangent of y/x will be computed
```

Example Use
```
angle = atan2(y, x);
```

Returns
Provided both arguments *x* and *y* are nonzero, *atan2()* returns an angle whose tangent is equal to *x*. However, if both arguments are zero, a domain error may occur.

See Also
```
atan(), tan()
```

atexit() ✦ function

Purpose
Use *atexit()* to set up a stack of up to 32 (this is the minimum number specified by ANSI C) functions that the system will call in a "last-in, first-out" manner when your program terminates normally. Note that the functions passed to *atexit()* cannot take any arguments. This feature is useful for setting up housecleaning chores that may be performed upon program termination.

Syntax
```
#include <stdlib.h>
int atexit(void (*func)(void));
void (*func)(void);        Pointer to function to be called
```

Example Use
```
atexit(cleanup_all);
```

Returns
The *atexit()* function returns a zero if successful. Otherwise, it returns a nonzero value.

See Also
```
exit()
```

atof() ✦ function

Purpose
Use the *atof()* function to convert the argument string into a double value. A call to *atof()* is equivalent to the call *strtod(string, (char **)NULL)*.

Syntax
```
#include <stdlib.h>
double atof(const char *string);
const char *string;        String to be converted
```

Example Use
```
dbl_value = atof(input_string);
```

Returns
The *atof()* function returns the double-precision value after conversion.

See Also
```
atoi(), atol(), strtod(), NULL
```

atoi() ♦ function

Purpose
Use the *atoi()* function to convert the argument *string* into an *int* value. A call to *atoi()* is equivalent to the call *(int)strtol(string, (char **)NULL, 10)*.

Syntax
```
#include <stdlib.h>
long atoi(const char *string);
const char *string;         String to be converted
```

Example Use
```
int_value = atoi(input_string);
```

Returns
The *atoi()* function returns the integer value as an *int* variable.

See Also
```
atof(), atol(), strtol(), strtoul(), NULL
```

atol() ♦ function

Purpose
Use the *atol()* function to convert the argument *string* into a *long* integer value. A call to *atol()* is equivalent to the call *strol (string, (char**) NULL, 10)*.

Syntax
```
#include <stdlib.h>
long atol (const char*string);
const char* string;         String to be converted
```

Example Use
```
long_value = atol(input_string);
```

Returns
The *atol()* function returns the converted value as a long variable.

See Also
```
atof(), atoi(), strtol(), strtoul(), NULL
```

auto ◆ keyword

Purpose
Use the *auto* storage class specifier to declare temporary variables. These variables are created upon entering a block statement and destroyed upon exit. Local variables of a function have the *auto* storage class by default.

Syntax
```
auto <type> <varname>;
```

Example Use
```
/* the variables i, limit, and sum are created only when the if statement is
true-when the user presses a C */
#include <stdio.h>
main()
{
    int c;
    c = getchar();
    if(c == 'C')
    {
        auto int i, limit, sum;
        printf("Sum from 1 to ?");
        scanf(" %d",&limit);
        /* Compute sum from 1 to limit */
        for(i=0, sum=0; i <= limit; sum += i, i++);
        printf("\nSum from 1 to %d = %d\n", limit, sum);
    }
}
```

See Also
```
extern, register, static
```

\b ◆ escape sequence for backspace

Purpose
Use the *\b* escape sequence to move the cursor or print head back one space. Other effects depend on the hardware in use.

Example Use
```
/* backs up to start of last word printed */
for (pos = 1; pos < len(word); pos++)
    putc('\b');
```

See Also
```
printf(), cout, << (put-to stream operator), \r, \n
```

bad() ◆ function

Purpose
Use the *bad()* *ios* member function to determine if an invalid operation was attempted involving a stream, or an unrecoverable error occurred.

Syntax
```
#include <fstream.h>
<stream_name>.bad()
stream_name              stream to be accessed
```

Example Use
```
#include <fstream.h>
ifstream testfile; // declare an input file
if (testfile.bad()) cout << "Serious file error\n";
```

Returns
The *bad()* function returns a nonzero ("true") integer value if the *badbit* or *hardfail ios* flag bit has been set for the stream.

See Also
```
ios, istream, fail(), good(), rdstate(), setiosflags(), resetiosflags()
```

break ◆ keyword

Purpose
Use the *break* keyword to exit the innermost *do*, *while*, or *for* loop. It is also used to exit from a *switch* statement.

Syntax
```
break;
```

Example Use
```
/* add the numbers from 1 to 10 in an endless loop.
   Use break to exit the loop   */
sum = 0;
i = 0;
while(1)
{
    sum += i;
    i++;
    if(i > 10) break;
}
```

See Also
```
case, continue, do, for, switch, while
```

bsearch() ♦ function

Purpose
Use the *bsearch()* function to search a sorted array beginning at the address *base* and comprising *num* elements, each of size *width* bytes. The argument *key* points to the value being sought. Note that you can use the *qsort()* routine to sort the array before calling *bsearch()*.

Syntax
```
#include <stdlib.h>
void *bsearch(const void *key, const void *base, size_t num, size_t width,
int (*compare)(const void *elem1, const void *elem2));
const void *key;         Pointer to element value being searched for
const void *base;        Pointer to beginning of array being searched
size_t      num;         Number of elements in array
size_t      width;       Size of each element in bytes
int (*compare)(const void *elem1, const void *elem2);
                         Pointer to a function that compares two elements
                         elem1 and elem2 each of type const void *
```

Example Use
```
int mycompare(const void *, const void *);
result = (char **) bsearch((const void *)keyword,
                    (const void *)envp,
                    (size_t)count,
                    (size_t)sizeof(char *),
                    mycompare);
```

Returns
The *bsearch()* function returns a pointer to the first occurrence of the value *key* in the array. If the value is not found, *bsearch()* returns a NULL.

See Also
qsort(), NULL, size_t

BUFSIZ ♦ predefined value

Purpose
The *BUFSIZ* predefined value gives the size of the buffer used by *setbuf()*. It is defined in *stdio.h*.

See Also
FOPEN_MAX

CHAPTER 10 ALPHABETICAL REFERENCE

calloc() ♦ function

Purpose

Use *calloc()* to allocate memory for an array of *num_elems* elements each of size *elem_size* bytes. All bytes of the allocated array will be initialized to zero. Note that C++ objects should be allocated with the *new* operator.

Syntax

```
#include <stdlib.h>
void *calloc(size_t num_elems, size_t elem_size);
size_t   num_elems;              Number of elements
size_t   elem_size;              Size of each element in bytes
```

Example Use

```
p_int = (int *) calloc(100, sizeof(int));
```

Returns

The return value from *calloc()* is a pointer to *void*, representing the address of the allocated memory. If the memory allocation is unsuccessful because of insufficient space or bad values of the arguments, a *NULL* is returned.

See Also

```
free(), malloc(), realloc(), NULL, size_t
```

case ♦ keyword

Purpose

Use the *case* keyword to label cases in a *switch* statement. If the switch variable has the specified value, the statements associated with the case are executed. A *break* statement is used at the end of the statements for each case in order to prevent the next case from being executed, unless that behavior is intended.

Syntax

```
case <value> : <statement; ... >
```

Example Use

```
case 'A':
      do_choice_A();
      break;
```

See Also

```
default, switch
```

catch ◆ keyword

Purpose

Use the *catch* keyword to define an exception handler. An exception handler is a block of code designed to deal with a particular error (exception) usually involving an invalid index, argument, or data value. Note that the C++ exception-handling features are not yet widely implemented, and are not covered in *Master C++ for Windows*.

Syntax

```
catch (<Exception class>) {
    // Code to handle exceptions
    // that were tested by exception class
}
exception class contains functions for checking exceptions
```

Typically for exceptions involving a particular class, you define a nested class (subclass) with functions or operators that check values for validity. When some other part of the program wants to use the class being safeguarded with error checking, a block of code beginning with the keyword *try* performs some manipulation of the data. If an error is detected by your program during the processing of a *try* block construct, you can write a statement to *throw* the exception to a matching *catch* exception handler defined immediately following the *try* block. A *catch* block must immediately follow either a *try* block or another *catch* block.

Example Use

```
class Counter {
    int total;
public:
    class Range { }; // exception class
    int show_total() {
            if (total >= 0 && total <= MAX_TOT)
                        return total;       // total is in range
        throw Range();                      // if executed, means that
                                            // it was out of range
    }
};
// Elsewhere in the program...
try { // Enclose function that will work with data
    check_total(total-n);
}
catch (Counter::Range) {
            // handler for Counter::Range exception
            // check_total() must have gotten an invalid
            // total in Counter::show_total()
            // Handle the exception here
    ...
    ...
}
```

See Also

throw, try

ceil() ◆ function

Purpose

Use the *ceil()* function to find the "ceiling" of a *double* argument *x*. The "ceiling" is the smallest integral value that is equal to or that just exceeds *x*. This can be used in rounding a *double* value *up* to the next integer.

Syntax
```
#include <math.h>
double ceil(double x);
double x;                  Variable whose "ceiling" is to be returned
```

Example Use
```
x_ceiling = ceil(4.1);  /* x_ceiling is 5.0 */
```

Returns

The return value is the "ceiling" of *x* expressed as a *double*.

See Also
```
floor()
```

cerr ◆ stream

Purpose

Use the *cerr* stream to receive error messages. *cerr* is the standard error stream, corresponding to *stderr* in the ANSI C library. By default, *cerr* is assigned to the screen, but it can be redirected.

Syntax
```
#include <iostream.h>
cerr << <message or value>
```

Example Use
```
if (pressure > red_line)
    cerr << "Gonna blow!" << endl;
```

See Also
```
<< (insertion operator), cin, clog, cout
```

char ◆ keyword

Purpose

Use the *char* type specifier to declare character variables and arrays. A character variable actually stores the character's ASCII code number in the machine's character set.

A *signed char* has a range between –128 and 127, while a regular *char* (occasionally called *unsigned char*) has a range of 0 through 255.

Syntax
```
char <varname>;
```

Example Use
```
/* declare a character, a pointer to a char, and an array of characters */
    char c, *p_c, string[80];
```

See Also
```
double, float, int, long, short, signed, unsigned
```

CHAR_BIT ✦ predefined value

Purpose
The *CHAR_BIT* predefined value gives the maximum number of bits in *char*. It is defined in *limits.h*.

See Also
```
CHAR_MAX, CHAR_MIN
```

CHAR_MAX ✦ predefined value

Purpose
The *CHAR_MAX* predefined value gives the maximum value of a *char*. It is defined in *limits.h*.

See Also
```
CHAR_MIN, CHAR_BIT
```

CHAR_MIN ✦ predefined value

Purpose
The *CHAR_MIN* predefined value gives the minimum value of a *char*. It is defined in *limits.h*.

See Also
```
CHAR_MAX, CHAR_BIT
```

CHAPTER 10   ALPHABETICAL REFERENCE

cin ◆ stream

Purpose

Use the *cin* stream as an input source for your program. *cin* is the standard input stream, corresponding to *stdin* in the ANSI C library. By default *cin* is assigned to the console (keyboard), but it can be redirected. Typically, the extraction stream operator >> is used to get data from *cin* and store it in an object. In C++ 2.0 *cin* has predefined operators for handling the following data types: *short, int, long, float, double, long double, char,* and *char *.*

Syntax

```
cin >> <receiving variable>;
```

Example Use

```
int age;
...
cin >> age;// Get user's age from keyboard
```

Returns

cin passes the incoming data via the >> (extraction) operator to the receiving variable.

See Also

`cerr, clog, cout, >> (extraction operator), sprintf()`

class ◆ keyword

Purpose

Use the *class* keyword to begin the definition of a class. A class is the specification for an object to be manipulated by the program. A class can contain declarations of values (data members) and ways of working with the values (function members). A class can be derived from one or more "parent" classes. The keywords *private, public,* and *protected* control access from the rest of the program to the data and functions included in the class.

Syntax

```
class <class_name> : <derivation> <base_class> ...{
                     How derived and base class (optional)
member declaration   One or more data members and/or member functions
...
};
```

Begin the class definition with the keyword *class*, followed by the name of the class, which will be the name of the data type for objects of the class. (You can have an unnamed class, but this is usually not useful.) If the class is derived from one or more base classes, follow the class name with a colon and the name(s) of the base classes, separated by commas. If desired, the name of any base class can be preceded by the keyword *public, private,* or *protected* to specify the access the class will have to members of the base class. (See the entries for these keywords for more information.)

The rest of the body of the class definition consists of declarations of the data members and/or member functions of the class. These follow the usual rules for declarations, and again the keywords *public, private,* or *protected* can be used to specify the degree of access to the items in the following declarations.

A class can be nested inside another class definition. If this is done, the contents of the nested class are accessible only within the enclosing class.

The structure and syntax of a *class* is the same as that of a *struct*, except that access to a *class* is private by default and access to a *struct* is public by default.

Example Use
```
class planet : public sky_object {
      private:                                      // restricted data
                  float mass;
                  float radius;
                  float density;
                  Point position;
                  planet (stats_array[]);    // constructor
                  ~planet ();                 // destructor
                  Point calc_position();
      public:                                       // functions for outside access
                  Mag calc_magnitude(Point view);
};
```

See Also
private, protected, public, struct, typedef, union

clear() ◆ function

Purpose
Use the *clear()* ios member function to set the values of the error bits of a stream according to the integer value you supply. (If you specify 0 or do not give an argument, all error bits will be cleared.) A typical use is to set an error flag if a problem is encountered or to clear the error bits after a problem has been handled.

Syntax
```
#include <iostream.h>
<stream_name>.clear(intval);
stream_name              name of stream to be affected
intval                   integer value for setting bits
```

Example Use
```
ifstream my_input;
...                          // some stream operations
my_input.clear(0);           // clears all error bits
my_input.clear(ios::failbit|my_input.rdstate());
```

The second call to *clear()* in the previous example uses the | (bitwise *OR*) operator to "or" the flag values returned by *rdstate()* with the current value of *failbit*. The result is to set *failbit* without affecting the other flags for the stream.

See Also
```
ios, rdstate(), fail()
```

clearerr()   function

Purpose
Use *clearerr()* to reset the error and end-of-file indicators of the ANSI C stream specified by the stream pointer *stream*. (Note that *ios* member functions such as *clear()* are used to set or clear error bits for C++ streams.)

Syntax
```
#include <stdio.h>
void clearerr(FILE *stream);
FILE *stream;    Pointer to stream whose error flag is being cleared
```

Example Use
```
clearerr(outfile);
```

See Also
```
ferror(), feof(), FILE
```

CLK_TCK   predefined value

Purpose
The *CLK_TCK* predefined value gives the number of clock ticks per second returned by the *clock()* function. It is defined in *time.h*.

See Also
```
clock()
```

clock()   function

Purpose
Use *clock()* to obtain the amount of processor time since the machine was started in "number of ticks." The constant CLK_TCK, defined in *time.h*, is the number of ticks per second, so the value returned by *clock* should be divided by CLK_TCK to get the elapsed processor time in seconds.

Syntax
```
#include <time.h>
clock_t clock(void);
```

Example Use
```
ticks_now = clock();
```

Returns

If the processor time is available to *clock()*, it returns the current time in ticks, cast as a value of type *clock_t* which is defined in *time.h*. Otherwise, it returns the value –1, cast as *clock_t*.

See Also
```
difftime(), time(), CLK_TCK, clock_t
```

clock_t ✦ predefined data type

Purpose

The *clock_t* data type is capable of holding the value of the time returned by the *clock* function. It is defined in *time.h*.

See Also
```
time_t, tm
```

clog ✦ stream

Purpose

Use the predefined *clog* C++ stream to direct output to "standard error." While this output goes by default to the screen, it can be reassigned to another destination (such as a disk file). *clog* is the same as *cerr* except that *clog* is fully buffered.

Syntax
```
#include <iostream.h>
```

Example Use
```
clog << "Error number " << errno << "has occurred." << endl;
```

See Also
```
cerr, cout, ostream, errno
```

close() ✦ function

Purpose

Use the *close()* ios member function to properly close a C++ file and the associated stream. Any data in the buffer will be flushed before the file is closed.

CHAPTER 10   ALPHABETICAL REFERENCE

Syntax

```
#include <fstream.h>
<filename>.close()
filename                   name of file to close
```

Example Use

```
ofstream output_file;      // declare an output file
                           // open file and write data to it
output_file.close();       // close the file
```

See Also

open(), flush(), fclose() (ANSI C streams)

---

const ◆ keyword

Purpose

Use the *const* type qualifier to indicate that the variable that follows may not be modified by the program. (You can, however, initialize the constant at the time of declaration, as shown in the following examples.) You cannot later assign a value to a *const*, increment it, or decrement it. Declaring constants can protect key values from change, accommodate data in read-only memory, or improve optimization in some compilers by assuring the compiler that a value will not be changed later. *const* guarantees only that you the programmer will not change the value later; the value may in some cases be changed by the operation of the hardware. You can declare such a hardware-dependent value to be *const volatile*.

Use of *const* is preferable to using *#define* with a numeric literal, because the compiler doesn't provide type-checking in the latter case.

Syntax

```
const <name> = <value>
```

Example Use

```
const short x = 32;           /* x is constant */
const int *p_i = 2048;        /* value pointed to by p_i is constant */
int *const p_c_i = &total;    /* pointer p_c_i is constant*/
```

See Also

volatile, #define

---

continue ◆ keyword

Purpose

Use the *continue* keyword to skip execution of the body of a loop. It is equivalent to executing a *goto* to move to the end of the loop. After skipping the rest of the body of the loop, control returns to the loop condition, which is checked as usual. The *continue* statement affects the innermost loop in which it appears.

Syntax
```
continue;
```

Example Use
```
/* The statement sum += i; will be skipped when i is 5, giving the sum of
the numbers from 1 to 10, excluding 5 */
for(i=0, sum=0; i <= 10, i++)
{
    if(i == 5) continue;
    sum += i;
}
```

See Also
for, if, while

cos() ◆ function

Purpose
Use the *cos()* function to compute the cosine of *double* argument x, which must be expressed in radians. You can convert an angle from degrees to radians by dividing it by 57.29578.

Syntax
```
#include <math.h>
double cos(double x);
double x;                  Angle in radians whose cosine is to be computed
```

Example Use
```
cos_angle = cos(ang_radian);
```

Returns
The *cos()* function returns the cosine of x. If the value of x is large in magnitude, the result may be very imprecise.

See Also
acos(), sin()

cosh() ◆ function

Purpose
Use the *cosh()* function to compute the hyperbolic cosine of x.

Syntax

```
#include <math.h>
double cosh(double x);
double x;              Variable whose hyperbolic cosine is to be computed
```

Example Use

```
result = cosh(x);
```

Returns

Normally, *cosh()* returns the hyperbolic cosine of *x*. If the value of the result is too large (a *double* variable can be as large as 10^{308}), a range error will occur.

See Also

sinh()

cout ♦ stream

Purpose

Use the *cout* C++ stream to output data. *cout* corresponds to the *stdout* (standard output) stream in ANSI C. By default, *cout* is assigned to the screen, but it can be redirected. Typically, the *insertion stream* operator << is used to put the value of a variable, literal, or constant in the output stream. In C++ 2.0, *cout* has predefined operators for the following data types: *short, int, long, float, double, long double, char*, and *char* ∗, plus (new with 2.0) *void* ∗ (for pointer values).

Syntax

```
#include <iostream.h>
cout << <data>
data                   numeric or string constant, literal, variable, or
                       user-defined class object
```

Example Use

```
cout << "Welcome to Master C++\n";    // string output
cout << total;                        // output value of variable total
```

See Also

ostream, >> (stream extraction operator)

__cplusplus ♦ predefined macro

Purpose

Use the *__cplusplus* macro when you need to compile or link something depending on whether the program being compiled is a C program or a C++ program. Most compilers automatically define *__cplusplus* if C++ compilation has been set.

Syntax

```
<test> _ _cplusplus        test is #ifdef, #ifndef, etc.
```

Example Use

```
#ifndef _ _cplusplus  /* not compiling C++ */
    #error C++ must be used for this program!
#endif
```

Returns

The state of _ _*cplusplus* is communicated by whether it is defined or not: if it is defined, the compiler mode is C++.

See Also

_ _STDC_ _

---

ctime()   ♦   function

Purpose

Use the *ctime()* function to convert to a character string the value of time stored in the variable of type *time_t* at the address *timer*. Calling *ctime()* is equivalent to the call *asctime(localtime(timer))*.

Syntax

```
#include <time.h>
char *ctime(const time_t *timer);
const time_t  *timer;       Pointer to calendar time
```

Example Use

```
printf("Current time = %s\n", ctime(&bintime));
```

Returns

The *ctime()* function returns the pointer to the string.

See Also

asctime(), time(), time_t

_ _DATE_ _   ♦   predefined macro

Purpose

Use the _ _*DATE*_ _ predefined macro to display the date of translation of the source file by the preprocessor. This macro inserts a string constant into the file of the form "MMM DD YYYY" (such as "Jun 15 1990").

Example Use

```
printf("Compiled on: ");
printf(_ _DATE_ _);
```

See Also

_ _FILE_ _, _ _TIME_ _, _ _LINE_ _, _ _STDC_ _

DBL_DIG ✦ predefined value

Purpose

The *DBL_DIG* predefined value gives the number of significant decimal digits in a *double* value. It is defined in *float.h*.

See Also

DBL_EPSILON, DBL_MANT_DIG, DBL_MIN, DBL_MIN_10_EXP, DBL_MIN_EXP, DBL_MAX, DBL_MAX_10_EXP, DBL_MAX_EXP

DBL_EPSILON ✦ predefined value

Purpose

The *DBL_EPSILON* predefined value gives the smallest positive *double* value x such that $1+x \ne 1$. It is defined in *float.h*.

See Also

DBL_DIG, DBL_MANT_DIG, DBL_MIN, DBL_MIN_10_EXP, DBL_MIN_EXP, DBL_MAX, DBL_MAX_10_EXP, DBL_MAX_EXP

DBL_MANT_DIG ✦ predefined value

Purpose

The *DBL_MANT_DIG* predefined value gives the number of base *FLT_RADIX* digits in the mantissa of a *double*. It is defined in *float.h*.

See Also

DBL_DIG, DBL_EPSILON, DBL_MIN, DBL_MIN_10_EXP, DBL_MIN_EXP, DBL_MAX, DBL_MAX_10_EXP, DBL_MAX_EXP

DBL_MAX ✦ predefined value

Purpose

The *DBL_MAX* predefined value gives the maximum representable finite value that can be stored in a *double*. It is defined in *float.h*.

See Also

`DBL_DIG, DBL_MANT_DIG, DBL_EPSILON, DBL_MIN, DBL_MIN_10_EXP, DBL_MIN_EXP DBL_MAX_10_EXP, DBL_MAX_EXP`

DBL_MAX_10_EXP ♦ predefined value

Purpose

The *DBL_MAX_10_EXP* predefined value gives the maximum integer such that 10 raised to that power is representable in a *double*.

See Also

`DBL_DIG, DBL_MANT_DIG, DBL_EPSILON, DBL_MIN, DBL_MIN_10_EXP, DBL_MIN_EXP, DBL_MAX, DBL_MAX_EXP`

DBL_MAX_EXP ♦ predefined value

Purpose

The *DBL_MAX_EXP* predefined value gives the maximum integer such that FLT_RADIX raised to that power is representable in a *double*. It is defined in *float.h*.

See Also

`DBL_DIG, DBL_MANT_DIG, DBL_EPSILON, DBL_MIN, DBL_MIN_10_EXP, DBL_MIN_EXP, DBL_MAX, DBL_MAX_10_EXP`

DBL_MIN ♦ predefined value

Purpose

The *DBL_MIN* predefined value gives the minimum, positive floating-point number that can be stored in a *double*. It is defined in *float.h*.

See Also

`DBL_DIG, DBL_MANT_DIG, DBL_EPSILON, DBL_MIN_10_EXP, DBL_MIN_EXP, DBL_MAX, DBL_MAX_10_EXP, DBL_MAX_EXP`

DBL_MIN_10_EXP ♦ predefined value

Purpose

The *DBL_MIN_10_EXP* predefined value gives the minimum negative integer such that 10 raised to that power is representable in a *double*. It is defined in *float.h*.

CHAPTER 10 ALPHABETICAL REFERENCE

See Also

`DBL_DIG, DBL_MANT_DIG, DBL_EPSILON, DBL_MIN, DBL_MIN_EXP, DBL_MAX, DBL_MAX_10_EXP, DBL_MAX_EXP`

DBL_MIN_EXP ◆ predefined value

Purpose

The *DBL_MIN_EXP* predefined value gives the minimum negative integer such that FLT_RADIX raised to that power minus 1 is representable in a *double*.

See Also

`DBL_DIG, DBL_MANT_DIG, DBL_EPSILON, DBL_MIN, DBL_MIN_10_EXP, DBL_MAX, DBL_MAX_10_EXP, DBL_MAX_EXP`

dec ◆ manipulator

Purpose

Use the *dec* C++ stream manipulator to set the conversion base format flag for a stream to decimal. The conversion base is used to control the base used in inputting or displaying numbers using the specified stream.

Syntax

```
#include <iostream.h>
ostream << dec;            set base to decimal for output stream
istream >> dec;            set base to decimal for input stream
```

Example Use

```
int num = &H20;        // set num to hex 20
cout << dec << num;    // outputs value 32 decimal
```

dec is equivalent to *setbase(10)*

See Also

`hex, oct, setbase()`

default ◆ keyword

Purpose

Use *default* as the label in a *switch* statement to mark code that will be executed when none of the *case* labels match the *switch* expression.

Syntax

```
default: <statement; ..>
```

239

Example Use
```
default: printf("Unknown command!\n");
```

See Also
```
case, switch
```

#define ◆ preprocessor definition directive

Purpose

Use the *#define* directive to define a symbol or a macro. A definition such as *#define PI 3.14159* simply tells the preprocessor to replace each occurrence of *PI* in the source code with the numeric literal *3.14159*. A macro is a more flexible definition with one or more parameters that control what is actually put into the source code. For example, *#define SQUARE(x) ((x)*(x))* allows you to use a statement such as *SQUARE(2)* in your code; the result of this statement is to place *((2)*(2))* or 4 in the code. You can redefine a macro with the same expression as often as you want. (Note that ANSI C and C++ prefer the use of the *const* keyword to simple defined values because a *const* is automatically guarded against having its value changed by the program. C++ practice prefers the use of inline functions to macros because the former provide full argument checking.)

Example Use
```
#define ZOOM(v, r)      ((v)*(r))
ZOOM(4, 8)              /* puts 4 * 8 or 32 in the code */
```

See Also
```
# (string-making operator),  ## (token-pasting operator)
```

defined ◆ preprocessor operator

Purpose

Use the *defined* preprocessor operator to determine whether a preprocessor symbol or macro is defined in the current program. Typically, this is used to control conditional compilation.

Syntax
```
#if defined (symbol)       true if symbol is defined
#if !defined (symbol)      true if symbol is not defined
```

Note that *#ifdef* is an alternate form of *#if defined* and *#ifndef* is an alternate form of *#if !defined*.

Example Use
```
#if defined (NON_STANDARD)
    #include "ourdefs.h"
#endif
```

delete ♦ operator

Purpose

Use the *delete* operator to deallocate (free up) the memory being used by an object. You can use the *delete* operator with any standard data type. You can also use it in a destructor to free up an object of a class. *delete* is not usually needed for simple data types that go out of scope, but it is needed when a pointer goes out of scope, because with pointers the object pointed to is not automatically deallocated.

When you *delete* a class object the object's destructor is automatically called. You can overload the *delete* operator to provide special memory management for an object.

Note that *delete* should be used only to free memory that was originally allocated with the *new* operator, and should not be used with objects that were created by ANSI C functions of the *malloc()* family. C++ does guarantee that deleting a 0 (null) pointer will be harmless. You cannot *delete* using a pointer to *const* because a constant cannot be altered.

Syntax

```
delete <pointer>; or
delete <[elements]> <cast expression>;      to delete an array of objects
pointer                                      pointer to object to be deallocated
[elements]                                   number of array elements
```

Example Use

```
delete this_object;          // delete a single object
delete [255] flags;          // delete each of 255 elements of
                             // flags (which could be a simple array or
                             // an array of class objects)
```

Note that C++ 2.0 specifies that you can use empty brackets ([]) to *delete* all elements of an array. Not all compilers currently support this specification, however.

See Also

new, malloc() functions (for ANSI C)

difftime() ♦ function

Purpose

Use the *difftime()* function to compute the difference between two time values *time2* and *time1*, both of type *time_t*.

Syntax

```
#include <time.h>
double difftime(time_t time2, time_t time1);
time_t time2;         Value of time from which time1 will be subtracted
time_t time1;         Value of time to be subtracted from time2
```

Example Use
```
seconds_used = difftime(oldtime, newtime);
```

Returns
The *difftime()* function returns the elapsed time, *time2-time1*, in seconds as a double-precision number.

See Also
```
clock(), time(), time_t
```

div() ♦ function

Purpose
Use the *div()* function to divide the first integer *numer* by the second one *denom* and obtain the resulting quotient and remainder packed in a structure of type *div_t*. The structure of type *div_t* is defined in *stdlib.h* as

```
typedef struct
{
    int quot;     /* The quotient */
    int rem;      /* The remainder */
} div_t;
```

Syntax
```
#include <stdlib.h>
div_t div(int numer, int denom);
int numer;          Numerator
int denom;          Denominator
```

Example Use
```
result = div(32, 5);
/* result.quot = 6 and result.rem = 2 */
```

Returns
The *div()* function returns a structure of type *div_t* containing the quotient and remainder of the division.

See Also
```
ldiv(), div_t
```

div_t ♦ predefined data type

Purpose
The *div_t* data type can hold the value returned by the *div* function. It is defined in *stdlib.h*.

See Also
```
div()
```

do ✦ keyword

Purpose
Use the *do* keyword with *while* to form iterative loops where the statement or statements in the body are executed until the expression evaluates to 0 (false). The expression is evaluated after each execution of the loop body. Note that a *do...while* statement is always executed at least once. Because the entire *do...while* structure counts as a statement, it must end with a semicolon.

Syntax
```
do
{
    statement;
    ...
}
while(condition);
```

if there is only one statement in the body the loop can be written:

```
do statement while (condition);
```

Example Use
```
do
{
    sum += i;
    i++;
}
while(i >= 10);
```

See Also
```
for, if, while
```

double ✦ keyword

Purpose
Use the *double* type specifier to declare double-precision floating-point variables and arrays. In most implementations, the *double* type is stored in twice as many bytes as *float*, though this is not required by the ANSI standard.

Syntax
```
double <varname>;
```

Example Use

```
/* declare a double, a pointer to a
    double, and an array of doubles */
    double d, *p_d, dvars[80];
```

See Also

`char, float, int, long, short, signed, unsigned`

EDOM ◆ predefined value

Purpose

The *EDOM* constant indicates an invalid argument (or "domain") error. It is defined in *errno.h*.

See Also

`ERANGE`

#elif ◆ preprocessor else-if directive

Purpose

Use the *#elif* directive to specify an alternate branch for conditional compilation.

Syntax

See *#if*

Example Use

See *#if*

See Also

`#if, #else, #endif`

else ◆ keyword

Purpose

Use the *else* keyword as part of an *if* statement when you want to specify statements to be executed if the condition is false (0). When *if...else* statements are "nested," a particular *else* is always associated with the first preceding *if* that does not have an *else*.

Syntax

```
if (condition)
    statement_1;
else
    statement_2;
```

where *statement_1* is executed if the *expression* is not equal to zero, otherwise *statement_2* is executed.

Example Use

See *if* for an example.

See Also

```
if, default, #else (preprocessor else operator)
```

#else ◆ preprocessor directive

Purpose

Use the *#else* directive to specify an alternate branch for conditional compilation.

Syntax

See *#if*

Example Use

See *#if*

See Also

```
#if, #elif, #endif
```

#endif ◆ preprocessor directive

Purpose

Use the *#endif* preprocessor directive to mark the end of an *#if* preprocessor directive.

Syntax

See *#if*

Example Use

See *#if*

See Also

```
#if, #else, #elif
```

endl ◆ manipulator

Purpose

Use the *endl* manipulator to send a newline character to a C++ output stream. This action also flushes the line (sends any pending characters in the line to the stream).

Syntax

```
#include <iostream.h>
<output_stream> << endl;
output stream              stream for output (usually cout)
```

Example Use

```
cout << "This is a line." << endl;
```

The example is equivalent to:

```
cout << "This is a line." << "\n";
```

but it is a bit easier to write.

Returns

As with all manipulators, *endl* returns a reference to the stream object, allowing cascading of output.

See Also

ends, flush, \n (escape sequence for newline)

ends ◆ manipulator

Purpose

Use the *ends* manipulator to insert the string-terminating null character (ASCII 0) and flush pending characters. You can use this to create an "official" C/C++ string from a series of characters.

Syntax

```
#include <iostream.h>
<output_stream> << ends;
output stream              stream for output
```

Example Use

```
ofstream names;   // set up an output stream
for (int str = 1; str <= numstrs; str++)
        names << phrases[str] << ends;
```

Each phrase in the char array *phrases* is sent to the output and followed by a string terminator. The result is a file of strings.

Returns

As with all manipulators, *ends* returns a reference to the stream object, allowing cascading of output.

See Also

endl

enum ♦ keyword

Purpose

Use the *enum* keyword to define a set of related values, often values that are considered to be in a particular order. This is an integral data type that can take its values from a list of enumerated constants.

Syntax

```
enum identifier { enumerated_list };    declare an enumerated type
                                        and a list of values
enum identifier var1, var2;             declare two variables to be of this type
```

Example Use

```
/* make traffic_signal the name of an enumerated type, with the values red,
yellow, and green */
enum traffic_signal {red = 10, yellow = 20, green = 30};

/* declare signal_1 to be a variable of the traffic_signal type and p_signal
to be a pointer to data of the traffic_signal type */

enum traffic_signal signal_1, *p_signal;
```

See Also

typedef

EOF ♦ predefined value

Purpose

The *EOF* integer constant indicates "end-of-file." It usually has a value of –1, and is defined in *stdio.h*.

Example Use

```
while (datafile.get(ch) != EOF)
        cout << ch;
```

See Also

eof() (C++ member function)

eof() ♦ function

Purpose

Use the *eof()* ios member function with a C++ input stream (*istream*) to determine whether you have reached the end of the file.

Syntax

```
#include <iostream.h>
int eof()
<input_stream>.eof()
```

Example Use

```
while (!cin.eof())
{
// process the file
}
```

The expression *!cin.eof()* becomes false when *eof()* returns a "true" value indicating end of file. The *while* loop is then exited, ending processing of the file.

Returns

The *eof()* function returns a nonzero (true) value if the end of the file has been reached (as indicated by the *eofbit ios* status bit having been set). Otherwise, *eof()* returns a zero (false).

See Also

`ios, bad(), fail(), ! and * (stream status operators)`

errno ♦ predefined value

Purpose

The *errno* predefined variable is a code indicating the last error that occurred. It is defined in *errno.h* and the values are dependent on the compiler and operating system. Some commonly encountered values under MS-DOS are shown in Table 10-1.

Table 10-1

CONSTANT	VALUE	MEANING
ENOENT	2	No such file or directory
ENOPATH	3	Path not found
EMFILE	4	Too many open files
EACCES	5	Permission denied
EBADF	6	Bad file number
EINVDRV	15	Invalid drive specified
ECURDIR	16	Attempted to remove current directory
ENMFILE	18	No more files
EEXIST	35	File already exists

See Also
```
perror(), cerr, clog
```

#error ◆ preprocessor directive

Purpose
Use the *#error* preprocessor directive to produce a diagnostic message during compilation.

Syntax
```
#error <message text>
```

Example Use
```
#if defined(WRONG_OPTION)
    #error Recompile with correct option
#endif
```

See Also
```
#if, #else, #elif, #endif, defined
```

exit() ◆ function

Purpose
Use the *exit()* function to terminate your program normally by flushing file buffers, closing files, and invoking functions set up with *atexit()*. A value of 0 or EXIT_SUCCESS for *status* means a normal exit, whereas the value of EXIT_FAILURE is used to indicate errors.

Syntax
```
#include <stdlib.h>
void exit(int status);
int status;              Exit status code
```

Example Use
```
exit(EXIT_SUCCESS);
```

See Also
```
abort(), atexit(), EXIT_FAILURE, EXIT_SUCCESS
```

EXIT_FAILURE ◆ predefined value

Purpose
The *EXIT_FAILURE* status code can be used with *exit()* to indicate that the program ended with an error. It is defined in *stdlib.h*.

See Also
EXIT_SUCCESS

EXIT_SUCCESS ✦ predefined value

Purpose
The *EXIT_SUCCESS* status code can be used with *exit()* to indicate that the program executed successfully. It is defined in *stdlib.h*.

See Also
EXIT_FAILURE

exp() ✦ function

Purpose
Use the *exp()* function to compute the exponential of the *double* variable x. The exponential of a variable x is e^x where e is the base of natural logarithms (e = 2.7182818).

Syntax
```
#include <math.h>
double exp(double x);
double x;           Variable whose exponential is to be computed
```

Example Use
```
y = exp(x);
```

Returns
Normally, *exp* returns the exponential of x. If the value of the result is too large, a range error occurs.

See Also
log

extern ✦ keyword

Purpose
Use the *extern* keyword to tell the compiler that a variable or a function is defined in another module (a separate file) and that you want to use it in the current module. The data item or function must be declared in one of the program modules without the *static* or the *extern* qualifier.

Syntax
```
extern <type> <varname>;
```

Example Use

```
/* In the example below the variables current_state and state_table are
shared between FILE 1 and FILE 2. They are defined in FILE 1, and declared
to be extern in FILE 2 */

/* FILE1 */
int current_state, state_table[MAXSTATE][MAXSYMB];

/* following is reference to variable declared in file2 */
extern void next_state(int in_symbol);
main()
{
  int in_symbol;
  ...
  current_state = 0;
  next_state(in_symbol);
  ...
}

/*   FILE2 */
void next_state(int in_symbol)
{
/* following declaration is referenced in file1 */
extern int current_state,state_table[MAXSTATE] [MAXSYMB];
if ( current_state == 0 ) ...
   ...
   current_state = state_table[current_state]
   [in_symbol];
   ...
}
```

See Also
static

\f ◆ escape sequence for form feed

Purpose

Use the \f (form feed) escape sequence to start a new page on the printer. On most systems the form feed displays as a single character rather than affecting the screen display.

Example Use

```
printf("%s", footer);
printf('\f'); /* start a new page */
printf("%s", header);
```

See Also
printf(), cout, form), << (insertion stream operator)

fabs() ◆ function

Purpose
Use the *fabs()* function to obtain the absolute value of its argument, which must be a double value.

Syntax
```
#include <math.h>
double fabs(double x);
double x;          Variable whose absolute value is to be returned
```

Example Use
```
y = fabs(-5.15); /* y will be 5.15 */
```

Returns
The return value is of type *double* with a positive value which is the absolute value of *x*.

See Also
abs()

fail() ◆ function

Purpose
Use the *fail()* ios member function to check whether a C++ file stream access has encountered an error.

Syntax
```
#include <iostream.h>
<input_stream>.fail();
Example Use
istream input; // input stream
...
if (input.fail()) handle_error();
// deal with error if encountered
```

Returns
The *fail()* function returns a nonzero (true) value if the *ios failbit*, *badbit*, or *hardfail* status bit has been set, indicating an error. Otherwise, *fail()* returns a 0 (false).

See Also
```
ios, bad(), eof(), ! and * (stream status operators)
```

fclose() ◆ function

Purpose
Use the *fclose()* function to close the ANSI C stream specified by *stream*. If the stream was open for writing, the contents of the buffer associated with the stream is written to the file ("flushed") before the file is closed. If it was open for reading, any unread data in the buffer are discarded. Note that you should use the member function *close()* to close a C++ file stream.

Syntax
```
#include <stdio.h>
int fclose(FILE *stream);
FILE *stream;              Pointer to stream to be closed
```

Example Use
```
fclose(infile);
```

Returns
fclose() returns 0 if the stream was successfully closed; otherwise, it returns EOF.

See Also
```
fopen(), fflush(), EOF, FILE
```

feof() ◆ function

Purpose
Use the *feof()* function to determine whether *stream*'s end-of-file indicator is set. When an error is returned from a read operation, you can call *feof()* to determine if the error occurred because you tried to read past the end-of-file. Note: You should use *eof()* or another *ios* status function to check for end-of-file on a C++ stream.

Syntax
```
#include <stdio.h>
int feof(FILE *stream);
FILE *stream;              Pointer to FILE data structure associated
                           with the stream whose status is being checked
```

Example Use
```
if (feof(infile) != 0) printf("File ended\n");
```

Returns
feof() returns a nonzero if and only if the end-of-file indicator is set for *stream*.

See Also
```
clearerr(), ferror(), rewind(), FILE; ios (for C++ streams)
```

ferror() ♦ function

Purpose
Use *ferror()* to determine if the error indicator is set for the specified *stream*. Note that you should use *ios* member functions to check for errors in C++ streams.

Syntax
```
#include <stdio.h>
int ferror(FILE *stream);
FILE *stream;            Pointer to FILE data structure associated
                         with the stream whose status is being checked
```

Example Use
```
if (ferror(infile) != 0) printf("Error detected\n");
```

Returns
ferror() returns a nonzero value if and only if the error indicator is set for *stream*.

See Also
```
clearerr(), feof(), FILE, ios (for C++ streams)
```

fflush() ♦ function

Purpose
Use the *fflush()* function to flush the current contents of the buffer associated with the ANSI C stream specified by *stream*. If the file is open for write operations, the "flushing" involves writing the contents of the buffer to the file. Otherwise, the buffer is cleared. If *stream* is NULL, the flushing action is performed on all open streams. Note that this function is used with C streams, not C++ streams, for which the *flush()* manipulator can be used.

Syntax
```
#include <stdio.h>
int fflush(FILE *stream);
FILE *stream;            Pointer to stream whose buffer is being flushed
```

Example Use
```
fflush(stdin);
```

Returns

If the flushing is successful, *fflush* returns a 0. In case of an error, it returns the constant EOF defined in *stdio.h*.

See Also
```
fopen(), fclose(), setbuf(), setvbuf(), EOF, FILE, NULL
```

fgetc() ♦ function

Purpose

Use *fgetc* to read a single character from the ANSI C stream specified by the pointer *stream*. The character is read from the current position in the stream. After reading the character, the current position is advanced to the next character. Note: This function is used with C streams, not C++ streams.

Syntax
```
#include <stdio.h>
int fgetc(FILE *stream);
FILE *stream;          Pointer to stream from which a character is to be read
```

Example Use
```
char_read = fgetc(infile);
```

Returns

If there are no errors, *fgetc()* returns the character read, as an unsigned char converted to an *int*. Otherwise, it returns the constant *EOF*. You should call *ferror()* and *feof()* to determine if there really was an error or the file simply reached its end.

See Also
```
getc(), getchar(), fputc(), putc(), putchar(), EOF, FILE, stdin
```

fgetpos() ♦ function

Purpose

Use the *fgetpos()* function to get and save the current position indicator of the stream specified by the argument *stream* in the *fpos_t* data object *current_pos*. This value can be used only by the companion function *fsetpos()* to reposition the stream to its position at the time of the call to *fgetpos()*. Note: This function is used with C streams, not with C++ streams, for which the functions *tellp()* and *tellg()* can be used.

Syntax

```
#include <stdio.h>
int fgetpos(FILE *stream, fpos_t *current_pos);
FILE *stream;                   Pointer to stream whose current position is
                                requested
fpos_t *current_pos;            Pointer to variable where file's current
                                position is requested
```

Example Use

```
fgetpos(infile, &curpos);
```

Returns

If successful, *fgetpos()* returns a 0. In case of error, it returns a nonzero value and sets the global variable *errno* to an implementation-defined error constant.

See Also

```
fsetpos(), errno, fpos_t
```

fgets() ◆ function

Purpose

Use the *fgets()* function to read a line from the ANSI C stream specified by *stream*. The line is read into the character array *string* until a newline (\n) character is encountered, an end-of-file condition occurs, or the number of characters read reaches one less than the value given in the argument *maxchar*. A null character is written to *string* immediately after the last character. Note that the equivalent function for C++ file streams is *getline()*.

Syntax

```
#include <stdio.h>
char *fgets(char *string, int maxchar, FILE *stream);
char *string;                   Pointer to buffer where characters will be stored
int maxchar;                    Maximum number of characters that can be stored
FILE *stream;                   Pointer to stream from which a line is read
```

Example Use

```
fgets(buffer, 80, infile);
```

Returns

If there are no errors, *fgets()* returns the argument *string*. Otherwise, it returns a NULL. You can call *ferror()* and *feof()* to determine whether the error is genuine or it occurred because the file reached its end.

See Also

```
gets(), fputs(), puts(), FILE, NULL
```

CHAPTER 10   ALPHABETICAL REFERENCE

FILE ✦ predefined data type

Purpose

The *FILE* data type contains the information needed to perform standard C file I/O. It is defined in *stdio.h*. Note that in C++ the stream functions defined in *iostream.h* are preferred.

See Also

`EOF, FILENAME_MAX`

_ _FILE_ _ ✦ predefined macro

Purpose

Use the _ _*FILE*_ _ predefined macro to display the name of the source file being translated by the preprocessor.

Example Use

```
printf("Now preprocessing: ");
printf(_ _FILE_ _);
```

See Also

`_ _DATE_ _, _ _TIME_ _, _ _LINE_ _, _ _STDC_ _`

filebuf ✦ class

Purpose

The *filebuf* class is derived from the *streambuf* class and adds data structures and member functions needed to adapt the general stream buffer mechanism to files. *filebuf* is defined in *fstream.h*.

See Also

`streambuf, ios, iostream.h, fstream.h`

FILENAME_MAX ✦ predefined value

Purpose

The *FILENAME_MAX* predefined value gives the maximum length of a filename string, and is dependent on the operating system in use. It is defined in *stdio.h*.

See Also

`FILE`

fill() function

Purpose

Use the *fill()* ios member function to set the character that will be used to fill leading spaces in numeric quantities. By default the fill character is a space.

Syntax

```
#include <iostream.h>
fill();                          returns fill character
fill(<char>);                    to set fill character and return old fill
                                 character
```

Example Use

```
char fchar = fill();             // store old fill char. in fchar
fill('*');                       // set fill char to *
int check_amount = 1000;
cout.width(8);                   // set number width to 8
cout << check_amount;            // displays ****1000
```

The way a number is padded is also affected by the settings of *ios* format flags such as *ios::width*, which is set to 8 by the *width()* manipulator. The *ios::adjustfield* flag determines where numbers will be padded by specifying their justification; *ios::left* can also be used for left justification (padding to right) or *ios::right* for right justification (padding to left).

The *setfill()* function can also be used to specify a fill character. This function takes an *int* or *const char* value.

Returns

If *fill()* is called without an argument, it returns the current fill character. If it is called with an argument, it sets the fill character to that argument and also returns the previous fill character. Therefore, the previous example could be written:

```
char fchar = fill ('*');
```

See Also

```
ios (formatting flags), width(), setfill()
```

flags() function

Purpose

Use the *flags()* ios member function to return and/or set the *ios* formatting flags for a C++ stream. The *ios* formatting flags are listed in the entry for *ios*. Typically, you set flags by providing a value of type *long* that provides a *mask value* that sets one or more flags while leaving the remaining ones untouched.

Syntax

```
<stream_name>.flags();           to get current flags
<stream.name>.flags(<longval>);  to set flags and return previous flag values
```

Example Use

```
long old_flags = cout.flags(); // get current flags
cout.flags(old_flags ^ ios::dec | ios::hex | ios::showbase);
```

All conflicting flags have to be accounted for when *flags()* is used. First, the old flags are saved by getting them from a call to *flags()* with no argument. The next call to *flags()* uses the bitwise exclusive OR operator (^) to clear the flag for decimal output. This is then *ORed* with the flags for hex output and for displaying the base, to provide the desired output.

As a practical matter, the *setf()* and *unsetf()* functions are easier and more convenient to use because they allow you to specify just the flag you want to set or clear, and they take care of the "bit-twiddling" for you. The *setiosflags()* and *resetiosflags()* functions provide yet another way to set or clear *ios* format flags.

Returns

When called without an argument, *flags()* returns the current *long* value containing the flag settings. When called with a *long* argument (normally a logical expression using the predefined *ios* mask values as shown), *flags()* returns the *previous long* flag value.

See Also

```
ios (formatting flags), setf(), unsetf(), setiosflags(), resetiosflags()
```

float ◆ keyword

Purpose

Use the *float* data type specifier to declare single-precision floating-point variables and arrays.

Syntax

```
float <varname>;
```

Example Use

```
/* declare a float, a pointer to a
    float, and an array of float */
float f, *p_f, fvars[100];
```

See Also

```
char, double, int, long, short, signed, unsigned
```

floor() ♦ function

Purpose
Use the *floor()* function to get the "floor" of a *double* argument x. The "floor" is the largest integral value that is less than or equal to x. This can be used in rounding a double down to the preceding integer.

Syntax
```
#include <math.h>
double floor(double x);
double x;                    Variable whose "floor" is to be returned
```

Example Use
```
x = floor(4.15);   /* x will be 4.0 */
```

Returns
The return value is the "floor" of x expressed as a *double*.

See Also
```
ceil()
```

FLT_DIG ♦ predefined value

Purpose
The *FLT_DIG* predefined value gives the number of significant decimal digits in a *float* value. It is defined in *float.h*.

See Also
```
FLT_EPSILON, FLT_MANT_DIG, FLT_MIN, FLT_MIN_10_EXP, FLT_MIN_EXP, FLT_MAX,
FLT_MAX_10_EXP, FLT_MAX_EXP, FLT_RADIX
```

FLT_EPSILON ♦ predefined value

Purpose
The *FLT_EPSILON* predefined value gives the smallest positive *float* value such that 1+x != 1. It is defined in *float.h*.

See Also
```
FLT_DIG, FLT_MANT_DIG, FLT_MIN, FLT_MIN_10_EXP, FLT_MIN_EXP, FLT_MAX,
FLT_MAX_10_EXP, FLT_MAX_EXP, FLT_RADIX
```

FLT_MANT_DIG ✦ predefined value

Purpose

The *FLT_MANT_DIG* predefined value gives the number of base *FLT_RADIX* digits in the mantissa of a *float*. It is defined in *float.h*.

See Also

`FLT_DIG, FLT_EPSILON, FLT_MIN, FLT_MIN_10_EXP, FLT_MIN_10, FLT_MAX, FLT_MAX_10_EXP, FLT_MAX_EXP, FLT_RADIX`

FLT_MAX ✦ predefined value

Purpose

The *FLT_MAX* predefined value gives the maximum, representable finite value that can be stored in a *float*. It is defined in *float.h*.

See Also

`FLT_DIG, FLT_MANT_DIG, FLT_EPSILON, FLT_MIN, FLT_MIN_10_EXP, FLT_MIN_10, FLT_MAX_10_EXP, FLT_MAX_EXP, FLT_RADIX`

FLT_MAX_10_EXP ✦ predefined value

Purpose

The *FLT_MAX_10_EXP* predefined value gives the maximum integer such that 10 raised to that power is representable in a *float*. It is defined in *float.h*.

See Also

`FLT_DIG, FLT_MANT_DIG, FLT_EPSILON, FLT_MIN, FLT_MIN_10_EXP, FLT_MIN_EXP, FLT_MAX, FLT_MAX_EXP, FLT_RADIX`

FLT_MAX_EXP ✦ predefined value

Purpose

The *FLT_MAX_EXP* predefined value gives the maximum integer such that *FLT_RADIX* raised to that power is representable in a *float*. It is defined in *float.h*.

See Also

`FLT_DIG, FLT_MANT_DIG, FLT_EPSILON, FLT_MIN, FLT_MIN_10_EXP, FLT_MIN_EXP, FLT_MAX, FLT_MAX_10_EXP, FLT_RADIX`

FLT_MIN ♦ predefined value

Purpose

The *FLT_MIN* predefined value gives the minimum, positive floating-point number that can be stored in a *float*. It is defined in *float.h*.

See Also

`FLT_DIG, FLT_MANT_DIG, FLT_EPSILON, FLT_MIN_10_EXP, FLT_MIN_EXP, FLT_MAX, FLT_MAX_10_EXP, FLT_MAX_EXP, FLT_RADIX`

FLT_MIN_10_EXP ♦ predefined value

Purpose

The *FLT_MIN_10_EXP* predefined value gives the minimum negative integer such that 10 raised to that power is representable in a *float*. It is defined in *float.h*.

See Also

`FLT_DIG, FLT_MANT_DIG, FLT_EPSILON, FLT_MIN, FLT_MIN_EXP, FLT_MAX, FLT_MAX_10_EXP, FLT_MAX_EXP, FLT_RADIX`

FLT_MIN_EXP ♦ predefined value

Purpose

The *FLT_MIN_EXP* predefined value gives the minimum negative integer such that FLT_RADIX raised to that power minus 1 is representable in a *float*. It is defined in *float.h*.

See Also

`FLT_DIG, FLT_MANT_DIG, FLT_EPSILON, FLT_MIN, FLT_MIN_10_EXP, FLT_MAX, FLT_MAX_10_EXP, FLT_MAX_EXP, FLT_RADIX`

FLT_RADIX ♦ predefined value

Purpose

The *FLT_RADIX* predefined value gives the radix of the exponent used for numeric representation (usually 2 for binary exponent). It is defined in *float.h*.

See Also

`FLT_DIG, FLT_MANT_DIG, FLT_EPSILON, FLT_MIN, FLT_MIN_EXP, FLT_MIN_10_EXP, FLT_MAX, FLT_MAX_10_EXP, FLT_MAX_EXP`

FLT_ROUNDS ✦ predefined value

Purpose

The *FLT_ROUNDS* predefined value gives a constant that indicates how floating-point values are rounded. The possible values are −1 (indeterminate), 0 (toward 0), 1 (to nearest representable value), 2 (toward positive infinity), and 3 (toward negative infinity). It is defined in *float.h*.

See Also

FLT_DIG, FLT_MANT_DIG, FLT_EPSILON, FLT_MIN, FLT_MIN_EXP, FLT_MIN_10_EXP, FLT_MAX, FLT_MAX_10_EXP, FLT_MAX_EXP, FLT_RADIX

flush ✦ manipulator

Purpose

Use the *flush* C++ stream manipulator to flush an output stream (that is, send any data waiting in the stream buffer to the file).

Syntax

```
#include <iostream.h>
<output_stream> << flush;
```

Example Use

```
cout << flush;   // send remaining data to output
```

Returns

As with all manipulators, *flush* returns a reference to the stream so that it can be "cascaded" with other output.

See Also

endl, ends, close()

fmod() ✦ function

Purpose

Use the *fmod()* function to compute the floating-point remainder after dividing the floating-point number *x* by *y* and ensuring that the quotient is the largest possible integral value. If this quotient is *n*, then *fmod()* returns the value *r* computed from the expression r = x − n*y. The entire operation is equivalent to:

```
double n, r;
...
...
n = floor(x/y);
r = x - n*y;
```

Syntax

```
#include <math.h>
double fmod(double x, double y);
double x, y;                The remainder after the division x/y is returned
```

Example Use

```
rem = fmod(24.95, 5.5); /* rem will be 2.95 */
```

Returns

When *y* is zero, *fmod()* returns a zero. Otherwise, it returns the remainder as previously described.

See Also

floor()

fopen() ♦ function

Purpose

Use the *fopen()* function to open the file whose name is in the string *filename* and associate a stream with it. The argument *access_mode* contains one of the strings in Table 10-2.

Table 10-2

ACCESS_MODE	INTERPRETATION
"r"	Open a text file for reading. Fail if file does not exist.
"w"	If file exists, open and truncate it to zero length. Otherwise, create the file and open it for writing in the text mode.
"a"	Open text file for appending—writing at the end of file. Create file if it does not already exist.
"rb"	Same as "r," but binary mode.
"wb"	Same as "w," but binary mode.
"ab"	Same as "a," but binary mode.
"r+"	Open text file for updating—reading as well as writing.
"w+"	If file exists, open it and truncate it to zero length. Otherwise, create it and open it for updating.
"a+"	Open text file for appending. Create file if it does not already exist.
"r+b" or "rb+"	Open binary file for updating.
"w+b" or "wb+"	If file exists, truncate to zero length; else create a binary file for update operations.
"a+b" or "ab+"	Open or create binary file for appending.

Note that the *fopen()* function is used with C file streams, not C++ streams. Use the *ios* member function *open()* to open a C++ file stream.

Syntax
```
#include <stdio.h>
FILE *fopen(const char *filename, const char *access_mode);
const char   *filename;       Name of file to be opened
const char   *access_mode;    A character string denoting whether file is
                              being opened for read, write, or append
```

Example Use
```
input_file = fopen("data.in", "rb");
```

Returns
If the file is successfully opened, *fopen()* returns a pointer to the FILE data structure that controls the stream. The FILE structure is allocated elsewhere and you do not have to allocate it. In case of an error, *fopen()* returns NULL.

See Also
`fclose(), freopen(), setbuf(), setvbuf(), FILE, NULL`

FOPEN_MAX ✦ predefined value

Purpose
The *FOPEN_MAX* predefined value gives the maximum number of files that can be open simultaneously. This value is dependent on the operating system. It is defined in *stdio.h*.

See Also
`BUFSIZ, FILENAME_MAX`

for ✦ keyword

Purpose
Use the *for* keyword to create a loop that will be executed a specified number of times. Usually an index variable is set to a starting value and progressively varied each time the body of the loop is executed. The index variable is compared to a specified condition before each execution of the loop body. When the condition is satisfied (evaluates as 1 or true), the body of the loop is not executed and control resumes with the statement following the end of the loop.

Syntax
```
for (initialization; condition; varying statement);
```

where the *initialization* is evaluated once at the beginning of the loop, and the *varying statement* is executed until the *condition* evaluates to 0 (false). The statement for varying the loop index is evaluated after each execution of *statement*.

Example Use
```
/* add the numbers from 1 to limit, all inside
   the loop specifications */

for(i=0, sum=0; i <= limit; sum += i, i++);
   printf("\nSum from 1 to %d = %d\n", limit, sum);
```

Notice that there can be more than one statement in each part of the loop specification, with successive statements in a group being separated with commas. Here the initialization is i = 0, sum = 0; and the varying statements are sum + = i, i ++.

A *for* loop does not need to have a statement in the body; if the *printf()* statement in the preceding example were omitted, the loop would still function correctly and accumulate the sum.

See Also
```
break, continue, if, switch, , (sequential evaluation operator)
```

form()   function

Purpose
The *form()* function was provided in C++ 1.2 as a general-purpose formatting facility. It accepted essentially the same specifiers as the *sprintf()* C library function. Because *form()* is no longer supported in C++ 2.X, the expanded range of overloaded versions of the extraction and insertion operators and manipulators should be used to construct the desired format.

See Also
```
<< and >> operators, cout, cin, get(), getline(), read(), readline(), setf(),
unset(), sprintf()
```

fpos_t   predefined data type

Purpose
The *fpos_t* data type contains information enabling the specification of each unique position in a file. It is defined in *stdio.h*.

See Also
```
fseek(), ftell()
```

fprintf() ✦ function

Purpose

Use the *fprintf()* function to format and write character strings and values of variables to the stream specified by the argument *stream*. See reference entry for *printf()* for a description of the argument *format_string*. Note that this function is used with C streams, not C++ streams, which use *ios* member functions such as *write()* or the insertion operator <<.

Syntax

```
#include <stdio.h>
int fprintf(FILE *stream, const char * format _string,...);
FILE *stream;                    Pointer to output stream
const char *format_string;       A character string which describes the
                                 format to be used
...                              A variable number of arguments depending on
                                 the number of items being printed
```

Example Use

```
fprintf(resultfile, "The result is %f\n", result);
```

Returns

The *fprintf()* function returns the number of characters it has printed. In case of error, it returns a negative value.

See Also

```
printf(), vfprintf(), vprintf(), sprintf(), vsprintf(), FILE, <<, write()
(C++ streams)
```

fputc() ✦ function

Purpose

Use *fputc()* to write the single character *c* to the stream specified by *stream*. Note that this function is used with C streams, not C++ streams, which use *ios* member functions such as *put()*.

Syntax

```
#include <stdio.h>
int fputc(int c, FILE *stream);
int c;                Character to be written
FILE *stream;         Pointer to output stream
```

Example Use

```
fputc('X', p_datafile);
```

Returns

If there are no errors, *fputc()* returns the character written. Otherwise, it returns the constant *EOF*. You should call *ferror()* to determine if there really was an error or if the integer argument *c* just happened to be equal to EOF.

See Also

fgetc(), getc(), getchar(), putc(), puts(), EOF, FILE, put() (C++ streams)

---

fputs()   ◆   function

Purpose

Use the *fputs()* function to write the C string given by *string* to the stream specified by *stream*. Note that this function is used with C streams, not C++ streams, which can use the insertion operator << for this purpose.

Syntax

```
#include <stdio.h>
int fputs(const char *string, FILE *stream);
const char *string;        Null ('\0') terminated character string to be output
FILE *stream;              Pointer to stream to which the string is output
```

Example Use

```
fputs("Sample Input Data", p_datafile);
```

Returns

The *fputs()* function returns a nonnegative value if all goes well. In case of error, it returns the constant EOF.

See Also

fgets(), gets(), puts(), EOF, FILE, << (C++ streams)

---

fread()   ◆   function

Purpose

Use the *fread()* function to read the number of data items specified by *count*, each of the size given by the argument *size*, from the current position in *stream*. The current position of *stream* is updated after the read. Note that this function is used with C streams, not C++ streams.

Syntax

```
#include <stdio.h>
size_t fread(void *buffer, size_t size, size_t count,
                           FILE *stream);
void *buffer;              Pointer to buffer where fread will store
                           the bytes it reads
```

```
size_t size;            Size in bytes of each data item
size_t count;           Maximum number of items to be read
FILE *stream;           Pointer to stream from which data items
                        are to be read
```

Example Use
```
numread = fread(buffer, sizeof(char), 80, infile);
```

Returns

The *fread()* function returns the number of items it successfully read. If the return value is less than you expected, you can call *ferror()* and *feof()* to determine if a read error has occurred or if end-of-file has been reached.

See Also
```
fopen(), fwrite(), fclose(), FILE, size_t
```

free() ♦ function

Purpose

Use the *free()* function to deallocate (return to the pool of free memory) a block of memory which was allocated earlier by *malloc()*, *calloc()*, or *realloc()*. The address of the block is specified by the argument *mem_address*, which is a pointer to the starting byte of the block. A *NULL* pointer argument is ignored by *free()*. Note that C++ objects are normally deallocated via their class destructor and the *delete* operator.

Syntax
```
#include <stdlib.h>
void free(void *mem_address);
void *mem_address;          Pointer to block of memory to be released
```

Example Use
```
free(buffer);
```

See Also
```
calloc(), malloc(), realloc(), NULL, delete (C++ objects)
```

freopen() ♦ function

Purpose

Use the *freopen()* function to close *stream* and open another file whose name is in the string *filename* and attach *stream* to it. For example, you can use *freopen()* to redirect I/O from the preopened file *stdout* to a file of your choice. See *fopen()* for a description of the argument *access_mode*. The error indicator of *stream* will be cleared after the reopening. Note that this function is used for C streams, not C++ streams.

Syntax

```
#include <stdio.h>
FILE *freopen(const char *filename, const char *access_mode, FILE *stream);
const char *filename;          Name of file to be reopened including
                               drive and directory specification
const char *access_mode;       A character string denoting whether file is
                               being reopened for read, write, or append
FILE *stream;                  Pointer to stream to be reopened
```

Example Use

```
freopen("output.txt", "w", stdout);
/* Redirect stdout to a file */
```

Returns

If all goes well, *freopen()* returns a pointer to the newly opened file. This returned pointer will be the same as the argument *stream*. In case of error, a NULL is returned.

See Also

```
fopen(), fclose(), FILE, NULL, stdout
```

frexp() ✦ function

Purpose

Use the *frexp()* function to break down the floating-point number x into a mantissa m whose absolute value lies between 0.5 and 1.0, and an integer exponent n, so that $x = m\,2^n$. The integer exponent n is stored by *frexp()* in the location whose address is given in the argument *expptr*. If x is zero, the exponent will also be zero.

Syntax

```
#include <math.h>
double frexp(double x, int *expptr);
double x;              Floating-point argument to be decomposed
int *expptr;           Pointer to an integer where the exponent
                       will be returned
```

Example Use

```
mantissa = frexp(5.1, &exponent);
/* mantissa will be 0.6375, exponent = 3 */
```

Returns

Normally, *frexp()* returns the mantissa m computed as previously described. When x is zero, *frexp()* returns zero as the mantissa.

See Also

```
ldexp(), modf()
```

fscanf() ♦ function

Purpose

Use the *fscanf()* function to read characters from *stream*, convert them to values according to format specifications embedded in the argument *format_string*, and finally store the values into variables whose addresses are provided in the variable length argument list. See *scanf()* for more details on the argument *format_string*. Note that this function is normally used with C streams. Use *ios* member functions such as *getline()* with C++ streams.

Syntax

```
#include <stdio.h>
int fscanf(FILE *stream, const char* format_string,...);
FILE *stream;                     Pointer to the stream from which reading
                                  will occur
const char *format_string;        A character string which describes
                                  the format to be used
...                               Variable number of arguments representing
                                  addresses of variables whose values are being read
```

Example Use

```
fscanf(infile, "Date: %d/%d/%d", &month, &day,&year);
```

Returns

The *fscanf()* function returns the number of input items that were successfully read, converted, and saved in variables. The count does not include items that were read and ignored. If an end-of-file is encountered during read, the return value will be equal to the constant EOF (defined in *stdio.h*).

See Also

```
scanf(), sscanf(), eof(), FILE, getline() (C++ streams)
```

fseek() ♦ function

Purpose

Use the *fseek()* function to reposition *stream* to the location specified by *offset* with respect to the argument *origin*. The constants which are valid values of *origin* are shown in Table 10-3.

Table 10-3

ORIGIN	INTERPRETATION OF CONSTANT
SEEK_SET	Beginning of file
SEEK_CUR	Current position in the file
SEEK_END	End of file

Note that the *fseek()* function is used with C streams, not C++ streams. For C++ streams, use *ios* member functions *seekg()* (to set the read position) or *seekp* (to set the write position).

Syntax
```
#include <stdio.h>=
int fseek(FILE *stream, long offset, int origin);
FILE *stream;            Pointer to stream whose current position
                         is to be set
long offset;             Offset of new position (in bytes) from origin
int origin;              A constant indicating the position from
                         which to offset
```

Example Use
```
fseek(infile, 0L, SEEK_SET); /* Go to the beginning*/
```

Returns
fseek() returns a nonzero value only if it fails to position the stream.

See Also
```
fgetpos(), fsetpos(), ftell(), FILE, SEEK_SET, SEEK_CUR, SEEK_END, seekg(),
seekp() (for C++ streams)
```

fsetpos() ♦ function

Purpose
Use the *fsetpos()* function to set the position where reading or writing will take place in *stream*. The new position is specified in a *fpos_t* data object whose address is in *current_pos*. For file position, you should use a value obtained by an earlier call to *fgetpos()*. Note that this function is used with C streams, not C++ streams. Use *seekg()* to set the read position for a C++ stream, or *seekp()* to set the write position.

Syntax
```
#include <stdio.h>
int fsetpos(FILE *stream, const fpos_t *current_pos);
FILE *stream;                 Pointer to stream whose current position
                              is to be set
const fpos_t *current_pos;    Pointer to location containing new value of
                              file position
```

Example Use
```
fsetpos(infile, &curpos);
```

Returns
If successful, *fsetpos()* clears the end-of-file indicator of *stream*, and returns zero. Otherwise, the return value will be nonzero and the global variable *errno* will be set to an implementation-defined error constant.

See Also
fgetpos(), FILE, errno, fpos_t, setg(), setp() (C++ streams)

fstream ♦ class

Purpose
Use the *fstream* class to declare a stream object for use with a file. The *fstream* class is derived from the *fstreambase* and *iostream* classes. See the *ios* and *open()* entries for more information on opening files, and the *istream* and *ostream* entries for more information on input and output files.

Syntax
```
#include <fstream.h>
fstream <object_name> ; or
fstream <handle_no>; or
fstream <object_name>, <"filename">, <ios::mode>, <filebuf::mode>;
object_name              name of stream object in program
handle_no                integer handle number (e.g., for DOS)
"filename"               filename acceptable to operating system
ios::open_mode           read, write, etc. mode (see ios entry)
                         (optional; default is ios::in)
filebuf::mode            file protection mode (always filebuf::openprot in
                         current DOS implementations; check for others)
```

If you declare an *fstream* with just the object name, you must use the *fstream* ::open() function to open the file before use. The use of a file handle number assumes that this handle has already been set up with the operating system. Because there is currently only one file protection mode in *filebuf* and the constructor defaults to it, you normally don't have to use this parameter at all.

Example Use
```
fstream test_input;                         // create object, must open file
                                            // before use
fstream(5);                                 // use file handle 5 in operating
                                            // system
fstream(input, "datafile");                 // create object "input"
                                            // and associate it with
                                            // "datafile" on disk
fstream(datastream, "specdev", ios::binary); //
                                            // declare object "datastream",
                                            // associate it with actual file
                                            // "specdev", and open in
                                            // explicit binary mode
```

See Also
iostream.h, ios, fstream.h, fstreambase, istream, ostream

fstreambase ♦ class

Purpose

The *fstreambase* is, as the name suggests, the base class for *fstream*, providing file-related facilities and declared in *fstream.h*. *fstreambase* is derived from the more general *ios* class. In turn the input file (*ifstream*) is derived from *fstreambase* and *istream*, and the output file (*ofstream*) classes are dervied from *fstreambase* and *ostream*.

Syntax
```
#include <fstream.h>
```

See Also
```
ios, filebuf, fstream, ifstream, ofstream
```

fstream.h ♦ header file

Purpose

Use the *fstream.h* header file to include the file-related classes such as *ifstream* and *ofstream* and member functions such as *close()* and *open()*. Because the *fstream.h* header file includes the directive *#include <iostream.h>*, you do not need to include *iostream.h* separately in order to use the general *ios* formatting and stream state functions.

Syntax
```
#include <fstream.h>
```

See Also
```
iostream.h, stream.h, iomanip.h, filebuf
```

ftell() ♦ function

Purpose

Use the *ftell()* function to obtain the current position of *stream*. The position is expressed as a byte offset from the beginning of the file. Note that this function is used with C streams, not C++ streams. Use *tellg()* to obtain the current read position in a C++ stream, or *tellp()* to get the write position.

Syntax
```
#include <stdio.h>
long int ftell(FILE *stream);
FILE *stream;     Pointer to stream whose current position is to be returned
```

Example Use
```
curpos = ftell(infile));
```

Returns

If successful, *ftell()* returns a long integer containing the number of bytes the current position of *stream* is offset from the beginning of the file. In case of error, *ftell()* returns −1. Also, the global variable *errno* is set to an implementation-defined constant.

See Also

fgetpos(), fseek(), fsetpos(), FILE, errno, tellg(), tellp() (C++ streams)

fwrite() ✦ function

Purpose

Use the *fwrite()* function to write the number of data items specified by *count*, each of the size given by *size*, from *buffer* to the current position in *stream*. The current position of *stream* is updated after the write. Note that this function is used with C streams, not C++ streams. Use the *write()* ios member function to write binary data to a C++ stream.

Syntax

```
#include <stdio.h>
size_t fwrite(const void *buffer, size_t size, size_t count, FILE *stream);
const void *buffer;      Pointer to buffer in memory from where
                         fwrite will get the bytes it writes
size_t size;             Size in bytes of each data item
size_t count;            Maximum number of items to be written
FILE *stream;            Pointer to stream to which the data items
                         are to be written
```

Example Use

```
numwrite = fwrite(buffer, sizeof(char), 80, outfile);
```

Returns

The *fwrite()* function returns the number of items it actually wrote. If the return value is less than what you expect, an error may have occurred. Use *ferror()* to verify this.

See Also

fopen(), fread(), fclose(), FILE, size_t, write() (C++ streams)

get() ✦ function

Purpose

Use the *get()* ios member function with an *istream* object in C++ to get a single character or a series of characters from a stream.

Syntax

```
#include <iostream.h>
<stream>.get (char* string, int numchars, char term_char = '\n');  for
string input                      string in which characters are to be stored
char * string;                    maximum number of characters to read
int numchars;                     character at which to stop reading (default
char term_char;                   is newline)

<stream>.get(char onechar&);      for binary or single-character input
char onechar int                  single-char or binary value
<stream>.get();                   for single-char or binary input; returns
                                  integer
```

As usual all forms are called by referencing the stream object (for example, *cin.get(C);*). The first form of *get()* shown in the example reads up to a newline or until one less than the number of characters specified have been read. (You can specify a character other than newline as input terminator; in any case, the terminating character is not included in the string, but the string is ended with a null character.)

The second form of *get()* reads any single character (even whitespace) or a char-sized binary value. The third form works like the second, but returns the integer equivalent of the character rather than a reference to the *istream*. (In Borland/Turbo C++, this version, when used with *cin*, waits until you have pressed ENTER after typing a character. It also treats CTRL-C as a system break.)

Example Use

```
char * name;                      // string to hold name
cout << "Enter your name and press enter ";
cin.get (name, 40);               // read up to 40 chars.
                                  // or newline
cin.get (name, 20, '\t');         // read up to 20
                                  // characters or a tab
char choice;
cin.get(choice);                  // get single character
```

Returns

The *get()* function returns a reference to the *istream* object, except for the *int get()* version, which returns the *int* value of the character input.

See Also

read(), getline(), peek()

---

getc() ♦ macro

Purpose

Using the *getc()* macro to read a single character from *stream*. *getc()* is identical to *fgetc()*, except that it is implemented as a macro. This means you should not provide it an argument that may cause any side effects. Note: Use this macro for C streams; use the *get() ios* member function for C++ streams.

Syntax

```
#include <stdio.h>
int getc(FILE *stream);
FILE *stream;          Pointer to stream from which a character is to read
```

Example Use

```
in_char = getc(p_txtfile);
```

Returns

The *getc()* macro returns the character read as an integer value. A return value of *EOF* indicates an error.

See Also

fgetc(), fputc(), getchar(), putc(), putchar(), EOF, FILE; get() (C++ streams)

getchar() ♦ macro

Purpose

Use the *getchar()* macro to read a single character from the preopened file *stdin* which is normally connected to your keyboard input. Note that *getchar()* is identical to *getc()* with *stream* set to *stdin*. (Use the *ios* member function *get()* to read a single character from a C++ stream.)

Syntax

```
#include <stdio.h>
int getchar(void);
```

Example Use

```
c = getchar();
```

Returns

The *getchar()* macro returns the character read from *stdin* as an integer value. In case of any error, the return value is equal to the constant EOF.

See Also

fgetc(), fputc(), getc(), putc(), putchar(), EOF, stdin, get() (C++ streams) getenv()

getenv() ♦ function

Purpose

Use *getenv()* to get the definition of the environment variable *varname* from the environment of the process.

Syntax

```
#include <stdlib.h>
char *getenv(const char *varname);
const char *varname;        Name of environment variable to look for
```

Example Use

```
current_path = getenv("PATH");
```

Returns

If *varname* is found, *getenv* returns a pointer to the string value of *varname*. If *varname* is undefined, *getenv()* will return a *NULL*. Predefined environment variables vary with the operating system in use.

See Also

argc, argv

getline() ♦ function

Purpose

Use the *getline()* *ios* member function to get a line of input. You can specify the total number of characters to be read and/or the character at which to terminate input. *getline()* produces the same effect with a string as *get()* except that *getline()* includes the terminating character (usually a newline) before appending the string-terminating null character. Note that your string object must allow for the extra character, as shown in the example.

Syntax

```
#include <iostream.h>
<stream>.getline(char* string, int numchars, char term_char = '\n');
char* string;               string to receive input
int numchars;               maximum chars. to input
char term_char;             character at which to terminate input
```

Example Use

```
char command[80];           // array to hold command
cin.getline(command, 79);   // command up to 79 chars.
                            // must make room for terminating character
```

Returns

The *getline()* function returns a reference to the *istream* object.

See Also

get(), read()

gets() ✦ function

Purpose

Use *gets()* to read a line from the standard input file *stdin* into the string *buffer*. The reading continues until *gets()* encounters a newline character or end-of-file. At this point, it replaces the newline character with a null character (\0) and creates a C-style string. You must allocate room for the buffer in which the characters will be stored. Note that *fgets()* performs similarly, but unlike *gets()*, it retains the newline character in the final string. Also note that *gets()* should not be used with C++ streams; use the *ios* member function *getline()* instead.

Syntax

```
#include <stdio.h>
char *gets(char *buffer);
char *buffer;              Buffer where string will be stored
```

Example Use

```
gets(command_line);
```

Returns

If successful, *gets()* returns *buffer*. Otherwise, it returns a NULL.

See Also

fgets(), fputs(), puts(), NULL, stdin, getline() (C++ streams)

gmtime() ✦ function

Purpose

Use the *gmtime()* function to break down a time value of type *time_t* stored at the location *time* into year, month, day, hour, minutes, seconds, and several other fields that it saves in a structure of type *tm* maintained internally. The structure *tm* is defined in *time.h* and shown in the entry for *asctime()*. The fields setting up *gmtime* will correspond to Greenwich Mean Time (GMT).

Syntax

```
#include <time.h>
struct tm *gmtime(const time_t *time);
const time_t *time;         Pointer to calendar time
```

Example Use

```
t_gmt = gmtime(&bintime);
```

Returns

The *gmtime()* function returns a pointer to the *tm* structure where the converted time is stored. If GMT is not available, it returns a NULL.

See Also

```
asctime(), localtime(), time(), NULL, time_t, tm
```

good()   function

Purpose

Use the *good()* *ios* member function to check whether any error involving a stream has occurred.

Syntax

```
<stream_name>.good()
```

Example Use

```
while (cin.good()) {
// process the input
}
```

Returns

The *good()* function returns a nonzero (true) value if no *ios* error bits have been set for the stream. If one or more error bits have been set, *good()* returns a 0 (false).

See Also

```
ios, bad(), fail()
```

goto   keyword

Purpose

Use the *goto* keyword to jump unconditionally to a label in the current function. The label ends in a colon. If the *goto* is executed, control jumps to the code following the specified label.

Use of *goto* is not recommended for most applications because it makes it hard to follow the flow of execution in the program.

Syntax

```
goto <label>;
```

Example Use

```
if (system_price > 6000.0) goto TooExpensive;
    ...
TooExpensive:
    seek_alternative();
```

hex ◆ manipulator

Purpose

Use the *hex* C++ stream manipulator to set the conversion format flag for a stream to hexadecimal (base 16). The conversion format controls the base in which numbers will be output to or input from the stream. Note: *hex* is equivalent to *setbase(16)*.

Syntax
```
#include <iostream.h>
ostream << hex;          set base to hexadecimal for output stream
istream >> hex;          set base to hexadecimal for input stream
```

Example Use
```
int n = 255;
cout << hex << n; // outputs 'ff'
```

Returns

The *hex* manipulator returns a reference to the stream. This allows the manipulator to both change the stream state and pass a value along a chain of input or output.

See Also
```
dec, oct, setbase()
```

HUGE_VAL ◆ predefined value

Purpose

The value *HUGE_VAL* is a predefined *double* expression that evaluates to a very large value (for use as a return value by math functions when the computed result is too large). It is defined in *math.h*.

See Also
```
INT_MAX, DBL_MAX, FLT_MAX
```

if ◆ keyword

Purpose

Use *if* to execute code only when certain conditions hold true. You can use *if* alone or with *else* to specify multiple alternatives.

Syntax
```
if (<condition>)
    <statement; ...>
or
```

continued on next page

continued from previous page

```
if (<condition>)
    <statement_1>;
else
    <statement_2>;
```

The statement following the *if* is executed if *condition* is true (not equal to 0). When an *else* is present, statement_2 is executed if *condition* is false (equal to 0).

Example Use

```
if (x <= y)  smaller = x;
else smaller = y;
...
```

If *x* is less than or equal to *y*, then *smaller* is assigned the value *x*. Otherwise, (else), *smaller* is assigned the value *y*.

See Also
else

#if ♦ preprocessor conditional directive

Purpose

Use the *#if* preprocessor directive to control which parts of your code will be compiled under which conditions.

Syntax

```
#if <condition1>
    <directive1>
#elif <condition2>
    <directive2>
...
#else
    <default_directive>
#endif
```

If *condition1* is true, *directive1* is executed by the preprocessor; otherwise, if *condition2* is true, *directive2* is executed. If neither *condition1* nor *condition2* is true, then *default_directive* is executed. You can have no *#elif* or more than one of them; you can omit *#else* but not have more than one *#else*.

Example Use

```
#if !defined(FILE_1_INCLUDED)
    #include <file1.h>
#elif defined(INCLUDE_FILE_2)
    #include <file2.h>
#else
    #include <file3.h>
#endif
```

See Also
defined (preprocessor condition), #include

#ifdef ◆ preprocessor directive

Purpose
Use the *#ifdef* preprocessor directive to determine whether a preprocessor symbol or macro is defined in the current program. The *#ifdef* directive is equivalent to *#ifdefined*.

Syntax
#ifdef (<SYMBOL>)

Example Use
```
#ifdef (NON_STANDARD)
    #include "ourdefs.h"
#endif
```

See Also
defined (preprocessor operator), #ifndef

#ifndef ◆ preprocessor directive

Purpose
Use the *#ifndef* preprocessor directive to determine whether a preprocessor symbol or macro is not defined in the current program. *#ifndef* is equivalent to *#if!defined*.

Syntax
#ifndef (<SYMBOL>)

Example Use
```
#ifndef (COPROCESSOR)
      #include "emulate.h"
#endif
```

See Also
defined (preprocessor operator), #ifdef

ifstream ◆ class

Purpose
Use the *ifstream* class to declare an input stream object. The *ifstream* class is derived from the *istream* class and adds file-related functions and the extraction (>>) operator. See the *ios* and *open()* entries for more information on opening files. The input file *cin* is predefined for standard input (by default, the keyboard).

Syntax

```
#include <fstream.h>
ifstream <object_name> ; or
ifstream <handle_no>; or
ifstream (<object_name>, <"filename">, <ios::mode>, <filebuf::mode>);
object_name                    name of stream object in program
handle_no                      integer handle number (e.g. for DOS)
"filename"                     filename acceptable to operating system
ios::open_mode                 read, write, etc. mode (see ios entry)
                               (optional; default is ios::in)
filebuf::mode                  file protection mode (always
                               filebuf::openprot in current DOS
                               implementations; check for others)
```

If you declare an *ifstream* with just the object name, you must use the *ifstream::open()* function to open the file before use. The use of a file handle number assumes that this handle has already been set up with the operating system. Because there is currently only one file protection mode in *filebuf* and the constructor defaults to it, you normally don't have to use this parameter at all.

Example Use

```
ifstream test_input;        // create object, must open file
                            // before use
ifstream(5);                // use file handle 5 in operating
                            // system
ifstream(input, "datafile"); // create object "input"
// and associate it with "datafile" on disk
ifstream(datastream, "specdev", ios::binary);
// declare object "datastream", associate it with
// actual file "specdev", and open in explicit binary
// mode
```

See Also

iostream.h, ios, fstream.h, fstreambase, istream, ostream

---

ignore()   ✦   function

Purpose

Use the *ignore()* function with an *istream* (C++ input stream) to skip over (ignore) the specified number of input characters. This is a binary mode operation that treats whitespace (tabs, form feeds, etc.) as just another character value.

Syntax

```
#include <iostream.h>
<istream>.ignore(int numchars = 1, int delim = EOF);
numchars                       number of characters to skip over
delim                          delimiter character indicating end-of-file
                               (default is standard EOF value)
```

Example Use

```
ifstream infile ("data.txt", ios::in);    // set up file
infile.ignore(80, CR);                    // skip 80 chars. but stop at
                                          // a CR if found
```

The preceding example supposes that a file "data.txt" has a first line that you want to skip, and that the line is not longer than 80 characters. If the line is shorter, skipping will stop when the carriage return character is encountered. (CR is assumed to be a constant with the value 13.)

Returns

The *ignore()* function returns a reference to the *istream*, allowing its operation to be combined with other input operations.

See Also

```
istream, cin, >> (extraction operator), get(), getline()
```

#include ♦ preprocessor directive

Purpose

Use the *#include* preprocessor directive to have the preprocessor read a header file (sometimes called an "include file") into the source code. The contents of the included file will be compiled along with the original source file.

Syntax

```
#include <filename>     /* read file from default directory */
#include "filename"     /* read file from same directory as source
                          code-details vary with implementation */
```

Example Use

```
#include <stdio.h>
```

inline ♦ keyword

Purpose

Use the *inline* keyword to have a function's code inserted in the object file each time the function is called. Use of *inline* functions increases the size of the object program, but can speed up the program by removing the overhead involved in function calls. The effects of using an *inline* function are similar to those of using macros, but an *inline* function is safer to use as it is a true function with a prototype and full data type-checking is performed.

Syntax

```
inline <type> <func_name> (<arg>..._) {<function definition>;}
    // standalone inline function
```

continued on next page

continued from previous page

```
<type> <func_name> (<arg>...) {function definition;}
    // implicit inline function defined in a class
type                        return type of function
func_name                   name of the function
arg                         function argument(s) (optional)
function definition         statement(s) implementing the function
```

There are two ways to use inline functions. You can declare a stand-alone function (one that is not a member of a class) as inline by preceding its declaration with the *inline* keyword and following the declaration with the function's definition code enclosed in curly braces ({ }). Stand-alone inline functions must be declared *and* defined before any call is made to the function.

You can also declare a class member function to be *implicitly* inline. You do this by including the function's definition in curly braces ({ }) immediately following the function's declaration. (The only difference from an explicit inline declaration is that the keyword *inline* is omitted.)

The inline function mechanism is really suitable only for very short, simple functions usually consisting of a single line of code. The degree to which functions declared *inline* are actually placed inline is compiler-dependent.

Example Use
```
inline int triple (int num) { return num * 3;} //standalone
class runner
{
...
public
int triple (int bases) { return bases * 3;}
...
}; // implicit in member function
```

See Also
#define, register

int ◆ keyword

Purpose
Use the *int* type specifier to declare integer variables and arrays. The size qualifiers *short* and *long* should be used to declare an integer of desired size. The size of an *int* is implementation-dependent.

Syntax
```
int <varname>;
```

Example Use
```
int i, x[100];
```

See Also
char, double, float, long, short, signed, unsigned

INT_MAX ✦ predefined value

Purpose

The predefined value *INT_MAX* is the maximum value of an *int*. It is defined in *limits.h*.

See Also

`HUGE_VAL, DBL_MAX, FLT_MAX`

INT_MIN ✦ predefined value

Purpose

The predefined value *INT_MIN* is the minimum value of an *int*. It is defined in *limits.h*.

See Also

`DBL_MIN, FLT_MIN`

_IOFBF ✦ predefined value

Purpose

The predefined value *_IOFBF* indicates "full buffering" when used with *setvbuf()*. It is defined in *stdio.h*.

See Also

`_IOLBF, _IONBF, setvbuf()`

_IOLBF ✦ predefined value

Purpose

The predefined value *_IOLBF* indicates "line buffering" when used with *setvbuf()*. It is defined in *stdio.h*.

See Also

`_IOFBF, _IONBF, setvbuf()`

iomanip.h ✦ header file

Purpose

Include the *iomanip.h* header file in your program when you want to use stream manipulator functions that take parameters (arguments). The manipulator functions that require *iomanip.h* are *setbase()*, *resetiosflags()*, *setiosflags()*, *setfill()*, *setprecision()*, and *setw()*.

Syntax
```
#include <iomanip.h>
```

Example Use
```
#include <iostream.h>     // for general stream functions
#include <iomanip.h>      // for manipulators that take
                          // parameters
cout << setw(8);          // set output width to 8
cout << 100;              // display '100' in 8 char.
                          // field
```

See Also
iostream.h, fstream.h, ios, setbase(), resetiosflags(), setiosflags(), setfill(), setprecision(), setw(), << (insertion operator), >> (extraction operator), cin, cout

_IONBF ♦ predefined value

Purpose
The predefined value *_IONBF* indicates "no buffering" when used with *setvbuf()*. It is defined in *stdio.h*.

See Also
_IOFBF, _IOLBF, setvbf()

ios ♦ class

Purpose
The *ios* class provides the basic interface to a *streambuf* and includes a variety of status flags. The member functions of *ios* are usually not used directly. Rather, the stream is accessed through the appropriate class derived from *ios: istream* (for input from a stream) and *ostream* (for output to a stream), and *fstream* and its derivatives for streams related to disk files.

Formatting Status Flags
ios provides all input and output streams with the flags shown in Table 10-4, which have the indicated effects when set.

Table 10-4

FLAG	EFFECT WHEN SET
Flags for Positioning Output	
skipws	Skip whitespace (space, tab, etc.) chars. on input
left	Padding before value
right	Padding after value (default)
internal	Padding after sign or base indicator
Base for Numeric Output	
dec	Convert numeric values to decimal (base 10) (default)
oct	Convert numeric values to octal (base 8)
hex	Convert numeric values to hexadecimal (base 16)
showbase	Include base indicator in output (off by default)
uppercase	Show base, exponent indicators in uppercase (off by default)
Sign and Decimal Format	
showpos	Show + for positive numbers (off by default)
showpoint	Always show decimal point in floating-point output (off by default)
scientific	Use scientific notation (for example, 1.2345E4) (off by default)
fixed	Use standard decimal notation (for example, 123.45) (default)
Flushing Stream After Output (Insertion)	
unitbuf	Flush all streams after insertion
stdio	Flush stdout, stderr after insertion

IOS File Stream Opening Modes

The *ios* class also provides a set of modes that determine how a file stream will be opened.

Table 10-5

MODE	EFFECT
in	Open for input (default for *ifstream* objects)
out	Open for output (default for *ofstream* objects)
app	Open for append, start writing at end of file
ate	Open and position at end of file
trunc	Create file; if file already exists, truncate to length 0
nocreate	Open file if file already exists, otherwise fail
noreplace	If truncation requested, fail rather than truncate if file exists
binary	Open in explicit binary mode

The file opening modes given in Table 10-5 are used with the *ios open()* member function and are similar to those used with the standard C function *fopen()*. As with the formatting flags, the file opening modes can be combined using the bitwise OR (|) operator.

File Positioning Specifiers

The *ios* class provides three enumerated values that specify how the current read and/or write position for the file will be set.

Table 10-6

POSITION	EFFECT
beg	Seek relative to file beginning
cur	Seek relative to the current position
end	Seek relative to the end of file

These specifiers (shown in Table 10-6) are used with the *seekg()* and *seekp()* functions for positioning the file's read and write positions, respectively. See the entries for *seekg()* and *seekp()* for details.

Stream Error Status Values

The *ios* class provides five flags that are set automatically depending on the result of an attempt to access a file stream.

Table 10-7

FLAG	SET WHEN
goodbit	No errors encountered with stream
eofbit	End of file was reached
failbit	Error encountered and *failbit*, *badbit*, or *hardfail* was set
badbit	Last operation was invalid (not defined or not allowed)
hardfail	An irrevocable error occurred

The flags shown in Table 10-7 are actually masks that test appropriate bits in a status value called *state*. The flags are not generally used directly: the functions *good()*, *eof()*, *fail()*, and *bad()* test the indicated bits conveniently. Once an error has occurred, no further operations with that stream will succeed until the error bit(s) are cleared: this is usually done with the *clear()* function.

Syntax

```
#include iostream.h
ios::<flagname>                        to refer to an ios flag
ios::<flagname>|ios::<flagname>| ...   to combine flags
```

See the entries for *flags()*, *setf()*, *setiosflags()*, and *resetiosflags()* for examples of setting the ios formatting flags. See the entry for *open()* for syntax using the file opening mode flags. See the entries for *seekg()* and *seekp()* for use of the file position specifiers. For the stream error status flags, see the entries for *rdstate()* and *clear()* as well as specific bit-testing functions such as *eof()* and *failbit()*.

Note that you can set an integer value to the bitwise *OR* of several flags, for example:

```
const int io_opts = ios::left | ios::showpoint | ios::fixed;
```

These options specify that values will be left-adjusted, fixed-point, with the decimal point always shown. This technique can also be used for the other type of *ios* flags.

Example Use

```
// set some ios format flags
cout.flags(ios::hex | ios::showbase);      // base 16 with
                                            // base indicator
setf(ios::left, ios::adjustfield);          // pad output to
                                            // left
// use ios file open specifiers
fstream my_input;
myfile.open("input.txt",ios::in,filebuf::openprot);
...
// set file read position
seekg(1, ios::end);                         // set read point to char. just
                                            // before end of file
// test for EOF using stream status values
if (cin.ios::state & ios::eofbit)
     return (MyEOFValue);
...
```

See Also

istream, ostream, iostream, iostream.h, stream.h, fstream, fstreambase, fstream.h, iomanip.h, (as well as other entries mentioned in the text)

iostream ♦ class

Purpose

The *iostream* class is used for I/O operations in which a stream is used "bidirectionally"—that is, for both input and output. The *iostream* class is derived from the *istream* and *ostream* classes (which are in turn derived from the *ios* class).

Syntax

```
#include <iostream.h>
```

See Also

ios, istream, ostream, stream.h, iostream.h, fstream, fstreambase, fstream.h, istream, ostream, iomanip.h

iostream.h ✦ header file

Purpose

Use the *iostream.h* header file to include C++ stream I/O in your program. *iostream.h* contains the basic classes for streams in C++ version 2.0 or later. Older compilers that support version 1.0 or 1.2 use only the file *stream.h*.

Syntax

```
#include <iostream.h>     For C++ 2.0 or later stream I/O
```

See Also

fstream, fstreambase, fstream.h, istream, ostream, iomanip.h

isalnum(), isalpha(), iscntrl(), isdigit(), isgraph(), islower(), isprint(), ispunct(),

isspace(), isupper(), isxdigit() ✦ macros

Purpose

Use this group of macros to check for specific properties of the character *c*, such as whether it is a control character, a digit, lowercase, printable, and so on. Table 10-8 shows the test performed by each of the functions. Note that some compilers may implement these tests as functions rather than as macros.

Table 10-8

MACRO NAME	TESTS FOR
isalnum()	Alphanumeric character
isalpha()	Character in alphabet
iscntrl()	Control character
isdigit()	Decimal digit
isgraph()	Printable character excluding the space
islower()	Lowercase letter
isprint()	Printable character including space
ispunct()	Punctuation character
isspace()	Whitespace character. In "C" locale these are space, form feed (\f), newline (\n), carriage return (\r), horizontal tab (\t), and vertical tab (\v)
isupper()	Uppercase letter
isxdigit()	Hexadecimal digit

CHAPTER 10   ALPHABETICAL REFERENCE

Syntax
```
#include <ctype.h>
int isalnum(int c);
int isalpha(int c);
int iscntrl(int c);
int isdigit(int c);
int isgraph(int c);
int islower(int c);
int isprint(int c);
int ispunct(int c);
int isspace(int c);
int isupper(int c);
int isxdigit(int c);
int c;                    Character to be tested
```

Example Use
```
if(isprint(c) != 0) printf("%c is printable\n", c);
if(isdigit(c) != 0) printf("%c is a digit\n", c);
if(iscntrl(c) != 0) printf("%d is a control char\n"",c);
```

Returns
Each macro returns a nonzero value if the *c* satisfies the criterion for that function. Otherwise, it returns a zero.

See Also
`int, char`

istream ✦ class

Purpose
Use the member functions of the *istream* class for both unformatted and formatted input from a stream (such as from *cin*, the standard input stream, to obtain keyboard input). The *istream* class is derived from the base class *ios*, from which it gets its interface to a *streambuf*. In turn the class *istream_withassign* is derived from *istream* in order to provide the four standard streams (*cin*, *cout*, *cerr*, and *clog*). Note that in C++ 2.X streams connected to disk files must be handled using an *fstream* object such as an *ifstream* or *ofstream*.

Syntax
```
#include <iostream.h>
```

See Also
`cin, >> (extraction operator), iostream.h, stream.h, fstream, fstreambase, fstream.h, ostream, iomanip.h`

jmp_buf ◆ predefined data type

Purpose

The *jmp_buf* struct type is capable of holding information necessary to restore a calling environment. It is defined in *setjmp.h*.

See Also
```
longjmp(), setjmp()
```

L_tmpnam ◆ predefined value

Purpose

The predefined value *L_tmpnam* is the size of a char array large enough to hold temporary file names generated by *tmpnam()*. It is defined in *stdio.h*.

See Also
```
tmpnam(), FILENAME_MAX
```

labs() ◆ function

Purpose

Use the *labs()* function to get the absolute value of the long integer *n*.

Syntax
```
#include <stdlib.h>
long labs(long n);
long n;                    Long integer whose absolute value is returned
```

Example Use
```
lresult = labs(-65540L); /* result will be 65540 */
```

Returns

The long integer returned by *labs()* is the absolute value of *n*.

See Also
```
abs(), fabs()
```

LC_ALL ◆ predefined value

Purpose

The predefined constant *LC_ALL* indicates the program's entire locale (aspects that depend on country-specific formats). It is defined in *locale.h*.

See Also
LC_COLLATE, LC_CTYPE, LC_MONETARY, LC_NUMERIC, LC_TIME

LC_COLLATE ✦ predefined value

Purpose
The predefined constant *LC_COLLATE* affects the behavior of *strcoll()* and *strxfrm()*. It is defined in *locale.h*.

See Also
LC_ALL, LC_CTYPE, LC_MONETARY, LC_NUMERIC, LC_TIME, strcoll(), strxfrm()

LC_CTYPE ✦ predefined value

Purpose
The predefined constant *LC_CTYPE* affects the behavior of all locale-aware character handling routines. It is defined in *locale.h*.

See Also
LC_ALL, LC_COLLATE, LC_MONETARY, LC_NUMERIC, LC_TIME,

LC_MONETARY ✦ predefined value

Purpose
The predefined constant *LC_MONETARY* affects monetary formatting information returned by *localeconv*. It is defined in *locale.h*.

See Also
LC_ALL, LC_COLLATE, LC_CTYPE, LC_NUMERIC, LC_TIME, localeconv()

LC_NUMERIC ✦ predefined value

Purpose
The predefined constant *LC_NUMERIC* affects the locale-specific, decimal point formatting information returned by *localeconv*. It is defined in *locale.h*.

See Also
LC_ALL, LC_COLLATE, LC_CTYPE, LC_TIME, LC_MONETARY, localeconv()

LC_TIME ♦ predefined value

Purpose
The predefined constant LC_TIME affects the behavior of the *strftime()* function. It is defined in *locale.h*.

See Also
LC_ALL, LC_COLLATE, LC_CTYPE, LC_NUMERIC, LC_MONETARY, strftime()

lconv ♦ predefined data type

Purpose
The *lconv* struct holds strings to be used in formatting numeric and monetary values for a specified locale. It is defined in *locale.h*.

See Also
localeconv(), LC_NUMERIC, LC_MONETARY

LDBL_DIG ♦ predefined value

Purpose
The predefined value LDBL_DIG is the number of significant decimal digits in a *long double* value. It is defined in *float.h*.

See Also
LDBL_EPSILON, LDBL_MANT_DIG, LDBL_MIN, LDBL_MIN_10_EXP, LDBL_MIN_EXP, LDBL_MAX, LDBL_MAX_10_EXP, LDBL_MAX_EXP

LDBL_EPSILON ♦ predefined value

Purpose
The LDBL_EPSILON predefined value gives the smallest positive *long double* value *x* such that *1+x != 1*. It is defined in *float.h*.

See Also
LDBL_DIG, LDBL_MANT_DIG, LDBL_MIN, LDBL_MIN_10_EXP, LDBL_MIN_EXP, LDBL_MAX, LDBL_MAX_10_EXP, LDBL_MAX_EXP

LDBL_MANT_DIG ◆ predefined value

Purpose

The *LDBL_MANT_DIG* predefined value gives the number of base LDBL_RADIX digits in the mantissa of a *long double*. It is in *float.h*.

See Also

```
LDBL_DIG, LDBL_EPSILON, LDBL_MIN, LDBL_MIN_10_EXP, LDBL_MIN_10,LDBL_MAX,
LDBL_MAX_10_EXP, LDBL_MAX_EXP
```

LDBL_MAX ◆ predefined value

Purpose

The *LDBL_MAX* predefined value gives the maximum representable finite value that can be stored in a *long double*. It is defined in *float.h*.

See Also

```
LDBL_DIG, LDBL_MANT_DIG, LDBL_EPSILON, LDBL_MIN, LDBL_MIN_10_EXP,
LDBL_MIN_EXP, LDBL_MAX_10_EXP, LDBL_MAX_EXP
```

LDBL_MAX_10_EXP ◆ predefined value

Purpose

The *LDBL_MAX_10_EXP* predefined value gives the maximum integer such that 10 raised to that power is representable in a *long double*.

See Also

```
LDBL_DIG, LDBL_MANT_DIG, LDBL_EPSILON, LDBL_MIN, LDBL_MIN_10_EXP,
LDBL_MIN_EXP, LDBL_MAX, LDBL_MAX_EXP
```

LDBL_MAX_EXP ◆ predefined value

Purpose

The *LDBL_MAX_EXP* predefined value gives the maximum integer such that LDBL_RADIX raised to that power is representable in a *long double*. It is defined in *float.h*.

See Also

```
LDBL_DIG, LDBL_MANT_DIG, LDBL_EPSILON, LDBL_MIN, LDBL_MIN_10_EXP,
LDBL_MIN_EXP, LDBL_MAX, LDBL_MAX_10_EXP
```

LDBL_MIN ♦ predefined value

Purpose
The *LDBL_MIN* predefined value gives the minimum, positive, long floating-point number that can be stored in a *long double*. It is defined in *float.h*.

See Also
LDBL_DIG, LDBL_MANT_DIG, LDBL_EPSILON, LDBL_MIN_10_EXP, LDBL_MIN_EXP, LDBL_MAX, LDBL_MAX_10_EXP, LDBL_MAX_EXP

LDBL_MIN_10_EXP ♦ predefined value

Purpose
The *LDBL_MIN_10_EXP* predefined value gives the minimum negative integer such that 10 raised to that power is representable in a *long double*. It is defined in *float.h*.

See Also
LDBL_DIG, LDBL_MANT_DIG, LDBL_EPSILON, LDBL_MIN, LDBL_MIN_EXP, LDBL_MAX, LDBL_MAX_10_EXP, LDBL_MAX_EXP

LDBL_MIN_EXP ♦ predefined value

Purpose
The *LDBL_MIN_EXP* predefined value gives the minimum negative integer such that LDBL_RADIX raised to that power minus 1 is representable in a *long double*. It is defined in *float.h*.

See Also
LDBL_DIG, LDBL_MANT_DIG, LDBL_EPSILON, LDBL_MIN, LDBL_MIN_10_EXP, LDBL_MAX, LDBL_MAX_10_EXP, LDBL_MAX_EXP

ldexp() ♦ function

Purpose
Use the *ldexp()* function to compute and obtain the floating-point number equal to x times 2^{exp}.

Syntax
```
#include <math.h>
double ldexp(double x, int exp);
double x;                Floating-point value of the mantissa
int exp;                 Integer exponent
```

Example Use
```
value = ldexp(0.6375, 3); /* value will be 5.1 */
```

Returns
Normally *ldexp()* returns the value computed as previously described. When the result is too large, a range error may occur.

See Also
frexp(), modf()

ldiv() ♦ function

Purpose
Use the *ldiv()* function to divide the long integer *numer* by another long integer *denom* and obtain the resulting quotient and remainder packed in a structure of type *ldiv_t*. The structure type *ldiv_t* is defined in *stdlib.h* as:

```
typedef struct
{
    long quot;   /* The quotient */
    long rem;    /* The remainder */
} ldiv_t;
```

Syntax
```
#include <stdlib.h>
ldiv_t ldiv(long numer, long denom);
long numer;                Numerator
long denom;                Denominator
```

Example Use
```
lresult = ldiv(65540L, 65536L);
/* lresult.quot = 1, lresult.rem = 4 */
```

Returns
The *ldiv()* function returns a structure of type *ldiv_t* containing the quotient and remainder of the division.

See Also
div(), ldiv_t

ldiv_t ♦ predefined data type

Purpose
The *ldiv_t* data type can hold the value returned by *ldiv()*. It is defined in *stdlib.h*.

See Also
```
ldiv(), div_t
```

#line ◆ preprocessor line numbering directive

Purpose
Use the *#line* preprocessor directive to set the current line number for this location in the source code. This can be used as a debugging aid.

__LINE__ ◆ predefined macro

Purpose
Use the __LINE__ predefined macro to display or check the number of the line currently being translated by the preprocessor.

Example Use
```
printf("%d",__LINE__);
```

See Also
```
__DATE__, __TIME__, __FILE__, __STDC__
```

localeconv() ◆ function

Purpose
Use the *localeconv()* function to obtain detailed information on formatting monetary and numeric values according to the rules of the current locale. Note that many compilers support only the "C" locale at this time. Table 10-9 lists the categories of locale information that may be available.

Table 10-9 Locale Information

LOCALE CATEGORY	PARTS OF PROGRAM AFFECTED
LC_ALL	The entire program's locale-specific parts (all categories shown)
LC_COLLATE	Behavior of the routines *strcoll* and *strxfrm*
LC_CTYPE	Behavior of the character handling functions and multibyte functions
LC_MONETARY	Monetary formatting information returned by the *localeconv()* function
LC_NUMERIC	Decimal point character for the formatted output routines (for example, *printf()* and the data conversion functions, and the nonmonetary formatting information returned by the *localeconv()* function
LC_TIME	Behavior of the *strftime()* function

Syntax

```
#include <locale.h>
struct lconv *localeconv(void);
```

Example Use

```
p_lconv = localeconv();
```

Returns

The *localeconv()* function returns a pointer to a statically allocated *lconv* structure whose fields are filled in with formatting information appropriate for the current locale. Use *setlocale()* to set the current locale. The *lconv* structure is declared in *locale.h* as follows:

```
struct lconv
{
    char *decimal_point;        /* Decimal point character for nonmonetary
                                   quantities */
    char *thousands_sep;        /* Separator for groups of digits to the
                                   left of decimal point for nonmonetary
                                   quantities */
    char *grouping;             /* Size of each group of digits in
                                   nonmonetary quantities */
    char *int_curr_symbol;      /* International currency symbol for the
                                   current locale */
    char *currency_symbol;      /* Local currency symbol for the current
                                   locale */
    char *mon_decimal_point;    /* Decimal point character for monetary
                                   quantities */
    char *mon_thousands_sep;    /* Separator for groups of digits to the
                                   left of decimal point for monetary quantities */
    char *mon_grouping;         /* Size of each group of digits in monetary
                                   quantities */
    char *positive_sign;        /* String denoting sign for nonnegative
                                   monetary quantities */
    char *negative_sign;        /* String denoting sign for negative
                                   monetary quantities */
    char int_frac_digits;       /* Number of digits to the right of decimal
                                   point for internationally formatted monetary
                                   quantities*/
    char frac_digits;           /* Number of digits to the right of decimal
                                   point in formatted monetary quantities */
    char p_cs_precedes;         /* 1 = currency_symbol precedes, 0 = succeeds
                                   positive value */
    char p_sep_by_space;        /* 1 = space, 0 = no space between
                                   currency_symbol and positive formatted values */
    char n_cs_precedes;         /* 1 = currency_symbol precedes, 0 = succeeds
                                   negative value */
    char n_sep_by_space;        /* 1 = space, 0 = no space between
                                   currency_symbol and negative formatted values */
    char p_sign_posn;           /* Position of positive_sign in positive
                                   monetary quantities */
    char n_sign_posn;           /* Position of negative_sign in negative
                                   monetary quantities */
};
```

See Also
setlocale(), lconv()

localtime() ◆ function

Purpose
Use the *localtime()* function to break down the value of time of type *time_t* stored at the location *time* into year, month, day, hour, minutes, seconds, and several other fields that it saves in a structure of type *tm* maintained internally. The structure *tm* is defined in *time.h* and is shown in the reference pages on *asctime()*. The fields set up by *localtime()* will correspond to the local time.

Syntax
```
#include <time.h>
struct tm *localtime (const time_t *time);
const time_t *time;         Pointer to stored calendar time
```

Example Use
```
t_local = localtime(&bintime);
```

Returns
The *localtime()* function returns a pointer to the *tm* structure where the converted time is stored.

See Also
asctime(), gmtime(), time(), time_t, tm

log() and log10() ◆ functions

Purpose
Use the *log()* and *log10()* functions, respectively, to compute the natural logarithm and logarithm to the base 10 of the positive *double* variable x.

Syntax
```
#include <math.h>
double log(double x);
double log10(double x);
double x;                   Variable whose logarithm is to be computed
```

Example Use
```
y = log(2);        /* y = 0.693147 */
a = log10(2);      /* a = 0.30103  */
```

Returns

For positive *x*, *log()* and *log10()* return the logarithm of *x*. If *x* is negative, a domain error occurs. If *x* is zero, a range error occurs.

See Also

`exp(), pow()`

long ✦ keyword

Purpose

Use the *long* type specifier as a size qualifier for *int* and *unsigned int* variables. Note that *long* alone means *signed long int*. A *long* qualifier indicates that the integer data type is at least 32 bits, and is often twice as long as an *int*.

Example Use

`long filepos; unsigned long timer_tick;`

See Also

`char, double, float, int, short, signed, unsigned`

LONG_MAX ✦ predefined value

Purpose

The *LONG_MAX* predefined value is the maximum value of a *long int*. It is defined in *limits.h*.

See Also

`LONG_MIN`

LONG_MIN ✦ predefined value

Purpose

The *LONG_MIN* predefined value is the minimum value of a *long int*. It is defined in *limits.h*.

See Also

`LONG_MAX`

longjmp() ♦ function

Purpose

Use the *longjmp()* function to restore the calling environment to that contained in the *jmp_buf* struct env. This environment must have been saved by an earlier call to *setjmp()*. *longjmp()* restores all local variables (except the ones declared *volatile*) to their previous states and returns as if from the last call to *setjmp()* with the return value *retval*. Because *longjmp()* jumps to the return address of the last matching call to *setjmp*, you must make sure that the call to *longjmp()* occurs before the function where you had called *setjmp()* has returned.

Syntax

```
#include <setjmp.h>
void longjmp(jmp_buf env, int retval);
jmp_buf env;              Struct data type where the calling environment
                          is stored
int retval;               Value that will appear to be returned by the
                          earlier call to setjmp
```

Example Use

```
longjmp(stack_env, 1);
```

See Also

setjmp(), jmp_buf()

malloc() ♦ function

Purpose

Use the *malloc()* function to allocate a specified number of bytes. Note that you should use the *new* operator instead of a *malloc()* type function to allocate space for a C++ object.

Syntax

```
#include <stdlib.h>
void *malloc(size_t num_bytes);
size_t num_bytes;   Number of bytes needed
```

Example Use

```
buffer = (char *)malloc(100*sizeof(char));
```

Returns

The *malloc()* function returns a pointer which is the starting address of the memory allocated. If the memory allocation is unsuccessful because of insufficient space or bad values of the arguments, a *NULL* is returned.

See Also
free(), calloc(), realloc(), NULL, size_t

MB_CUR_MAX ◆ predefined value

Purpose
The *MB_CUR_MAX* predefined value is the maximum length of a multibyte character for the current locale. It is defined in *stdlib.h*, and is always less than *MB_LEN_MAX*.

See Also
MB_LEN_MAX

MB_LEN_MAX ◆ predefined value

Purpose
The *MB_LEN_MAX* predefined value is the maximum number of bytes in a multibyte character. It is defined in *limits.h*.

See Also
MB_CUR_MAX

mblen() ◆ function

Purpose
Use the *mblen()* function to obtain the number of bytes that make up a single, multibyte character. Note that some otherwise ANSI-compliant compilers do not support multibyte characters.

Syntax
```
#include <stdlib.h>
int mblen(const char *s, size_t n);
const char *s;            Pointer to multibyte character whose length is
                          to be determined
size_t n;                 Maximum number of bytes expected to comprise a
                          multibyte character (MB_CUR_MAX is a good choice
                          for this argument)
```

Example Use
```
mbsize = mblen(p_mbchar, MB_CUR_MAX);
```

Returns
If *s* is NULL, *mblen()* returns a 0 or a nonzero depending on whether multibyte encodings have state dependencies or not. If *s* is not NULL, *mblen()* returns the

number of bytes that comprise the multibyte character provided the next *n* or fewer characters form a valid multibyte character. Otherwise, it returns −1.

See Also
mbtowc(), mbstowcs(), wctomb(), wcstombs(), MB_CUR_MAX, NULL, size_t

mbtowc() ◆ function

Purpose

Use the *mbtowc()* function to convert a multibyte character at *s* to *wchar_t* type and store the result in the array *pwchar*. If *pwchar* is NULL, *mbtowc* will not save the resulting wide character. Also, *mbtowc()* will check at most *n* characters in *s* when trying to locate a valid multibyte character. Note that some otherwise ANSI-compliant compilers do not support multibyte characters.

Syntax
```
#include <stdlib.h>
int mbtowc(wchar_t *pwchar, const char *s, size_t n);
wchar_t *pwchar;              Pointer to array where the wide character
                              equivalent of multibyte character will be stored
const char *s;                Pointer to multibyte character to be converted to
                              wide character format
size_t n;                     Maximum number of bytes expected to comprise a
                              multibyte character (MB_CUR_MAX is a good choice
                              for this argument)
```

Example Use
```
mdc_size = mbtowc(pwc, mbchar, MB_CUR_MAX);
```

Returns

If *s* is NULL, *mbtowc()* will return a 0 or a nonzero depending on whether multibyte encodings have state dependencies or not. If *s* is not NULL, *mbtowc()* returns the number of bytes that comprise the multibyte character provided the next *n* or fewer characters form a valid multibyte character. Otherwise, it returns −1.

See Also
mblen(), mbstowcs(), wctomb(), wcstombs(), MB_CUR_MAX, NULL, size_t, wchar_t

mbstowcs() ◆ function

Purpose

Use the *mbstowcs()* function to convert a sequence of multibyte characters in *mbs* into a sequence of codes of *wchar_t* type and store at most *n* such codes in the array *pwcs*. Note that some otherwise ANSI-compliant compilers do not support multibyte characters.

Syntax
```
#include <stdlib.h>
size_t mbstowcs(wchar_t *pwcs, const char *mbs, size_t n);
wchar_t *pwcs;          Pointer to array where wide character results
                        will be stored
const char *mbs;        Pointer to array of multibyte characters being
                        converted to wide character
size_t  n;              Maximum number of wide characers to be stored
                        in pwcs
```

Example Use
```
mbstowcs(wc_array, mb_array, 10);
```

Returns
If successful, *mbstowcs()* returns the number of wide characters it stored in *pwcs*. If it encountered less than *n* multibyte characters, it returns –1 cast as *size_t*.

See Also
```
mblen(), mbtowc(), wctomb(), wcstombs(), size_t, wchar_t
```

memchr() ◆ function

Purpose
Use the *memchr()* function to search through the first *count* bytes in the buffer at the address *buffer* and find the first occurrence of the character *c*.

Syntax
```
#include <string.h>
void *memchr(const void *buffer, int c, size_t#count);
const void *buffer;     Pointer to buffer in which search takes place
int c;                  Character to look for
size_t count;           Maximum number of bytes to be examined
```

Example Use
```
/* Look for the first occurrence of 'I' in a 100 byte buffer */
first_i = memchr(start_address, 'I', 100);
```

Returns
If *memchr()* finds the character *c*, it will return a pointer to this character in *buffer*. Otherwise, *memchr()* returns a NULL.

See Also
```
memcmp(), strchr(), NULL, size_t
```

memcmp() ♦ function

Purpose
Use the *memcmp()* function to compare the first *count* bytes of the two buffers *buffer1*, *buffer2*.

Syntax
```
#include <string.h>
int memcmp(const void *buffer1, const void *buffer2, size_t count);
const void *buffer1;      Pointer to first buffer
const void *buffer2;      Pointer to second buffer
size_t count;             Number of bytes to be compared
```

Example Use
```
if (memcmp(buffer1, buffer2, sizeof(buffer1)) == 0)
printf("The buffers are identical\n");
```

Returns
The *memcmp()* function returns an integer less than, equal to, or greater than zero according to whether the string *buffer1* is less than, equal to, or greater than the string *buffer2*.

See Also
`strcoll(), strcmp(), strncmp(), size_t`

memcpy() ♦ function

Purpose
Use the *memcpy()* function to copy *count* bytes from the buffer at address *source* to another buffer at *dest*. The behavior of *memcpy()* is undefined if the source and destination buffers overlap. (If this situation is anticipated, use *memmove()* instead.)

Syntax
```
#include <string.h>
void *memcpy(void *dest, const void *source, size_t count);
void   *dest;             Pointer to buffer to which data will be copied
const void *source;       Pointer to buffer from which data will be copied
size_t  count;            Maximum number of bytes to be copied
```

Example Use
```
memcpy(dest, src, 80);    /* Copy 80 bytes from scr to dest */
```

Returns
The *memcpy()* function returns a pointer to the destination buffer *dest*.

See Also
`memmove(), strcpy(), strncpy(), size_t`

memmove() ◆ function

Purpose
Use the *memmove()* function to copy *count* bytes from the buffer at address *source* to another buffer at *dest*. Parts of the source and destination buffers may overlap. (If you can guarantee that there's no overlap, *memcpy()* is faster.)

Syntax
```
#include <string.h>
void *memmove(void *dest, const void *source, size_t count);
void *dest;             Pointer to buffer to which data will be copied
const void  *source;    Pointer to buffer from which data will be copied
size_t  count;          Maximum number of bytes to be copied
```

Example Use
```
memmove(dest, src, sizeof(src));
```

Returns
The *memmove()* function returns a pointer to the destination buffer *dest*.

See Also
`memcpy(), strcpy(), strncpy(), size_t`

memset() ◆ function

Purpose
Use the *memset()* function to set the first *count* bytes in the *buffer* to the character *c*.

Syntax
```
#include <string.h>
void *memset(void *buffer, int c, size_t count);
void *buffer;           Pointer to memory where bytes are to be set
int c;                  Each byte in buffer will be set to this character
size_t count;           Maximum number of bytes to be set
```

Example Use
```
memset(big_buffer, '\0', 2048);
```

Returns
The *memset()* function returns the argument *buffer*.

See Also
memcpy(), memmove(), strcpy(), strncpy(), size_t

mktime() ♦ function

Purpose
Use the *mktime()* function to convert the local time currently in the structure of type *tm* at the address *timeptr* to a value of type *time_t*. Essentially, the local time given in the form of year, month, day, etc. will be converted to the number of seconds elapsed since 00:00:00 hours GMT, January 1, 1970. This is the same format in which *time* returns the current time and is the format used in the argument to the functions *ctime*, *difftime*, and *localtime*.

Two fields in the structure of type *tm* are ignored by *mktime*. These are the fields *tm_wday* and *tm_yday*, denoting respectively the day of the week and the day of the year. The *mktime()* function will set the fields in the *tm* structure to appropriate values before returning.

Syntax
```
#include <time.h>
time_t mktime(struct tm *timeptr);
struct tm *timeptr;         Pointer to structure of type tm where local time
                            is stored
```

Example Use
```
bintime = mktime(&timebuf);
```

Returns
If successful, *mktime()* will return the current contents of *timeptr* encoded as a value of type *time_t*. If the local time in *timeptr* cannot be handled by *mktime()*, the return value will be a –1 cast to the type *time_t*.

See Also
asctime(), time(), time_t, tm

modf() ♦ function

Purpose
Use the *modf()* function to separate the floating-point number *x* into its fractional part and its integral part. The integer part is returned as a floating-point value in the location whose address is given in the argument *intptr*.

Syntax
```
#include <math.h>
```

```
double modf(double x, double *intptr);
double x;                  Floating-point value to be decomposed
double *intptr;            Integral part of x is returned here
```

Example Use
```
fraction = modf(24.95, &int_part);
/* fraction is .95 */
```

Returns
The *modf()* function returns the signed fractional part of *x*.

See Also
frexp(), ldexp()

\n ◆ escape sequence for newline

Purpose
Use the \n (newline) escape sequence to move the cursor or print head to the beginning of the next line. (The difference between \r (carriage return) and \n is that a carriage return moves the cursor or print head to the beginning of the *current* line.)

With C++ streams you can use the *endl* manipulator to send a newline to the output.

Example Use
```
printf("This string is on one line\n");
printf("and this one goes on the next line.");
```

See Also
printf(), \r, endl()

NDEBUG ◆ predefined value

Purpose
The *NDEBUG* value by default is not defined. If it is defined, *assert()* will be ignored.

See Also
assert()

new ◆ operator

Purpose
Use the *new* operator to allocate memory for a user-defined object. *new* offers a service similar to that provided by the *malloc()* family of functions in the standard C

library, but with superior management through use of the class hierarchy. *new* is often used in class constructors and for creating dynamic arrays (arrays whose size is determined at runtime). Note that memory allocated with *new* must be deallocated (freed) using *delete*.

Syntax

```
<type>* <ptr_name> = new <type_name>                      single object
<type>* <ptr_name> = new <array_name> <[elements]...>     array
<type>*                 pointer to a valid data type
<ptr_name>              name of pointer to be returned
type_name               type of object or variable to be created
array_name              name of array to be created
elements                number of array elements (repeat if array has more
                        than one dimension)
```

Example Use

```
int* next_block = new int;      // allocate integer-sized object
char *string = new char[21];    // allocate a string buffer 21 bytes long
```

Returns

The address of the newly allocated object is stored in the supplied pointer (you can use a previously defined pointer if you want). If insufficient memory is available for the new object, a null (0) pointer is returned.

See Also

```
delete, malloc(), free()
```

NULL ✦ predefined pointer

Purpose

The value *NULL* indicates an implementation-defined null pointer constant. It is defined in *locale.h*, *stddef.h*, *stdio.h*, *stdlib.h*, *string.h*, and *time.h*. This is more accurate than casting a pointer to a value of 0, which looks like an address, while *NULL* means "doesn't point to anything at all."

See Also

```
* (pointer dereferencing operator)
```

oct ✦ manipulator

Purpose

Use the *oct* C++ stream manipulator to have numeric values output in octal (base 8) notation. The effect of *oct* is equivalent to a call to *setbase(8)*.

Syntax

```
<output_stream> << oct;
```

Example Use

```
cout << 32 << oct; // outputs 40
```

Returns

The *oct* manipulator returns a reference to the stream object with which it is used. This allows *oct* to be used as part of a "cascade" of output as shown.

See Also

```
dec, hex, setbase()
```

offsetof ♦ predefined macro

Purpose

The predefined *offsetof* macro has the form *offsetof(structure_type, member)* and returns a *size_t* value that is the offset in bytes, of the *member* from the beginning of a structure. It can be used to manipulate the structure directly. It is defined in *stddef.h*.

See Also

```
struct, union, . (member access operator),
-> (pointer member access operator)
```

ofstream ♦ class

Purpose

Use an object of the *ofstream* class for an output file (typically a disk file). You can open the *ofstream* as you declare it or use the *open()* function later. *ofstream* inherits the insertion operator (>>) from *ostream*, making it easy to send data of any defined type to the file. See the entry for *fstream* for details.

Syntax

```
#include <fstream.h>
ofstream <object_name> ; or
ofstream (<handle_no>); or
ofstream (<object_name>, <"filename">, <ios::mode>, <filebuf::mode>);
object_name           name of stream object in program
handle_no             integer handle number (e.g., for DOS)
"filename"            file name acceptable to operating system
ios::open_mode        read, write, etc. mode (see ios entry)
                      (optional; default is ios::out)
filebuf::mode         file protection mode (always filebuf::openprot in
                      current DOS implementations; check for others)
```

If you declare an *ofstream* with just the object name, you must use the *ofstream::open()* function to open the file before use. The use of a file handle number assumes that this handle has already been set up with the operating system. Because there is currently only one file protection mode in *filebuf* and the constructor defaults to it, you normally don't have to use this parameter at all.

Example Use
```
ofstream results;                        // create object, must open file before use
ofstream(3);                             // use file handle 3 in operating system
ofstream(output, "datafile");            // create object "output" and associate it
                                         // with "datafile" on disk
ofstream(datafeed, "specdev", ios::binary);
                                         // creates output file "datafeed," associ-
                                         // ates it with device "specdev" and opens
                                         // in explicit binary mode.
```

See Also
fstream, ostream, istream, ifstream, cout, << (insertion operator), open()

open()   function

Purpose
Use the *ios* member function *open()* to open a C++ file stream for input or output. *open()* is used with a previously declared stream object (usually an *ifstream* for input or an *ofstream* for output).

Syntax
```
#include <fstream.h>
<stream_name>.open(<filename>,<open_mode>,<protection_mode>);
stream_name            Name of stream to be used for file
filename               actual file name used by operating system
open_mode              how file is to be accessed (see ios entry
                       for list of file modes)
protection_mode        degree of file protection (defined in fstream
                       class)
```

Most compilers have only the value *filebuf::openprot* for the protection_mode, so this parameter can be omitted.

Example Use
```
ofstream my_output;                      // declare an output file
ofstream.open("datafile", ios::out);     // open for output
```

Note that you can declare and open a file in one statement by using the constructor for *fstream* with one of its derivative classes, for example:

```
ofstream my_output("datafile",ios::out)  // equivalent to above two statements
```

See Also
ios, fstream, ifstream, ofstream

ostream ✦ class

Purpose
The *ostream* class is used for output to a C++ stream such as *cout*, the standard output stream that is usually assigned to the screen. The *ostream* class is derived from the *ios* class. The *ostream_withassign* class is in turn derived from *ostream* to provide the four predefined standard streams (*cin*, *cout*, *cerr*, and *clog*) and stream assignment operators.

Syntax
```
#include <iostream.h>
ostream <stream_name>;
```

See Also
ios, istream, iostream.h, stream.h, cout, << (insertion operator), iomanip.h

peek() ✦ function

Purpose
Use the *peek()* ios member function to get the value of the next character in the input stream without removing it from the stream. This allows you to test the validity of the input without processing it.

Syntax
```
#include <iostream.h>
char_var = <stream>.peek();
char_var                    character variable to receive peeked value
```

Example Use
```
char ch;
while ((ch = cin.peek()) != '*') {
        cin.get(ch);
        cout << ch;
        }
// echoes characters typed until "*" is
// entered (due to buffering, doesn't
// respond until <Enter> is pressed)
```

Returns
The *peek()* function returns a copy of the *char* value found in the input.

See Also
get(), getline(), cin, >> (insertion operator)

perror() ♦ function

Purpose
Use the *perror()* function to construct an error message by concatenating your message provided in the argument *string* with that from the system message corresponding to the current value in the global variable *errno*, and print the message to *stderr*.

Syntax
```
#include <stdio.h>
void perror(const char *string);
const char *string;        Your part of the message
```

Example Use
```
perror("Error closing file");
```

See Also
matherr(), errno, stderr

pow() ♦ function

Purpose
The *pow()* function computes the value of *x* raised to the power *y*. Neither *x* nor *y* may be zero and when *x* is negative, *y* must be an integer.

Syntax
```
#include <math.h>
double pow(double x, double y);
double x, y;              x raised to the power y will be computed
```

Example Use
```
x = pow(2.0, 3.0); /* x will be 8.0 */
```

Returns
When both *x* and *y* are nonzero positive numbers, *pow* returns the value *x* raised to the power *y*. If *x* is nonzero and *y* is zero, the return value is 1.

See Also
log(), log10(), sqrt()

#pragma ✦ preprocessor directive

Purpose

Use the *#pragma* directive to instruct the compiler in some way. Details are implementation-dependent. Typically, pragmas control the kinds of optimization to be performed, whether the intrinsic form of functions should be compiled, and other characteristics of the compiler.

Syntax

```
#pragma <pragma_name (arguments...)>
```

Example Use

```
#pragma loop_opt(on)     /* turns on loop optimization for Microsoft C
                            Compiler 5.1 or later */
```

printf() ✦ function

Purpose

Use *printf()* to write character strings and values of variables, formatted in a specified manner, to the standard output file *stdout*, normally the screen. The value of each argument is formatted according to the codes embedded in the string *format_string*. The formatting command for each variable consists of a percent sign (%) followed by a single letter denoting the type of variable being printed. The complete format specification is of the following form:

```
%[Flags][Width].[Precision][Size][Type]
```

Table 10-10 summarizes each component of the format string. The subsequent tables explain the *Size, Flag,* and *Type* fields, respectively.

Table 10-10 Format String

FIELD	EXPLANATION
Flags (Optional)	One or more of the characters -, +, # or a blank space to specify justification, appearance of plus/minus signs and of the decimal point in the values printed (see following explanation).
Width (Optional)	A number to indicate how many characters, at a minimum, must be used to print the value.
Precision (Optional)	Another number specifying how many characters, at most, can be used in printing the value. When printing integer variables, this is the minimum number of digits used.
Size (Optional)	This is a character that modifies the *Type* field which comes next. One of the characters 'h,' 'l,' or 'L' appears in this field. This field is used to differentiate between short and long integers, and between *float* and *double*. A summary of this field is shown in Table 10-11.
Type (Required)	A letter to indicate the type of variable being printed. Table 10-13 lists the possible characters and their meanings.

Table 10-11 Size Field

PREFIX	WHEN TO USE
h	Use when printing integers using *Type* d, i, o, x, or X to indicate that the argument is a short integer. Also, use with *Type* u to indicate that the variable being printed is a short unsigned integer.
l	Use when printing integers or unsigned integers with a *Type* field of d, i, o, u, x, or X to specify that the variable to be printed is a long integer.
L	Use when the floating-point variable being printed is a long double and the *Type* specifier is one of e, E, f, g, or G.

Table 10-12 Flag Field

FLAG	MEANING
–	Left-justify output value within the field.
+	If the output value is numeric, print a + or a –, according to the sign of the value.
space	Positive numerical values are prefixed with blank spaces. This flag is ignored if the + flag also appears.
#	When used in printing variables of type o, x, or X (i.e. octal or hexadecimal), nonzero output values are prefixed with 0, 0x, or 0X, respectively. When the *Type* field in the format specification is e, E, f, g, or G, this flag forces the printing of a decimal point. For a g or a G in the *Type* field, all trailing zeros will be printed.
0	For d, i, o, u, x, X, e, f, g, or G *Type* leading zeros will be printed. This flag is ignored if the – flag also appears.

Table 10-13 Type Field

SPECIFIER	DATA TYPE	RESULTING OUTPUT FORMAT
c	char	Single character.
d	int	Signed decimal integer as a sequence of digits with or without a sign depending on the Flags used. *printf ("%d", 95);* prints *95*.
e	double or float	Signed value in the scientific format. For example, *–1.234567e+002*.
E	double or float	Signed value in the scientific format, exponent letter capitalized, the previous example will print *–1.234567E+002* if the %E format is used.

Table 10-13 (continued)

SPECIFIER	DATA TYPE	RESULTING OUTPUT FORMAT
f	double or float	Signed value in the format, (*sign*)(*digits*).(*digits*), the example for *Type* e will print *−123.456700* if the *%f* format is used. The number of digits that come before the decimal point depends on the magnitude of the variable, and the number of digits that come after the decimal point depends on the *Precision* field in the format specification. The default precision is 6. Therefore, a *%f* format alone always produces six digits after the decimal point, but a *%.3f* will print the value *−123.457* which is *−123.4567* rounded off to three decimal places.
g	double or float	Signed value printed using one of *e* or *f* format. The format that generates the most compact output for the given *Precision* and value is selected. The *e* format is used only when the exponent is less than *−4* or when it is greater than the value of the *Precision* field. Printing the value *−123.4567* using a *%g* format will result in *−123.457* because the *g* format rounds off the number.
G	double or float	Signed value printed using the *g* format, but with the letter *G* in place of *e* whenever exponents are printed.
i	int	Signed decimal integer as a sequence of digits with or without a sign depending on the *Flags* field.
n	pointer to int	This is not really a printing format. The argument corresponding to this format is a pointer *to an integer*. Before returning, the *printf()* function will store in this integer the total number of characters it has printed thus far to the output file or to the file's buffer.
o	unsigned	Octal digits without any sign.
p	pointer to void	The address is printed in an implementation-defined format.
u	unsigned	Unsigned decimal integer as a sequence of digits.
x	unsigned	Hexadecimal digits using lowercase letters, *abcdef*.
X	unsigned	Hexadecimal digits using uppercase letters, *ABCDEF*.
%	—	Prints *a %*.

C++ programmers should use the streams formatting facilities instead of *printf()* for output formatting. The multiple overloaded versions of operator << for the basic data types produce reasonable default formatting, and a selection of manipulators and flags are available for tailoring the format of output.

Syntax

```
#include <stdio.h>
int printf(const char *format_string,...);
const char *format_string;     A character string which describes the
                               format to be used.
...                            A variable number of arguments depending on
                               the number of items being printed
```

Example Use

```
printf("The product of %d and %d is %d\n", x, y, x*y);
```

Returns

The *printf()* function returns the number of characters it has printed. In case of error, it returns a negative value.

See Also

fprintf(), sprintf(), vfprintf(), vprintf(), vsprintf(), stdout, cout, << (insertion operator), ios, flags(), setflags()

private ◆ keyword

Purpose

Use the *private* keyword to restrict access to the data or member functions of a class. *private* class members can only be used by member functions of the same class. By default, members of a class are *private* unless they follow the keywords *public* or *protected*. (In a *struct*, access is *public* by default.)

You can also use the keyword *private* to restrict access to a base class by a derived class. When this is done, the *public* and *protected* members of the base class become *private* members of the derived class (and, therefore, cannot be accessed from outside it). The *private* members of the base class are not inherited at all.

Syntax

```
class <classname> {
<member>...
};                             members private by default

class <classname> {
...
private:
<member>
...
};                             members explicitly private

class <derived_class> private <base_class>
...                            private derivation from base class
```

Example Use
```
class point {
int X, Y;
long color;              // these members are private
public:
point()                  // public members start here
...
};

class checking : private account {
...
}; // private derivation from "account" class
```

See Also
class, struct, public, protected

protected ♦ keyword

Purpose
Use the *protected* keyword to provide limited access to a class' member functions or to a base class from a derived class. Members in the *protected* section of a class can be accessed only by the class' member functions. When a class is derived from a class with a *protected* section, members of the derived class can access the *protected* members of the base class, but cannot access *private* members.

Syntax
```
class <classname< {
...
protected:
members...               these members are protected
...
};
class <derived_class> : protected <base_class> [
...
};                       derived can access protected members of base, but
                         not private members
```

Example Use
```
class acct_data {
char name [40];
...
protected:
long acct_number;
...
};                       // acct_number is protected

class cust_data : protected acct_data {
...
};                       // cust_data can access acct_number in
                         // acct_data
```

321

See Also
`private, protected, class, struct`

ptrdiff_t ♦ predefined data type

Purpose
The *ptrdiff_t* data type is a signed integral type that can hold the result of subtracting one pointer from another. It is defined in *stddef.h*.

See Also
`* (pointer-to)`

public ♦ keyword

Purpose
Use the *public* keyword to allow access to class members from outside the class, or to allow derived classes access to all but private members of the base class. *public* is the least restrictive access to a C++ object, and should be used carefully. Typically, a class' data members are made *private* (absent a strong reason to do otherwise), and a group of *public* member functions are used to provide access to the data from outside the class. Put another way, the *public* part of a class defines its interface to the outside world. By default all members of a *struct* are *public*, but all members of a class are *private*.

Syntax
```
class <classname> {
...
public:
members...              these members are public
...
};

class <derived_class> : public <base_class> {
...
}                       derived class can access all but private members
                        of the base class
```

Note that when a class has *public* derivation, any *public* members of the base class are also *public* in the derived class, and, therefore, can be accessed there by the rest of the program. *protected* members of the base class remain *protected* in the derived class, while *private* members of the base class are not inherited.

Example Use
```
class grab_bag {
```

```
    int internal_status;
public:
    container contents;
    ...
}; // "contents" publicly accessible

class purse : public grab_bag {
    ...
}; users of "purse" can access "contents"
```

See Also
```
private, protected, class, struct
```

put() ◆ function

Purpose

Use the *ios* member function *put()* to insert a character (or a character-sized binary value) into a C++ output stream.

Syntax
```
#include <iostream.h>
<output_stream>.put(<charvar>);
output_stream           an ostream object (or derivative)
charvar                 a variable of type char
```

Example Use
```
char chout;
cout.put(chout);
```

Returns

The *put()* function returns a reference to the output stream.

See Also
```
cout, << (insertion operator), putc(), putchar() (for ANSI C streams)
```

putback() ◆ function

Purpose

Use the *stream* member function *putback()* to "push" a character back into a C++ input stream. This can be done if it is decided that the program should not process the character and should return it so it is available for another part of the program to use. (See the entry for *peek()* for an alternative way to accomplish this procedure.)

Syntax
```
#include <istream>
<input_stream>.putback(charvar);
charvar                 a variable of type char
```

Example Use

```
ifstream input;
char inchar;
...
input.get(inchar);
// check the character
// can't process, so put it back
input.putback(inchar);
...
```

Returns

The *putback()* function returns a reference to the *istream* object from which the character was obtained.

See Also

```
istream, cin, << (insertion operator), peek()
```

putc() ✦ predefined macro

Purpose

Use the *putc()* macro to write a single character *c* to an ANSI C stream. *putc()* is equivalent to *fputc()*, except that it is implemented as a macro. (For C++ streams, the *ios* member function *put()* should be used for single-character output.)

Syntax

```
#include <stdio.h>
int putc(int c, FILE *stream);
int   c;                    Character to be written
FILE *stream;               Pointer to stream to which the character is written
```

Example Use

```
putc('*', outfile);
```

Returns

The *putc()* macro returns the character written. A return value of *EOF* indicates an error. The *ferror()* function should be called to determine if there was an error.

See Also

```
fgetc(), fputc(), getc(), getchar(), putchar(), EOF, FILE, put() (C++ streams)
```

putchar() ✦ predefined macro

Purpose

Use the *putchar()* macro to write the character *c* to the preopened stream *stdout* which is initially connected to your display. *putchar()* is equivalent to *putc()* with the second argument set to *stdout*. (For C++ streams, the *ios* member function *put()* should be used with *cout* for single-character output to the standard output stream.)

Syntax
```
#include <stdio.h>
int putchar(int c);
int c;                     Character to be written
```

Example Use
```
putchar('?');
```

Returns
The *putchar()* macro returns the character written to *stdout*. In case of any error, the return value is equal to the constant EOF.

See Also
fgetc(), fputc(), getc(), getchar(), putc(), EOF, stdout, cout, put() (C++ streams)

puts()   function

Purpose
Use the *puts()* function to output the null-terminated string *string* to the standard output stream *stdout*. The terminating null character (\0) is replaced by a newline (\n) in the output. (You can output a string to the C++ standard output stream by using the *ios* member function *write()* with the *cout* stream.)

Syntax
```
#include <stdio.h>
int puts(const char *string);
const char    *string;     Null-terminated string to be output
```

Example Use
```
puts("Do you really want to quit?");
```

Returns
If successful, *puts()* returns a nonnegative value. Otherwise, it returns EOF to indicate error.

See Also
fgets(), fputs(), gets(), EOF, stdout, cout, <<, write() (for C++ streams)

qsort() ◆ function

Purpose

Use the *qsort()* function to sort an array beginning at the address *base* and comprising *num* elements, each of size *width* bytes. During the sort, *qsort()* compares pairs of elements from the array by calling a routine whose address you provide in the argument *compare*. This function should accept two arguments *elem1* and *elem2*, each a pointer to an element in the array. Internally your comparison routine can call upon *strcmp()* or other appropriate functions to perform the comparison.

Syntax

```
#include <stdlib.h>
void qsort(const void *base, size_t num, size_t
width, int (*compare)(const void *elem1, const void *elem2));
const void *base;          Pointer to beginning of array being sorted
size_t      num;           Number of elements in array
size_t      width;         Size of each element in bytes
int  (*compare)(const void *elem1, const void *elem2);
                           Pointer to a function that compares two elements
                           elem1 and elem2 each of type const void *
```

Example Use

```
int compare(void *, const void *);
qsort((void *) envp, (size_t)count, (size_t)sizeof(char *), compare);
```

See Also

bsearch(), size_t

\r ◆ escape sequence for carriage return

Purpose

Use the \r escape sequence to move the cursor or print head to the beginning of the current line. To move to the beginning of the *next* line, use \n (newline).

Example Use

```
printf("Let's start over\r"); /* cursor goes over L*/
```

See Also

printf(), \n, cout, << (insertion operator) for C++ streams

raise() ◆ function

Purpose

Use *raise()* to "raise a signal" that creates an exception condition corresponding to the number *signum*. The exception will be handled by invoking a routine that was set

CHAPTER 10 ALPHABETICAL REFERENCE

up earlier by calling the function *signal*. The *abort()* function uses *raise()* to create the exception *SIGABRT* to initiate actions to be taken when aborting a program. Note that C++ now provides an alternative exception-handling mechanism, although it is not yet supported by all compilers.

Syntax
```
#include <signal.h>
int    raise(int signum);
int    signum;                 Signal number to be raised
```

Example Use
```
raise(SIGABRT);
```

Returns
If successful, *raise()* returns a zero. Otherwise, it returns a nonzero value.

See Also
```
abort(), signal(), SIGABRT, catch(), throw(), try() (for C++ exceptions)
```

rand() ◆ function

Purpose
The *rand()* function generates a pseudo random integer with a value between 0 and the constant RAND_MAX defined in *stdlib.h*. The "seed" or the starting point of the pseudo random integers can be set by calling *srand*.

Syntax
```
#include <stdlib.h>
int rand(void);
```

Example Use
```
random_value = rand();
```

Returns
The *rand()* function returns the pseudo random integer it generates.

See Also
```
srand(), RAND_MAX
```

RAND_MAX ◆ predefined value

Purpose
The predefined value *RAND_MAX* is the maximum integral value returned by the *rand()* function. It is defined in *stdlib.h*.

See Also
rand()

rdstate() ◆ function

Purpose
Use the *ios* member function *rdstate()* to return the error status of a C++ stream. The stream state flags are returned in a single integer; a return value of 0 means that no error bit has been set and, therefore, the stream is OK. See the entry for *ios* for a description of the error bits and their meanings. The functions *good()*, *eof()*, *fail()*, and *bad()* can be used to examine specific error flags.

Syntax
```
#include <iostream.h>
int <stream>.rdstate();
```

Example Use
```
int strflags;
while (cin.rdstate() == 0) {
        // process while no stream errors
        ...
}
```

Returns
The *rdstate()* function returns an integer whose component bits correspond to the stream error flags. You can use the *ios* bit values and logical operators to examine the integer returned by *rdstate()* for particular bit values.

See Also
iostream, ios, clear(), fail(), good(), eof(), bad()

read() ◆ function

Purpose
Use the *ios* member function *read()* to read a specified amount of character data (or character-sized binary data) from a stream.

Syntax
```
#include <iostream.h>
<input_stream>.read(char* data, int num_bytes);
```

Example Use
```
char mystring [81];      // leave room for end of string character
cin.read(mystring, 80);
```

Note that *read()* doesn't pay any particular regard to whitespace, CR/LF, or the end-of-string null character. Everything is read in just as it is found. This means that you can use *read()* to read arbitrary binary data as long as the destination object is a string (array of *char*) with a sufficient number of elements to hold the data. In the previous example, the string *mystring* is declared to 81 elements, allowing 80 characters for the string plus room for a null character that can be added later to make a standard C++ string. Note that input from *cin* won't stop after the user presses [ENTER]. All typed characters will be accepted until 80 characters have been typed or an interrupt character (typically [CTRL]-[C]) is received.

Returns

The *read()* function returns a reference to the input stream used.

See Also

```
istream, ios, cin, >> (extraction operator), get(), getline(), write()
```

realloc()   function

Purpose

Use the *realloc()* function to alter the size of a previously allocated block of memory to the new size given in the argument *newsize*. The address of the block is specified by the pointer *mem_address*. This pointer must be either NULL or a value returned by an earlier call to *malloc()*, *calloc()*, or *realloc()*. If the argument *mem_address* is a NULL, then *realloc()* behaves like *malloc()* and allocates a new block of memory of size *newsize*. The memory block of altered size may not be located at the same address any more, but the contents of the block (up to the old size) is guaranteed to be unchanged.

Note that C++ provides an alternative (and superior) memory allocation mechanism using the *new* and *delete* operators with class constructors and destructors.

Syntax

```
#include <stdlib.h>
void *realloc(void *mem_address, size_t newsize);
void *mem_address;         Pointer to the block of memory whose size is to
                           be altered
size_t   newsize;          New size of the block in bytes
```

Example Use

```
new_buffer = realloc(old_buffer, old_size+100);
```

Returns

The *realloc()* function returns the address of the block of memory. If *realloc()* fails, the pointer will be unchanged and it will return a NULL.

register ◆ keyword

Purpose
Use *register* as a storage classifier for integer data types to inform the compiler that the access to that data object should be as fast as possible. At its discretion, the compiler may use a CPU register to store that variable.

Syntax
```
register <type> <varname>;
type                        an integer type (such as char, int, or long)
```

Example Use
```
register int i;
```

See Also
auto, extern, static

remove() ◆ function

Purpose
Use *remove()* to delete a file specified by the name *file_name*.

Syntax
```
#include <stdio.h>
int remove(const char *file_name);
const char *file_name;    Name of file to be deleted
```

Example Use
```
remove("/usr/tmp/tmp01234"); /* Delete temporary file */
```

Returns
If *remove()* successfully deletes the specified file, it returns a zero. Otherwise, the return value is nonzero.

See Also
rename()

rename() ◆ function

Purpose
Use *rename()* to change the name of a file from *oldname* to *newname*.

Syntax

```
#include <stdio.h>
int rename(const char *oldname, const char *newname);
const char *oldname;         Current file name
const char *newname;         New file name
```

Example Use

```
/* Copy test.exe from /usr/tmp to /usr/bin and give it a new name */
rename("/usr/tmp/test.exe","/usr/bin/grview.exe");
```

Returns

If *rename()* is successful, it returns a zero. In case of an error, it returns a nonzero value.

See Also

fopen(), fclose(), remove()

---

resetiosflags() ◆ manipulator

Purpose

Use the *resetiosflags()* manipulator to clear specified *ios* format flags for a C++ stream. The flags corresponding to the bits set in *flag_vals* will be cleared. Typically, the flag masks enumerated in the *ios* class are used with the bitwise OR (|) to specify the flags to be cleared. Note that *resetiosflags()* takes the same *long* argument as *unsetf()*, which also clears the flags set in the long value. The difference between the two functions is that *resetiosflags()* returns a reference to the stream used, while *unsetf()* returns a *long* value representing the status of the format flags before clearing.

Syntax

```
output_stream << resetiosflags(<long flag_vals>);      or
input_stream >> resetiosflags(<long flag_vals>);
output_stream,              ostream or istream object
input_stream
long flag_vals              a long int value whose bits correspond to the
                            flags you want to clear
```

Example Use

```
#include <iostream.h>
#include <iomanip.h>         // needed for manipulators with
                             // arguments
cout << resetiosflags(ios::scientific | ios::uppercase);
```

Use of the *OR* operator ensures that only the bits representing "scientific notation" and "uppercase base and exponent indicator" are set in the value passed to *resetiosflags()*. These are, therefore, the flags that will be cleared.

Returns

The *resetiosflags()* manipulator returns a reference to the input or output stream used.

See Also

ios, istream, ostream, iomanip.h, setiosflags(), setf(), unsetf(), flags()

return ◆ keyword

Purpose

Use *return* to terminate execution of the current function and return control to the caller. Optionally, specify a value to be returned to the caller.

Syntax

```
return; or
return <expression>;
```

If the function returns a value, use the statement *return <expression>* to return the value represented by the *<expression>*.

Example Use

```
/* Return the maximum of two integers */
int findmax(int a, int b)
{
    if(a >= b)
        return a;
    else
        return b;
}
```

See Also

break, continue, goto

scanf() ◆ function

Purpose

Use *scanf()* to read characters from the standard input file *stdin* and convert the strings to values of variables according to the format specified in the string *format_string*. For each variable's address included in the argument list to *scanf*, there must be a format specification embedded in the *format_string*. The format specification for each variable is of the following form: %[*][Width][Size][Type] where Type is one of the specifiers for data types listed in the entry for *printf()*.

Normally, strings read using the %s format are assumed to be delimited by blank spaces. When you want to read a string delimited by any character other than those in a specific set, you can specify the set of characters within brackets and use this in place of the letter s in the format specification. On the other hand, if the first character inside the brackets is a caret (^), the set is assumed to show the characters that terminate the string. For example, %[^\"'] will read a string delimited by single or double quote characters.

Table 10-14 summarizes the purpose of each field in the format specification used by *scanf()*.

Table 10-14 Format String

FIELD	EXPLANATION
% (Required)	Indicates the beginning of a format specification. Use %% to read a percentage sign from the input.
* (Optional)	The characters representing the value are read according to the format specification, but the value is not stored. It is not necessary to give an argument corresponding to this format specification.
Width (Optional)	A positive value specifying the maximum number of characters to be read for the value of this variable.
Size (Optional)	A character that modifies the *Type* field that comes next. One of the characters h, l, or L appears in this field to differentiate between short and long integers, and between *float* and *double*. A summary of this field is shown in Table 10-15.
Type (Required)	A letter that indicates the type of variable being read. Table 10-16 lists the possible characters and their meanings.

Table 10-15 Size Field

PREFIX	WHEN TO USE
h	Use when reading integers using *Type* d, i, or n to indicate that the argument is a short integer. Also, use with *Type* o, u, and x to indicate that the variable being read is an unsigned integer.
l	Use when reading integers or unsigned integers with a *Type* field of d, i, or n to specify that the variable to be read is a long integer. Also use with o, u, and x to read values into unsigned long integers and for floating-point variables (when the *Type* field is e, f, or g) to a *double* rather than a *float*.
L	Use with e, f, and g to indicate that the variable is a *long double*.

Table 10-16 Type Field

TYPE SPECIFIER	C++ DATA TYPE	EXPECTED INPUT
c	Pointer to char	Single character. Whitespace characters (space, tab, newline) will be read in this format.
d	Pointer to int	Decimal integer.

continued on next page

Table 10-16 (continued)

TYPE SPECIFIER	C++ DATA TYPE	EXPECTED INPUT
e f g	Pointer to float	Signed value in the scientific format—for example, −1.234567e+002 and 9.876543e−002 or in the format "(sign)(digits).(digits)"—for example, −1.234567 and 9.876543.
i	Pointer to int	Decimal, hexadecimal, or octal integer.
n	Pointer to int	This is not a reading format. The argument corresponding to this format is a pointer to an integer. Before returning, the *scanf()* function stores in this integer the number of characters it has read thus far from the input file or the input file's buffer.
o	Pointer to int	Octal digits without a sign.
p	Pointer to an address	Implementation-defined format for pointer.
s	Pointer to an array of characters large enough to hold input string plus a terminating null (\0)	Character string.
u	Pointer to unsigned int	Unsigned decimal integer.
x	Pointer to int	Hexadecimal digits.

Syntax

```
#include <stdio.h>
int scanf(const char *format_string, <address>...
const char *format_string;     Character string that describes the format
                               to be used
address...                     variable number of arguments representing
                               addresses of variables whose values are
                               being used
```

Example Use

```
scanf("%d:%d:%d", &hour, &minute, &second);
```

Returns

The *scanf()* function returns the number of input items that were successfully read, converted, and saved in variables. This does not include the items that were read and ignored. A return value equal to the constant EOF (defined in *stdio.h*) means that an end-of-file was encountered during the read operation.

Note that for C++ streams, the use of *ios* member functions and the overloaded extraction operator (>>) is preferable to *scanf()* and related ANSI C library functions.

See Also
fscanf(), sscanf(), ios, cin, >> (extraction operator for C++)

SEEK_CUR ✦ predefined value

Purpose
The constant *SEEK_CUR* indicates "relative to current position" when positioning the file pointer with *fseek()*. It is defined in *stdio.h*. The equivalent specifier for C++ streams (used with *setg()* and *setp()*) is *ios::cur*.

See Also
SEEK_END, SEEK_SET, ios (ios::cur), setg(), setp() (for C++)

SEEK_END ✦ predefined value

Purpose
The constant *SEEK_END* indicates "relative to end of file" when positioning the file pointer with *fseek*. It is defined in *stdio.h*. The equivalent for C++ streams (used with *setg()* and *setp()*) is *ios::end*.

See Also
SEEK_CUR, SEEK_SET; ios (ios::end), setg(), setp() (for C++)

seekg() ✦ function

Purpose
Use the *seekg()* *istream* member function to reposition the location from which the next data will be read from a C++ file stream. You can position the new location to an absolute location or to a specified number of bytes before or after the beginning, current position, or end of the file.

Syntax
```
#include <iostream.h>
<istream>.seekg(<absolute_position>); or
<istream>.seekg(int num_bytes, position_from);
istream                 input stream; object of class fstream or derivative
long absolute_position  typically value returned from tellg()
num_bytes               number of bytes to move read position
position_from           location in file from which to position
```

If you want to set the read position to an absolute location in the file, follow *setg()* with the position as a *long* (*streampos*) value in parentheses. You can save a position by calling *tellg()* and then using *setg()* later to return to that position. You can also use the *ios* enumerated values *beg*, *cur*, and *end* to indicate the beginning, current position, and end of the file, respectively.

You can also specify an offset (the number of bytes to move the position) followed by the location from which to move. (This is again, one of the enumerations *ios::beg*, *ios::cur, or ios:end.*)

Example Use

```
istream input_file;
input_file.seekg(0, ios::beg);      // position to very
                                    // beginning of file
input_file.seekg(5, ios::cur);      // skip next five
                                    // bytes
input_file.seekg(-20,ios::end);     // position to 20
                                    // bytes before end of file
```

Returns

The *seekg()* function returns a reference to the input stream.

See Also

ios, istream, seekp(), tellg(), tellp()

seekp()   ✦   function

Purpose

Use the *seekp() iostream* member function to reposition the location from which the next data will be written to a C++ file stream. You can position the new location to an absolute location or to a specified number of bytes before or after the beginning, current position, or end of the file.

Syntax

```
#include <iostream.h>
<ostream>.seekp(<absolute_position>); or
<ostream>.seekp(int num_bytes, position_from);
ostream                             output stream; an of object of class
                                    ostream or derivative
long absolute_position              typically value returned from tellp()
num_bytes                           number of bytes to move write position
position_from                       location in file from which to position
```

If you want to set the write position to an absolute location in the file, follow *setp()* with the position as a *long* (*streampos*) value in parentheses. You can save a position by calling *tellg()* or *tellp()* and then use *setp()* later to return to that position. You can also use the *ios* enumerated values *beg*, *cur*, and *end* to indicate the beginning, current position, and end of the file, respectively.

You can also specify an offset (the number of bytes to move the position) followed by the location from which to move. (This is again, one of the enumerations *ios::beg*, *ios::cur*, or *ios:end*.)

Example Use
```
ostream output_file;
output_file.seekg(0, ios::beg);         // position to very
                                        // beginning of file-rewrite file
output_file.seekg(-reclen, ios::cur);   // rewrite
                                        // current record if at end
```

Returns
The *seekp()* function returns a reference to the input stream.

See Also
ios, istream, seekg(), tellg(), tellp()

SEEK_SET   ✦   predefined value

Purpose
The constant *SEEK_SET* indicates "relative to start of file" when positioning the file pointer with *fseek*. It is defined in *stdio.h*. The equivalent specifier for C++ streams (used with *setg()* and *setp()*) is *ios::beg*.

See Also
SEEK_CUR, SEEK_END, ios (ios::beg), setg(), setp() (for C++)

setbase()   ✦   manipulator

Purpose
Use the *setbase()* manipulator to set the base to be used for displaying numeric values. You can set the base to 0, 8, 10, or 16; the default is base 10. Note: alternate manipulators to set the numeric base are *dec* (base 10), *hex* (base 16), and *oct* (base 8).

Syntax
```
#include <iostream.h>
#include <iomanip.h>
<output_stream> << setbase(base);
```

Example Use
```
ostream my_output;
my_output << 24 << setbase(8); displays 30
```

See Also
dec, hex, oct

setbuf() ◆ function

Purpose

Use the *setbuf()* function to assign buffer, of size *BUFSIZ*, instead of the system-allocated one for use by *stream* for buffering. Calling *setbuf()* is equivalent to using *setvbuf()* with *_IOFBF* and *BUFSIZ* as the third and the fourth arguments, respectively. If *buffer* is NULL, the third argument will be *_IONBF*. (For C++ streams, set up a *streambuf* for derivative class rather than using *setbuf()*.)

Syntax

```
#include <stdio.h>
void setbuf(FILE *stream, char *buffer);
FILE *stream;              Pointer to stream whose buffer is being set
char *buffer;              Pointer to buffer (or NULL if no buffering is to
                           be done)
```

Example Use

```
setbuf(infile, mybuffer);
```

See Also

setvbuf(), BUFSIZ, FILE, _IOFBF, _IONBF, NULL, streambuf (C++)

setf() ◆ function

Purpose

Use the *setf()* *ios* member function to set an *ios* C++ stream format flag. You can use *setf()* with a mask value (enumerated in *ios*) to set a specified flag without disturbing the others. (This makes *setf()* easier and safer to use than *flags()*, which affects bits throughout the flags value.)

Some flags are arranged as groups of settings. For example, *ios::left*, *ios::right*, and *ios::internal* control adjustment (justification) of output. When you want to set one flag in a group, use the flag enumerator that you want to set followed by the group (*ios::adjustfield*, *ios::basefield*, or *ios::floatfield*). In this syntax, *setf()* clears all bits in the specified group and then sets the specified flag. See the *ios* entry for descriptions of the flags and flag groups.

Syntax

```
<stream>.setf(mask); or
<stream>.setf(mask, group_specifier);
mask                     a flag mask enumerated in ios
group_specifier          ios::adjustfield, ios::basefield, or ios::floatfield
```

Example Use

```
cout.setf(ios::left, ios::adjustfield);    // sets left justification of output
datastream.setf(ios::showbase);            // sets the showbase flag (not part
                                           // of a group)
```

Returns

The *setf()* function returns a long value containing the *ios* format flag values as they were before the new bit(s) were set.

See Also

flags(), unsetf(), setiosflags(), resetiosflags()

setfill() ✦ manipulator

Purpose

Use the *setfill()* manipulator to set the fill character to be used for padding values displayed from a C++ output stream. (Note that the *ios* member function *fill()* is an alternative for this purpose; *fill()* returns the previous fill character, but the *setfill()* manipulator is more convenient for use when cascading output to a stream.)

Syntax

```
#include <iostream.h>
#include <iomanip.h>
output_stream << setfill(fillchar);
fillchar                 character to use for padding
```

Example Use

```
ostream checkdata;
checkdata << setfill('#');
```

Returns

The *setfill()* manipulator returns a reference to the output stream.

See Also

fill()

setiosflags() ✦ manipulator

Purpose

Use the *ios setiosflags()* manipulator to set a stream's format flag bits according to the *long* value specified. (Nonmanipulator functions are also available for this purpose: see *flags()* and *setf()*.)

Syntax

```
#include <iostream.h>
#include <iomanip.h>
input_stream >> setiosflags(flagvals); or
output_stream << setiosflags(flagvals);
flagvals                 a long value containing the flag bits to be set
```

Example Use

```
// set up long flag value with ios enums
long flagvals = (ios::hex | ios::showbase);
// set the hex and showbase flags
cout << setiosflags(flagvals);
```

Returns

The *setiosflags()* manipulator returns a reference to the stream used.

See Also

```
resetiosflags(), flags(), setf(), unsetf()
```

setjmp()   ♦   predefined macro

Purpose

Use the *setjmp()* macro to save a stack environment in the *jmp_buf* struct named *env* before calling another function. This environment can subsequently be restored by a call to *longjmp()*, achieving the effect of a nonlocal *goto*. When *longjmp()* is called at a later time with the saved calling environment, it restores all stack-based local variables in the routine to the values they had when *setjmp()* was called and jumps to the return address that *setjmp()* had saved. For all intents and purposes, this will feel like a return, one more time, from the last call to *setjmp()*. Note that this process does not guarantee the proper restoration of register-based and *volatile* variables.

Syntax

```
#include <setjmp.h>
int setjmp(jmp_buf env);
jmp_buf env;              Struct data type where the current calling
                          environment is stored
```

Example Use

```
if (setjmp(env) != 0) printf("Returned from longjmp\n");
```

Returns

After saving the stack environment, *setjmp()* returns a zero. When *longjmp()* is called with the environment saved by this particular call to *setjmp()*, the effect is the same as returning from *setjmp()* again, this time with the second argument of *longjmp()* as the return value.

See Also

```
longjmp(), jmp_buf
```

setlocale() ◆ function

Purpose
Use *setlocale()* to define the locale named in the string *locale_name* for the locale-dependent aspects of your program specified by the argument *category*. The *category* can take one of the values shown in the table in the entry for *localeconv()*.

Syntax
```
#include <locale.h>
char *setlocale(int category, const char *locale_name);
int    category;         Indicates the parts of your program's locale-
                         dependent aspects for which you are defining a
                         locale, one of: LC_ALL, LC_COLLATE, LC_CTYPE,
                         LC_MONETARY, LC_NUMERIC, or LC_TIME
char   *locale_name;     The name of locale that will control the specified
                         category
```

Example Use
```
setlocale(LC_ALL, "C");
```

Returns
If *locale_name* is not NULL and *setlocale()* is successful, it returns the string associated with the specified category for the new locale. Otherwise, *setlocale()* returns a NULL and the program's locale is not changed.

See Also
localeconv(), LC_ALL, LC_COLLATE, LC_CTYPE, LC_MONETARY, LC_NUMERIC, LC_TIME, NULL

setprecision() ◆ manipulator

Purpose
Use the *setprecision()* manipulator to specify the number of digits of precision for floating-point numeric values in a stream.

Syntax
```
#include <iostream.h>
#include <iomanip.h>
output_stream << setprecision(digits);
digits                   number of digits of precision
```

It is of course not meaningful to set a precision greater than the inherent precision of the data type involved. See the entries for *float* and *double* for details.

Example Use
```
ostream output;
output << setprecision(6); // 6 digit precision
```

Returns

The *setprecision()* manipulator returns a reference to the stream used.

See Also

```
ios (formatting flags), setw()
```

setvbuf() ✦ function

Purpose

Use the *setvbuf()* function to assign buffer of a size *buf_size* to *stream*. You can also control the type of buffering to be used or turn off buffering for *stream* by specifying appropriate constants for the argument *buf_mode*. If *buf_mode* is *_IOFBF*, the I/O operations with the stream will be fully buffered. If it is *_IOFBF*, buffering will be done one line at a time. Setting *buf_mode* to *_IONBF* causes I/O to be unbuffered. (For C++ a *streambuf* or derivative class would probably be used.)

Syntax

```
#include <stdio.h>
int setvbuf(FILE *stream, char *buffer, int buf_mode, size_t buf_size);
FILE *stream;              Pointer to stream whose buffer is being set
char *buffer;              Pointer to buffer (or NULL if no buffering
                           requested)
int buf_mode;              Mode of buffering desired
size_t buf_size;           size of buffer in bytes, if any assigned
```

Example Use

```
setvbuf(infile, buffer, _IOFBF, 2048);
```

Returns

If successful, *setvbuf()* returns a 0. In case of bad parameters or other errors, the return value will be nonzero.

See Also

```
setbuf(), FILE, _IOFBF, _IOLBF, _IONBF, NULL, size_t
```

setw() ✦ manipulator

Purpose

Use the *ios setw()* manipulator to specify the total field width for output from a C++ stream. Note that the *ios* flags *ios::left*, *ios::right*, and *ios::internal* determine how values will be padded within the specified field width. If a value is longer than the width specified, the full value will be displayed, overflowing the field.

Syntax

```
#include <iostream.h>
#include <iomanip.h>
output_stream << setw(characters);
characters               integer width in characters
```

Example Use

```
cout << setw(10); // 10 character field
```

Returns

The *setw()* manipulator returns a reference to the stream used.

See Also

```
ios (formatting flags), setprecision()
```

short ◆ keyword

Purpose

Use *short* as a size qualifier for *int* and *unsigned int* variables. Note that *short* alone means *signed short int*. A *short* qualifier indicates that the integer data type is at least two bytes in size; on some systems it may be longer.

Syntax

```
short <integer_type> <varname>;
```

Example Use

```
short offset;
unsigned short array_index;
```

See Also

```
char, double, float, int, long, signed, unsigned
```

SHRT_MAX ◆ predefined value

Purpose

The predefined value SHRT_MAX is the maximum value of a *short int*. It is defined in *limits.h*.

See Also

SHRT_MIN

SHRT_MIN ✦ predefined value

Purpose
The predefined value *SHRT_MIN* is the minimum value of a *short int*. It is defined in *limits.h*.

See Also
SHRT_MAX

sig_atomic_t ✦ predefined data type

Purpose
The *sig_atomic_t* data type allows access as a single entity even in the presence of hardware and software interrupts. It is defined in *signal.h*.

See Also
SIGINT

SIG_DFL ✦ predefined value

Purpose
The constant *SIG_DFL* indicates default handling of a signal. It is defined in *signal.h*.

See Also
SIG_ERR, SIG_IGN, SIGABRT, SIGFPE, SIGILL, SIGINT, SIGSEGV, SIGTERM

SIG_ERR ✦ predefined value

Purpose
The constant *SIG_ERR* indicates error return from the signal function. It is defined in *signal.h*.

See Also
SIG_DFL, SIG_IGN, SIGABRT, SIGFPE, SIGILL, SIGINT, SIGSEGV, SIGTERM

SIG_IGN ✦ predefined value

Purpose
The constant *SIG_IGN* indicates that a signal should be ignored. It is defined in *signal.h*.

See Also
SIG_ERR, SIG_DFL, SIGABRT, SIGFPE, SIGILL, SIGINT, SIGSEGV, SIGTERM

SIGABRT ◆ predefined value

Purpose
The constant *SIGABRT* indicates that a program aborted. It is defined in *signal.h*.

See Also
SIG_ERR, SIG_DFL, SIGIGN, SIGFPE, SIGILL, SIGINT, SIGSEGV, SIGTERM

SIGSEGV ◆ predefined value

Purpose
The constant *SIGSEGV* indicates that an invalid storage address was accessed. It is defined in *signal.h*.

See Also
SIG_ERR, SIG_DFL, SIGIGN, SIGABRT, SIGFPE, SIGILL, SIGINT, SIGTERM

SIGFPE ◆ predefined value

Purpose
The constant *SIGFPE* indicates that a division by zero, an overflow, or another floating-point error has occurred. It is defined in *signal.h*.

See Also
SIG_ERR, SIG_DFL, SIGIGN, SIGABRT, SIGILL, SIGINT, SIGSEGV, SIGTERM

SIGILL ◆ predefined value

Purpose
The constant *SIGILL* indicates that an illegal instruction has been encountered. It is defined in *signal.h*.

See Also
SIG_ERR, SIG_DFL, SIGIGN, SIGABRT, SIGFPE, SIGINT, SIGSEGV, SIGTERM

SIGINT ✦ predefined value

Purpose
The constant *SIGINT* indicates that the user has attempted to get the attention of (interrupt) the program by pressing a key such as CTRL-C. It is defined in *signal.h*.

See Also
SIG_ERR, SIG_DFL, SIGIGN, SIGABRT, SIGFPE, SIGILL, SIGSEGV, SIGTERM

signal() ✦ function

Purpose
Use the *signal()* function to set up the routine *func* as the handler for the exception or signal number *signum*. The handler is expected to accept the signal number as an argument. The signal number *signum* must be one of the constants shown in Table 10-17. These constants are defined in the include file *signal.h*. If you want to ignore a signal, use *SIG_IGN* as the second argument to *signal()*. Specifying *SIG_DFL* as the second argument sets up the implementation-defined default handling for the signal.

Table 10-17 Signal Number

SIGNAL	EXCEPTION CONDITION
SIGABRT	Abnormal termination of program, for example, by calling the abort function.
SIGFPE	Floating-point error, such as overflow, division by zero, etc.
SIGILL	Illegal instruction in the program.
SIGINT	Generated when user presses a key designed to get the attention of the operating system. For example, pressing CTRL-C in UNIX or MS-DOS would generate this signal.
SIGSEGV	Illegal memory access.
SIGTERM	Termination request sent to the program.

Note that recent implementations of C++ provide a separate exception-handling mechanism using the keywords *catch*, *throw*, and *try*.

Syntax
```
#include <signal.h>
void (*signal(int signum, void (*func)(int)))(int);
int signum;              Signal number for which a handler is being set up
void (*func)(int);       Pointer to handler that can accept an integer argument
```

Example Use
```
if(signal(SIGINT, ctrlc_handler) == SIG_ERR)
   {
     perror("signal failed");
     exit(0);
   }
```

Returns

If successful, *signal()* returns the pointer to the previous handler. In case of error, it returns the constant *SIG_ERR* and sets the global variable *errno* to an implementation-defined error constant.

See Also

```
abort(), raise(), SIG_DFL, SIG_IGN, errno, catch, throw, try (for C++)
```

signed ✦ keyword

Purpose

Use the *signed* qualifier to indicate that data stored in an integral type (*int*, *char*) is signed. For example, a *signed char* can take values between −127 to +127 whereas an *unsigned char* can hold values from 0 to 255. The *int* and *char* types are *signed* by default.

Example Use

```
int i;   /* signed by default */
signed long int x;   /* signed long integer */
```

See Also

```
char, double, float, int, long, short, unsigned
```

SIGTERM ✦ predefined value

Purpose

The constant *SIGTERM* indicates a signal that is sent to a program to terminate it. It is defined in *signal.h*.

See Also

```
SIG_ERR, SIG_DFL, SIGIGN, SIGABRT, SIGFPE, SIGILL, SIGINT, SIGSEGV
```

sin() ✦ function

Purpose

Use the *sin()* function to compute the sine of *double* argument *x* which represents an angle in radians. You can convert an angle from degrees to radians by dividing it by 57.29578.

Syntax

```
#include <math.h>
double sin(double x);
double x;                Angle in radians whose sine is to be computed
```

Example Use
```
y = sin(x);
```

Returns
The *sin()* function returns the sine of *x*. If the value of *x* is large in magnitude, the result may be very imprecise.

See Also
```
asin(), cos()
```

sinh() ♦ function

Purpose
Use the *sinh()* function to compute the hyperbolic sine of a *double* variable *x*.

Syntax
```
#include <math.h>
double sinh(double x);
double x;               Variable whose hyperbolic sine is to be computed
```

Example Use
```
a = sinh(b);
```

Returns
Normally, *sinh()* returns the hyperbolic sine of *x*. If the result is too large (a *double* variable can be as large as approximately 10^{308}), a range error will occur.

See Also
```
cosh(), tanh()
```

size_t ♦ predefined data type

Purpose
The *size_t* data type is an unsigned integral type that is returned by the *sizeof* operator. It is defined in *stdlib.h*.

See Also
```
sizeof
```

sizeof ♦ operator

Purpose
Use the *sizeof* operator to determine the number of bytes that are used to store a particular variable or type of data. When applied to an array (with a reference to

CHAPTER 10   ALPHABETICAL REFERENCE

element [0]), *sizeof* returns the total size of the array; when applied to a pointer, *sizeof* returns the size of the pointer itself, not the size of the data to which it points. When applied to a C++ reference variable, *sizeof* returns the size of the referenced object. When applied to a class, *sizeof* returns the total size of an object of that class.

Example Use
```
image_size = sizeof(image_array[0]);
```

See Also
* (pointer dereferencing operator), & (address-of operator), & (C++ reference operator), this

sprintf()   ♦   function

Purpose

Use the *sprintf()* function to format and write the values of specified variables to the string given in *p_string*. See *printf()* for a description of *format_string*. Note that C++ programmers generally use the specialized in-memory string formatting functions in the *strstreambuf* class and its derivatives together with other stream functions.

Syntax
```
#include <stdio.h>
int sprintf(char *p_string, const char *format_string,
<argument ...>;
char *p_string;                       pointer to an array of characters where
                                      sprintf() sends its formatted output
const char *format_string;            A character string which describes the
                                      format to be used
argument ...                          A variable number of arguments depending on
                                      the number of items being printed
```

Example Use
```
sprintf(buffer, "FY 88 Profit = %.2f\n", profit);
```

Returns

The *sprintf()* function returns the number of characters it has stored in the buffer, not counting the terminating null character (\0).

See Also
fprintf(), printf(), vfprintf(), vprintf(), vsprintf()

sqrt()   ♦   function

Purpose

Use the *sqrt()* function to compute the square root of a nonnegative *double* variable *x*.

Syntax

```
#include <math.h>
double sqrt(double x);
double x;                  Variable whose square root is to be computed
```

Example Use

```
sqrt_2 = sqrt(2.0); /* sqrt_2 = 1.414 */
```

Returns

The *sqrt()* function returns the square root of *x*. However, if *x* is negative, a domain error occurs.

See Also

```
pow()
```

srand() ♦ function

Purpose

Use the *srand()* function to set the "seed" or the starting point of the random-number-generation algorithm used by the function *rand()*. If *seed* is 1, the random number generator is initialized to its default starting point. This will generate the sequence that is produced when *rand()* is called without any prior calls to *srand()*. Any other value of *seed* sets a random starting point for the pseudo random sequence to be generated by *rand()*. To generate randomly selected random sequences, you can use a function that returns the current time from the operating system and use the time value (modified if necessary) for *seed*.

Syntax

```
#include <stdlib.h>
void srand(unsigned seed);
unsigned seed;             Starting point for random number generator
```

Example Use

```
srand(new_seed);
```

See Also

```
rand()
```

sscanf() ♦ function

Purpose

Use *sscanf()* to read characters from *buffer* and convert and store them in C variables according to the formats specified in the string *format_string*. See *scanf()* for a description of the *format_string* argument. Note that C++ programs usually use the overloaded extraction operator (>>) for this purpose.

Syntax

```
#include <stdio.h>
int sscanf(const char *buffer, const char *format_string, <argument...>);
const char *buffer;           Pointer to buffer from which characters will
                              be read and converted to values of variables
const char *format_string;    A character string which describes the
                              format to be used
argument...                   Variable number of arguments representing
                              addresses of variables whose values are
                              being read
```

Example Use

```
sscanf(buffer, "Name: %s Age: %d", name, &age);
```

Returns

The *sscanf()* function returns the number of fields that were successfully read, converted, and assigned to variables. The count excludes items that were read and ignored. If the string ends before completing the read operation, the return value will be the constant *EOF*.

See Also

```
fscanf(), scanf(), EOF
```

static ◆ keyword

Purpose

Use *static* to localize the declaration of a data item or a function to a program module (file). You can use this to "hide" functions and data from other modules. Static variables have permanent storage; they retain their values throughout the life of the program.

Syntax

```
static <type> <varname>
```

Example Use

In the following example, each file has its own copy of the variable *current_index*. Each copy is initialized once, and each retains its last-stored value throughout the execution of the program.

```
/*   FILE1 */
static int current_index = 0;
 main()
{

   ...
   current_index = 1;
   ...
}
 /*   FILE2 */
```

continued on next page

continued from previous page

```
static int current_index = 0;
void some_function(void)
{
   if ( current_index == 0 ) ...
   ...
   current_index = 2;
   ...
}
```

See Also
auto, extern

_ _STDC_ _ ♦ predefined macro

Purpose

Use the _ _STDC_ _ predefined macro to check whether the compiler in use complies with the ANSI standard. This macro should supply a decimal constant 1 to indicate conformance.

Example Use
```
IF (_ _STDC_ _)
    printf("ANSI standard compiler.\n");
else
    printf("Not an ANSI standard compiler.\n");
```

See Also
_ _FILE_ _, _ _LINE_ _, _ _DATE_ _, _ _TIME_ _

stderr ♦ predefined stream

Purpose

The *stderr* predefined pointer points to the standard error stream. It is defined in *stdio.h*. The equivalent C++ stream is *cerr*.

See Also
stdin, stdout, cerr (C++ standard error stream)

stdin ♦ predefined stream

Purpose

The *stdin* predefined pointer points to the standard input stream—by default, the keyboard. It is defined in *stdio.h*. The equivalent C++ stream is *cin*.

See Also
stderr, stdout, cin (C++ standard input stream)

stdout ✦ predefined stream

Purpose

The *stdout* predefined pointer points to the standard output stream—by default, the screen. It is defined in *stdio.h*. The equivalent C++ stream is *cout*.

See Also

```
stderr, stdin, cout (C++ standard output stream)
```

strcmp() ✦ function

Purpose

Use the *strcmp()* function to compare the strings *string1* and *string2*.

Syntax

```
#include <string.h>
int strcmp(const char *string1, const char *string2);
const char *string1;        First null-terminated string
const char *string2;        Second null-terminated string
```

Example Use

```
if( strcmp(username, "root") != 0 ) exit(EXIT_FAILURE);
```

Returns

The *strcmp()* function returns an integer greater than, equal to, or less than 0 depending on whether *string1* is greater than, equal to, or less than *string2*.

See Also

```
memcmp(), strcoll(), strncmp(), EXIT_FAILURE, EXIT_SUCCESS
```

strcoll() ✦ function

Purpose

Use the *strcoll()* function to compare the strings *string1* and *string2* after interpreting both depending on the character collating sequence selected by the LC_COLLATE category of the current locale.

Syntax

```
#include <string.h>
int strcoll(const char *string1, const char *string2);
const char *string1;        First null-terminated string
const char *string2;        Second null-terminated string
```

Example Use

```
if( strcoll(username, rootname) != 0 ) exit(EXIT_FAILURE);
```

Returns

The *strcoll()* function returns an integer greater than, equal to, or less than 0 depending on whether *string1* is greater than, equal to, or less than *string2* when both are interpreted as appropriate to the current locale.

See Also
memcmp(), strncmp(), EXIT_FAILURE, EXIT_SUCCESS, LC_COLLATE

strcpy() ♦ function

Purpose

Use the *strcpy()* function to copy the null-terminated string *string2* to the string *string1*. The terminating null character (\0) of the second string is also copied so that *string1* becomes a copy of *string2*.

Syntax
```
#include <string.h>
char *strcpy(char *string1, const char *string2);
char *string1;             Destination string
const char *string2;       String to be copied to the first one
```

Example Use
```
strcpy(command, "resize");
```

Returns

The *strcpy()* function returns a pointer to the copied string which is *string1*.

See Also
memcpy(), memmove(), strncpy()

strcspn() ♦ function

Purpose

Use the *strcspn()* function to compute the length of the maximum initial segment of *string1* that consists entirely of characters not in *string2*. This is the first substring in *string1* that does not "span" the character set *string2*.

Syntax
```
#include <string.h>
size_t strcspn(const char *string1, const char *string2);
const char *string1;       String to be searched
const char *string2;       String describing set of characters to be located
```

Example Use
```
first_q = strcspn(soliloquy, "q"); /*first_q = 6 */
```

CHAPTER 10 ALPHABETICAL REFERENCE

Returns

If successful, the *strcspn()* function returns the length of the segment.

See Also

`strchr(), strpbrk(), strspn(), strrchr(), size_t`

streambuf ✦ class

Purpose

Use the *streambuf* class to handle unformatted operations with streams. The *streambuf* member functions are not generally used directly. Rather, *streambuf* is a base class for deriving two classes: *filebuf* for file-related stream operations and *strstreambuf* for formatting strings in memory. Note that in C++ 2.X, most *streambuf* member functions have been made protected and access is now done through the derived classes such as *istream* and *ostream*.

Syntax

`#include <iostream.h>`

See Also

`iostream.h, stream.h, fstream, fstreambase, fstream.h, istream, ostream, iomanip.h`

stream.h ✦ header file

Purpose

Use the *stream.h* header file for stream I/O in C++ versions prior to 2.0. Note: Most compilers available today support C++ version 2.0 (or later). With these compilers you should use the *iostream.h* header file instead, because the latter includes expanded and improved stream features.

Syntax

`#include stream.h  For pre-2.0 C++ streams`

See Also

`iostream.h, fstream, fstreambase, fstream.h, istream, ostream, iomanip.h`

strerror() ✦ function

Purpose

Use the *strerror()* function to obtain the system error message corresponding to the error number given in the argument *errnum*. Note that *strerror* only returns the error message, printing the message is up to you.

Syntax

```
#include <string.h>
char *strerror(int errnum);
int errnum;       Error number
```

Example Use

```
error_message = strerror(errno);
```

Returns

The *strerror()* function returns a pointer to the error message. The text of the message is implementation-dependent.

See Also

`perror(), errno`

strftime() ◆ function

Purpose

Use the *strftime()* function to format a time in the *tm* structure whose address is in *timeptr* into a string whose address is provided in *str*. At most *maxsize* characters will be placed in the string. The formatting is done according to the formatting codes given in the string *format_string*. As with *sprintf()*, the formatting codes begin with a % and are explained in Table 10-18. The argument *format_string* is expected to be in multibyte characters. Characters that do not begin with a % are copied unchanged to *str*. The LC_TIME category of the program's locale affects the behavior of *strftime*.

Table 10-18 Formatting Codes

FORMAT	REPLACED BY
%a	Current locale's abbreviated name for the weekday
%A	Current locale's full name for the weekday
%b	Current locale's abbreviated name for the month
%B	Current locale's full name for the month
%c	Date and time representation appropriate for the locale
%d	Day of the month as a decimal number (01-31)
%H	Hour in a 24-hour clock as a decimal number (00-23)
%I	Hour in a 12-hour clock as a decimal number (01-12)
%j	Day of the year as a decimal number (001-366)
%m	Month as a decimal number (01-12)
%M	Minute as a decimal number (00-59)
%P	Current locale's AM/PM indicator

FORMAT	REPLACED BY
%S	Second as a decimal number (00-60)
%U	Week of the year as a decimal number (Sunday is taken as the first day of a week) (00-53)
%w	Weekday as a decimal number (Sunday is 0, 0-6)
%W	Week of the year as a decimal number (Monday is taken as the first day of a week) (00-53)
%x	Date representation for current locale
%X	Time representation for current locale
%y	Year without the century as a decimal number (00-99)
%Y	Year with the century as a decimal number
%z	Name of time zone (or nothing if time zone is unknown)
%%	A percent sign (%)

Syntax

```
#include <time.h>
size_t strftime(char *str, size_t maxsize, const char *format_string, const struct tm *timeptr);
```

char *str;	Pointer to array of characters where result is placed
size_t maxsize;	Maximum number of characters in str
const char *format_string;	Formatting codes for converting the time to a string
const struct tm *timeptr;	Pointer to structure containing broken-down time

Example Use

```
/* Produce the standard output: Thu Jul 21 19:02:39 1999 */
strftime(s, 80, "%a %b %c\n", &tptr);
```

Returns

The *strtime()* function returns the total number of characters it placed in *str*, including the terminating null character. If the number of characters exceed *maxsize*, *strftime()* returns 0 and the contents of the array *str* are indeterminate.

See Also

asctime(), ctime(), gmtime(), localtime(), time(), LC_TIME, size_t, tm

strlen() ♦ function

Purpose

Use *strlen()* to find the length of *string* in bytes, not counting the terminating null character (\0).

Syntax

```
#include <string.h>
size_t strlen(const char *string);
const char *string;    Null-terminated string whose length is to be returned
```

Example Use

```
length = strlen(name);
```

Returns

The *strlen()* function returns the number of characters in *string* that precede the terminating null character.

See Also

```
strcspn(), size_t
```

strncat() ♦ function

Purpose

Use the *strncat()* function to append the first n characters of *string2* to *string1*, and terminate the resulting string with a null character (\0). The terminating null of the first string is removed and *string1* becomes the concatenation of the old *string1* and the first *n* characters of *string2*.

Syntax

```
#include <string.h>
char *strncat(char *string1, const char *string2, size_t n);
char *string1;          Destination string
const char *string2;    String whose first n characters are to be appended
                        to the first one
size_t n;               Number of characters of string2 to be appended to
                        string1
```

Example Use

```
char id[16] = "ID";
strncat(id, name, 10);
/* id is first 10 char of name */
```

Returns

The *strncat()* function returns a pointer to the concatenated string, *string1*.

See Also

```
strcat(), strcpy(), strncpy(), size_t
```

strncmp() ♦ function

Purpose
Use the *strncmp()* function to compare at most the first *n* characters of the null-terminated strings *string1* and *string2*.

Syntax
```
#include <string.h>
int strncmp(const char *string1, const char *string2, size_t n);
const char *string1;        First string
const char *string2;        Second string
size_t n;                   Number of characters of above strings to be compared
```

Example Use
```
if(strncmp(command, "quit", 4) == 0) quit_program();
```

Returns
The *strncmp()* function returns an integer greater than, equal to, or less than 0 depending on whether the first *n* characters of *string1* are greater than, equal to, or less than *string2*.

See Also
memcmp(), strcmp(), strcoll(), size_t

strncpy() ♦ function

Purpose
Use the *strncpy()* function to copy the first *n* characters of the null-terminated string *string2* to the buffer whose address is given by *string1*. The copy is placed starting at the first character position of *string1*. If *n* is less than the length of *string2*, no terminating null character (\0) is appended to *string1*. However, if *n* exceeds the length of *string2*, *string1* is padded with null characters so that it is exactly *n* bytes long. You should avoid situations where the *n* bytes following *string1* overlap *string2*, because the behavior of *strcpy()* with such arguments is not guaranteed to be correct.

Syntax
```
#include <string.h>
char *strncpy(char *string1, const char *string2, size_t n);
char *string1;              Destination string
const char *string2;        String whose first n characters are to be copied
                            to the first one
size_t n;                   Number of characters to be copied
```

Example Use
```
strncpy(fname, "tmp12345678", 8);
/* fname = "tmp12345" */
```

Returns

The *strncpy()* function returns a pointer to *string1*.

See Also
```
memcpy(), memmove(), strcat(), strncat(), strcpy(), size_t
```

strpbrk() ◆ function

Purpose

Use the *strpbrk()* function to locate the first occurrence in *string1* of any character in *string2*.

Syntax
```
#include <string.h>
char *strpbrk(const char *string1, const char *string2);
const char *string1;        String to be searched
const char *string2;        String describing set of characters to be located
```

Example Use
```
first_vowel = strpbrk(word, "aeiou");
```

Returns

If successful, the *strpbrk()* function returns a pointer to the first occurrence of any character from *string2* in *string1*. If the search fails, *strpbrk()* returns a NULL.

See Also
```
strchr(), strcspn(), strrchr(), strspn(), NULL
```

strrchr() ◆ function

Purpose

Use the *strrchr()* function to locate the last occurrence of the character *c* in the null-terminated string *string*. The terminating null character (\0) is included in the search and the null character can also be the character to be located.

Syntax
```
#include <string.h>
char *strrchr(const char *string, int c);
const char *string;         String to be searched
int c;                      Character to be located
```

CHAPTER 10 ALPHABETICAL REFERENCE

Example Use
```
char line_cost[] =
                "10 units at $1.20 ea. = $12.00"; total_cost =
                strrchr(line_cost, '$'');
/* Now total_cost will be the string "$12.00" */
```

Returns
If the character *c* is found, *strrchr()* returns a pointer to the last occurrence of *c* in *string*. If the search fails, *strrchr()* returns a NULL.

See Also
strchr(), strcspn(), strpbrk(), strspn(), NULL

strspn() ◆ function

Purpose
Use the *strspn()* function to compute the length of the maximum initial segment of *string1* that consists entirely of characters from the string *string2*. This is the first substring in *string1* that "spans" the character set *string2*.

Syntax
```
#include <string.h>
size_t strspn(const char *string1, const char *string2);
const char *string1;       String to be searched
const char *string2;       String describing set of characters
```

Example Use
```
char *input = "280ZX"";
first_nondigit_at = strspn(input, "1234567890");
/* first_nondigit_at will be  3 */
```

Returns
The *strspn()* function returns the length of the segment.

See Also
strcspn(), strpbrk(), size_t

strstr() ◆ function

Purpose
Use the *strstr()* function to locate the first occurrence of string *string2* in *string1*.

361

Syntax

```
#include <string.h>
char *strstr(const char *string1, const char *string2);
const char *string1;        String to be searched
const char *string2;        String to be located
```

Example Use

```
char input[]= "The account number is ACEG-88-07-11";
acc_no = strstr(input, "ACEG");     /* Now the string acc_no will be
                                       ACEG-88-07-11" */
```

Returns

If successful, the *strstr()* function returns a pointer to the first occurrence of *string2* as a substring in *string1*. If the search fails, *strstr()* returns a NULL.

See Also

strchr(), strcspn(), strpbrk(), NULL

---

strtod() ◆ function

Purpose

Use the *strtod()* function to convert *string* to a double-precision value. The string is expected to be of the form:

[whitespace][sign][digits.digits][exponent_letter][sign][digits]

where *whitespace* refers to (optional) blanks and tab characters, *sign* is a + or a − and the *digits* are decimal digits. The *exponent_letter* can be any one of d, D, e, or E (no matter which exponent letter is used, the exponent always denotes a power of 10). If there is a decimal point without any preceding digit, there must be at least one digit following it. The *strtod()* function will begin the conversion process with the first character of *string* and continue until it finds a character that does not fit the preceding form. Then it sets *endptr* to point to the leftover string, provided that *endptr* is not equal to NULL.

Syntax

```
#include <stdlib.h>
double strtod(const char *string, char **endptr);
const char    *string;      Pointer to character array from which
                            double-precision value will be extracted
char **endptr;              On return points to character in string where
                            conversion stopped
```

Example Use

```
dbl_value = strtod(input_string, &endptr);
```

Returns

The *strtod()* function returns the double-precision value as long as it is not too large. If it is too large, there will be an overflow and the return value will be the constant *HUGE_VAL* with the same sign as the number represented in *string*. Also, on overflow, the global variable *errno* is set to the constant *ERANGE*.

See Also
```
atof(), strtol(), strtoul(), HUGE_VAL, NULL, errno
```

strtok() ♦ function

Purpose

Use the *strtok()* function to retrieve a "token" or substring from *string1*. The token is marked by delimiting characters given in the second string argument *string2*. All tokens in a particular string *string1* can be extracted through successive calls to *strtok()* as follows. Make the first call to *strtok()* with the string to be "tokenized" as the first argument. Provide as second argument a string composed from the delimiting characters. After that, call *strtok()* with a *NULL* as the first argument and the delimiting characters appropriate for that token in the second string. This will tell *strtok()* to continue returning tokens from the old *string1*.

Note that the set of delimiters can change in each call to *strtok()*. Also, in the process of separating tokens, *strtok()* will modify the string *string1*. It will insert null characters in the place of delimiters to convert tokens to strings.

Syntax
```
#include <string.h>
char *strtok(char *string1, const char *string2);
char *string1;             String from which tokens are returned
const char *string2;       String describing set of characters that delimit
                           tokens
```

Example Use
```
next_token = strtok(input, '\t');
```

Returns

The first call to *strtok()* with the argument *string1* will return a pointer to the first token. Subsequent calls with a *NULL* as the first argument will return the next token. When there are no more tokens left, *strtok()* returns a *NULL*.

See Also
```
strcspn(), strpbrk(), strspn(), NULL
```

strtol() ♦ function

Purpose

Use the *strtol()* function to convert *string* to a long integer value. The string is expected to be of the form:

```
[whitespace][sign][0][x or X][digits]
```

where *whitespace* refers to (optional) blanks and tab characters, *sign* is a + or a − and the digits are decimal digits. The string is expected to contain a representation of the long integer using the argument *radix* as the base of the number system. However, if *radix* is given as zero, *strtol()* will use the first character in *string* to determine the radix of the value. The rules are indicated in Table 10-19.

Table 10-19 Base of the Number System

FIRST CHARACTER	NEXT CHARACTER	RADIX SELECTED
0	0 thru 7	Radix 8 is used, i.e., octal digits expected.
0	x or X	Radix 16, i.e., hexadecimal digits expected.
1 thru 9	—	Radix 10, decimal digits only expected.

Of course, other radices may be explicitly specified via the argument *radix*. The letters "a" through "z" (or "A" through "Z") are assigned values 10 through 35. For a specified radix, *strtol()* expects only those letters whose assigned values are less than the *radix*.

The *strtol()* function will begin the conversion process with the first character of *string* and continue until it finds a character that meets the requirements. Then, before returning, *strtol()* sets *endptr* to point to that character, provided it is not a null pointer.

Syntax

```
#include <stdlib.h>
long strtol(const char *string, char **endptr, int radix);
const char *string;       Pointer to character array from which the long
                          integer value will be extracted
char **endptr;            On return points to character in string where
                          conversion stopped
int radix;                Radix in which the value is expressed in the
                          string (radix must be in the range 2 to 36)
```

Example Use

```
value = strtol(input, &endptr, radix);
```

Returns

The *strtol()* function returns the long integer value except when it will cause an overflow. In case of overflow, *strtol* sets *errno* to ERANGE and returns either *LONG_MIN* or *LONG_MAX* depending on whether the value was negative or positive.

See Also
atol(), strtoul(), LONG_MIN, LONG_MAX, errno

strtoul() ◆ function

Purpose
Use the *strtoul()* function to convert a character string to an unsigned long integer. The string is expected to be of the same form as in *strtol()*. The conversion also proceeds in the same manner with *endptr* set to point to the character where conversion stopped, provided that *endptr* is not null.

Syntax
```
#include <stdlib.h>          For function declaration
#include <limits.h>          For the definition of the constants LONG_MIN,
                             LONG_MAX
#include <math.h>            For the definition of ERANGE

unsigned long strtoul(const char *string, char **endptr, int radix);
const char   *string;        Pointer to character array from which the unsigned
                             long value will be extracted.
char **endptr;               On return points to character in string where
                             conversion stopped
int radix;                   Radix in which the value is expressed in the
                             string (radix must be in the range 2 to 36)
```

Example Use
```
value = strtoul(input_string, &stop_at, radix);
```

Returns
The *strtoul()* function returns the unsigned long integer value except when it will cause an overflow. In case of overflow, *strtoul()* sets *errno* to ERANGE and returns the value ULONG_MAX.

See Also
atol(), strtol(), LONG_MIN, LONG_MAX, ULONG_MAX, errno

struct ◆ keyword

Purpose
Use the *struct* keyword to group related data items of different types together and to give the group a name by which you can refer to it later. Note that in C++, a *struct* has identical syntax to a *class* and can contain member functions as well as data members. The only difference is in default access: by default members of a *struct* have *public* access (are available to any part of the program that is in scope), while the default for a *class* is *private* access (data members accessible only to member functions of the same class).

Syntax

```
/* declare a structure */
struct structure_name
{
        type item_1;
        type item_2;
        ...
        type func1 (type);
        type func2 (type);
        ...
};
/*declare items of that structure type */
structure_name object_name;
```

Note that the more awkward C-style *struct* variable declaration syntax:

```
struct structure_name struct_1, struct_2;
```

is not needed in C++.

Similarly, the alternative C-style declaration:

```
struct
{
   <type> <member_name>
   ...
} var_name ... ;
```

is seldom used in C++. In C++ *structs* are usually used only to hold data that needs to be accessed from many places in the program.

Example Use

```
/* define a structure to be used in a linked list. It contains several
members including one that is a pointer to itself */
struct node
{
    int node_type;
    char node_name[16];
    struct node *next;
};
node *p_node, first_node;
```

See Also

union, . (member reference operator), -> (pointer member reference operator), class (C++)

strxfrm()   ♦   function

Purpose

Use the *strxfrm()* function to transform *string2* to a new form *string1* such that if *strcmp()* is applied to two transformed strings, the returned result is the same as that returned when *strcoll()* is applied to the original strings. No more than *maxchr* characters will be placed in *string1*. If *maxchr* is 0, *string1* can be a *NULL*. In this case, the return value will be the length of the transformed version of *string2*.

Syntax
```
#include <string.h>
size_t strxfrm(char *string1, char *string2, size_t maxchr);
char string1;              String where transformed version of  string2 is
                           returned
char *string2;             String to be transformed
size_t  maxchr;            Maximum number of characters to be placed in
                           string1
```

Example Use
```
strxfrm(s_xfrm, s_original);
```

Returns
The *strxfrm()* function returns the length of the transformed string, not counting the terminating null character. If the return value is *maxchr*, the contents of *string1* may be unusable.

See Also
```
strcmp(), strcoll(), NULL, size_t
```

switch ◆ keyword

Purpose
Use the *switch* statement to perform a multipath branch depending on the value of an expression. In such cases, the *switch* structure is more readable than a series of nested *if...else if* statements.

Syntax
```
switch (expression)
  {
  case <value> : statement; ...
  ...
  default: statement; ...
}
```

Use *case* labels inside the statement to indicate what to do for each expected value of the expression. Use *break* to separate the code of one *case* label from another. A *default* label marks code to be executed if none of the *case* labels match the expression.

Example Use
```
/* Execute different routines depending on the value of the command. Note
the use of break statements to keep the execution from falling through one
case label to another */
switch (command)
```

continued on next page

continued from previous page

```
{
    case 'Q': exit(0);
    case 'C': connect();
              break;
    case 'S': sendfile();
              break;
    case 'P': newparams();
              break;
    case '?': showparams();
              break;
    case 'H': printf(helplist);
              break;
    default:  printf("Unknown command!\n");
}
```

See Also
`break, case, default`

system()   function

Purpose
Use *system()* to execute the operating system command contained in *string* from your program. If *string* is *NULL*, *system()* returns a nonzero value only if a command processor (for example, the UNIX shell) is present in the environment.

Syntax
```
#include <stdlib.h>
int system(const char *string);
const char *string;     command to be executed
```

Example Use
```
system("ls");           /* UNIX command to list files in current directory */
```

Returns
If *string* is not *NULL*, *system()* will return an implementation-defined value.

See Also
`NULL`

\t   escape sequence for horizontal tab

Purpose
Use the \t escape sequence to move the cursor to the next horizontal tab position on the current line. Tab positions are typically found at positions 1, 9, 17, 25, 32, and so on, but this can vary from one system to another.

Example Use

```
/* Print table headers:
Name            Street          City            Zip */
printf("Name\t\tStreet\t\tCity\t\t\tZip");
```

See Also
printf(), \v

tan() ♦ function

Purpose
Use the *tan()* function to compute the tangent of an angle *x* whose value is expressed in radians. You can convert an angle from degrees to radians by dividing it by 57.29578.

Syntax
```
#include <math.h>
double tan(double x);
double x;               angle in radians whose tangent is to be computed
```

Example Use
```
y = tan(x);
```

Returns
The *tan()* function returns the tangent of *x*. If the value of *x* is large in magnitude, the result may be very imprecise.

See Also
atan(), atan2(), cos(), sin()

tanh() ♦ function

Purpose
Use the *tanh()* function to compute the hyperbolic tangent of a *double* variable *x*.

Syntax
```
#include <math.h>
double tanh(double x);
double x;               Variable whose hyperbolic tangent is to be computed
```

Example Use
```
a = tanh(b);
```

Returns

The *tanh()* function returns the hyperbolic tangent of *x*.

See Also

cosh(), sinh()

tellg() ◆ function

Purpose

Use the *tellg()* ios member function to obtain the current read position for a C++ stream. This is the location in the file where the next character will be read. This function is useful for saving the current read position before working elsewhere in the file.

Syntax

```
#include <iostream.h>
streampos <stream>.tellg();
```

Example Use

```
fstream datafile;
streampos current_pos = datafile.tellg();
```

Returns

The *tellg()* function returns the read position as a value of type *streampos*, which is actually a *typedef long*.

See Also

ios, tellp(), setg(), setp()

tellp() ◆ function

Purpose

Use the *tellp()* ios member function to obtain the current write position for a C++ stream. This is the location in the file where the next character will be written. This function is useful for saving the current write position before reading or writing elsewhere in the file.

Syntax

```
#include <iostream.h>
streampos <stream>.tellp();
```

Example Use

```
fstream datafile;
streampos writepos = datafile.tellp();
```

Returns

The *tellp()* function returns the current write position as a value of type *streampos*. This is actually a *typedef long*.

See Also

```
ios, tellg(), setg(), setp()
```

template ◆ keyword

Purpose

Use the *template* keyword to create sophisticated macro definition statements for functions and classes. Note that this feature is not yet implemented by many C++ compilers and is not covered in *Master C++ for Windows*.

Syntax

```
<type name> fnct_name(. . .) { . . . }    functon template
<type name> class_name { . . . }   class template
```

The <type name> is usually a *class,* so any data type will be allowed. However, the template definition can be more restrictive and can specify data types such as *int*, *double*, or a specific object class.

Example Use

```
template <class TYPE>  TYPE Add(TYPE x, TYPE y)
{
    return(x + y);
}
```

Whenever the *Add()* template function is used, the C++ compiler examines the arguments passed to the function and creates a real function definition replacing the TYPE parameter with the argument types used. For example, using the *Add()* template function as follows:

```
double d = Add(2.0, 3.0);
int i = Add(2, 3);
```

would cause the C++ compiler to create the following function defintions:

```
double Add(double x, double y)
   {
           return(x + y);
   }

   int Add(int x, int y)
   {
           return(x + y);
   }
```

The *template* keyword operates in a similar fashion with class definitions. For example, consider the following vector template class definition:

```
template <class TYPE, int SIZE> struct vector
{
  TYPE elem[SIZE];
  vector<TYPE, SIZE>& operator+=(vector<TYPE,
  SIZE>& x)
  {
  for(unsigned n = 0; n < SIZE; n++)
        elem[n] += x.elem[n];
  }
};
```

This is a template class for a vector object. The vector can be any dimension and can use any data type depending on the TYPE and SIZE parameters used in the declaration. For example, a three-dimensional type double vector called d_v3 is declared as follows:

```
vector<double, 3>  d_v3;
```

See Also
```
typedef, class, struct, union
```

terminate()   ♦   function

Purpose

Use the *terminate()* function to abandon exception handling (for example, if the stack has been corrupted or reliable behavior cannot be assured for some other reason). Note that C++ exception handling is a recent addition to the language and may not be supported by all compilers. It is not discussed in *Master C++ for Windows*.

When called, *terminate()* calls the last function given as an argument to another special function called *set_terminate()*.

Syntax
```
#include <except.h>
void terminate();
```

Example Use
```
if !stackchk terminate(); // stack corrupt
```

See Also
```
catch, throw, try, unexpected()
```

this   ♦   keyword

Purpose

Use the *this* special pointer to refer to the object currently being executed. That is, returning *this* from a class object's member function returns a pointer to the object.

Note that *this* is handled automatically by C++; you should not declare it, nor examine its address.

Syntax
```
this
```

Example Use
```
return this; // return pointer to this object
```

Returns
The *this* pointer points to the object in which it was used. If you want to return the object itself rather than a pointer to it, use * *this*.

See Also
```
:: (scope resolution operator)
```

throw ◆ keyword

Purpose
Use the *throw* keyword to call the defined exception handler, usually passing an object to it. The data type of the object is matched to one of the *catch* exception handlers defined immediately following the most recently entered *try* block for execution. If a *throw* is executed within a *catch* exception handler, the same object is thrown to the next most recently entered *try* block. If there is no *catch* exception handler matching the thrown object or no *try* block has been entered, then the *unexpected()* function is executed.

When control is passed to the *catch* exception handler or to the *unexpected()* function from a *throw* statement, the destructors for all automatic objects created after entering the *try*-block-associated exception handler are called. In addition, all function call return addresses placed after entering the *try* block are removed. The C language equivalent of a *throw* statement is the *longjmp()* library function. Entering a *try* block can be considered the equivalent of calling the *setjmp()* function. Note that exception handling is a recent addition to C++ and may not be supported by all compilers. This feature is not discussed in *Master C++ for Windows*.

Syntax
```
throw (object);
throw;                    only within a 'catch' handler
object                    object (such as a message string) to pass to
                          exception handler
```

Example Use
See entry for *catch* for an example.

See Also
```
catch, try, terminate(), unexpected(), longjmp(), setjmp()
```

time() ♦ function

Purpose

Use the *time()* function to get the current date and time (calendar time) encoded as an implementation-dependent value of type *time_t*. If the pointer *timeptr* is not null, the encoded time is copied to the location whose address is in *timeptr*.

Syntax
```
#include <time.h>
time_t time(time_t *timeptr);
time_t *timeptr;            Pointer to variable where result will be returned
```

Example Use
```
time(&bintime);
```

Returns

The *time()* function returns the calendar time encoded in an implementation-dependent manner.

See Also
```
ctime(), gmtime(), localtime(), time_t
```

_ _TIME_ _ ♦ predefined macro

Purpose

Use the _ _TIME_ _ predefined macro to display the time at which the source file is being translated by the preprocessor. The time is inserted as a string with the form "HH:MM:SS."

Example Use
```
printf("at");
printf(_ _TIME_ _);
```

See Also
```
_ _DATE_ _, _ _FILE_ _, _ _LINE_ _, _ _STDC_ _
```

time_t ♦ predefined data type

Purpose

The *time_t* data type holds the value returned by the *time()* function. It is defined in *time.h*.

See Also
time(), tm

tm ✦ predefined data type

Purpose
The struct *tm* holds the components of a calendar time. It is defined in *time.h*.

See Also
time_t, time()

TMP_MAX ✦ predefined value

Purpose
The predefined value *TMP_MAX* is the minimum number of unique names that can be had from *tmpnam*. It is defined in *stdio.h*.

See Also
FILENAME_MAX

tmpfile() ✦ function

Purpose
Use the *tmpfile()* function to open a temporary file for binary read/write operations (wb+ mode). The file will be automatically deleted when your program terminates normally or when you close the file.

Syntax
```
#include <stdio.h>
FILE *tmpfile(void);
```

Example Use
```
p_tfile = tmpfile();
```

Returns
The *tmpfile()* function returns a pointer to the stream associated with the temporary file it opens. In case of error, this pointer will be NULL.

See Also
fclose(), tmpnam(), FILE, NULL

tmpnam() ♦ function

Purpose
Use the *tmpnam()* function to generate a temporary file name in the string *file_name* which must have enough room to hold at least *L_tmpnam* (a constant defined in *stdio.h*) characters. You can generate up to *TMP_MAX* (another constant defined in *stdio.h*) unique file names with *tmpnam*.

Syntax
```
#include <stdio.h>
char *tmpnam(char *file_name);
char *file_name;           Pointer to string where file name will be returned
```

Example Use
```
tmpnam(tfilename);
```

Returns
The *tmpnam()* function returns a pointer to the name generated. If the argument to *tmpnam()* is *NULL*, the return pointer will point to an internal static buffer. If the generated name is not unique, it returns a *NULL*.

See Also
tmpfile(), L_tmpnam, NULL, TMP_MAX

tolower() ♦ function

Purpose
Use the *tolower()* function to convert the uppercase letter *c* to lowercase.

Syntax
```
#include <ctype.h>
int tolower(int c);
int c;                     Character to be converted
```

Example Use
```
c = tolower('Q'); /* c will become 'q' */
```

Returns
The *tolower()* function returns the lowercase letter corresponding to *c* if there is one. Otherwise, the argument is returned unchanged.

See Also
toupper()

toupper() ♦ function

Purpose
Use the *toupper()* function to convert the lowercase letter *c* to uppercase.

Syntax
```
#include <ctype.h>
int toupper(int c);
int c;                   Character to be converted
```

Example Use
```
c = toupper('q'); /* c will become 'Q' */
```

Returns
The *toupper()* function returns the uppercase letter corresponding to *c* if there is one. Otherwise, the argument is returned unchanged.

See Also
`tolower()`

try ♦ keyword

Purpose
Use the *try* keyword to establish an entry point for exceptions thrown using the *throw* keyword. If an exception is thrown, then the destructors for any automatic objects created after entering the *try* block are called and function call return addresses removed from the stack. A *try* block is normally followed by one or more *catch* exception handler definitions. The C language equivalent to a *try* block with multiple exception handlers is as follows:

```
jmp_buf jumper;
int exception;

if(!(exception = setjmp(jumper)))
{   // Entry into the 'try' block
    . . .
}
else
{
    switch(exception)
    {
            case Catch_Def_1:
            . . .
            case Catch_Def_2:
            . . .
            default:
            unexpected();

    }
}
```

Syntax

```
try {
...
}
catch (<type>)
...
```

Example Use

See the entry for *catch* for an example.

See Also

```
catch, throw, unexpected()
```

type() ♦ type cast operator

Purpose

Use the *type cast operator* to make a value have a specified data type. The desired type is placed in parentheses.

Syntax

```
type (value); or
(type) value /* makes value have type */
```

The first (function-style) syntax is preferred by most C++ programmers.

Example Use

```
int i = 1;
/* convert i to type double */
double(i);     /* C++-style syntax */
(double) i;    /* C-style syntax */
```

typedef ♦ keyword

Purpose

Use *typedef* to give a new name to an existing data type. This can improve the readability of your program as well as make declarations simpler to type.

Syntax

```
typedef existing_type new_name;
```

Example Use

```
typedef int (*P_FUNC)();
/* you can now use P_FUNC as a data type that means "pointer to a function
returning an integer" */
```

See Also

```
enum
```

UCHAR_MAX ♦ predefined value

Purpose
The predefined value UCHAR_MAX is the maximum value of an *unsigned char*. It is defined in *limits.h*.

See Also
UINT_MAX, USHRT_MAX

UINT_MAX ♦ predefined value

Purpose
The predefined value UINT_MAX is the maximum value of an *unsigned int*. It is defined in *limits.h*.

See Also
UCHAR_MAX, USHRT_MAX

ULONG_MAX ♦ predefined value

Purpose
The predefined value ULONG_MAX is the maximum value of an *unsigned long int*. It is defined in *limits.h*.

See Also
UINT_MAX, USHRT_MAX

#undef ♦ preprocessor directive

Purpose
Use the *#undef* preprocessor directive to remove a symbol or macro definition currently existing in the program.

Syntax
```
#undef symbol
```

Example Use
```
#undef DEBUG /* removes definition of DEBUG */
```

See Also
#define, #ifdef, #ifndef, defined

unexpected() ♦ function

Purpose

The *unexpected()* function is called when no *catch* handler is found in the most recently entered *try* block that matches the exception thrown by the *throw* keyword. The *unexpected()* function in turn calls the function set by the last call to *set_unexpected()* function. If the *unexpected()* function is executed before any call has been made to *set_unexpected()*, then the *terminate()* function is executed.

The *unexpected()* function is a predefined function pointer which points to the *terminate()* function and is set by the *set_unexpected()* function. It cannot be defined. It is also not normally called directly.

Example Use

See the entry for *catch* for an example of exception handling.

See Also

```
catch, throw(), try, terminate()
```

ungetc() ♦ function

Purpose

Use the *ungetc()* function to push the character *c* back onto *stream*. The characters that are pushed back will be returned to subsequent read operations on *stream* in the reverse order of their pushing. You can push any character except the constant *EOF*.

Because *ungetc()* pushes the character into the stream's buffer, any operation that tampers with the buffer or the file's current position (for example, *fseek()*, *fsetpos()*, or *rewind()*), may discard the pushed-back characters.

Note that the equivalent function for C++ streams is the *ios* member function *putback()*.

Syntax

```
#include <stdio.h>
int ungetc(int c, FILE *stream);
int c;                    Character to be pushed into the file's buffer
FILE *stream;             Pointer to stream onto which the character is
                          pushed back
```

Example Use

```
ungetc(last_char, infile);
```

Returns

If there are no errors, *ungetc()* returns the character it pushed back. Otherwise, it returns the constant EOF to indicate an error.

See Also

`fgetc()`, `fputc()`, `getc()`, `getchar()`, `putc()`, `putchar()`, `EOF`, `putback()` (for C++ streams)

union ◆ keyword

Purpose

Use *union* to allocate storage for several data items at the same location. This is useful when a program needs to access the same item of data in different ways. The declaration of *union* is identical to that of *struct*, except that in a *union* all data items in the declaration share the same storage location.

In C++ a *union* may have a constructor or destructor as well as other member functions. *unions* cannot be *virtual*, and they can neither be derived nor serve as a base class. An object of a *class* that has a constructor or destructor cannot be a member of a *union*. A union can have no *static* data members.

Syntax

```
union <union_name>
{
    <type> <member_name>;
    ...
};
```

union_name (sometimes called the union's "tag") can be omitted, in which case variables of the union type must be declared in the same statement as the union definition.

```
union (<type> <member_name>...)
{
// you can initialize members here
// if you don't use a constructor
} var_name ... ;
```

Example Use

```
/* Declare a union that stores a short in the same location as an array of
two characters. Each individual byte of the short stored in the union x can
be accessed by x.bytes[0] and x.bytes[1]*/
union short_u
{
    short sh_val;
    char  bytes[2];
};
short_u x;
```

See Also

`struct`, `class`

unsetf() ♦ function

Purpose

Use the *unsetf()* *ios* member function to clear the specified *ios* formatting flags. *unsetf()* is convenient because it clears only the flag specified in the *ios* enumerated mask without affecting other flags. See the *ios* entry for a description of the flag enumerations.

Syntax

```
#include <iostream.h>
long unsetf(longflagvals);
flagvals                        long value with flag bits
```

Example Use

```
cout.unsetf(ios::showbase);
// clear the showbase flag
// so base and exponent letters won't be shown
```

Returns

The *unsetf()* function returns a *long* value containing the flag values prior to unsetting.

See Also

```
setf(), flags(), setiosflags(), resetiosflags()
```

unsigned ♦ keyword

Purpose

Use the *unsigned* qualifier with integer data types (*char*, *int*, *short int*, and *long int*) to tell the compiler that the variable will be used to store nonnegative values only. This effectively doubles the maximum value that can be stored in that variable. Another useful feature is that arithmetic involving *unsigned* integers can never overflow because all operations are performed modulo a number that is one greater than the largest value that can be represented by that unsigned type.

Syntax

```
unsigned <integer type> <varname>;
```

Example Use

```
unsigned char data[1000];
unsigned long file_pos;
unsigned i;     /* equivalent to unsigned int i */
```

See Also

```
char, double, float, int, long, short
```

USHRT_MAX ◆ predefined value

Purpose
The predefined value *USHRT_MAX* is the maximum value of an *unsigned short int*. It is defined in *limits.h*.

See Also
UINT_MAX, CHAR_MAX

\v ◆ escape sequence for vertical tab

Purpose
Use the \v escape sequence to move the cursor to the next vertical tab position. This does not work with most video displays or some printers.

Example Use
```
printf("\vf\va\vl\vl\vi\vn\vg");
```

See Also
printf, \n, \t

va_arg(), va_end(), va_start() ◆ predefined macros

Purpose
Use the *va_start()*, *va_arg()*, and *va_end()* macros to access the arguments of a function when it takes a fixed number of required arguments followed by a variable number of optional arguments. The required arguments are in standard style and accessed by parameter name. The optional arguments are accessed using the macros *va_start()*, *va_arg()*, and *va_end()*. See the CBT for a step-by-step description.

Syntax
```
#include <stdarg.h>
<type> va_arg(va_list arg_ptr, <type>);
void va_end(va_list arg_ptr);
void va_start(va_list arg_ptr, prev_param);
va_list arg_ptr;         Pointer to list of arguments
prev_param               Name of parameter just preceding first optional
                         argument
<type>                   Type of argument to be retrieved, for example char*
```

Example Use
```
va_start(argp, firstint);
first_x = firstint;
next_x = va_arg(argp, int);
```

Returns

The *va_arg()* macro returns a pointer to the next argument of a given type. The *va_start()* macro sets a pointer to the beginning of the list of arguments.

See Also
```
vfprintf(), vprintf(), vsprintf()
```

va_list ✦ predefined data type

Purpose

The *va_list()* data type hold macros needed by the macros *va_start()*, *va_arg()*, and *va_end()*. These macros are used to allow functions to accept a variable number of parameters. It is defined in *stdarg.h*.

See Also
```
va_arg(), va_start(), va_end()
```

vfprintf() ✦ function

Purpose

Use the *vfprintf()* function to write formatted output to an ANSI C-type *stream*, just as *fprintf()* would, except that *vfprintf()* accepts a pointer to the list of variables (in *arg_pointer*) rather than the variables themselves, allowing a variable number of items to be printed. See *printf()* for a detailed description of the *format_string* argument.

Syntax
```
#include <stdarg.h>
#include <stdio.h>
int vfprintf(FILE *stream, const char *format_string, va_list arg_pointer);
FILE *stream;                       Pointer to stream to which the output goes
const char *format_string;          A character string which describes the
                                    format to be used
va_list arg_pointer;                Pointer to a list containing a variable
                                    number of arguments that are being printed
```

Example Use
```
vfprintf(stderr, p_format, p_arg);
```

Returns

The *vfprintf()* function returns the number of characters it has printed, excluding the terminating null character (\0).

See Also
```
printf(), sprintf(), vprintf(), vsprintf(), va_arg(), va_end(), FILE, stderr
```

virtual ✦ keyword

Purpose

Use the keyword *virtual* for a member function in a base class to specify that the function will be able to "pass through" a call to the appropriate derived class at runtime. This will assure that the version of a member function that will be called will be determined by the type of the actual object, not the type of a pointer to that object.

Syntax

```
virtual<type> <member_func_name> () {
... member function definition
}
type                       function return type
member_func_name           name of member function to be declared virtual
```

Example Use

```
class base_class {
...
virtual void membfunc (int& num) {
return scale(num, numeric::scale);
}
```

See Also

static, class, derived

void ✦ keyword

Purpose

Use the data type *void* in a function declaration to indicate the nonexistence of a return value or the fact that the function uses no arguments. You can also use *void ** to declare a pointer to any type of data object.

Syntax

```
void func (void);
```

The first *void*, if present, indicates that *func* does not return a value. The second *void*, if present, indicates that *func* takes no arguments.

Example Use

```
void a_function(void *buffer);
int get_something(void);
extern void *p_buf;
```

See Also

char, int, double, float

volatile ♦ keyword

Purpose

Use the *volatile* type qualifier to inform the compiler that the variable which follows may be modified by factors outside the control of your program. For example, the contents of a register in the real-time clock in your system will be such a variable. The *volatile* qualifier warns the compiler that actions performed on *volatile* data must not be "optimized out." You can use the qualifier *const* together with *volatile* to qualify objects that must not be changed by your program, yet that may change due to external factors.

Syntax

```
volatile <type> <varname>;
```

Example Use

```
/* The code below shows the declaration of the register in a real-time
clock. It says that our code cannot change the contents (*p_rt_clock), but
the contents may change by itself. We are, however, free to modify the
pointer p_rt_clock to point to another long int */

const volatile long *p_rt_clock = CLOCK_ADDRESS;
```

See Also

const

vprintf() ♦ function

Purpose

Use the *vprintf()* function to perform the same functions as *printf()*, that is, write formatted output to the ANSI C stream *stdout*, when you have only a pointer to the list of variables to be printed (in *arg_pointer*) rather than the variables themselves. This allows a variable number of arguments to be printed. The *format_string* is described under *printf()*.

Syntax

```
#include <stdarg.h>
#include <stdio.h>
int vprintf(const char *format_string, va_list arg_pointer);
const char *format_string;      A character string which describes the
                                format to be used
va_list arg_pointer;            Pointer to a list containing a variable
                                number of arguments that are being printed
```

Example Use

```
vprintf(p_format, p_arg);
```

Returns

The *vprintf()* function returns the number of characters it has printed, excluding the terminating null character (\0).

See Also

fprintf(), printf(), sprintf(), vfprintf(), va_arg(), va_end(), stdout

vsprintf()   ◆   function

Purpose

Use the *vsprintf()* function to perform the same function as *sprintf()*, i.e., write formatted output to the string *p_string*, except that *vsprintf()* accepts a pointer to a list of variables (in *arg_pointer*) rather than the variables themselves. Therefore, a variable number of arguments can be formatted. See *printf()* for a description of the *format_string* argument.

Syntax

```
#include <stdarg.h>
#include <stdio.h>
int vsprintf(char *p_string, const#char*format_string, va_list arg_pointer);
char *p_string;                    Pointer to an array of characters where
                                   vsprintf() sends its formatted output
const char *format_string;         A character string which describes the
                                   format to be used
va_list arg_pointer;               Pointer to a list containing a variable
                                   number of arguments that are being printed
```

Example Use

```
vsprintf(err_msg, p_format, p_arg);
```

Returns

The *vsprintf()* function returns the number of characters it has printed, excluding the terminating null character (\0).

See Also

fprintf(), printf(), sprintf(), vfprintf(), vprintf(), va_arg(), va_end()

wchar_t   ◆   predefined data type

Purpose

The *wchar_t* data type can hold the entire range of values necessary to represent the largest extended character set supported by the compiler. It is defined in *stdlib.h*.

See Also
char

wcstombs() ♦ function

Purpose
Use the *wcstombs()* function to convert a sequence of codes of *wchar_t* type given in the array *pwcs* into a sequence of multibyte characters and to store at most *n* such bytes in the array *mbs*.

Syntax
```
#include <stdlib.h>
size_t wcstombs(char *mbs, const wchar_t *pwcs, size_t n);
const char *mbs;        Pointer to array where multibyte characters will
                        be stored
wchar_t *pwcs;          Pointer to array of wide characters to be
                        converted to multibyte format
size_t n;               Maximum number of multibyte characters to be
                        stored in mbs
```

Example Use
```
wcstombs(mb_array, wc_array, 10*MB_CUR_MAX);
```

Returns
If successful, the *wcstombs()* function returns the number of bytes it stored in mbs, not including a terminating null character, if any. If *wcstombs()* encountered a wide character code that does not correspond to a valid multibyte character, it returns −1 cast as *size_t*.

See Also
mblen(), mbtowc(), mbstowcs(), wctomb(), MB_CUR_MAX, size_t, wchar_t

wctomb() ♦ function

Purpose
Use the *wctomb()* function to convert *wchar*, a character of *wchar_t* type to a multibyte character and store the result in the array *s*. At most, *MB_CUR_MAX* characters will be stored in the array *s*.

Syntax
```
#include <stdlib.h>
int wctomb(char *s, wchar_t wchar);
char *s;                Pointer to start of array where the multibyte
                        equivalent of wchar will be returned
wchar_t  wchar;         Wide character to be converted to multibyte format
```

Example Use
```
wctomb(mb_char, wchar);
```

Returns
If *s* is *NULL*, *wctomb()* will return a 0 or a nonzero depending on whether multibyte encodings have state dependencies or not. If *s* is not *NULL*, *wctomb* returns the number of bytes that comprise the multibyte character corresponding to the wide character *wchar*. If *wchar* does not correspond to a valid multibyte character, it returns −1.

See Also
mblen(), mbtowc(), mbstowcs(), wcstombs(), MB_CUR_MAX, NULL, wchar_t

while ◆ keyword

Purpose
Use the *while* statement to construct a loop that tests a condition and continues to execute the specified statements as long as the condition is true (not 0). Unlike the case of the *do...while* loop, the condition in the *while* statement is checked first, and then the body of the loop is executed if the condition is true.

Syntax
```
while (<condition>)
{
    statement;
    ...
}
```

A *while* loop with only one statement in the body is sometimes written as:
```
while (condition) statement;
```

Example Use
```
/* add up the numbers from 1 through 10 */
sum = 0;
i = 0;
while(i <= 10)
{
    sum += i;
    i++;
}
```

See Also
do, for, if, switch

width() ♦ function

Purpose

Use the *width()* *ios* member function to set the output width for a C++ stream. (Note that the *setwidth()* manipulator is an alternate method for accomplishing this function.)

The *ios flags ios::left, ios::ight*, and *ios::internal* specify how values will be padded and adjusted within the specified width. Note that if a numeric value exceeds the width specified, the full number will still be displayed, overflowing the field.

Syntax

```
#include <iostream.h>
<stream>.width(chars); or
<stream>.width();          just returns current width
chars                      integer number of characters
```

Example Use

```
cout.width(10); // set output field width to 10
```

Returns

If called without an argument, the *width()* function returns the current width. If called with an argument, it sets the width to that argument and returns the previous width.

See Also

ios, setw(), setprecision()

write() ♦ function

Purpose

Use the *write()* *ios* member function to insert the specified number of characters or bytes of binary data into the specified stream.

Syntax

```
#include <iostream.h>
<output_stream>.write(buffer, num_chars);
buffer              array of characters from which to write
num_chars           integer number of characters to write
```

Example Use

```
char message [80];
...
cout.write(message, 40);       // write first chars. from
                               // message buffer
```

Remember that *write()* doesn't care about the contents of the characters, so any sort of binary data that fits into the array can also be written.

Returns

The *write()* function returns a reference to the output stream.

See Also

```
ostream, << (insertion operator), get(), getline()
```

ws ♦ manipulator

Purpose

Use the *ws* manipulator to "eat" any whitespace characters coming from the input stream rather than storing them in the destination object.

Syntax

```
#include <iostream.h>
input_stream >> ws;
```

Example Use

```
cin >> ws >> input;      // put cin in "input" but throw
                         // away spaces, tabs, etc.
```

Returns

The *ws* manipulator returns a reference to the input stream used.

See Also

```
endl, ends
```

A

MASTER C++ FOR WINDOWS COMMAND REFERENCE

This appendix explains the commands located at the top of the screen in the Toolbar. Not all of these options appear in the Toolbar at the same time, and they are sometimes grayed out; some are context sensitive and are displayed only in certain modes. For example, Note and Example appear and are enabled in the Toolbar only when a *Note* or *Example* window is available for the screen you are using; Progress is only enabled at menu screens.

TOOLBAR COMMANDS

The following commands can appear in the Toolbar. They are listed in the order in which they appear on the screen.

Exit

The Exit button exits from *Master C++ for Windows* after confirming your intentions. Exit remembers where in the software you quit, so the next time you start, *Master C++ for Windows* will return to that location.

Help

The Help command provides access to the Help window.

Forward

Forward moves to the next screen in the lesson.

Back

Back moves you back a screen to the previous lesson. If you are at the first screen, Back will take you to the point where you entered the current lesson.

Refresh

The Refresh button replays a sound, video, or animation sequence when one is available at the current course location.

Progress

Master C++ for Windows saves a record of your progress in a special file. Select this Toolbar button to see this record. A graphical chart will display your scores and times for each section.

Options

The Options button causes a drop-down menu to appear containing the Calc, Print, Goal, Goto, and Settings buttons.

Calc

The Calc button (under Options) provides access to a calculator.

Print

The Print button (under Options) is used to print the current screen or an entire lesson.

Goal

The Goal button (under Options) brings up the *Objective* window, which identifies the main topics covered in the associated lesson and the time required by an average beginner to complete the lesson.

Goto

The Goto button (under Options) is used to move directly to a particular section in a lesson, without having to navigate the menu system. This might be useful if, for example, you are selecting topics of interest from the course map.

Settings

The Settings button (under Options) allows you to set options such as course personality and career orientation.

APPENDIX A   COMMAND REFERENCE

Glossary

Glossary provides online access to a collection of terms and concepts related to the C++ language. When you access the Glossary, you are requested to type in the name of the word in which you are interested. If the word is not available, a list of similar spellings is presented. Once the word is found, a definition is displayed, and you can choose to see a related lesson.

Note

The animated Note button is displayed on the Toolbar when a special *Note* window is available containing additional information relevant to the current concept. Once the *Note* window is displayed, you can close it by clicking in the upper-left corner of the box or on the Note button.

Example

The Example button is activated and animated on the Toolbar when a special *Example* window is available, containing related examples for the current screen. When the *Example* window is displayed, you can close it by clicking in the upper-left corner of the box or on the Example button. The Example button will continue to flash, and you can reread the example if you want. Some screens may have both a Note and an Example available.

Edit Answer

This button allows editing of the answer fields.

Memo

The Memo button brings up the *Memo* window, which allows you to make notes to yourself during the course. These notes are preserved from session to session.

B
FURTHER READING

There are three important areas in which you may want to do further reading on C++. First, there is the C++ language itself—both nuances of object-oriented programming and practical coding techniques. Second, there is the mastery of the features of your chosen C++ compiler and its associated tools and class libraries. Finally, there is useful lore inherited from the established C programming community—especially the use of extensive function libraries such as those specified in ANSI C and enhanced in Borland/Turbo C++, Visual C++, and others.

In this appendix we mention only a few titles that we think might be particularly useful to users of *Master C++ for Windows*. Although we concentrate on titles from The Waite Group, we acknowledge that a wide variety of excellent books from other publishers are available, dealing with the philosophy of object-oriented programming and with particular programming applications.

C++ IN GENERAL

The C Programming Language by Brian W. Kernighan and Dennis W. Ritchie (Prentice-Hall, 1978. Second Edition, 1988) essentially defined the C language for a generation of programmers. In similar fashion, Bjarne Stroustrup, main developer of the C++ language, has written *The C Programming Language* (Addison-Wesley, 1986. Second Edition, 1991). In addition to covering version 2.0 of the language, the second edition adds extensive commentary on OOP philosophy and design issues. Further details on language nuances can be found in *The Annotated C++ Reference Manual* (Addison-Wesley, 1990).

C++ Primer Plus by Stephen Prata (Waite Group Press, 1991. Second Edition, 1995) is a step-by-step tutorial that teaches "generic" (AT&T 2.0) C++ and object-oriented programming, from the ground up. There is some discussion of C++ compilation under both DOS and UNIX, but the example programs are not tied to any particular compiler or platform.

C++ COMPILERS AND DEVELOPMENT ENVIRONMENTS

The best-selling C++ compilers today are undoubtedly the Borland products Borland C++ and Turbo C++. Borland C++ is essentially the "professional" version and includes support for 32-bit Windows programming. Turbo C++ for Windows is aimed more at students. Either is fine for learning the C++ language.

Object-Oriented Programming in C++ by Robert Lafore (Waite Group Press, 1991. Second Edition, 1994) has detailed but easy-to-follow tutorials on both the C++ language and matters specific to Borland's compilers and DOS. The tutorials in *Master C++ for Windows* have been adapted from this book.

The Waite Group's *Borland C++ Developer's Bible* (Waite Group Press, May 1992) is a detailed reference to the use of Borland compiler, linker, and other tools for developing both DOS and Windows applications. A fractal generation program provides an extensive example.

RESOURCES FROM C

The ANSI C library included in Borland/Turbo C++ is covered extensively in The Waite Group's *Turbo C++ Bible* (Sams, 1990). This book contains both tutorials on aspects of C++ programming and a complete reference entry for each library function. The Waite Group's *Turbo C++ Bible* can serve as an expansion of the *Master C++ for Windows* printed reference in two ways: The individual entries are longer, with complete program examples; and the numerous special functions that Borland has added to the ANSI library are also covered.

If you want to learn the ANSI C language, we recommend *Master C* (Waite Group Press, 1990), the predecessor of *Master C++ for Windows*. The reference manual for *Master C* includes alphabetical entries for all ANSI C library functions.

INDEX

! error check, 175, 177
! logical NOT operator, 45, 168, 170, 193
! stream status operator, 193
!= not-equal-to operator, 168, 170, 194
format flag, 318
preprocessor directives, 44, 165, 170-172
string-making operator, 171, 194
token-pasting operator, 171, 194-195
% modulus operator, 168, 169-170, 195
% prefix, 317, 332-333, 356
%= assignment operator, 168, 170
& address-of operator, 168, 195
& bitwise AND operator, 169-170, 195-196
& reference operator, 196
  <type>& reference-to, 168
&= assignment operator, 168, 170, 196
&& logical AND operator, 45, 168, 170, 196-197
( ) function call operator, 169-170, 197
( ) for precedence override, 170
* dereferencing operator, 52-53, 197
* error check, 175, 177
* indirection operator, 168, 197
* multiplication operator, 167, 169-170, 198
* operator, overloading, 126-127, 170
* stream status pointer operator, 198
*= assignment operator, 168, 170
+ addition operator, 168, 170, 198-199
+ format flag, 318
+ operator, overloading, 122-125, 170
+ unary plus operator, 168-169, 199
++ increment operator, 91, 168, 169-170, 199-200

+= assignment operator, 168, 170
, sequential evaluation operator, 169-170, 200
- format flag, 318
– negation operator, 168, 200
- subtraction operator, 168, 170, 201
-- decrement operator, 91, 168, 169-170, 201
-= assignment operator, 168, 170
-> member selection operator, 168-170, 201-202
->* class member selection operator, 168-170, 202-203
. member selection operator, 168-170, 204
.* class member selection operator, 168-169, 204
/ division operator, 167, 169-170, 205
/* */ C comments, 205
// C++ comments, 205-206
/= assignment operator, 168, 170
0 format flag, 318
:: scope resolution operator, 52, 169, 206
; semicolon, use of, 44, 82
< less-than operator, 127-128, 168, 170, 207
<< insertion (put-to) operator, 169, 175, 177, 207
<< left shift operator, 169-170, 208
<<= assignment operator, 168, 170
<= less-than-or-equal-to operator, 168, 170, 208
= assignment operator, 153-154, 168, 170, 208-209
== equal-to operator, 123-124, 168, 170, 209
> greater-than operator, 168, 170, 209-210
>= greater-than-or-equal-to operator, 168, 170
>> extraction (get from) operator, 169, 175, 177, 210
>> right shift operator, 169-170, 211
>>= assignment operator, 168, 170

?: conditional operator, 169-170, 213
[] array element operator, 168-170, 211
\ backslash, 172-173
\" (print "), 173
\0<octal digits>, 173
\? (print ?), 173
\\ (print \), 173
\' (print '), 173
^ bitwise XOR operator, 169-170, 211-212
^= assignment operator, 168, 170
_ underscore, 172
{ } braces, 82
| bitwise OR operator, 169-170, 212
|= assignment operator, 168, 170
|| logical OR operator, 45, 168, 170, 212
~ bitwise negation operator, 169-170, 213

A

\a (alert), 173, 213-214
achievement data, 36-37. *See also* progress information
ANSI C, 166, 398
ANSI C function library, 4, 44, 165-166, 173-188, 398
answer analysis, 7-8, 32
answer judging, 7
answers, 31-36
argc, 215
arguments, 47
argv, 216
arithmetic operators, 44, 167-170
array notation, 53
arrays, 49-50
asm keyword, 217
assert.h, 174
assignment operators, 54, 168, 170
associativity, 169-170
auto keyword, 222
automatic variables, 47

399

B

\b (backspace), 173, 222
Back button, 23, 394
backup files, 83
badbit, 290
BAK extension, 83
base class, 51, 54
binary calculator, 9, 24
binary operators, 50
bitwise operators, 169-170, 195-196, 211-213
book contents, 4
Bookmark, 7, 27
books on C++, 397-398
Borland C++ compiler, 67-68, 74-79, 397-398
Borland compilers, 67-79, 397-398
braces ({ }), 82
branching statements, 45
break keyword, 223
break statements, 45
BUFSIZ, 224
button bar, 21-27, 393-395

C

C++ compilers, 67-79, 397-398
C++ language, 3-4
C++ standard, 166
C++ streams library, 49, 55
Calc button, 24, 394
calculator, online, 9, 24, 394
case keyword, 225
case sensitivity, 13-14, 32-33, 82
catch keyword, 226
CBT (computer-based training), 3, 7, 37
cerr, 227
CHAR_BIT, 228
char keyword, 227-228
CHAR_MAX, 228
CHAR_MIN, 228
character conversion functions, 184-185
character string, 49
cin, 55, 229
class hierarchy, 51-52
class keyword, 229
class library, 56, 166, 173, 175-176
class template, 57
classes, 42, 44, 46, 48-49, 229-230
    address, 118-119
    base, 51, 54
    bigdata, 154
    Countadd, 130-131
    Counter, 122-123, 130
    derived, 51, 54, 130-131
    Distance, 135-138

classes *continued*
    filebuf, 175, 257
    fracpri, 111-112, 114-115, 119-120, 124-125, 127-129, 134, 144, 151-152, 156-158
    fstream, 175, 273
    fstreambase, 175, 274
    ifstream, 283-284
    ios, 176, 288-291
    iostream, 176, 291
    istream, 176, 293
    item, 131-132, 148-149
    linklist, 159-160
    objfile, 161
    ofstream, 176, 313-314
    ostream, 176, 315
    person, 145, 147
    predefined, 165, 173, 175-176
    Queue, 121-122
    storage, 47
    streambuf, 176, 355
    String, 142-143
    target, 113-114, 126-127
    time, 108-109
CLK_TCK, 231
clock_t, 232
clog, 232
code reusability, 42
code sections, 36
command reference, 21-27, 393-395
compilers, 67-79, 397-398
compiling, 43, 83
complex.h, 174
compressed format, 14-15, 61-62
computer-based training (CBT), 3, 7, 37
concatenation, 51
conceptual errors, 85
console mode, 68
const keyword, 172, 233
constants, 172
constructor, 48, 181
constructor, copy, 54, 155
containership, 52
continue keyword, 233-234
continue statements, 45
copy constructors, 54, 155
course map, 41-57
Course Personality, 8, 24
cout, 55, 82, 175, 235
cpp extension, 80
ctype.h, 174

D

data conversion functions, 182
data types, predefined, 165, 172
database functions, 187

date functions, 187-188. *See also* functions
DBL_DIG, 237
DBL_EPSILON, 237
DBL_MANT_DIG, 237
DBL_MAX, 237-238
DBL_MAX_10_EXP, 238
DBL_MAX_EXP, 238
DBL_MIN, 238
DBL_MIN_10_EXP, 238-239
DBL_MIN_EXP, 239
debugging, 76, 311
dec (decimal) manipulator, 175, 239, 289
decimal calculator, 9, 24
decision statements, 45
decrement operator, 91, 168, 169-170, 201
def files, 81
default keyword, 239-240
#define directive, 171, 240
defined, 240-241
definition, 47
delete operator, 169, 241
dereferencing pointers, 52-53
derivation, 42, 51-52, 130-131
derived class, 51, 54, 130-131
destructor, 48, 181
dimension, 49
div_t, 242-243
divisor, greatest common (GCD), 93, 107
do keyword, 243
do while loop, 45
DOS case sensitivity, 13-14
DOS text mode, 68
double keyword, 243-244
dummy variable, 91-92

E

EasyWin, 68, 79-80
Edit Answer button, 26, 395
editor, using, 82-83
EDOM, 244
element, 49
#elif (else if) directive, 171, 244
#else directive, 171, 245
else keyword, 244-245
encapsulation, 42
#endif directive, 171, 245
endl, 175, 245-246
ends, 175, 246
enum keyword, 247
enumerated variables, 46
EOF, 247
eofbit, 290
errno, 248-249
errno.h, 174

INDEX

#error directive, 171, 249
error handling, 179-180
error status values, 290
errors, programming, 84-85
escape sequences, 165, 172-173
Euclid's algorithm, 93, 107
Example button, 24-26, 395
exception handling, 57, 179-180,
    226, 373, 377, 380
exceptions, 57, 179-180
EXE extension, 84
EXE files, 84
exercises. *See also* exercises (by
    .cpp file name) *and* review
    exercises
  address class, 118-119
  address/name, 80-83, 89-90
  bigdata class, 154
  change maker, 96-97
  character input, 101
  clear screen, 100
  coin changer, 96-97
  compare counters, 123-124
  compare strings, 117-118
  compare text files, 158-159
  compass rose, 97-98
  computer speed, 91-92
  concatenation, 142-143
  convert measurements, 90-91
  Countadd class, 130-131
  counter, add to, 122-123,
    130-131
  Counter class, 122-123, 130
  counter, compare, 123-124
  database inventory, 131-133,
    148-151
  disk, read from, 157-161
  disk, write to, 156-157,
    159-161
  Distance class, 135-138
  distances, 135-140
  fracpri class, 111-112,
    114-115, 119-120,
    124-125, 127-129, 134,
    144, 151-152, 156-158
  fracpri structure, 98-99,
    101-104
  fractions, 98-99, 101-104
    adding, 105-107, 114-116,
      124-126, 151-153
    array of, 119-120,
      156-158
    class. *See* exercises, fracpri
      class
    compare, 127-128
    converting, 128-130
    lowest term, 107-108,
      114-116
    negative, 134-135

exercises, fractions *continued*
    pointers, 144
  friend function, 151-153
  greatest common divisor,
    93-94, 107-108
  hardware database, 131-133,
    148-151
  increment operator (++), 91
  inheritance, 130-131, 138
  input/output, 135-137
  item class, 131-132, 148-149
  light-years to inches, 90-91
  linked list, 145-146, 159-161
  linklist class, 159-160
  maximum value, 116-117
  memory allocation, 153-155
  NIM game, 92-93, 112-113
  number from digits, 95
  objfile class, 161-162
  person class, 145, 147
  pointers, 140-141
    array, 144
    passing, 141-142
  queue, 121-122
  Queue class, 121-122
  radar, 99-100, 113-114,
    126-127
  range/bearing, 99-100,
    113-114, 126-127
  read from disk, 157-161
  reverse characters, 90
  stock data, 102-104
  stock prices, 98-99, 101-102,
    111-112
  String class, 142-143
  string concatenation, 142-143
  target class, 113-114, 126-127
  time class, 108-109
  time constructor, 109-110
  time structure, 95-96
  TV remote control, 94-95,
    104-105, 110-111
  virtual functions, 146-151
  write to disk, 156-157,
    159-161
  addarr, 118-119
  addfracs, 105-107, 114
  address1, 89-90
  address2, 90
  bigcopy, 155-156
  bigequal, 153-155
  changer, 96-97
  clear, 100
  compstr, 117-118
  concat, 142
  counplus, 130-131
  countadd, 122-123
  countcmp, 123-124
  engliop, 135-137

exercises *continued*
  exer1, 80-83
  fracarr, 119-120
  fracfren, 151-153
  fracin, 157-158
  fracladd, 114-116, 119, 124
  fracclass, 111-112, 114, 134,
    144
  fraclow, 107-108, 144
  fracomp, 127-128
  fraconv, 128-130
  fracout, 156-157
  fracplus, 124-127
  fracstr, 98-99
  fraction, 101-102, 105
  gcd, 93-94, 107
  getachar, 101
  hardware, 131-133, 148
  incagain, 91
  lightyrs, 90-91
  linkdisk, 159-161
  linkpers, 145-146
  makenumb, 95, 104
  negengl, 137-140
  negfrac, 134-135
  nim, 92-93, 112
  nimclass, 112-113
  objfile, 161-162
  ocomp, 158-159
  ptrfracs, 144
  ptrtest, 140-141
  queue, 121-122
  radar, 99-100, 113
  rbclass, 113-114, 126
  rbtimes, 126-127
  remclass, 110-111
  remote, 94-95, 104
  remote2, 104-105, 110
  revlets, 90
  rose, 97-98
  scores, 116-117
  speedtst, 91-92
  stocks, 102-104
  stringca, 142-143
  timclass, 108-109
  timconst, 109-110
  timestrc, 95-96, 108
  virthard, 148-151
  virtpez, 146-148
  weight, 141-142
Exit button, 26-27, 393
EXIT_FAILURE, 249-250
EXIT_SUCCESS, 250
expressions, 44
extensibility, 42
extensions
  .BAK, 83
  .cpp, 80
  .def, 81

extensions *continued*
  .EXE, 84
  .h, 174
  .hpp, 174
  .ide, 80
  .rc, 81
extern keyword, 250
external variables, 47

F

\f (form feed/new page), 173, 251
failbit, 290
feedback, 7-8, 32
feedback personality, 8, 24
fencepost error, 85
file extensions. *See* extensions
file input/output functions, 178-179
file opening modes, 289
file position, 290
FILE type, 257
filebuf class, 175, 257
FILENAME_MAX, 257
files, 55
first in first out (FIFO), 121
float keyword, 259
float.h, 174
FLT_DIG, 260
FLT_EPSILON, 260
FLT_MANT_DIG, 261
FLT_MAX, 261
FLT_MAX_10_EXP, 261
FLT_MAX_EXP, 261
FLT_MIN, 262
FLT_MIN_10_EXP, 262
FLT_MIN_EXP, 262
FLT_RADIX, 262
FLT_ROUNDS, 263
flush, 263
FOPEN_MAX, 265
for keyword, 265-266
for loop, 45
format flags, 288-289, 317-318
format size, 317-318, 333
format types, 317-319, 333-334
format width, 317, 333
Forward button, 23, 394
10fpos_t, 266
friend, 54
fstream class, 175, 273
fstream.h, 174-175, 274
fstreambase class, 175, 274
function library, 165-166, 173-188
function template, 57
functions, 47-48. *See also* macros
  ! (error check), 175, 177
  * (error check), 175, 177

functions *continued*
  << (put value), 175, 177
  >> (get value), 175, 177
  abort, 180, 214
  abs, 183, 214
  acos, 183, 215
  Add (template), 371
  asctime, 188, 216-217
  asin, 183, 217
  assert, 180, 218-219
  atan, 183, 219
  atan2, 183, 219-220
  atexit, 180, 220
  atof, 182, 220-221
  atoi, 182, 221
  atol, 182, 221-222
  bad, 175, 223
  bsearch, 187, 224
  calloc, 182, 225
  ceil, 183, 227
  cerr, 175
  character conversion, 184-185
  cin, 175
  clear, 100, 175, 230-231
  clearerr, 178, 231
  clock, 188, 231-232
  clog, 175
  close, 175, 232-233
  compstr, 117-118
  cos, 183, 234
  cosh, 183, 234-235
  cout, 55, 82, 175
  ctime, 188, 236
  data conversion, 182
  database, 187
  date, 187-188
  dec, 175, 239
  difftime, 188, 241-242
  div, 183, 242
  endl, 175, 245-246
  ends, 175, 246
  eof, 175, 247-248
  exit, 180, 249
  exp, 183, 250
  fabs, 183, 252
  fail, 175, 252
  fclose, 178, 253
  feof, 178, 253-254
  ferror, 178, 254
  fflush, 178, 254-255
  fgetc, 178, 255
  fgetpos, 178, 255-256
  fgets, 178, 256
  file input/output, 178-179
  fill, 175, 258
  flags, 175, 258-259
  floor, 183, 260
  flush, 175
  fmod, 183, 263-264

functions *continued*
  fopen, 178, 264-265
  form, 266
  fprintf, 178, 267
  fputc, 178, 267-268
  fputs, 178, 268
  fraclow, 107-108, 114-116
  fread, 178, 268-269
  free, 182, 269
  freopen, 178, 269-270
  frexp, 183, 270
  fscanf, 271
  fseek, 178, 271-272
  fsetpos, 178, 272-273
  ftell, 178, 274-275
  fwrite, 178, 275
  get, 175, 275-276
  getachar, 101
  getc, 178, 276-277
  getch, 101
  getchar, 178, 277
  getche, 94-95
  getenv, 180, 277-278
  getline, 176, 278
  getmax, 116-117
  gets, 178, 279
  gmtime, 188, 279
  good, 176, 280
  hex, 176, 281
  ifstream, 176
  ignore, 176, 284-285
  inline, 172
  input/output, 174-179
  istream_, 176
  labs, 183, 294
  ldexp, 183, 298-299
  ldiv, 183, 299
  library, 165, 173-188
  locale, 179-180
  localeconv, 180, 300-302
  localtime, 188, 302
  log, 183, 302-303
  log10, 183, 302-303
  longjmp, 180, 304
  malloc, 182, 304-305
  math, 183-184
  mblen, 186, 305-306
  mbstowcs, 186, 306-307
  mbtowc, 186, 306
  memchr, 186, 307
  memcmp, 186, 308
  memcpy, 186, 308-309
  memmove, 186, 309
  memory allocation, 181-182
  memset, 186, 309-310
  mktime, 188, 310
  modf, 183, 310-311
  oct, 176, 312-313
  open, 176, 314-315

INDEX

functions *continued*
   ostream_, 176
   peek, 176, 315-316
   perror, 180, 316
   pow, 183, 316
   precision, 176
   printf, 178, 182, 317-320
   process control, 179-180
   put, 176, 323
   putback, 176, 323-324
   putc, 178, 324
   putchar, 178, 324-325
   puts, 178, 325
   qsort, 187, 326
   raise, 180, 326-327
   rand, 183, 327
   rdstate, 176, 328
   read, 176, 328-329
   realloc, 182, 329-330
   remove, 178, 330
   rename, 178, 330-331
   resetiosflags, 176, 331-332
   rewind, 178
   scanf, 178, 182, 332-335
   search, 187
   seekg, 176, 335-336
   seekp, 176, 336-337
   setbase, 176, 337
   setbuf, 178, 338
   setf, 176, 338-339
   setfill, 176, 339
   setiosflags, 176, 339-340
   setjmp, 180, 340
   setlocale, 180, 341
   setprecision, 176, 341-342
   setvbuf, 178, 342
   setw, 176, 342-343
   signal, 180, 346-347
   sin, 184, 347-348
   sinh, 184, 348
   sort, 187
   sprintf, 178, 182, 349
   sqrt, 184, 349-350
   srand, 184, 350
   sscanf, 182, 350-351
   strcat, 186
   strchr, 186
   strcmp, 186, 353
   strcoll, 186, 353-354
   strcpy, 186, 354
   strcspn, 186, 354-355
   stream input/out, 174-177
   strerror, 186, 355-356
   strftime, 188, 356-357
   strlen, 186, 357-358
   strncat, 186, 358
   strncmp, 186, 359
   strncpy, 186, 359-360
   strpbrk, 186, 360

functions *continued*
   strrchr, 186, 360-361
   strspn, 186, 361
   strstr, 186, 361-362
   strtod, 182, 362-363
   strtok, 186, 363
   strtol, 182, 364-365
   strtoul, 182, 365
   strxfrm, 186, 366-367
   system, 180, 368
   tan, 184, 369
   tanh, 184, 369-370
   tellg, 176, 370
   tellp, 176, 370-371
   terminate, 372
   text manipulation, 185-187
   time, 187-188, 374
   tmpfile, 375
   tmpnam, 376
   tolower, 184-185, 376
   toupper, 184-185, 377
   trigonometric, 183-184
   unexpected, 380
   ungetc, 380-381
   unsetf, 176, 382
   vfprintf, 384
   virtual, 54-55
   vprintf, 386-387
   vsprintf, 387
   wcstombs, 186, 388
   wctomb, 186, 388-389
   width, 176, 390
   write, 177, 390-391
   ws, 177, 391

G

Glossary button, 24, 395
Glossary, online, 6, 8, 24, 27, 37, 395
Goal button, 24, 394
goodbit, 290
Goto button, 394
goto keyword, 280
grammar, 32
grayed buttons, 22
greatest common divisor (GCD), 93, 107

H

h extension, 174
hard copy, 14, 38
hardfail, 290
hardware requirements, 4-5, 13-15
HAS A relationship, 52
header files, 44, 56, 172-174
   assert.h, 174
   complex.h, 174

header files *continued*
   ctype.h, 174
   errno.h, 174
   float.h, 174
   fstream.h, 174-175, 274
   iomanip.h, 174, 287-288
   iostream.h, 44, 174-175, 292
   limits.h, 174
   locale.h, 174, 180
   math.h, 174
   setjmp.h, 174, 180
   signal.h, 174, 180
   stdarg.h, 174
   stddef.h, 174
   stdlib.h, 174, 180, 182
   stream.h, 175, 355
   string.h, 174
   time.h, 174
Help button, 23, 394
hex manipulator, 176, 281, 289
hexadecimal calculator, 9, 24
hexadecimal notation, 173, 281
   \x<hexadecimal digits>, 173
highlighting, 14, 63
hints, 7-8, 33-34
hpp extension, 174
HUGE_VAL, 281

I

ide extension, 80
#if directive, 171, 282-283
if else statements, 45
if keyword, 281-282
if statements, 45
#ifdef directive, 171, 283
#ifndef directive, 171
ifstream class, 283-284
implementations, 4-5
#include directive, 44, 171-172, 285
include files. *See* header files
increment operator, 91, 168, 169-170, 199-200
index, 49
inheritance, 42, 51-52, 130-135
inline functions, 47, 172
inline keyword, 285-286
input/output (I/O), 55
input/output functions, 174-179
installation, 13-16
   problems, 61-62
instructional area, 21-22
int keyword, 286
INT_MAX, 287
INT_MIN, 287
Integrated Development Environment (IDE), 43, 68, 79-84

Intel memory models, 43
interactivity, in lessons, 5
_IOFBF, 287
_IOLBF, 287
iomanip.h, 174, 287-288
_IONBF, 288
ios class, 176, 288-291
ios flags, 317-318, 331-332, 339-340
iostream class, 176, 291
iostream.h, 44, 174-175, 292
is (macro prefix), 184, 292
IS A relationship, 52
istream class, 176, 293

J

jmp_buf, 294

K

keyboard commands, 83
keywords, 165-167
    const, 172
    asm, 217
    auto, 222
    break, 223
    case, 225
    catch, 226
    char, 227-228
    class, 229
    const, 233
    continue, 233-234
    default, 239-240
    do, 243
    double, 243-244
    else, 244-245
    enum, 247
    extern, 250
    float, 259
    for, 265-266
    goto, 280
    if, 281-282
    inline, 285-286
    int, 286
    long, 303
    public, 320-323
    private, 320-321
    protected, 321-322
    register, 330
    return, 332
    short, 343
    signed, 347
    static, 351-352
    struct, 365-366
    switch, 367-368
    template, 371-372
keywords *continued*
    this, 372-373

throw, 373-374
try, 377-378
typedef, 378
union, 381
unsigned, 382
void, 385
virtual, 385
volatile, 386
while, 389

L

L_tmpnam, 294
last in first out (LIFO), 121
LC_ALL, 294-295, 300
LC_COLLATE, 295, 300
LC_CTYPE, 295, 300
LC_MONETARY, 295, 300
LC_NUMERIC, 295, 300
LC_TIME, 296, 300
lconv structure, 296, 301
LDBL_DIG, 296
LDBL_EPSILON, 296
LDBL_MANT_DIG, 297
LDBL_MAX, 297
LDBL_MAX_10_EXP, 297
LDBL_MAX_EXP, 297
LDBL_MIN, 298
LDBL_MIN_10_EXP, 298
LDBL_MIN_EXP, 298
ldiv_t, 299-300
lesson sets, 5
    map, 41-57
    printing, 14, 38
libraries
    class, 56, 166, 173, 175-176
    function, 165-166, 173-188
    stream, 166, 174-177
library files, 44
limits.h, 174
#line directive, 172, 300
link errors, 84
linked lists, 145
linking, 43, 83
lists, 53, 145
locale, 179-180, 294-296, 300-301, 341
locale functions, 179-180
locale.h, 174, 180
logic errors, 85
logical operators
    AND (&&), 45, 168, 170, 196-197
    NOT (!), 45, 168, 170, 193
    OR (||), 45, 168, 170, 212
long keyword, 303
LONG_MAX, 303
LONG_MIN, 303
loops, 45-46

M

macros, 170-174. *See also* functions
    __cplusplus, 172, 235-236
    __DATE__, 172, 236-237
    __FILE__, 172, 257
    __LINE__, 172, 300
    __STDC__, 172, 352
    __TIME__, 172, 374
    assert, 180, 218-219
    character classification, 184-185, 292-293
    feof, 178, 253-254
    ferror, 178, 254
    getc, 178, 276-277
    getchar, 178, 277
    isalnum, 184, 292-293
    isalpha, 184, 292-293
    iscntrl, 184, 292-293
    isdigit, 185, 292-293
    isgraph, 185, 292-293
    islower, 185, 292-293
    isprint, 185, 292-293
    ispunct, 185, 292-293
    isspace, 185, 292-293
    isupper, 185, 292-293
    isxdigit, 185, 292-293
    offsetof, 313
    putc, 178, 324
    putchar, 178, 324-325
    setjmp, 180, 340
    va_arg, 181, 383-384
    va_end, 181, 383-384
    va_start, 181, 383-384
    variable argument, 181, 383-384
main menu, 20-21
main( ) function, 44
Make (compiling), 83
manipulators
    dec, 175, 239
    endl, 175, 245-246
    ends, 175, 246
    flush, 263
    hex, 176, 281
    oct, 176, 312-313
    resetiosflags, 176, 331-332
    setbase, 176, 337
    setfill, 176, 339
    setiosflags, 176, 339-340
    setprecision, 176, 341-342
    setw, 176, 342-343
    ws, 177, 391
mastery, defined, 7, 24, 27, 36
math functions, 183-184
math.h, 174
MB_CUR_MAX, 305
MB_LEN_MAX, 305

INDEX

members, 46
Memo button, 26, 395
memory
    allocation, 153-156, 181-182, 225, 304, 311-312, 329
    freeing, 241, 269
    models, 43, 72, 77
    pointers, 52-53
multibyte characters, 185-187, 306-307

N

\n (new line), 173, 311
navigation, 21-27
NDEBUG, 311
new operator, 169, 311-312
Note button, 25-26, 395
Notepad, 14
NULL, 312

O

object-oriented programming (OOP), 3, 42-43, 48, 397-398
Object-Oriented Programming in Turbo C++, 2nd Edition, 5-6, 21, 41, 398
Objective window, 24, 27, 394
objects, 42, 48-49
oct manipulator, 176, 289, 312-313
octal calculator, 9, 24
octal notation, 173, 312-313
offsetof, 313
ofstream class, 176, 313-314
OOP. *See* object-oriented programming
operations, order of, 91
operator associativity, 169-170
operator functions, 50
operator overloading, 50-51, 55, 137-138, 167, 170
    * operator, 126-127
    + operator, 122-125
    < operator, 127-128
    = operator, 153-154
    == operator, 123-124
operator precedence, 167, 169-170
operator redefining. *See* operator overloading
operators, 165, 167-170
    arithmetic, 44, 167-170
    assignment, 54, 168, 170
    binary, 50
    bitwise, 169-170, 195-196, 211-213
    data access, 168
    delete, 169, 241

operators, *continued*
    logical, 45, 168, 170, 193, 196-197, 212
    member selection, 168
    new, 169, 311-312
    relational, 45, 168, 170
    size, 168
    sizeof, 168-169, 348-349
    typecast, 169, 378
    unary, 50
    See also symbols at start of Index
Options button, 24, 394
ostream class, 176, 315
overloading operators. *See* operator overloading

P

parentheses, and operator precedence, 170
personality, feedback, 8, 24
pointers, 52-53, 140
polymorphism, 42
#pragma directive, 172, 317
precedence, 167, 169-170
precision, 317-318
preprocessor, 170-171
preprocessor directives, 44, 165, 170-172
Print button, 394
private access, 51, 56
private keyword, 320-321
private members, 48
problems, 61-63
procedural language, 42-43
process control functions, 179-180
program development, 36, 56, 67, 79-85
programming basics, 44
programs, multifile, 56
Progress button, 23, 394
Progress Detail controls, 24
progress information, 7, 36-37
    private, 24, 36
    saving, 26-27
    window, 23
projects, 80. *See also* exercises
protected access, 51
protected keyword, 321-322
prototype, 47
ptrdiff_t, 322
public access, 51, 56
public keyword, 322-323
public members, 48
punctuation, 32

Q

questions, 31-36
queue, 121

R

\r (carriage return), 173, 326
RAND_MAX, 327-328
rc files, 81
README.TXT file, 13-14
Recall mode, 5, 8, 27
redefining operators. *See* operator overloading
redirection, 55
reference alphabetization, 191
reference entry format, 192
references, 47
Refresh button, 23, 394
REGISTER directory, 36-37
register keyword, 330
registration, 15-16, 79
requirements, 4-5, 13-15, 62, 67
resetiosflags, 176, 331-332
resource files, 81
resources (C++), 397-398
return keyword, 332
reusability of code, 42
review exercises for
    Chapter 1 (none), 89
    Chapter 2 (none), 89
    Chapter 3, 89-91
    Chapter 4, 91-95
    Chapter 5, 95-100
    Chapter 6, 100-108
    Chapter 7, 108-116
    Chapter 8, 116-122
    Chapter 9, 122-130
    Chapter 10, 130-140
    Chapter 11 (none), 89
    Chapter 12, 140-146
    Chapter 13, 146-156
    Chapter 14, 156-162
    Chapter 15 (none), 89
    See also exercises
review sections, 6, 38

S

saving, 83
scores, 36-37. *See also* progress information
screen layout, 21-22
screen numbers, 22, 27
search functions, 187
SEEK_CUR, 271, 335
SEEK_END, 271, 335
SEEK_SET, 271, 337
segmented architecture, 43
semicolon, use of, 44, 82
setbase, 176, 337
setfill, 176, 339
setiosflags, 176, 339-340
setjmp, 340

setjmp.h, 174, 180
setprecision, 176, 341-342
Settings button, 24, 394
setup, 19
setw, 176, 342-343
short keyword, 343
SHRT_MAX, 343
SHRT_MIN, 344
sig_atomic_t, 344
SIG_DFL, 344
SIG_ERR, 344
SIG_IGN, 344-345
SIGABRT, 345-346
SIGFPE, 345-346
SIGILL, 345-346
SIGINT, 346
signal.h, 174, 180
signed keyword, 347
SIGSEGV, 345-346
SIGTERM, 346-347
size_t, 348
sizeof operator, 168-169, 348-349
software features, 5
software problems, 61-63
sort functions, 187, 326
source file, 80
space format flag, 318
spelling, 32
square root, 184, 349-350
stacks, 53, 121
statements, 44
static functions, 54
static keyword, 351-352
static variables, 47
status bar, 21-22, 27
stdarg.h, 174
stddef.h, 174
stderr, 352
stdin, 352
stdlib.h, 174, 180, 182
stdout, 353
storage classes, 47
stream errors, 290
stream.h, 175, 355
stream input/out functions, 174-177
streambuf class, 176, 355
streams, 55

streams library, 49, 55, 166, 174-177
string concatenation, 51
string manipulation functions, 49
string.h, 174
strings, 49
struct keyword, 365-366
structures, 46
switch keyword, 367-368
switch statements, 45
syntax errors, 84
system requirements, 4-5, 13-15

T

\t (horizontal tab), 173, 368-369
template keyword, 371-372
templates, 57
text manipulation functions, 185-187
text mode, 68
this keyword, 372-373
THIS pointer, 54
throw keyword, 373-374
time functions, 187-188. *See also* functions
time.h, 174
time requirements, 41-42
time_t, 374-375
tm structure, 375
TMP_MAX, 375
toolbar, 21-27, 393-395
trigonometric calculator, 9, 24
trigonometric functions, 183-184
troubleshooting, 61-63
try block, 57
try keyword, 377-378
Turbo C++ for Windows, 67-68, 70-74, 79
tutorials, 6
type cast operators, 169, 378
type casts, 44
type conversion, 50-51
type conversion functions, 50-51
type( ) operator, 169, 378
<type>& operator, 168
typedef keyword, 378
types, predefined, 165, 172

U

UCHAR_MAX, 379
UINT_MAX, 379
ULONG_MAX, 379
unary operators, 50
#undef directive, 172, 379
union keyword, 381
unsigned keyword, 382
USHRT_MAX, 383

V

\v (vertical tab), 173, 383
va_arg, 181, 383-384
va_end, 181, 383-384
va_list, 384
va_start, 181, 383-384
values, predefined, 165, 172
variables, 46-47
virtual functions, 54-55
virtual keyword, 385
void keyword, 385
volatile keyword, 386

W

wchar_t, 387-388
while keyword, 389
while loop, 45
whitespace manipulator, 177, 391
Windows Notepad, 14
Windows, required, 19
Windows version, 62
ws manipulator, 177, 391

X

\x<hexadecimal digits>, 173

Y

Z

ENVIRONMENTAL AWARENESS

Books have a substantial influence on the destruction of the forests of the Earth. For example, it takes 17 trees to produce one ton of paper. A first printing of 30,000 copies of a typical 480 page book consumes 108,000 pounds of paper which will require 918 trees!

Waite Group Press™ is against the clear-cutting of forests and supports reforestation of the Pacific Northwest of the United States and Canada, where most of this paper comes from. As a publisher with several hundred thousand books sold each year, we feel an obligation to give back to the planet. We will therefore support organizations which seek to preserve the forests of planet Earth.

WAITE GROUP PRESS™

OBJECT-ORIENTED PROGRAMMING IN C++ SECOND EDITION
Robert Lafore
The best-selling OOP programming book now incorporates the suggestions from an extensive survey of instructors—updated chapters on objects, classes, overloading, constructors, inheritance, and virtual functions, and the newest features of the C++ programming language including templates and exceptions. It's fully compatible with the newest Borland C++ 4.0 compilers and the disk includes all the programs and source code.

Available Now • 800 pages
ISBN: 1-878739-73-5
U.S. $34.95 Can. $48.95
1 – 3.5" disk

C++ PRIMER PLUS, SECOND EDITION
Stephen Prata
This friendly step-by-step tutorial is ideal for beginners—no previous knowledge of C is assumed. It teaches the basics of object-oriented programming (OOP) and shows how to use classes, inheritance, and polymorphism to build programs that are flexible, easily modified, and easily maintained. *C++ Primer Plus, Second Edition* is compatible with all versions of C++.

Available Now • 800 pages
ISBN: 1-878739-74-3
U.S. $32.95 Can. $48.95
1 - 3.5" Disk
Teacher's Handbook Available

VISUAL C++ HOW-TO
Scott Stanfield, Mickey Williams, Alan Light, and Ralph Arvesen
Here is a book for programmers of all levels, from beginner to expert, who want to take advantage of Microsoft's Visual C++ development environment. Using the reader-endorsed problem-solver format of The Waite Group's How-To series, this book provides a wealth of sophisticated Windows MFC programming techniques that may not be immediately apparent, but are quick and simple to use. The CD-ROM provided with the book contains all the How-To sample code, plus megabytes of custom controls and classes that extend the power of the MFC library. The wealth of tricks include adding a "push-pin" to keep a modeless dialog in place, creating a Bezier OLE server object, displaying a splash window when an app starts, and more than a hundred other practical solutions to frequently asked Foundation Class questions.

Available Now • 650 pages
ISBN: 1-878739-82-4
U.S. $44.95 Can. $62.95
1 - CD-ROM

Send for our unique catalog to get more information about these books, as well as about our outstanding and award-winning titles.

WAITE GROUP PRESS™

BLACK ART OF 3D GAME PROGRAMMING
André LaMothe

This hands-on, step-by-step guide covers all essential game-writing techniques, including wire-frame rendering, hidden surface removal, solid modeling and shading, input devices, artificial intelligence, modem communications, lighting, transformations, digitized VR sound and music—even voxel graphics. The CD-ROM includes a 3D modem-to-modem space combat simulator that you build from scratch.

Available Now • 1,000 pages
ISBN: 1-57169-004-2
U.S. $49.95 Can. 72.95
1 - CD-ROM

SIMPLE C++
Jeffrey M. Cogswell

Use POOP (Profound Object-Oriented Programming) to learn C++! Write simple programs to control ROBODOG in this entertaining, beginner-level programming book.

Available Now • 240 pages
ISBN: 1-878739-44-1
U.S. $16.95 Can. $23.95

LAFORE'S WINDOWS PROGRAMMING MADE EASY
Robert Lafore

Learn to write Windows programs with no prior knowledge of C++ or object-oriented programming. This book focuses on the essentials so that you're programming in no time!

Available now • 610 pages
ISBN: 1-878739-23-9
U.S. $29.95 Can. $41.95
1 - 3.5" disk

TO ORDER TOLL FREE CALL 1-800-368-9369
TELEPHONE 415-924-2575 • FAX 415-924-2576
OR SEND ORDER FORM TO: WAITE GROUP PRESS, 200 TAMAL PLAZA, CORTE MADERA, CA 94925

Qty	Book	US/Can Price	Total
___	OOP in Microsoft C++	$29.95/41.95	___
___	C++ Primer Plus, 2nd Ed.	$32.95/48.95	___
___	Visual C++ How-To	$44.95/62.95	___
___	Black Art of 3D Game Programming ☐ 3.5" ☐ 5.25" disks	$44.95/62.95	___
___	Simple C++ ☐ 3.5" ☐ 5.25" disks	$16.95/23.95	___
___	Lafore's Windows Programming	$29.95/41.95	___

Calif. residents add 7.25% Sales Tax ___

Shipping
USPS ($5 first book/$1 each add'l) ___
UPS Two Day ($10/$2) ___
Canada ($10/$4) ___
TOTAL ___

Ship to
Name _____
Company _____
Address _____
City, State, Zip _____
Phone _____

Payment Method
☐ Check Enclosed   ☐ VISA   ☐ MasterCard

Card# _____ Exp. Date _____

Signature _____

SATISFACTION GUARANTEED OR YOUR MONEY BACK.

This is a legal agreement between you, the end user and purchaser, and The Waite Group®, Inc., and the authors of the programs contained in the disk. By opening the sealed disk package, you are agreeing to be bound by the terms of this Agreement. If you do not agree with the terms of this Agreement, promptly return the unopened disk package and the accompanying items (including the related book and other written material) to the place you obtained them for a refund.

SOFTWARE LICENSE

1. The Waite Group, Inc. grants you the right to use one copy of the enclosed software programs (the programs) on a single computer system (whether a single CPU, part of a licensed network, or a terminal connected to a single CPU). Each concurrent user of the program must have exclusive use of the related Waite Group, Inc. written materials.

2. The program, including the copyrights in each program, is owned by the respective author and the copyright in the entire work is owned by The Waite Group, Inc. and they are therefore protected under the copyright laws of the United States and other nations, under international treaties. You may make only one copy of the disk containing the programs exclusively for backup or archival purposes, or you may transfer the programs to one hard disk drive, using the original for backup or archival purposes. You may make no other copies of the programs, and you may make no copies of all or any part of the related Waite Group, Inc. written materials.

3. You may not rent or lease the programs, but you may transfer ownership of the programs and related written materials (including any and all updates and earlier versions) if you keep no copies of either, and if you make sure the transferee agrees to the terms of this license.

4. You may not decompile, reverse engineer, disassemble, copy, create a derivative work, or otherwise use the programs except as stated in this Agreement.

GOVERNING LAW

This Agreement is governed by the laws of the State of California.

LIMITED WARRANTY

The following warranties shall be effective for 90 days from the date of purchase: (i) The Waite Group, Inc. warrants the enclosed disk to be free of defects in materials and workmanship under normal use; and (ii) The Waite Group, Inc. warrants that the programs, unless modified by the purchaser, will substantially perform the functions described in the documentation provided by The Waite Group, Inc. when operated on the designated hardware and operating system. The Waite Group, Inc. does not warrant that the programs will meet purchaser's requirements or that operation of a program will be uninterrupted or error-free. The program warranty does not cover any program that has been altered or changed in any way by anyone other than The Waite Group, Inc. The Waite Group, Inc. is not responsible for problems caused by changes in the operating characteristics of computer hardware or computer operating systems that are made after the release of the programs, nor for problems in the interaction of the programs with each other or other software.

THESE WARRANTIES ARE EXCLUSIVE AND IN LIEU OF ALL OTHER WARRANTIES OF MERCHANTABILITY OR FITNESS FOR A PARTICULAR PURPOSE OR OF ANY OTHER WARRANTY, WHETHER EXPRESS OR IMPLIED.

EXCLUSIVE REMEDY

The Waite Group, Inc. will replace any defective disk without charge if the defective disk is returned to The Waite Group, Inc. within 90 days from date of purchase.

This is Purchaser's sole and exclusive remedy for any breach of warranty or claim for contract, tort, or damages.

LIMITATION OF LIABILITY

THE WAITE GROUP, INC. AND THE AUTHORS OF THE PROGRAMS SHALL NOT IN ANY CASE BE LIABLE FOR SPECIAL, INCIDENTAL, CONSEQUENTIAL, INDIRECT, OR OTHER SIMILAR DAMAGES ARISING FROM ANY BREACH OF THESE WARRANTIES EVEN IF THE WAITE GROUP, INC. OR ITS AGENT HAS BEEN ADVISED OF THE POSSIBILITY OF SUCH DAMAGES.

THE LIABILITY FOR DAMAGES OF THE WAITE GROUP, INC. AND THE AUTHORS OF THE PROGRAMS UNDER THIS AGREEMENT SHALL IN NO EVENT EXCEED THE PURCHASE PRICE PAID.

COMPLETE AGREEMENT

This Agreement constitutes the complete agreement between The Waite Group, Inc. and the authors of the programs, and you, the purchaser.

Some states do not allow the exclusion or limitation of implied warranties or liability for incidental or consequential damages, so the above exclusions or limitations may not apply to you. This limited warranty gives you specific legal rights; you may have others, which vary from state to state.

SATISFACTION REPORT CARD

Please fill out this card if you wish to know of future updates to
Master C++, or to receive our catalog.

Company Name:

Last Name: **First Name:**   **Middle Initial:**

Street Address:

City: **State:**   **Zip:**

E-Mail address

Daytime telephone: ( )

Date product was acquired: Month   Day   Year   **Your Occupation:**

Overall, how would you rate *Master C++*?
- ☐ Excellent   ☐ Very Good   ☐ Good
- ☐ Fair   ☐ Below Average   ☐ Poor

What did you like MOST about this book?

What did you like LEAST about this book?

Please describe any problems you may have encountered with installing or using the disk:

How did you use this book (problem-solver, tutorial, reference...)?

What is your level of computer expertise?
- ☐ New   ☐ Dabbler   ☐ Hacker
- ☐ Power User   ☐ Programmer   ☐ Experienced Professional

What computer languages are you familiar with?

Please describe your computer hardware:
Computer _____ Hard disk _____
5.25" disk drives _____ 3.5" disk drives _____
Video card _____ Monitor _____
Printer _____ Peripherals _____
Sound board _____ CD ROM _____

Where did you buy this book?
- ☐ Bookstore (name):
- ☐ Discount store (name):
- ☐ Computer store (name):
- ☐ Catalog (name):
- ☐ Direct from WGP   ☐ Other

What price did you pay for this book?

What influenced your purchase of this book?
- ☐ Recommendation   ☐ Advertisement
- ☐ Magazine review   ☐ Store display
- ☐ Mailing   ☐ Book's format
- ☐ Reputation of Waite Group Press   ☐ Other

How many computer books do you buy each year?

How many other Waite Group books do you own?

What is your favorite Waite Group book?

Is there any program or subject you would like to see Waite Group Press cover in a similar approach?

Additional comments?

Please send to: Waite Group Press
200 Tamal Plaza
Corte Madera, CA 94925

☐ Check here for a free Waite Group catalog

SATISFACTION CARD

BEFORE YOU OPEN THE DISK OR CD-ROM PACKAGE ON THE FACING PAGE, CAREFULLY READ THE LICENSE AGREEMENT.

Opening this package indicates that you agree to abide by the license agreement found in the back of this book. If you do not agree with it, promptly return the unopened disk package (including the related book) to the place you obtained them for a refund.